THE HOUSE I LIVE IN

THE HOUSE I LIVE IN

———

RACE IN THE AMERICAN CENTURY

———

ROBERT J. NORRELL

OXFORD
UNIVERSITY PRESS

2005

OXFORD
UNIVERSITY PRESS

Oxford   New York

Auckland Bangkok Buenos Aires Cape Town Chennai
Dar es Salaam Delhi Hong Kong Istanbul Karachi Kolkata
Kuala Lumpur Madrid Melbourne Mexico City Mumbai Nairobi
São Paulo Shanghai Taipei Tokyo Toronto

Library of Congress Cataloging-in-Publication Data
Norrell, Robert J. (Robert Jefferson)
The house I live in : race in the American century / Robert J. Norrell.
p. cm.
Includes bibliographical references and index.
ISBN 13: 978-0-19-507345-4
ISBN 10: 0-19-507345-2
1. United States—Race relations—History. 2. Civil rights movements—United States—History.
3. African Americans—Civil rights—History. 4. African Americans—History—1877–1964.
5. African Americans—History—1964- I. Title.
E185.61.N879 2005
305.896'073'09—dc22
2004023280

Book design and composition by Mark McGarry, Texas Type & Book Works
Set in Dante

9 8 7 6 5 4 3 2 1
Printed in the United States of America
on acid-free paper

For Kelly

CONTENTS

ACKNOWLEDGMENTS

My greatest encouragement for this work came from the late Robert H. Wiebe, who befriended me in 1984–85 when we were both visitors at the University of Cambridge. I was awed by Bob's bibliography and inspired by his commitment to address big questions about American history. He never failed to encourage me to think deeply and alternatively about the nature of the American experience and to bring forward the large interpretive questions. He cautioned me about the practical reality that synthetic treatments had gone out of favor after the 1960s, but he so provoked me that I have been trying ever since 1985 to create one. I hope that this book in a small way can be a tribute to Bob's memory.

A number of friends have encouraged me in this project, especially Thomas Childers, David Colburn, James C. Cobb, Charles Eagles, Lorri Glover, John Griffiths, Gerry McCauley, the late August Meier, and Clarence Walker. For years Cleophus Thomas, Jr., has provoked me in conversation to think about the issues addressed herein. Anthony Badger invited me to give the Special Lectures in History at the University of Newcastle in 1991, an opportunity that forced me to make a first attempt at what would eventually become this book. I am indebted to W. Fitzhugh Brundage, Gaines Foster, Paul Gorman, David B. Parker, and

Mary Rolinson for help on particular matters of interpretation. Andrea Watson at the University of Alabama Library provided invaluable assistance in locating images to illustrate this book.

Paul M. Gaston, Daniel Feller, and Charles Eagles all read an earlier draft and provided much-needed correctives about points of interpretation. Professor Gaston's encouragement over the decades has sustained me in many ways. Paul Zwier was especially encouraging after his reading. Ernest Freeberg's extensive commentary raised many good questions that resulted in improvements. George Frederickson's instructive comments saved me from some errors. Peter Ginna was extraordinarily patient in waiting for this book and then made a number of excellent suggestions for improving the manuscript. Lawrence F. Kohl's critique of the manuscript was as ruthless as it was intelligent, but he more than anyone else understood the kind of book I wanted to produce, and I am much in his debt for his contribution to this effort.

My wife Kelly has supported me for a long time and in return gotten only the dubious reward of living with me. Thus it is in long overdue recognition of her daily encouragement and affection that I dedicate this book to her.

PREFACE

Most Americans celebrate the civil rights movement of the 1950s and 1960s as an era of great reform and national revival. At that time we as a nation addressed and conquered some of the worst aspects of our race relations. Now treated as a historical subject worthy of an entire college course at major universities, the civil rights movement offers compelling drama and teaches important lessons. Its most prominent message has been that African Americans, by challenging forthrightly the bitter racism of white southerners, triumphed over several centuries of oppression. The unavoidable conclusion is that the oppressors yielded when blacks and sympathetic whites finally and firmly renounced them. No statement of the efficacy of protest is more powerful than the lines of the now famous freedom song "Eyes on the Prize":

> *I know one thing we did right*
> *Was the day we started to fight*

As the success of the documentary film *Eyes on the Prize* demonstrated, the civil rights movement has captured our historical imagination in part because it suggested that it did one thing right—protest.

Most of the writing about the civil rights movement has focused on those who engaged in protest, especially such leaders as Martin Luther King, Jr. Compelling descriptions of men and women engaged in struggle have come from scholars, journalists, and many participants themselves. One might easily deduce from what has been written that the movement began in 1955 when blacks in Montgomery first committed themselves to mass protest in the bus boycott; that a sustained effort to attack segregation appeared in 1960 and continued uninterrupted through 1965; and that in 1966 the commitment to protest failed, done in by divisions among protestors and a turn to reaction among whites.

The powerful and easily comprehensible narrative line overlooks some important realities and basic questions. Since emancipation African Americans had often protested their mistreatment. Why did protests become more visible and more effective in the 1950s and 1960s? Many African Americans remained committed to protest after 1965, but their efforts did not yield significant positive results. The conventional view that protest worked between 1955 and 1965 is correct, but why was that so? What made direct-action protests successful during one moment of American history but not another? Most important, what part of the civil rights agenda was left unfinished?

This essay on race relations in twentieth-century America will attempt to answer questions about how and why changes occurred, and why some things did not change. I offer a broad view of the quest for equal rights for African Americans and connect those efforts to big, evolving structural realities of the twentieth century. I argue that Americans act most basically to get security and status, needs that operate within both material and psychological realms. The quest for status and security has consistently taken the form of racial competition for economic opportunity, political power, and the use of physical space. Until the 1960s, whites generally behaved as a group whose color gave it a superior status to other groups, but especially to blacks, whom whites have treated as a group of inferior, or pariah, status. Whites' pursuit of superior status over blacks provides the most basic explanation for the relentless discrimination and exploitation of African Americans in the United States.[1]

Americans typically justify our pursuit of security and status—which we often think of in terms of wealth and prestige—with ideological reasoning. Just as important, our ideological commitments set directions for, and even limits on, our pursuit of security and status. This work suggests ideological explanations for many of the changes in race relations that occur before, during, and after the civil rights movement. Although these ideological commitments have always been complex and evolutionary, this work asserts that four central ideologies have shaped American race relations.

Americans have been deeply committed to our creed of democratic values—liberty, democracy, and equality. Derived mainly from the Revolutionary ideology, Americans' democratic values underwent redefinition during the Civil War, which brought the end of slavery and thus radically new meanings for freedom and equality. Abraham Lincoln helped his countrymen understand new meanings in order to include blacks in the promises of citizenship. After the war, however, the authority of democratic values over race relations waned, and their meanings contracted in ways so detrimental to blacks that they were practically meaningless to the next three generations of African Americans. And yet many African Americans, and some whites still imbued with the Lincoln spirit, never forgot the promise of freedom and equality that had been made. During the twentieth century, the Great Depression and World War II forced a new consideration of the meaning of democratic values and ultimately the most expansive definition yet of freedom, equality, and democracy. In the 1950s, black protest leaders, and especially Martin Luther King, Jr., appealed to the broadened understandings to impel protest and change.

Americans often have been equally and sometimes more determined in our embrace of the ideologies of race, especially white supremacy. This ideology was based not just on the belief that people of African, Asian, and Indian descent were inferior in intelligence and morality to those of European origin, but also on the faith that whites should maintain sufficient economic and political power always to impose their will on people of color. Over the course of the nineteenth century, white supremacy evolved to a much stronger and more all-inclusive ideology than it had been in colonial America, reaching its clearest expression and greatest authority in the United States at about the turn of the twentieth century. How the ideology of white supremacy was addressed and overcome during the twentieth century is the central concern of this book.

A third ideological influence shaping the course of race relations has been American state nationalism. Lincoln's redefinition of democratic values had behind it the rapid expansion of the power of the national government during the Civil War. That phase of American nationalism expired quickly after the war, and with it went the authoritative influence of democratic values over race relations. The surge of American honor that came with the United States's rise to world power in 1898 and then continued during World War I had remarkably little positive effect on human relations. But the United States's participation in World War II vastly strengthened American state nationalism, and it had a direct impact on domestic race relations. For most white Americans, the huge commitment to fighting racist regimes in Germany and Japan heightened sensitivity to American bigotry. Adolf Hitler, it was said, gave racism a bad name. The war encouraged black activism for civil rights in many ways: In addition to the ideological ascent of democratic values and the undermining of racist thought, it gave African Americans their best opportunities yet for economic and institutional uplift. The war also caused the first serious questioning of antiblack stereotyping in popular culture and brought about a drastic reduction of such cultural usage in wartime and postwar America.

Thus, in a great many ways, the intensification of American nationalism in the mid-twentieth century, perhaps best encompassed in the publisher Henry Luce's notion of "the American Century," led to the civil rights movement. But in no way is American triumphalism warranted: The Cold War presented powerful obstacles to race reform, even while many Americans noted the damage done to our reputation by white-supremacist excesses in the South.

A fourth ideological influence has been ethnic nationalism, and there are two distinctive forms that have shaped American race relations. First, a southern white nationalism emerged in the post–Civil War South. This

strain of thinking created myths about the prewar South, the war experience, and Reconstruction. The myths promoted a sense of white southern distinctiveness in opposition to both the United States government
and white southerners' ethnic enemies, African Americans. White
nationalism animated southerners' political discourse, their cultural
expressions, and their racial policies from the 1870s through the 1930s.
World War II, I argue, brought the demise of white southern nationalism. Black nationalism found its first popular expression in the Garvey
movement of the 1920s, but it was effectively pushed into the background as the drive for integration dominated black thought for the next
three decades. During the 1960s black nationalism again found a popular
following in the Black Power and black consciousness movements, which
continued into subsequent decades. By then black nationalism, like white
nationalism earlier, had engendered intense opposition from Americans
who believed that ethnic nationalism of any kind was antithetical to
American nationalism and democratic values.

How in fact were these ideological commitments converted into
action that brought changes in race relations? Americans' ideologies have
been reflected in political discourse, protest action, popular culture, and
the outlets of mass communication. The renderings of values in those
arenas clarified conflicts within our national ideological construct. The
presentations of racial images in American popular culture, it is argued
here, supported white supremacy into the 1940s, but thereafter the popular culture rejected it in favor of democratic values. There was no
national movement for civil rights until activists could create a mass,
national appeal to African Americans, which they were able to do in part
because of television and other changes in mass communications.
Another part of the answer lay in the remarkable ability of the civil rights
leadership to insist on its ideological understandings in order to press for
change. Martin Luther King, Jr.'s use of language as symbolic action
pointed the way for millions of black protestors to demonstrate the
incompatibility between white supremacy and democratic values.

Separated into three parts, this work begins with the promise of
equality made by Abraham Lincoln and then quickly explores how it was

rejected and replaced by white-supremacist authority. We must explore the intense racial competition for status in order to understand the structures that had to be overcome. To see what the civil rights movement accomplished, we need to explore the system of segregation that it challenged. Similarly, to comprehend the power of ideology that liberated later on, we must examine the ideologies that upheld racial exploitation. Soon, however, the book turns to the dynamics in the early twentieth century that made possible the fundamental changes several decades later.

Part two begins the story of struggle against white supremacy and its institutions. I assert that the civil rights movement began in 1938 with a confluence of national and local events. World War II animated much of the change, but the Cold War slowed it down. This part of the work recounts the *Eyes on the Prize* drama, with special attention to how Americans perceived the well-known events of the civil rights movement. It explores the ways that democratic values were presented as the means to overcome violent white supremacy. Here also we see how the power of the national government was brought to bear against segregation and how new developments in popular culture and mass communication enabled racial change.

Part three follows the history of American race relations from 1965 to the end of the century, a time that has been cast mostly in terms of failure, of lost opportunities and failed commitments. This work addresses most of the crucial post–civil rights issues, and I reach relatively positive conclusions about the nature of human relations in the late twentieth century, though the bitter debate about the meaning of equality is explored in detail. Post–civil rights events more often reflected the overall success of the civil rights movement than its failure, especially in the ways that so many Americans who previously had experienced discrimination now took advantage of new opportunities and in the manner that so many whites embraced the promise of freedom and equality for African Americans.[2] There are exceptions to this estimation that I explore herein, but the larger truth of it is sustained. By the end of the twentieth century, "the house we live in" was closer than ever to fulfilling the promise of its democratic values.

The focus here is mainly on relations between blacks and whites, though connections are made to white attitudes toward other minority populations. Beyond the historic significance of African slavery to the settlement of North America, there was a demographic destiny to American race relations set by the overwhelming significance of African Americans as the main minority group in American life. In 1880, for example, the U.S. census counted 6.5 million African Americans, 94,000 Chinese immigrants, 45,000 Indians, and 52,000 Mexican immigrants in a total population of almost 50 million. At the time, African Americans composed about 13 percent of the U.S. population—almost their percentage today—and the other groups only one- or two-tenths of 1 percent. Asian and Hispanic populations grew in significance in the American population over the course of the twentieth century, with most of the growth coming after 1965. Today those groups represent about 4 and 13 percent, respectively, of the U.S. population, and thus more attention is paid to the other minorities as the book reaches the end of the twentieth century. By that time a new demographic destiny was reinforcing the ideological changes that had occurred in the United States as a result of the civil rights movement.

This book suggests that in fact there was more than one thing Americans did right to overcome our legacy of racial exploitation. The day we started to fight actually occurred much earlier than the freedom song assumed. Indeed, the story of the civil rights movement is a much longer and richer narrative than we have often thought. And like so many compelling sagas of American history, it began during the dark times of the Civil War.

THE HOUSE I LIVE IN

PART ONE

THE HIDDEN HONOR
OF A PARIAH PEOPLE, 1861–1937

CHAPTER 1

THE MOVING WHITE LINE

THE BURDEN OF an awful year weighed heavily on Abraham Lincoln when in late November 1862 he sat down to write his annual message to Congress to report on the state of the Union. It was, to say the least, a difficult duty. President Lincoln had been struggling, without much success, to win the civil war that had begun in 1861 between the northern and southern states. His generals had failed to attack the Confederate Army as aggressively as he thought they should, and the lists of dead northern soldiers mounted higher on his desk. There had been about 20,000 casualties at Shiloh in Tennessee in April, and almost 25,000 at Antietam in Maryland in September. The Confederates had won big battles, and many northerners howled condemnations of Lincoln's apparently failed war leadership. In October he had announced his intention to free slaves in the rebellious Confederate states on the first day of 1863, a controversial action because many northerners did not want the freed slaves coming to their states. The editors of the *New York World* advised their readers that the coming congressional elections would decide "whether a swarthy inundation of Negro laborers and paupers shall flood the North, accumulating new burdens on taxpayers, cheapening white labor by black competition . . . , and raising dangerous questions of political and social equality." The campaign slogan of the Ohio Democratic Party in 1862 was "The Constitution as it is, the Union as it was, *and the Niggers where they are.*" On Election Day, Lincoln's Republican Party did indeed lose many seats in the U.S. Congress, a fact that the *New York Times* attributed to a "want of confidence" in the president.[1]

In the message that finally came from his pen, Lincoln recounted at length the Union's problems and offered policies he hoped would bring better days. For the coming emancipation, he proposed to compensate slaveholders who freed their slaves, a policy meant to get Confederates to give up the fight. He rejected the widespread fear among white northerners that emancipation would bring a flood of blacks to the North. "If the [freed slaves] stay in their old places, they jostle no white laborers; if they leave their old places, they leave them open to white laborers," the president contended without actually confronting the possibility of a massive northward migration. At the end, he moved to ground on which he was more certain when he explained to Americans that they were caught in a moment of profound importance. "Fellow citizens," he declared, "the fiery trial through which we pass will light us down in honor or dishonor to the last generation." A place of honor would be reserved only for those who preserved the American nation, for to Abraham Lincoln it was the highest achievement of human progress, and he meant to save it. "In giving freedom to the slave, we assure freedom to the free—honorable alike in what we give and what we preserve. We shall nobly save or meanly lose the last, best hope of earth."[2]

Abraham Lincoln's definition of American nationality in moral terms may seem dated, even naive, to some in the twenty-first century. Many people today would say that there are no *American* beliefs or values, because the United States is a society of many cultures, each of which holds independent and sometimes competing ideas about what to believe. Lincoln's thinking, however, was consistent with an older tradition that has recognized universal values in American life, and it conforms to moral impulses that have periodically resurged, even in the age of moral relativism. From the country's beginning, foreign visitors and some introspective Americans have explored what values might be attached to "the American character." Lacking the common ethnic or tribal past that most European nations had, Americans strived to establish a national identity by setting common values, beliefs to which all could subscribe regardless of their disparate origins. The self-conscious act of articulating values probably caused Americans to vest greater importance in *national* beliefs.[3]

Lincoln believed that Thomas Jefferson had done more than any other to proclaim American national ideals. To Jefferson, the highest American ideals were liberty and equality. It was "self-evident" that all men were equal in the sight of God and that each had an "unalienable," natural right to liberty. "Freedom of religion, freedom of the press, and freedom of person," he said in his first speech as president, were "the creed of our political faith, the text of civil instruction." If liberty meant freedom from governmental oppression, and if political equality meant one citizen's having the same rights as the next, then democracy was the

President Abraham Lincoln. *Courtesy Library of Congress.*

protector of both liberty and equality. "I know no safe depository of the ultimate powers of the society but the people themselves," he wrote. In his second inaugural address in 1805, Jefferson congratulated his fellow Americans on the achievement of "civil and religious liberty unassailed, law and order preserved; equality of rights maintained, and that state of property, equal or unequal, which results to every man from his own industry." We had said what we believed and then, according to Jefferson, we had lived up to those beliefs.[4]

An unrealistic, even romantic view of American character can result if "ideals" are not distinguished from "values." Jefferson created a model for an American character that elevated liberty, equality, and democracy as its highest ideals, but despite the optimism of his second inaugural, he knew that Americans often failed to conform to model behavior. Things other than ideals often drive people. Human beings want security and status—basic desires that are not judged to be idealistic by their fellows. The needs and desires that motivate the main actions of human beings are their values. If people really value something, they act to acquire it or keep it, and the things that they believe in most have the largest control over their behavior. Values encompass the full range of motivations, both high-minded ideals and selfish desires, and thus an analysis of values provides a more realistic view of Americans' behavior.

But because Americans had created a national community—a sense of being a people—by embracing certain beliefs, they became a peculiarly ideological group that relied on ideas and common beliefs to explain their behavior. Thus even when their basic motive was to advance their status or increase their security, Americans have tended to justify their actions with ideological explanations. This does not mean that Americans' ideology has been vacuous or false. Rather it means their ideology has to be taken seriously, examined closely, and connected to the more fundamental drive for security and status. When Americans have spoken of their "values," they usually have meant their ideology—or some part of their ideology.

A more realistic assessment of Americans' ideology than Thomas Jefferson's came from the Frenchman Alexis de Tocqueville, who visited the United States in 1831 and 1832 and later wrote what has been the most influential analysis of it, *Democracy in America*. Tocqueville believed that liberty and equality had been advanced to higher levels in the United States than in Europe. The distinctive feature of American life was the great equality that existed among the people—a general equality of condition and a corresponding celebration of equality as the society's highest virtue. But Tocqueville also saw that the commitment to equality led Americans to enforce a sameness of opinion and belief. This uniformity of thought was made all the more confining by the overwhelming commitment to majority rule, which could mean oppression of minorities. Because Americans measured status in material terms, Tocqueville discovered the paradox that American equality naturally begat *inequality*. He observed that the desire to stay equal with a neighbor spurred a general race for material success, and that some did become rich. "I know of no country where love of money has such a grip on men's hearts and where stronger scorn is expressed for the theory of the permanent equality of property," he wrote.[5]

Thus the most influential early interpreters described an American character formed mainly by the values of liberty, equality, and democracy. Liberty meant that Americans had the ability to do what they wanted without artificial barriers set by government or hierarchical authority. Equality was defined in several ways, according to the sphere of action: It meant a political system in which one citizen had about the same power as the next; a social order in which no aristocracy or inherited status was respected; and an economic system in which everyone had about the same chance to gain security and wealth. Democracy empowered every citizen to influence governmental authority over the society. Although often exalted in highly moral tones, these values could and did justify selfish action. In the critical eye of Tocqueville, liberty in America could encourage pursuit of materialism and disregard of the common good; equality did foster a uniformity of ideas and behavior; and democracy could result in an unwillingness to stand against the majority.

Anyone defining national character wrestled with the reality of race, especially as they imagined America's future. Like almost all white

Americans in his time, Thomas Jefferson believed that blacks were intellectually inferior to whites, though he did think they might be equal in moral sensibility. Jefferson decided that there could be no comfortable, permanent place for black people in American society, that they would have to be colonized outside the United States. In the 1780s Jefferson cited reasons why he doubted that the United States could become a free, interracial society: "Deep rooted prejudices entertained by the whites; ten thousand recollections by the blacks of the injuries they have sustained; . . . the real distinctions which nature has made; and many other circumstances, will divide us into parties, and produce convulsions which will probably never end but in the extermination of the one or the other race." Tocqueville was equally pessimistic about the future of race relations in the United States. He believed that the end of slavery in the South would likely result in the "most horrible" of wars between the races and the probable extinction of one race, concluding finally, "I do not think that the white and black races will ever be brought anywhere to live on a footing of equality." He further observed that whites in the North were even more hostile to blacks than were white southerners. Indeed, "race prejudice seems stronger in those states that have abolished slavery than in those where it still exists, and nowhere is it more intolerant than in those states where slavery was never known."[6]

The democracy observed by Tocqueville fully accommodated white supremacy, a commitment that went beyond a cultural prejudice to a firmly held assumption that whites must dominate blacks in all spheres of an interracial society. The Democratic Party in the North supported pro-slavery candidates, used specifically racial appeals to excite its supporters, and loudly condemned abolitionism as "niggerology." The Republican Party emerged in the 1850s not out of sympathy for blacks but from the commitment to giving white working men the chance for economic opportunity in the West without having to compete against slave labor. Its spokesman Abraham Lincoln shared Jefferson's and Tocqueville's skepticism about whether blacks and whites could ever live together as equal and free citizens. He also favored colonization. "Separation of the races is the only perfect preventive of amalgamation," he wrote, and it was both "morally right" and practical for all "to transfer the African to his native clime." Lincoln despised slavery, but when accused of being overly fond of blacks, he said he was not for "social and political equality of the white and black races," nor had he "ever...been in favor of making voters or jurors of negroes, nor of qualifying them to hold office, nor to intermarry with white people."[7]

Americans of a less thoughtful nature than Abraham Lincoln had embraced white supremacy with more aggressive determination. Throughout the 1830s and 1840s, mobs of whites in northern cities attempted to drive blacks from their midst with violent attacks. The influx of poor Irish immigrants in the 1840s and 1850s fueled much of the antiblack animosity, as the Irish attempted to force blacks out of workplaces and thus use a "whiteness" strategy to elevate their own status. Subject to intense cultural prejudice among Anglo-Americans, located at the bottom of the economic order, the Irish made pariahs of African Americans in order to insure that there was a group with lower status than they had. At the same time, white southerners insisted that racial inequality was the basis for a "white man's democracy." The North and South agreed on the goal of white democracy, but they divided on how to achieve it. Most southerners believed slavery made democracy possible, whereas most northerners believed slavery made it *impossible*.[8]

As discordant as it sounds amid the sweeter tones of liberty, equality, and democracy, white supremacy surely represented a basic value embraced by most white Americans at the middle of the nineteenth century, and their hold on it seemed to tighten year by year.

Discussions of the American character often presumed the existence of a fundamental belief in nationalism, a commitment to the honor and prestige of the nation-state created in 1776. For Abraham Lincoln, all considerations of the meaning of freedom took place in the context of his ultimate faith in the ideal of America the nation. For much of early American history, nationalism was expressed mainly in the belief in greatness ordained by God to the European Americans who occupied North America. The United States was the new Israel. For the first decades of the nineteenth century, American nationalism was reflected in the citizenry's great faith in their national government, even if the government in Washington impinged rarely on their lives. Nationalism acquired more specific meaning in the mid-nineteenth century when commitments to American prestige surged and found expression in "manifest destiny," Americans' growing ambition to dominate the whole of the North American continent. But when Americans focused their ambitions westward, nationalistic feelings became enmeshed with the commitment to white supremacy and tangled in the sectional crisis that resulted in the Civil War.

By the 1840s, the meaning of American nationalism began to acquire distinctly sectional aspects. For many northerners, negative impressions of the South's character shaped the definition of American nationalism. As the North became politically and economically stronger, a "northern" nationalism emerged based on a belief that the region's greater commitment to equality and freedom made it inherently different from, and morally superior to, the South and its "Slave Power." This northern conception of American nationalism would be strengthened during the sectional crisis, brought to high intensity during the Civil War, and maintained in many quarters of the North even after the war.[9]

One can accept that most Americans embraced the same values and still acknowledge the diversity of belief within the society. Abraham Lincoln observed this in 1864: "We all declare for liberty; but in using the same *word* we do not mean the same *thing*. With some, the word liberty may mean for each man to do as he pleases with himself and the product of his labor; while with others the same word may mean for some men to do as they please with other men and the product of other men's labor. Here are two, not only different, but incompatible things, called by the same name—liberty." Similarly, equality could be broadly defined as the desire for an egalitarian social and political order, *and* it could be narrowly construed as one citizen's having the same rights as another before the law. Democracy might be understood to mean every citizen's having a say in government *and* the majority's ruling in political decisions. White supremacy made some Americans defend slavery fiercely and others condemn slavery just as adamantly. The elasticity of meaning gave

Black soldiers' contributions to the Union war effort earned them full citizenship rights. *Courtesy Library of Congress.*

these values acceptance and currency, at the same time that it created ambiguity and confusion about what Americans believed.[10]

It also resulted in conflicts in values. Liberty unchecked surely can lead to inequality, just as democratic majorities can trample on the liberty of minorities. Fervent nationalism can override any of the other fundamental beliefs, and white supremacy did indeed simply cancel liberty and equality for blacks. Throughout their history, Americans have managed to settle, reconcile, or ignore such conflicts in values.[11]

I

By the time he became a national figure in 1858, Abraham Lincoln believed that one conflict in American life had to be resolved: the United States had to find some new status for the African American in order to preserve the Union. That year he made his famous statement on the connection between slavery and the future of the nation: "'A house divided against itself cannot stand.' I believe this government cannot endure permanently half slave and half free. I do not expect the Union to be dissolved—I do not expect the house to fall—but I do expect it will cease to be divided. It will become all one thing, or all the other." By late 1862, when he struggled to explain to Congress how to cope with the war disaster, Lincoln had recognized that his commitment to save the Union would necessarily change American race relations. Although he doubted that white Americans would accept full racial equality anytime soon, Lincoln began to entertain the possibility, pushed strongly by the black abolitionist Frederick Douglass and others, that African Americans' support for the Union war effort made them deserving of full citizenship rights. Once the black man had gotten the brass letters U.S. on his chest and "a musket on his shoulder," Douglass declared, "there is no power on earth which can deny that he has earned the right to citizenship in the United States." In his last public speech, delivered from a White House balcony just three days before his assassination, the president publicly announced his support for suffrage for educated African Americans and "those who serve our cause as soldiers." From the crowd below came forth an angry voice: "That means nigger citizenship!" And then John Wilkes Booth made a vow: "That is the last speech he will ever make."[12]

Lincoln's most memorable statement about the war's meaning to Americans had come in his funeral oration at the dedication of the Gettysburg battlefield in November 1863, just a few months after the battle that began to turn the war in the North's favor. His opening premise in the Gettysburg Address was familiar—that the very nationality the Union was defending had been created to uphold freedom and equality: "Fourscore and seven years ago our fathers brought forth on this continent, a new nation, conceived in Liberty, and dedicated to the proposition that all men are created equal." The crisis of the moment would prove whether the nation and its values would survive: "Now we are engaged in a great civil war, testing whether that nation or any nation so conceived and so dedicated can long endure." Gettysburg had become a symbol for how many Americans were willing to sacrifice themselves so that their nation, and the values for which it stood, could live on: "We have come to dedicate a portion of that field, as a final resting place for those who here gave their lives that that nation might live." Those who survived now ought to make the same commitment to those values: "We here highly resolve that these dead shall not have died in vain; that this nation, under God, shall have a new birth of freedom; and that government of the people, by the people, for the people, shall not perish from the earth."[13]

In this speech Lincoln redefined the meaning of America's fundamental values. Although the Gettysburg Address clearly echoes the language of the Declaration of Independence, it was not a reiteration of it. Liberty, which had originally meant to Americans a freedom from oppressive government, now was expanded to mean also that every person, regardless of race, was free from slavery. Equality, which had originally meant that any citizen regardless of wealth or status was equal to any other citizen in political rights, would come to mean also that people of African descent had the same opportunity for citizenship as those whose ancestors came from Europe. Democracy, which had originally meant that citizens, not monarchs or aristocrats, held the main influence over government, would soon be understood to mean that all men, regardless of color, participated in governing the society. To be sure, these new meanings did not become instantly clear in 1863: they would emerge afterward as Americans sought understanding of the Civil War. Nevertheless, Lincoln at Gettysburg articulated a fundamental change in what Americans would believe thereafter.[14]

It was one thing to suggest that freedom and equality had new meanings, but it was quite another to persuade Americans that those new definitions must be applied. Much of Lincoln's greatness lay in his ability to inspire people, both during his lifetime and after his death, to accept his conception of those values. The Civil War itself was an event so costly that Americans needed to assign to it large benefits like "a new birth of freedom." Those who supported the Union during the Civil War had afterward the memory of suffering to make them embrace broader meanings for liberty, democracy, and equality. Many people took Lincoln's martyrdom as atonement for the sin of slavery, and the parallel to

Jesus was often made. A Republican campaigning for party candidates in 1868 read the Gettysburg Address to crowds and then proclaimed tearfully, "That is the voice of God speaking through the lips of Abraham Lincoln!" Had he died in vain? the speaker asked. "Let us here, every one, with uplifted hand declare before Almighty God that the precious gift of this great heritage, consecrated in the blood of our soldiers, shall never perish from the earth."[15]

For many generations after his death, Abraham Lincoln would symbolize the American creed to which he gave new meaning. He became the most revered American, his image an icon of the Union and its democratic values. Successive generations of Americans would invoke his name and his words to call forth American idealism, even when the times were generally inhospitable to Lincoln's values. The vast majority of Americans were no more willing to reject Lincoln's contribution to the national identity than they were George Washington's and the accomplishments of the American Revolution. Often the understanding of Lincoln's contribution was only superficial, but in every subsequent generation of Americans, some studied the Great Emancipator's words and deeds and found inspiration to live up to his definitions of national values.

Lincoln's determination to save the Union led directly to a much stronger national government. The founders of the United States, men deeply suspicious of political power, had divided authority between the states and the national government. Southerners had relied on the divided sovereignty to shape their different social order. Northern victory in the war represented a defeat for the southern notion of divided sovereignty, and at the same time it greatly increased federal power at the expense of the states. Now no state or region could legally withdraw or renounce a national law, and the national government could force a recalcitrant state to accept a national policy. The war itself had greatly expanded the federal government's actions and had created the beginnings of a bureaucratic state that could act forcefully in the future.

In the process, Americans' understanding of their nationalism was strengthened and made much more specific. Now nationalism meant that the United States was a nation strong enough to survive the ordeal of civil war and to establish a permanent republic. The wartime experience merged with the antebellum northern nationalism to constitute an intensely antisouthern sense of national honor. More than ever before, the United States was a nation upholding a commitment to liberty, equality, and democracy. By leading the Union to victory in war and defining the meaning of its outcome, Abraham Lincoln shaped what American nationalism would be long after 1865.

Lincoln's understanding of the new birth of freedom immediately faced a powerful challenge. The Confederates returned home from war and passed state laws that denied freedom to the emancipated African Americans. The "black codes" typically included laws that made a crime of vagrancy, gave any white the authority to arrest any black who did not fulfill a labor contract, and denied blacks the right to rent farm land—all laws designed to force blacks back to the fields. In 1866 violence against African Americans in the South further challenged the promise of freedom. In Memphis a riot of white policemen and firemen resulted in much death, injury, and property destruction among freed people. In New Orleans, whites determined to prevent black political influence in city politics attacked a political convention and killed thirty-four blacks. The black codes and the rampant violence demonstrated the need for a political force to check the old "Slave Power."[16]

Northern Republicans saw that left alone white southerners would make a mockery of the Union sacrifice—and the martyrdom of the Great Emancipator. In 1867 they initiated military rule that oversaw a "reconstruction" of the South consistent with the new meanings of American democratic values. Under the U.S. Army's supervision, new state constitutions created governments that enfranchised the freedmen. New elections were held, and the Republican Party won control in state after state. To prevent white southerners from obstructing the promise of equality, congressional Republicans wrote the Fourteenth Amendment to the Constitution, which forbade any state to "deprive any person of life, liberty, or property, without due process of law" or to "deny to any person within its jurisdiction the equal protection of the laws." It was ratified by the states, and freedom and equality were protected for the new black citizens. The Republicans then wrote the Fifteenth Amendment, which specifically promised African Americans the right to vote, and, once ratified, it ensured the meaning of democracy. These Reconstruction amendments to the Constitution solidified the shift of power to Washington and put the expanded meaning of American values into the organic law of the land.

With emancipation African Americans were able to contemplate themselves as true Americans, people accepted as citizens, and they could confront the meaning of American values. As slaves, blacks had naturally understood values in a radically different context from whites, but they nevertheless embraced American ideals. Liberty had the compelling meaning of freedom from slavery, and it was commonly understood in the language and symbols of the Old Testament. With freedom from slavery secured by the war, blacks began to interpret liberty in the economic sense that whites did. They appreciated land ownership as the crucial underpinning to individual autonomy, and they soon recognized the inherently competitive aspects of American freedom. Equality and democracy, which before the war meant something only to the small minority of free people in the North, acquired specific meanings during the Civil War as promises were made to African Americans about voting, citizenship rights, and equal treatment before the law.

The African-American experience naturally had fostered deep ambivalence about the American nation. During the 1850s some free and educated blacks had rejected completely any sense of national honor. "What, to the American slave, is your Fourth of July?" Frederick Douglass demanded to know of an Independence Day celebration in 1852. "A day that reveals to him, more than all other days of the year, the gross injustices and cruelty to which he is the constant victim." But a pride in the Union flourished among African Americans during and after the war. They became some of the most ardent of all state nationalists, because the Union had given them their freedom—or, in the case of so many, it had given them the opportunity to fight for their freedom. After the war the national government acted to protect their freedom and granted them citizenship rights. For generations afterward, African Americans had faith—often more than was warranted—that the national government was their friend and protector in a society where otherwise they found only perils.[17]

The post–Civil War years were a time of great optimism and movement for African Americans. Freedom meant mobility, though it was almost entirely movement within the South. Until well into the twentieth century, more than nine out of ten blacks lived in the South. Most slaves left their masters during or just after the war and moved about the countryside, often in search of separated loved ones. Freedom also meant the opportunity to establish independent black institutions, especially churches and schools. By 1867 the beginning of military Reconstruction suggested that democratic rights would be protected. African Americans turned their Union Leagues into local organizations of the Republican Party and began to pursue political power. They knew instinctively that democracy was now the tool for defending their new liberty and equality. For blacks at that moment, the future seemed to promise an altogether new world.

"Will the Negro work?" was the question asked constantly throughout the South in the immediate postwar years. Through 1865 and 1866, many waited for the announcement that the government in Washington would divide confiscated land in the South among the freedmen in forty-acre plots. They believed the widely circulated rumor that the government would award "forty acres and a mule" at Christmas 1865, but no such news came. Still they held out for economic independence, for freedom from the dominance of white men.[18]

II

For Daniel H. Smith of Noxubee County, Mississippi, freedom meant the ability to teach black children to read and write. Born a slave in Georgia, Smith had come to Noxubee after serving in the Union army during hot battles in Tennessee and Georgia. Since the war Smith's determined efforts for black education had kept him in hot spots in Mississippi. One white man had offered to help him start a school if Smith would send his wife to be the man's maid, but when Smith explained that his wife was unwilling, the man warned angrily that he "didn't ask no negro what they did" but "generally made negroes...do as [I] wanted them to do." An argument about national politics so enraged a white neighbor that he drew his pistol and shot at the Republican Smith. In 1870, Smith made still another attempt to conduct a school, and this effort seemed more promising because it was part of the new system of public education just enacted by the new Republican state government. Yet the danger escalated. Threatening letters signed "KKK" arrived at Smith's house, soon followed by twenty Klansmen with a late-night warning that there would

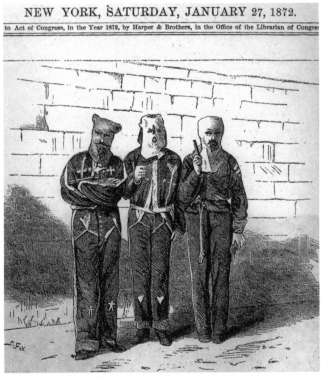

NEW YORK, SATURDAY, JANUARY 27, 1872.

to Act of Congress, in the Year 1872, by Harper & Brothers, in the Office of the Librarian of Congre

Klansmen terrorized black southerners in 1870–71. *Harper's Weekly*, January 27, 1872.

be "no damned negro schools nohow." Despite the harassment, Smith did begin a state-supported school in Noxubee County in the fall of 1870, and for a brief time black children enjoyed the long-desired education.[19]

But the apparent triumph of African Americans' ambitions seemed only to harden white opposition. That fall Noxubee blacks became the object of sustained violence, part of a reign of terror spreading over northeastern Mississippi. In the middle of the night, bands of mounted men wearing long white robes and hoods barked warnings not to vote, go to school, or rent land. They ordered some blacks to leave Mississippi altogether, and to show they meant business, they whipped men, women, and even children. At least fifteen African Americans were killed in Noxubee County, and about as many died in each of five nearby counties. Even Daniel Smith's determination finally had to give way before the unrelenting threats of violence. His black neighbors prevailed upon him to close the school. "The colored people commenced persuading me to quit," Smith later explained. "They said I had better, as they thought somebody would come and scare the children to death, and kill them, and me, maybe."[20]

The terrorism of 1870–71 dramatized whites' determination to reestablish their control in the face of the new Republican state government. A former Confederate Army captain who rode with the Noxubee Klan testified later that the organization's goal was "to make the negroes subservient, and make them fear [us]." The Klan generally believed that it was better "not to have negroes rent land at all, so that [whites] could always control the labor." A northern visitor found that the "feeling against any ownership of the soil by Negroes" was so strong among white Mississippians that the "man who should sell small tracts to them would be in actual personal danger." Daniel Smith reported that whites opposed black landownership because "if you suffer the colored people here to own land [whites] cannot get any laborers then, for where a colored man owns a piece of land, as many as can do will go to their land."[21]

In the United States, landownership had historically been viewed as the underpinning of republican citizenship, and thus to deny a person or group access to land was to take away the possibility of gaining citizen-

ship. Everyone, black and white, assumed that owning land was like voting or learning to read—a means to, and fulfillment of, the democratic
values that were promised to citizens. Landownership also represented
the most fundamental material measurement of status in American society, and thus it mattered greatly whether African Americans could
achieve it. In the specific context of Mississippi in 1870, the new Republican government had funded the public school system by putting new
taxes on land. The land tax seemed especially burdensome to Mississippians, because prior to the Civil War the bulk of state taxes were assessed
on slave property. The small farmers, who had rarely paid any taxes
before, now confronted a levy on their only real asset, their land. Many
were unable to pay it and took out their insecurity on blacks, whom they
viewed as the beneficiaries of the new taxes.[22]

The Noxubee events of 1870–71 revealed two crucial realities about
post–Civil War race relations in the United States. First, violence served as
the ever-present and final authority for enforcing white supremacy. Beatings and executions had been used to uphold discipline under slavery, and
now in freedom whites would apply these and other forms of brutality.
Various new institutions would emerge in this "free" society to impose
white supremacy, but upholding each one ultimately was the ability to
beat and kill any resistant African American without significant consequences. Second, schools provided a battleground over status between
blacks and whites. In the United States, education represented both preparation for republican citizenship and access to economic opportunity.
Blacks and whites, regardless of whether they had been to school, understood what education meant, and each racial group acted accordingly.
Blacks tried to get into schools, and whites worked to keep them out.

The violence of 1870–71 subsided and was followed by a few years of
relative calm in Mississippi. The U.S. government prosecuted seven hundred Klansmen in Mississippi for the reign of terror. More violence might
mean only more federal intervention in Mississippi, and some white
Democrats even began to call for political cooperation with African
Americans.[23]

But the violent white supremacists were only lying low. In 1875 they rose with a new vengeance that Democratic politicians called "the white line." In this strategy all whites stood together in a solid line against any black influence in politics. The white-line position of 1875 represented a more all-encompassing commitment to white supremacy than the Klan terrorism of 1870–71. Whereas the original adherents of the violent white-supremacist position had ridden at night wearing hoods, the proponents of the white line in 1875 marched in red-shirted rifle companies in the broad daylight. Bloody scenes recurred throughout Mississippi as the white line spread to every electoral precinct. On Election Day thousands of blacks were stopped at gunpoint from casting a ballot. The Republican governor appealed to President Ulysses S. Grant for military protection of the November state elections. None was forthcoming, as Lincoln's favorite general proved himself an unworthy protector of the Great Emancipator's values.[24]

Mississippi's white-line experience of 1875 was only the latest example of a kind of political terrorism that had already occurred in much of the South. Between 1869 and 1871, the white line had moved through Virginia, North Carolina, Tennessee, and Georgia. The white-line path of racial violence through Alabama in 1874 had been almost as bloody as Mississippi's would be in 1875. In South Carolina in 1876, Democratic rifle clubs used comparable violence to undermine black political influence in the one state that had elected a majority-black legislature during Reconstruction. By 1877, when the last federal troops were removed from the South and Reconstruction was finally over, virtually all of the old Confederacy was firmly in the control of political forces committed to the white line.[25]

If the Civil War and Reconstruction for a time had rearranged power between the states and the nation to benefit the cause of black freedom and equality, the withdrawal of federal power effectively put authority over African Americans back in its old place. Distracted by scandal, Ulysses Grant proved himself unable or unwilling to help the freedmen's cause, and his successor Rutherford Hays bargained away any remnant of Republican interest in African Americans in order to win the contested election in 1876. The Congress remained true to Lincoln's purposes longer, but after 1871 northern Republicans began losing their moral intensity about southern mistreatment of African Americans. Democratic takeover of the Congress in 1874 turned the legislative branch against racial equality. The House Democratic leader declared that blacks and whites were "not of the same race; we are so different that we ought not to compose one political community." The United States was "a white man's Government, made by the white man for the white man."[26]

By the mid-1870s white southerners had in effect restored state sovereignty that freed them to do as they wished with African Americans. They could deny citizenship rights, extract blacks' labor for their own benefit, and renounce the promises of the Fourteenth and Fifteenth Amendments, in deeds if not in so many words.

Whites justified such domination with a powerful new ideological claim. In the postwar years, white southerners developed the crucial characteristics of an ethnic nation. Since 1860 white southerners had formed a large part of their identity in opposition to a dominant political authority, the United States government. They had seen, conversely, the ways in which American nationalism had been defined effectively as "northern nationalism," the antithesis of southern life. Southerners had long since felt a keen consciousness of their geographical unity, a common aspect of ethnic nationalism. In the 1870s and 1880s, they made quick work of the creation of myths, which always support ethnic nationalism. They defined themselves by their common Anglo-Saxon "racial" blood, ignoring altogether their much more varied genetic inheritance. They imagined a glorious prewar South built on chivalry and Christian virtue. The fulfillment of Old South values was meant to be the Confederate States of America, but it was now the Lost Cause whose memory could be honored only by embodying its racial values in the benighted present. White southerners would expend much civic effort in the fifty years after the war memorializing the valor of the Confederate soldier. Reconstruction was the most recently created and most powerful myth: it was understood as the postwar atrocity of an occupying enemy in league with ethnic enemies, the African Americans, from which the homeland had to be redeemed.[27]

After the war, southern ethnic nationalism in effect replaced Confederate state nationalism as a central part of the ideology of white southerners. White southern nationalism, with its powerful emotional pull, separated the South ideologically from the rest of the nation, even when the vast majority of white Americans everywhere embraced the values of white supremacy. In the 1880s some elite southern businessmen, led by the Atlanta newspaper editor Henry Grady, would attempt to reconcile southerners to the North, but it is not clear that peace was made much beyond the hearts of corporation executives intent on doing business in national markets.[28]

White southern nationalism intensified the racial feeling of southerners by doubling the portion of white animus for blacks. Blacks were not only inferior human beings in their midst, they were also ethnic enemies, rivals for power and status. Southern nationalism demonized an "enemy" nation-state that explained whites' political and economic insecurity and thus justified the brutal domination of African Americans. And it alienated white southerners from the ideological bases—American democratic values—that during the Civil War had challenged the authority of white supremacy.

III

In the immediate postwar years, black-white relations were mainly established in the countryside where the vast majority of African Americans lived. By 1867 many freedmen had begun to reach a compromise with white landowners in an arrangement called sharecropping. Under sharecropping, a landowner provided a farmer with a house on a plot of land, usually fifteen to twenty acres, on which he planted, cultivated, and gathered a crop with less constant white supervision. The arrangement seemed to allow more autonomy to the black farmer than wage labor. The landlord provided the equipment, seed, and often the food to sustain the sharecropper and his family during the growing season. The sharecropper and the landlord thus jointly contributed to the production of

the crop, and after paying expenses they shared the money the sale of the
crop yielded. Although sharecropping appeared on the surface to have
been a fair partnership arrangement, in reality illiterate black farmers
were subject to the conspiracy of white landlords and merchants, who
always kept the books on the business arrangement. In slavery the white
man beat you with his whip, African Americans commonly said later in
the nineteenth century, but under sharecropping he beat you with his
pencil. Sharecropping perpetuated poverty and debt, especially as the
region's economy became increasingly dependent on one crop, cotton.
To make matters worse, the price of cotton declined almost continu-
ously during the last quarter of the nineteenth century, at the same time
that the southern population was growing rapidly. As a result, more and
more young white farmers joined the ranks of sharecroppers.[29]

The fact that both blacks and whites were caught in this bad system
intensified racial competition in rural areas. During the 1890s and early
1900s, whites terrorized black farmers from their homes and property.
Called "whitecapping" for the style of headwear the white farmers
donned, this violence was meant to enable whites to monopolize the
diminishing opportunities in depressed southern agriculture. In 1892 and
1893, in southwestern Mississippi, where the economic depression had
led to foreclosures on white farmers' land and where landless whites
could not get merchants and landlords to forego using black sharecroppers, whitecaps killed the livestock and burned the homes of black farmers newly moved into the area. Reported throughout the South between
1890 and World War I, whitecapping revealed the intensity of racial competition in the rural South.[30]

A rope stretched taut between a branch of a hackberry tree and the
neck of a black farmer became the most potent symbol of the white
line's final authority. In the 1890s lynchings of blacks increased to almost
two hundred per year in the South. The ritual execution of an African
American typically was justified by the need to protect white women
from black rapists. The Georgia suffragist Rebecca Felton told a gather-
ing of her state's farmers in 1897 that "if it takes lynching to protect
woman's dearest possession from drunken, ravening human beasts, then

I say lynch a thousand a week if it becomes necessary." But in fact the real cause most of the time was blacks' resistance to white domination in the economic struggle. The most common event precipitating a lynching was a dispute between a black man and a white man over a business matter that escalated into violence by the black man. According to Ida B. Wells, the outspoken black journalist from Tennessee, lynching was "an excuse to get rid of Negroes who were acquiring wealth and property," a means to "keep the nigger down." Sudden, violent death was the ultimate enforcement of white supremacy. "When the niggers get so that they are not afraid of being lynched," one white Mississippian declared, "it is time to put the fear in them."[31]

The poverty and insecurity of agricultural life pushed many African Americans away from the farm toward jobs in southern towns and cities. The black populations of Atlanta, Memphis, and Birmingham increased by half again each decade from the 1880s until World War I, and smaller cities and towns experienced only somewhat less dynamic growth. Two of every three black urban dwellers held domestic or service jobs, for which whites rarely competed. Within a few years after emancipation, some blacks found wage labor at tobacco factories and on railroad construction crews, and in the 1870s and 1880s they went to work at sawmills, iron furnaces, and coal mines. In those industries, the work was dirty, hot, backbreaking, and frequently dangerous, and the wages were low—about a dollar a day in the 1890s.[32]

Whites at first disdained such "Negro" jobs, but industrial work gradually attracted more frustrated white farmers, who brought the white line with them when they came to southern industries. It most often took the form of a barrier between black unskilled jobs and white skilled positions. In the industries employing many blacks, some African Americans inevitably acquired the knowledge to do skilled work, and employers often wanted to give them those jobs in order to increase the supply, and thus lower the cost, of skilled labor. In response, white workers agitated to monopolize the skilled positions, and generally they succeeded by simply refusing to work alongside blacks. White hate strikes to keep blacks out of skilled jobs occurred often enough in southern industries to be the most commonly cited reason by employers for not using black skilled labor. Similarly, almost all supervisory positions were reserved for whites. To put white men under a black man simply represented too large an affront to white status.

The sum total of black southerners' various experiences after they left the farm amounted to one plain reality: their opportunities for economic advancement were decidedly and intentionally inferior to white workers'. Whereas most white industrial workers during their careers moved up into higher-paying skilled and management positions, the large majority of blacks spent their entire working lives as unskilled laborers. The white line thus separated upwardly mobile white working men from blacks fixed—permanently, it often seemed—at the bottom of the socioeconomic order.

The brightest spot on the dark side of the white line resulted from the need for black business and professional people to serve the urban black community. Each southern town had a small contingent of teachers, ministers, undertakers, barbers, and beauticians who provided services to black people that no white business or professional person offered. Most southern cities were home to a few black doctors and dentists, insurance agents, and building contractors, and perhaps a lawyer or two. The black business and professional group almost never served whites, and thus blacks' economic opportunities were limited by the relatively weak buying power of urban African Americans. The benefit was that this black "middle class" operated relatively free of white authority and competition. Although this group represented a small portion, usually not more than about 5 percent of the black urban population, its existence proved that some African Americans could rise in the socioeconomic order—indeed above the economic position of many whites. These well-to-do blacks threatened the status position of whites, and their independence from white control meant that some blacks themselves might be able eventually to push the white line.[33]

For city residents black and white, the use of public accommodations became the everyday reminder of the white line. As southerners became more urbanized, whites attempted to order race relations in all public places by a formal separation. To be sure, much public separation of the races had been established prior to the migration to cities. During the late 1860s and 1870s, most African Americans voluntarily left churches where they had worshipped as slaves and formed all-black congregations. Virtually all schools formed for the freed people served only blacks. African Americans were usually denied access to hotels, restaurants, theaters, and parks, and if admitted, were put in a separate section. Republican-controlled Reconstruction governments enacted antidiscrimination laws, and public accommodations began to open up. During the 1870s and 1880s, African Americans sometimes used theaters, streetcars, and railroads on an equal basis with whites, especially in the upper South. But the more general pattern, and certainly the trend over time, was to provide separate racial accommodations. The usual choice for African Americans was between exclusion—and they continued to be denied access to many hotels, restaurants, and theaters—and inclusion in separate places.[34]

The dynamic character of the white line was witnessed most clearly in the competition for use of public transportation. In the 1880s whites began to agitate for separate seating on railroad cars, and most southern states passed laws requiring separate cars, or sections of cars, for first-class black passengers. Rather than provide a true dual service, the railroads usually relegated black passengers to the "smoking" cars on passenger trains, which were hardly separate, because white men partaking of smelly cigars, and often strong drink, were allowed to occupy that car with African Americans. In reality the racial separation on trains usually amounted only to a denial of first-class accommodation to blacks. African Americans naturally raised the matter of their Fourteenth Amendment rights' being denied in lawsuits challenging the separate-car laws. One case brought by a black Louisianan resulted in the 1896 U.S. Supreme Court decision *Plessy v. Ferguson*, which advanced a "separate but equal" doctrine that in the future would be the legal justification for all manner of racial distinctions.[35]

IV

Underlying the relentless movement of the white line to limit black freedom in the 1880s and 1890s was white Americans' thinking about race relations. Intellectuals and politicians writing to shape public opinion, from both North and South, turned increasingly hostile toward African Americans as they thought about the nation's future. Ideas about black inferiority were spread by popular culture and mass communications so broadly that by the end of the nineteenth century, fewer white Americans believed that racial equality was possible than had thought so in 1865. Much thinking about race derived in some way from the work of Charles Darwin. In *The Descent of Man* in 1871, Darwin wrote that "at some future period, not very distant as measured by centuries, the civilized races of man will almost certainly exterminate and replace the savage races throughout the world." Many commentators presumed that a competition for race survival in American society was well underway.[36]

In the immediate post–Civil War years, many whites presumed that blacks would not be able to survive in freedom—that ultimately they would die out in the absence of the care and concern of white masters. An inaccurate count in the 1870 census convinced some observers that the black population had stopped growing in the 1860s, and these commentators predicted that soon African Americans would fail to sustain their numbers. Much of this was wishful thinking on the part of southern whites, though the belief that blacks were dying out also comforted all those northern whites whose worst fear in the Civil War had been the possibility of mass movement of blacks northward. Another erroneously low count in the 1890 census reinforced the belief that blacks were on the road to extinction. As African Americans became more urban, one race "expert" surmised, they were more subject to tuberculosis, pneumonia, syphilis, and typhoid, and the disease factor combined with their propensity for "crime and immorality" to doom the race. Such conclusions were so widely accepted that in 1900, the chief statistician of the U.S. Census summarily declared that blacks would die en masse from "disease, vice, and profound discouragement" and that even those capable of rising to the "elevation of the white man's civilization will ultimately be merged and lost in the lower classes of whites, leaving almost no trace to mark their former existence."[37]

A belief that African Americans were degenerating into beasts bolstered the predictions of blacks' disappearance as a race. Most white Americans historically had viewed Africa and Africans as uncivilized, and an important corollary assumption held that slavery had provided the only civilizing influence that blacks in America had known. In 1889 a widely regarded historian declared that, once African Americans were freed from the governance of slavery, crime and sexual immorality among them had risen—as evidenced by the surge of rapes of white women. By the 1880s the assertions of black bestiality pervaded both the intellectual and popular sources of opinion, and in the 1890s even some of the South's most widely respected progressives had become pessimistic about blacks' behavior. In 1899 the South's staunchest white promoter of black education wrote that "when the interest and authority of owners was removed and former religious instruction was crippled or withdrawn, the negroes fell rapidly from what had been attained in slavery to a state of original fetishism."[38]

By the early 1890s readers of the leading American journals of opinion were regularly told that blacks ought not be in politics. Lord James Bryce, the British historian of the United States, maintained to the readers of the *North American Review* in 1891 that, while blacks were progressing in most areas, nine-tenths of them were "confessedly unfit" to vote. Since Reconstruction, Bryce surmised, "the Negroes have been unable to protect themselves in the exercise of the suffrage because they are naturally inferior to the whites—inferior in intelligence, in tenacity, in courage, in the power of organization." Even Frederick Douglass had conceded in the *Review* in 1884 that "for a time the social and political privileges of the colored people may decrease," though he thought blacks would "rise naturally and gradually" and hold permanently to the gains made.[39]

American popular culture had long reinforced such ideas about black physical and moral inferiority. The minstrel show had emerged in the

Zip Coon, left, and Jim Crow, right, were the main stereotypes in racist humor in the nineteenth century. *Courtesy Library of Congress.*

1830s as the leading form of mass entertainment, and its producers adopted antiblack stereotypes as the basis for the appeal. White actors "corked" their faces black to play the African-American parts. Every production incorporated the character of "Jim Crow," originated in the 1830s by an actor who mimicked a crippled black stable boy's awkward gait while he danced and sang a ditty:

> *W'eel about and turn about*
> *And do just so,*
> *Eb're time I w'eel about*
> *I jump Jim Crow.*

The Jim Crow character was stupid, superstitious, and slow moving. Another "Negro delineator" developed what would become Jim Crow's smarter companion on the minstrel stage, "Zip Coon," who was a criminal dandy, overdressed in a long-tailed coat and tights and outrageously outspoken in a nonsensical way. Jim Crow and Zip Coon typically served as the "endmen" in the minstrel show's comedy semicircle, and there they provided both the origin and the object of the antiblack humor. The mid-nineteenth-century minstrel shows featured music, commonly known as "darky songs," that romanticized life on the southern plantation. Stephen Foster, a Pennsylvanian, wrote many of the minstrel favorites—"Camptown Races," "My Old Kentucky Home," "Old Black Joe," and "Ring de Banjo." In the nineteenth century, almost any town with a railroad station and a hall received a touring minstrel company.[40]

Minstrel shows remained the most popular form of national touring entertainment until the 1890s, when the "vaudeville" variety show emerged. Vaudeville automatically adopted the minstrel characters. In the 1890s, Zip Coon became a more dangerous, razor-wielding persona, and all African Americans were presented as chicken stealing, promiscuous, and habitually violent. The main musical feature became the "coon song," which featured a bright melody and relentlessly racist lyrics. Popular titles included "No Coon Can Come Too Black for Me," "Who Dat Say Chicken in Dis Crowd?" and the perennial favorite, "All Coons Look Alike to Me," written by an African-American composer. Indeed, the minstrel stereotypes were so pervasive that talented black actors and musicians had to conform if they were to find work. In 1896, Bert Williams and George Walker, African Americans who had starred on the minstrel stage as Jim Crow and Zip Coon, developed a hugely successful vaudeville act billed as "Two Real Coons." In keeping with the tradition, they also blacked their faces for the stage.[41]

In the 1890s coon imagery suffused American advertising and mass communications. Cigar packages offered "coon" trading cards, and advertisements used coon images to sell a wide variety of products. Currier and Ives illustrations depicted the stereotypes, as did cartoon illustrations in some leading magazines of opinion. Newspaper comics serialized coon characters. One could not receive the most commonplace forms of communication in the 1890s without getting constant repetition of blacks stereotyped as lazy, stupid, and criminal.[42]

These men were convicts leased to an Alabama coal company. *Courtesy Birmingham Public Library.*

For the large majority of southerners who lived in rural areas, small-town newspapers were primary sources of white-supremacist thought. Small-town editors revealed "a general fear of the Negro," one historian has written, and they typically depicted an African American as a "wild, ignorant animal...black sensual fiend, whose intense hatred of the white race would cause him to strike with wild demoniacal fury at an unguarded moment." The newspapers commonly disparaged blacks physically, with references to unpleasant smell, "kinky" hair, and thick skulls. African Americans' morality was treated with great condescension: Black men were portrayed as predatory, black women as promiscuous, and black marriages as devoid of fidelity. Endless jokes alleged blacks' compulsion for chicken thievery and their affinity for mules. The most fundamental presumption of small-town and rural editors in the 1880s and 1890s was that a white man should always supervise blacks.[43]

One syndicated columnist had an especially wide influence on small-town newspapers. "Bill Arp" was the pen name of Charles Henry Smith, whose column appeared in perhaps half of all southern weeklies and many of the larger city dailies. Family-oriented, knowledgeable about history, and witty in portraying the oddities of human nature, Bill Arp appealed broadly, which made all the more significant his views about African Americans. He gave voice to many common myths of southern ethnic nationalism. He believed that whites in the South provided for blacks' basic needs, freeing them to enjoy life. In his Georgia community, "relations between the races are friendly and kind, and always will be." That was, Arp the southern nationalist added, "if the howling hypocrites of the north will let us alone." There simply was no place for African Americans in politics. Claiming that "the universal sentiment of the north is that he shall not rule up there, but shall have a fair chance to do it here," Arp responded, "We will not submit to the election of a Negro." As he moved through the 1890s, Arp focused increasingly on black crime. Georgia had nearly two thousand blacks in chains, but he insisted that the black man had "less excuse for crime" than a white man, because he needed less money and was "not cramped by society nor social temptations." Arp reported that nearly all black convicts were less than forty years old, and few had been slaves. "They have been to school, most of them, and most them are from the cities and towns. The old-time Negroes are not in the chain gang. They had no schooling but they had moral training.... Crime among the Negroes increases with their education."[44]

This intensely negative thinking about African Americans buttressed the white-supremacist impulses that pervaded southern society in the late nineteenth century. Had notions of black degeneracy and immorality been confined to intellectual discourse, or had blacks' alleged unfitness for political rights and education been limited to the minstrel stage, the ability of whites to insist on total authority over African Americans would have been weaker. But so many forms of expression—intellectual and political thought, popular entertainment, advertising, and mass communications—reinforced the message of black inferiority that popular culture clearly enhanced white dominance. Any effort to challenge white supremacy in the United States, or to combat the ever-growing white nationalism in the South, would have to address not just the political and economic forms of white dominion but also the authority of its pervasive cultural expressions.

V

During the 1890s white southerners codified their control over blacks though a system of segregation laws and measures to disfranchise blacks. The movement of southerners to town explained much of the perceived need: as more blacks and whites crowded into urban spaces, increased contacts raised the likelihood of racial conflict, and legally enforcing physical distance between the races was intended to reduce open clashes. Segregation laws also strengthened white authority in the face of rising challenges in the 1890s from a new generation of African Americans then coming to maturity, people who had never learned the deference taught in slavery. At the same time, young white southerners were more likely than their parents to view blacks as vicious, something supported entirely by the intellectual and cultural influences at the end of the nineteenth century.[45]

Segregation emerged also because the forces that opposed racial discrimination had weakened over time. The national government's concern for black rights had eroded greatly with the Republican Party's focus on the protection of business interests in the 1870s. When in 1890 Senator Henry Cabot Lodge of Massachusetts proposed legislation to enforce blacks' right to vote, white southerners reacted fiercely to such a "force bill." Its defeat made federal intervention less likely in the future, and the white South soon moved to codify white supremacy.[46]

Because the Fifteenth Amendment prevented states from simply out-lawing black voting, southern states contrived indirect means to disfran-chise blacks. Stepping forward first in 1890, Mississippians wrote a new constitution requiring that prospective voters be able to read the state constitution. Once registered, a citizen was required to pay an annual two-dollar poll tax for the privilege of voting. The new voting rules were remarkably effective: more than 90 percent of Mississippi's former black voters were disqualified within two years. South Carolina changed its vot-ing laws to similar effect in 1895, as did Louisiana in 1898, North Carolina in 1900, Alabama in 1901, Virginia in 1902, Georgia in 1908, and Oklahoma in 1910. The remaining southern states disfranchised with only a poll tax. The main concern was how to remove blacks without also disfranchising property-less, ignorant whites. Under the Mississippi constitution, voter registrars allowed illiterate whites to demonstrate that they "understood" the state constitution even if they could not read it, and they used the same requirement as the means to deny registration to literate blacks, whom they deemed unable to understand what they could read. Other states created loopholes for "unqualified" whites by accepting those whose grandfathers had fought in the Civil War, or those whom the regis-trars thought had "good character." But no exceptions were given for the poll tax, and mainly because of it the number of white voters in the South fell drastically after the disfranchising laws were enacted.[47]

Although disfranchisement had in fact created oligarchic rule mainly by planters, a white man's democracy remained the announced ideal of white southerners, and the Democratic Party tried to make it seem like reality. Democrats began to nominate their candidates in primaries rather than caucuses or conventions. Theirs was a "white" primary, which excluded by law the few remaining black voters—a biennial claim that a white man's democracy had come to pass.

Disfranchisement demonstrated one of the harshest ironies of post–Civil War America: democratic institutions—parties, conventions, elections, and constitutions—provided the most effective means to enforce white supremacy next to violence. Whites co-opted the demo-cratic process to impose their total dominance over African Americans. The more effectively whites used governmental institutions, the less need

they had for raw violence and the better they felt about their own domination. Indeed, white supremacy imposed by democratic sanction
seemed altogether legitimate to most whites.

Disfranchisement meant that blacks were essentially powerless in the
city governments that decided where parks, water and sewage services,
streetcar lines, and hospitals would go. Political impotence left African
Americans at the mercy of an unfair and often unforgiving criminal justice system in which virtually all policemen, jailers, judges, and attorneys
were white. Absence from the voting rolls kept African Americans off the
jury venire, and thus a "jury of peers" meant that only white men determined guilt or innocence. As the front-line enforcers of white supremacy,
white policemen in the South quickly resorted to violence; they could
beat or even kill blacks without much concern that they would be cen-
sured. Black men were commonly arrested in vagrancy "round-ups"
when white officials felt the need to force them to work or simply to
exert racial control. Once convicted, they then stood a good chance of
being sentenced to hard labor for an industrial corporation. Southern
states and many local governments leased their convicts to railroads,
lumber companies, and coal mines, where they often suffered under
appalling working and living conditions.[48]

Nowhere was the impact of disfranchisement greater than in black
schools. When public education was first made available to African
Americans during Reconstruction, black schools received funding about
equal to white schools. But as Daniel Smith's experience in Noxubee
County revealed, whites were intensely hostile to black education, and
they remained unsympathetic even after the Klan terrorism had subsided. White opposition became most apparent in the lesser amounts
spent on educating black children, and the racial disparity emerged as
blacks lost the right to vote. By 1900 southerners spent almost two and
one-half times as much on a white child as they did on a black child, and
the difference would increase in later years as the white man's democracy
became more entrenched. Throughout the South black children attended
class fewer months each school term than whites did. Their school buildings were smaller, less comfortable—indeed, totally dilapidated in many

These men were convicts leased to an Alabama coal
company. *Courtesy Birmingham Public Library.*

cases—and supplied with fewer books. Black teachers taught many more
students for much less pay.[49]

The white line between black and white schools marked a widening
disparity of quality that resulted in generations of relative ignorance
among African-American children and ensured that whites kept every
advantage in the future competition between the races.

VI

If conditions in the South were so bad and getting worse for African
Americans in the late nineteenth century, why did they stay in the South
rather than migrate en masse to the North? After 1860 the number of
blacks did rise in Philadelphia, New York, Washington, D.C., and

Chicago—most of that the in-migration of better-educated African Americans from the upper South, especially Virginia. After Reconstruction black southerners were in fact more likely to move west. Beginning in the 1870s with the "Exoduster" movement, thousands of southern blacks moved to Kansas, Oklahoma, and Arkansas. But in 1900, notwithstanding their frequent movements around rural areas and to southern towns and cities, almost 90 percent of African Americans still lived in the South.[50]

Some things were clearly better in the North. A substantial portion of the northern public—inheritors of the Lincoln and abolitionist traditions—still believed that blacks deserved citizenship. After ratification of the Fifteenth Amendment, African Americans in the North usually voted freely. They generally received better treatment in the criminal justice system than blacks in the South. Only some schools in the North were integrated, but the quality of the education given black children even in segregated schools was much more nearly equal to whites' than in the South. Few northerners assumed that they should appropriate the benefit of blacks' labor in the way that most white southerners did.[51]

But a white line did exist in the minds of white northerners, and its purpose mainly was to exclude blacks. Whereas most white southerners were willing to live and work among blacks in order to extract their labor, white northerners' dominant instinct was to keep blacks away from them. After the Civil War, the states of Indiana and Illinois continued to attempt to bar African Americans from living within their borders. Even after such efforts failed, extralegal actions kept blacks from living in parts of the North. In cities, black residences were usually confined to small, center-city enclaves. Hotels, restaurants, and saloons did not post the "white only" signs that became universal in the South, but African Americans were in fact excluded from many public places, and often the only way for a black person to know if he was welcome was to try to enter and risk the humiliation of rejection.[52]

The most important form of exclusion took place in the economic sphere, and there whites threw up an even higher barrier than in the South. African Americans in the North were most likely to find jobs as domestic servants—caterers, cooks, maids, waiters, and coachmen—

which was the work that most had done prior to the Civil War. But unlike in the South, where only blacks accepted domestic-service jobs in the late nineteenth century, they encountered in the North increasing competition for service jobs. After the Civil War, immigrants displaced blacks as coachmen and chambermaids in New York hotels and as cooks in restaurants. In the 1890s, Italian immigrants in that city and others would begin to take jobs from blacks as waiters, barbers, and whitewashers. In Boston, New York, Philadelphia, and Chicago, city governments rarely hired African Americans as firemen, street maintenance men, or garbage men. Municipal jobs frequently went to Irish Americans by way of political patronage through Democratic Party machines, and they represented good economic opportunities for the often-unskilled Irish. As American cities grew in the late nineteenth century, public employment grew with them, and the virtual exclusion of blacks from that sector of the economy became increasingly significant.[53]

Even more damaging was the denial of manufacturing jobs. Between 1865 and 1900, the American industrial economy grew to be the most powerful in the world, and that growth created a huge demand for industrial labor. Jobs in factories offered opportunities for upward economic mobility, especially among the millions of immigrants who arrived from Europe during those years. But African Americans were usually shut out of industrial jobs. They were rarely hired at textile mills in Philadelphia or steel plants in Pittsburgh or machine shops in Cincinnati or stockyards in Chicago. In all these cities African Americans came into direct competition with recent immigrants from Europe, and as a rule they lost the contest badly. Immigrants already at work in the plants pressed their bosses to hire friends and family members. In Pittsburgh, for example, where Polish or Italian immigrants dominated certain departments in steel mills, they insisted that their foreman hire a fellow Pole or Italian—probably the son, nephew, or cousin of one already working—when there was a job opening.[54]

The industrial employer who hired blacks ran into opposition from white workers. Between 1880 and 1900, there were at least fifty recorded hate strikes against northern companies that hired blacks. "In the North white mechanics and skilled laborers will not work at the same bench or on the same house with the colored mechanic," one industrialist observed in 1880. But in the 1890s, coal operators in Pennsylvania and Illinois and shippers in New York turned to black workers to break strikes. Labor unions in the North were stronger and even more discriminatory against blacks than in the South, where the relatively large supply of black artisans meant that some unions had to accept black members or face the possibility of employers' using only black labor. No such leverage existed in the North, and hence unions were freer to exclude blacks absolutely. Unions representing plasterers, carpenters, masons, and painters that accepted some black members in the South allowed almost none in the northern lodges. In 1880, Frederick Douglass wrote that "it is easier today to get a colored lad into a lawyer's office to study law, than into a blacksmith-shop to hammer iron."[55]

It is a harsh irony that, at a time when the United States was the fastest-growing industrial economy in the world and labor shortages were frequent and long-lasting, most white workers assumed that any job gains made by African Americans necessarily meant a loss of opportunity for white workers. Although that was a logical conclusion for workers to make when black strikebreakers took their jobs, by no means were all strikebreakers black, and this fear cannot account for the white monopoly imposed on most workplaces during normal times of labor-management peace. White workers' sense of labor competition overrode reality and reason, but it governed most industrial workplaces in the North nevertheless.

One consequence of the denial of economic opportunities was the much higher occurrence of crime among blacks than whites. Unable to find legitimate work that paid a decent wage, African Americans in northern cities often turned to vice—prostitution, gambling, and illegal drug and liquor trade—and theft. With the criminal economy went high incidences of assault and murder. A pattern of crime and violence was set in the nineteenth century, and it continued in subsequent generations through the twentieth century. Crime rates were also high among the first generation of Irish and Italian immigrants, but the succeeding generations among those groups, which much more easily found work in the industrial and service sectors, typically conformed to the lower propensity for crime and violence in the larger white population. Violent and criminal behavior by blacks reinforced the negative stereotypes that American popular culture so readily projected about blacks in the late nineteenth century, though the ugly images in the culture had originated largely independent of the northern urban developments.[56]

The African-American experience might today read very differently if black men and women had received the industrial labor opportunities that came with the massive growth of manufacturing in the North after the Civil War. Good jobs at decent wages, in communities where education was supported and political rights protected, could have changed the entire course of the black experience in the United States. Equal opportunities in northern industries surely would have accelerated the black migration out of southern poverty and oppression. Instead, while blacks languished on southern farms laboring unprofitably, a steady flow of immigrants from Europe took their places in the mines and mills and enjoyed the opportunities for economic advancement that came as the American industrial economy matured. Immigrants started their way up the ladder of wealth and status in the United States in large part because the abundant industrial jobs provided good opportunities to the first- and second-generation arrivals from Europe. By rights, far more of those opportunities should have gone to African Americans.

VII

By the end of the nineteenth century, the Lincoln revision of democratic values had effectively been canceled. American nationalism had dissipated, and with it went the ideological reinforcement that had been so authoritative during the Civil War. White southerners had developed a powerful ethnic nationalism that put them in ideological opposition at once to the national government and to their ethnic enemies, the African Americans. Darwinian thought had infused a special aggressiveness into the racial ideology of white Americans. Popular culture and mass communications spread the notions of race competition in vicious, easily accessible, and even entertaining forms. By 1900 the ideological authority of white supremacy and white nationalism had almost completely overridden the power of American democratic values to shape race relations. The Lincoln revision was in actuality a dead letter to most blacks.

How had the promise of the new birth of freedom been broken? Whites in the South had deployed violence in various forms to prevent blacks from pursuing economic, political, and educational opportunities. Death and destruction, or the threat of them, thwarted fair competition in each arena. Whites also seized dominant political power, gained ostensibly through democratic processes, to control the arenas of race competition. These two seemingly contradictory means, violence and democracy, had secured white dominance by the end of the nineteenth century. They would have to be overcome in the new century if blacks were to achieve any higher status. Or, the antiblack feelings in the North that kept African Americans confined in the South would have to be overridden.

As bleak as things were at the close of the nineteenth century, people at the time—black and white—knew that race relations in the United States were never fixed. At the start of the new century, new leaders were emerging to push the white line in unexpected directions. Some wanted to formalize even more blacks' inferior status. Others would attempt to reshape Americans' thinking about race and to reclaim Lincoln's understandings of democratic values. Notwithstanding the passing century's burden, the new leaders would move forward with determination to define for themselves the nature of race in twentieth-century America.

CHAPTER 2

THE NEW AND IMPROVED NEGRO

ONE MORNING IN October 1904, Congressman J. Thomas Heflin took the podium in front of a packed courtroom in the county courthouse at Tuskegee, Alabama. Heflin was campaigning for election in one of the important towns in his district, and the race had turned ugly. The previous night he and his Republican challenger had exchanged blows. At Tuskegee, however, Heflin turned his focus away from his opponent. "If the truth be told," one reporter observed, "Mr. Heflin devoted more of his remarks to Booker Washington and President Roosevelt than to all other subjects." The principal of Tuskegee Institute—by far the town's most famous resident—appeared to be an obsession of the congressman. Heflin railed against Washington's influence with Theodore Roosevelt, who had hosted Washington for dinner at the White House in 1901 in order to get the Tuskegeean's advice about patronage appointments in the South. "There they sat, Roosevelt and Booker," Heflin sneered, "and if some Czolgosz...had thrown a bomb under the table, no great harm would have been done the country." Here Heflin referred to Leon Czolgosz, the anarchist who had assassinated President William McKinley just weeks before the White House dinner. Heflin insisted that Washington was secretly scheming to get him defeated. "If Booker interferes in this thing there is a way of stopping him," he intimated to the courtroom crowd of three hundred, at the rear of which stood a number of blacks. "We have a way of influencing negroes down here when it becomes necessary." The threat of lynching was implied, but hardly anyone hearing the congressman could have missed his message.[1]

When Alabama was rewriting its constitution in 1901, Heflin had announced that he believed "God almighty intended the negro to be the servant of the white man." Freeing the slaves had put the nation on the road to race war: "Some day the clash will come, and I do not believe it is incumbent upon us to lift him up and educate him and put him on an equal footing that he may be armed and equipped when the combat comes." Now on the stump in 1904, Heflin explained that "we disfranchised the negro and we are going to keep him disfranchised." He drew a straight line from Washington's political influence to demands for social

Congressman Thomas Heflin. *Courtesy University of Alabama Special Collections.*

equality: "If Booker Washington didn't believe in social equality, he wouldn't do as he is doing."[2]

Heflin won the 1904 race and served eight terms in Congress and then two in the U.S. Senate. Booker Washington suffered in silence Heflin's threat of lynching, and no rope-wielding mob came for him. But Heflin's political success hurt Washington, who had enjoyed a warm relationship with Heflin's predecessor.

Heflin's denunciation reflected the recent decline in Washington's acceptance among whites. Starting in 1881, Washington had gained regional fame as the founder and builder of Tuskegee Institute, a school emphasizing industrial training among African Americans. He had risen to national prominence in 1895 on the reports of his speech at the Atlanta Exposition, a kind of economic fair for which he had been chosen as the lone African-American speaker. The most often cited passage of his brief "Negro address" to southern whites was the statement "In all things that are purely social we can be as separate as the fingers, yet one as the hand in all things essential to human progress." Washington would be credited with creating the "Atlanta Compromise," in which, many whites believed, African Americans gave up equal social and political rights for limited economic and educational opportunities. But in fact he was reiterating the consensus strategy among post-Reconstruction black leaders who had become increasingly pessimistic about the Republican Party and political activism in general. In the 1890s, African Americans strongly opposed disfranchisement, but by then they had already seen severe limits put on black political independence through terrorism and electoral fraud. As they turned in the late 1870s and 1880s more toward economic and moral development, black leaders emphasized self-help strategies and support of black businesses. By the time Washington made the Atlanta speech, the Tuskegee principal was ratifying an old reality. He got credit for creating something new largely because he was an eloquent spokesman who emerged at a moment when some white Americans were casting about for the black leader to replace Frederick Douglass, who had died a few months earlier.[3]

In the Atlanta speech, Washington began a sustained challenge to the ugly images then current in white intellectual and cultural presentations of beastly, immoral African Americans. The speech represented Washington's attempt to counter the presumption on the part of the white South, and much of the rest of the nation, that in freedom African Americans had declined in character and morality. He insisted that blacks were a people of "love and fidelity" to whites, a "faithful, law-abiding, and unresentful" people. The overarching message that Washington intended was not acceptance of disfranchisement and segregation but a belief in progress, in movement forward and upward.[4]

In the years after the Atlanta speech, Washington acted both openly and covertly to defend African-American civil and political rights. He organized political protests against disfranchisement efforts in several states, and when political action failed, he surreptitiously sponsored lawsuits to challenge voting discrimination. He also secretly brought suits against segregation on railroads, discrimination in jury selection, and peonage, at least some of which were successful. Washington's clandes-

Booker T. Washington. *Courtesy Library of Congress.*

tine manner was meant to shield him and his institution from southerners who did not suffer kindly challenges to white supremacy.[5]

But he also spoke publicly against the many wrongs done to blacks. In 1896, Washington told the *Washington Post* that forcing blacks "to ride in a 'Jim Crow' car that is far inferior to that used by the white people is a matter that cannot stand much longer against the increasing intelligence and prosperity of the colored people." In an 1898 speech at a Spanish-American War Peace Jubilee in Chicago before sixteen thousand people, Washington hoped the resurgent state nationalism might expand democratic values, as it had during the Civil War, when he asserted that the United States had won all its battles but the one to blot out racial prejudice. "Until we thus conquer ourselves, I make no empty statement when I say that we shall have, especially in the Southern part of our country, a cancer gnawing at the heart of the Republic, that shall one day prove as dangerous as an attack from an army without or within." In 1899 he made several widely published statements condemning lynching, including evidence showing that only a small portion of those lynched were charged with rape. It did not deter crime, Washington declared, but it did degrade whites who participated, and it gave the South a bad name throughout the world.[6]

As he became recognized after 1895 as the most prominent African American—and as he consciously accepted the role as leader of his race—Washington constantly tried to improve the image of African Americans. He was in effect challenging the ideology of white supremacy by contradicting the pervasive message of black degeneracy and criminality. The Negro as degenerative beast and rapist became an image so destructive that it had to be altered for the race to make progress. A more positive reputation for black Americans was needed to defuse some of the explosive feelings that had built up against blacks since Reconstruction, especially during the 1890s. In practice, creating an ideology to challenge white supremacy usually amounted to influencing what the public media reported about blacks. By the late 1890s, Washington frequently was sending press releases to both black and white newspapers that contradicted blacks' negative image by showing their economic and educational achievements.[7]

Washington should be understood as a kind of modern public-relations man who through his public utterances and his writings endeavored to change the image of the Negro by offering white America the "new and improved Negro." Washington's public-relations campaign relied on the simple strategy of presenting a competing image, one less threatening in all ways. This image of a new and improved Negro acknowledged, and corrected, a number of past mistakes. First, the Tuskegee principal criticized blacks for losing work skills acquired during slavery but suggested that they were now the hardest-working labor available. Skeptical of unions for their antiblack practices, Washington advised African Americans to be loyal to their white employers, and he insisted that they almost always were. Second, he said blacks in the past too often had shown a misplaced preference for highbrow arts, but now they were committed to practical education. Third, he believed that blacks during Reconstruction had been overly enamored of politics, but now they embraced an economic strategy. Rural landownership and entrepreneurship were their first goals. In short, Washington insisted that ordinary economic and moral virtues were not only the proper goals for African Americans but also the very ones they were now pursuing.[8]

Washington always portrayed blacks as embracing American ideology, an effort in part designed to reinvigorate the pro-black conscience that had existed in the North during the Civil War era. Washington idolized Abraham Lincoln, about whom he claimed to have read all that was written and to whom he said all blacks owed both physical and moral freedom, himself especially. He told blacks that Lincoln's life was a lesson on how hard work and honest character could take them from humble origins to a place where they could make great contributions to society. Washington's adoration of Lincoln was no doubt sincere, but it also served the practical purpose of solidifying his common ideological ground with northern philanthropists whose support he needed for black education in the South. The northern inheritors of the Lincoln and abolitionist legacies could act on their historic commitments by supporting Booker Washington's agenda.[9]

Washington made avoiding conflict a central part of his strategy. "Controversy equalizes wise men and fools, and the fools know it," he sometimes noted to close associates, quoting Oliver Wendell Holmes. Washington already knew what some modern-day public-relations experts teach public figures caught in the midst of controversy: answering criticism often only fuels a public-relations crisis. Thus he publicly ignored criticism of himself and the institute, whether it came from whites or blacks. Washington was almost always conciliatory to the white South because he believed that interracial harmony and white good will were prerequisites to black progress. For the same reason, he saw little value in direct-action protest and discouraged it. He usually emphasized the positive about both black and white southerners, and he typically just ignored contrary evidence, like the violent threats of Tom Heflin. Because he was purposely ambiguous in many public statements, however, blacks and whites interpreted Washington differently: When he disavowed "social equality," that meant to whites acceptance of white supremacy. To blacks it meant not eating or sleeping together.[10]

Running through all of Washington's public efforts to counter the intensely antiblack feeling in the South in the late 1890s was a defense of black education. In virtually every speech, magazine article, and newspaper interview and in many of the press releases sent out from Tuskegee, Washington dwelt on the great and growing value of African-American education. Having observed the removal of blacks from politics in Mississippi and South Carolina and having fought disfranchisement in Louisiana and lost, Washington by 1900 privately doubted that anything could halt the powerful momentum of the movement to take blacks' suffrage rights. The attack on black education that intensified over the course of the 1890s, however, represented an even more fundamental assault, one that Washington had to turn back or the main goal of his life would never be reached."[11]

Up from Slavery, Washington's autobiography published in 1901, represented his ultimate statement of black progress. "No one can come into contact with the race for twenty years as I have done in the heart of the South," he wrote, "without being convinced that the race is constantly making slow but sure progress materially, educationally, and morally." Washington had made himself, and he clearly understood that his life personified the progress that he wanted whites to believe about African Americans in general. Tuskegee Institute was to be seen as an objective demonstration of black progress. From the time that he emerged as a national figure and the leader of his race at Atlanta in 1895, Washington held fast to the idea that African Americans were going up, not down. "It is not within the province of human nature," Washington the public-relations man claimed, that "the man who is intelligent and virtuous, and owns and cultivates the best farm in the county, shall very long be denied the proper respect and consideration." Washington the realist had to know that was not true, but he was committed to presenting a new variety of Negro—one ready to meet the standards of material success that white Americans used to award status. Examined carefully, Washington's new and improved Negro implicitly was committed to the Darwinian struggle—and to winning it.[12]

Thus in his indirect, if not disingenuous way, Washington challenged the ideological positions of white southerners on several fronts. His emphasis on black progress countered the white supremacists' insistence on black degeneracy and criminality. His declaration of affection and loyalty to white southerners defied the white nationalists' belief that all blacks were their ethnic enemies. At the same time, Washington demonstrated to white northerners that he and his fellow blacks were loyal, patriotic Americans, the rightful and deserving inheritors of Lincoln's interpretation of democratic values. And, according to the Tuskegeean, African Americans accepted the inherently competitive nature of American society and wanted only a fair chance to prove themselves.

I

Washington's purposeful ambiguity and contradictions were lost on some whites, but not Tom Heflin and other white nationalists. Heflin was representative of a type of ethnic-nationalist leader common in the early-twentieth-century South. His competitive posture toward blacks closely resembled that of Governor James K. Vardaman of Mississippi, Senator Benjamin R. Tillman of South Carolina, Governor Hoke Smith of Georgia, and the North Carolina–born writer Thomas Dixon. All reflected the attitudes of a generation of white southerners who had little or no memory of the more paternalistic relationship between blacks and whites under slavery. One of Heflin's allies in the Alabama constitutional convention told that body that "we of the younger generation, we have known but one slavery, and that—slaves to the negro vote."[13]

Thomas Dixon contributed most to the advancement of southern ethnic nationalism in the new century. More than anyone else, he popularized the myth of how Reconstruction had exploited and degraded the white South. His writing, beginning with *The Leopard's Spots* in 1902, promoted the feelings of a region besieged by an aggressive outside force, the U.S. government. His novels made insistent demands for a white man's democracy in the South. "The beginning of Negro equality as a vital fact is the beginning of the end of this nation's life," Dixon's vigilante white-supremacist preacher wails in *Leopard's Spots*. "There is enough Negro blood here to make mulatto the whole Republic.... It's the one unsolved and unsolvable riddle of the coming century. *Can you build, in a Democracy, a nation inside a nation of two hostile races?*" Obviously not, the character answered, because "you cannot seek the Negro vote without asking him to your home sooner or later." Once the Negro is in your home, you will inevitably ask the Negro to dine, the preacher argued. "And if you seat him at your table, he has the right to ask your daughter's hand in marriage."[14]

The white-nationalist leaders were adamant that educating blacks was a dangerous thing. Tillman frequently declared that "it is foolish to my mind to disfranchise the Negro on account of illiteracy and turn right around and compel him to become literate." He denounced those who had helped establish black education in the South as "the biggest fools alive" and those who did not see that black educational progress threatened white political control as dolts plagued with "besotted ignorance." Dixon denounced Booker Washington's educational mission as a subterfuge to racial equality and amalgamation. Washington was not,

Dixon declared, "training Negroes to take their place in any industrial system of the South in which the white man can direct or control him." Quite the contrary, he said, "he is training them *all* to be masters of men, to be independent, to own and operate their own industries, plant their own fields, buy and sell their own goods, and in every shape and form destroy the last vestige of dependence on the white man for anything."[15]

Booker Washington's 1901 dinner at the White House represented to the white nationalist leaders a new alliance of their ethnic enemies with the U.S. government that historically had oppressed them. It suggested that the new president might restore the Republican commitment to black political power. It also reinforced the concern among many whites about the interest of northern philanthropy in black education, something that Washington had enthusiastically supported. As every white nationalist knew, northern involvement in the South could mean the restoration of Lincoln's values among southern blacks.

President Theodore Roosevelt. *Courtesy Library of Congress.*

The white-nationalist leaders had erupted in outrage at the White House dinner. "The action of President Roosevelt in entertaining that nigger," Ben Tillman announced, "will necessitate our killing a thousand niggers in the South before they will learn their place again." Vardaman proclaimed that Roosevelt had insulted every white man in America: "President Roosevelt takes this nigger bastard into his home, introduces him to his family and entertains him on terms of absolute social equality." Rebecca Felton, the Georgia white-supremacist suffragist, declared that Washington "was supposed to be a level-headed, educated colored man" but at the White House he "threw off the mask" and revealed that he was a "disintegrator and disorganizer of both races." Washington would be "wise to lift his Tuskegee plant and move northward while he is basking in Presidential favor." The editor of the *Memphis Scimitar* represented only the extreme of the nearly universal anger expressed in southern newspapers when he wrote that the White House dinner was the "most damnable outrage which has ever been perpetrated by any citizen of the United States," and that it taught a frightening lesson: "Any Nigger who happens to have a little more than the average amount of intelligence granted by the Creator of his race, and cash enough to pay the tailor and the barber, and the perfumer for scents enough to take away the nigger smell, has a perfect right to be received by the daughter of the white man among the guests in the parlor of his home." Almost immediately the White House dinner was memorialized with a coon song.

> *Coon, coon, coon,*
> *Booker Washington is his name;*
> *Coon, coon, coon*
> *Ain't that a measly shame?*
>
> *Coon, coon, coon,*
> *Morning, night, and noon,*
> *I think I'd class Mr. Roosevelt*
> *With a coon, coon, coon.*[16]

As threatening letters poured in to Tuskegee and rumors of Washington's impending assassination circulated, Tuskegee's principal forged ahead with the purpose that had taken him to the White House in the first place: the naming of federal appointments in the South. He made a protracted defense of Roosevelt's appointment of a black Republican to be collector of the port of Charleston against the determined opposition of Senator Tillman. All the while he was leading a vigorous, South-wide campaign against the spreading "lily-white" movement in the Republican Party, an effort of southern white Republicans to become as racially exclusive as the Democrats. Washington's political efforts provided southern politicians and editorialists with evidence of his interference in whites' control of politics in the South. Time and again, editorials decrying black political power referred back to the White House dinner, a perfect symbol of the way that black political influence led to demands for social equality.[17]

In 1904 and 1905 the white-nationalist leaders focused much fury on Washington. Vardaman wrote in a national magazine that he was just as opposed to Washington's voting "as I am to voting by the cocoanut-headed, chocolate-colored typical little coon, Andy Dotson, who blacks my shoes every morning." It was time, Vardaman insisted, to repeal the constitutional amendments "which gave the nigger the right to pollute politics" and to stop wasting money on black education: "More than $250,000,000 has been spent since the years 1861–65 by the white people of the North and the South in a foolish endeavor to make more of the nigger than God Almighty ever intended." He had asked the Mississippi legislature to remove its state constitutional guarantee of equal education in order that funding could be spent on "the white country boys and girls who are to rule Mississippi in the future."[18]

In June 1905, Thomas E. Watson, the populist Georgia congressman, charged in his magazine that Washington believed that "the black man is superior to the white." To give evidence of black progress, Washington had begun noting the rapid rise in black literacy, comparing their lower rates of illiteracy with those in European countries. Watson reported Washington's saying that "the negro race has developed more rapidly in the thirty years of its freedom than the Latin race has in one thousand years of freedom," though it is doubtful he did express it that way. "Why didn't you include *all the Negroes,* as you included *all* the Italians, *all* the Spaniards," Watson asked of Washington. "Why leave out your home folks in Africa, Doctor?" Does it not, Watson demanded, "occur to you that you may create a feeling of resentment among *all* the whites?" That, of course, was exactly what Watson was encouraging, resentment against Washington's assertion of black progress. Watson's attack was reprinted in many southern newspapers, and according to his biographer, it was more widely quoted in the South than anything he wrote.[19]

Then two months later, Thomas Dixon published in the *Saturday Evening Post* a less angry but more penetrating critique of Washington. A man of keen public-relations skills himself, Dixon had just delivered *The Clansman*, his second antiblack historical novel, and was then preparing his own stage version of it, which would soon tour the South. Thus Dixon stood to benefit from a newspaper controversy with Washington. In the article Dixon warned that Washington was building an independent black nation within the white man's America, which represented a great danger that inevitably would lead to destruction. Blacks were white southerners' ethnic enemies, and Washington was their sneaky leader. "Every pupil who passes through Mr. Washington's hands ceases forever to work under a white man. Not only so, but he goes forth trained under an evangelist to preach the doctrine of separation and independence." Dixon doubted that the southern white man would "allow the Negro to master his industrial system, take the bread from his mouth" but predicted that instead that "he will do exactly what his white neighbor in the North does when the Negro threatens his bread—kill him!"[20]

Just as Dixon's attack appeared, Booker Washington found himself in another firestorm, this one the result of a dinner with the department store magnate John Wanamaker in a New York hotel. Early accounts reported that Wanamaker's daughter entered the dining room on Washington's arm. Condemnation erupted from the southern press, and newspapers that historically had supported Washington now lost all restraint in denouncing him for practicing social equality. Events had turned so strongly against Washington that he broke his regular policy and answered some criticisms publicly. He had not escorted Miss Wanamaker to the table but admitted that he regularly dined with whites in the North. "When in the South I conform like all colored people to the customs of the South," he wrote to the *Advertiser*, "but when in the North, I have found it necessary . . . to come into contact with white people in the furtherance of my work in ways I do not in the South." He stopped short of any direct confrontation with his detractors.[21]

In the fall of 1905, as Dixon's play went from city to city playing to audiences that roared wildly in response to the melodramatic staging of Klan retribution during Reconstruction, Booker Washington traveled with Pinkerton detectives to protect his life from various assassination threats. At the time, Washington's white friends in the North, including the son and grandson of the abolitionist William Lloyd Garrison, worried among themselves about the possibilities of "the torch being applied . . . to Tuskegee in some sudden whirlwind of passion" and of Washington's becoming "a martyr to his cause." Washington did not openly acknowledge the real possibility of violence, but he did write a northern friend that "a large element of the South" had decided that "the education of the colored people shall go no further."[22]

Then in 1906 Roosevelt summarily dismissed from the United States Army three companies of African-American soldiers who were accused of shooting civilians in Brownsville, Texas. Listening only to the white army investigators, the president allowed the black soldiers no hearing and ignored the evidence that showed it unlikely that all—or perhaps any—of the black soldiers were guilty. Washington tried but failed to dissuade Roosevelt from the harsh action. One prominent African American told Washington that when he became Roosevelt's adviser, people believed that he guided the president, and thus "in the minds of many you are held responsible for the dismissal of the colored soldiers." Because Washington was known by the company he kept, his reputation among blacks declined with Roosevelt's betrayal.[23]

Just weeks after the Brownsville incident, whites in Atlanta assaulted blacks in the streets of the black business district and at streetcar stops, where they pulled black passengers out of cars to beat them mercilessly. White anger against blacks had been stirred by a bitter newspaper battle during a recently completed state election, but sheer envy of black success drove much of the frenzy. A young black Atlantan, armed and barricaded in his home, heard a shout from the mob heading toward his house: "That's where that nigger mail carrier lives! Let's burn it down! It's too nice for a nigger to live in!" To the common explanation among whites that the rioters were out to punish criminals, one black editor replied, "There is evidence that the mob was not after the worst Negroes so much as they were after the best."[24]

The Atlanta riot revealed the ugly truth about southern race relations in the very city in which Booker Washington had portrayed them as good and getting better. Once again, circumstances far beyond his control undermined his public-relations campaign. And once again Roosevelt betrayed him. In his annual message to Congress in 1906, the president focused on lynching as a central problem of race relations in the South and blamed African Americans for the South's lawlessness: "The greatest existing cause of lynching is the perpetration, especially by black men, of the hideous crime of rape." Try as he might, Washington could not overcome the assumption, even among supposed friends, of the "Negro as beast."[25]

II

By 1905, Washington also faced sharp criticism from his side of the color line. A contingent of African Americans had already rejected Washington's standing as *the* leader of black people. They disliked both his approach to race problems and his style of leadership. To some northern blacks especially, he was a sycophant to white racists by his unwillingness openly to demand political and civil rights. They were a small group, composed of a few hundred prosperous, educated families in the North and few dozen in the South, but they made themselves heard. William Monroe Trotter, editor of the *Boston Guardian*, openly challenged Washington at a 1903 meeting in Boston, an act that resulted in shouting and even fights in the audience. The "Boston riot" signaled the beginning of determined black opposition to Washington's leadership.[26]

It soon emerged that the most influential of his black detractors would be William Edward Burghardt Du Bois, the first African American to receive the doctor of philosophy from Harvard University and the leading scholar of the American black experience. At the same time that he offered realistic research on black material conditions, Du Bois held a mystical, romantic view of blacks' superior aesthetic and moral sensibilities. He believed that African peoples had a racial "soul" that was different from whites', which explained their distinctive senses and contributed to a unique duality in their existence. Du Bois made a famous statement on the ambiguity of the African-American identity: "One feels his two-ness—an American, a Negro, two souls, two thoughts, two unreconciled strivings, two warring ideals in one dark body."[27]

Du Bois started out as a friendly acquaintance of Washington, even considering an offer to teach at Tuskegee. In the 1890s, as he was rising to prominence in black intellectual circles, his own approach to black progress emphasized economic self-help and de-emphasized political action in the way that Washington and most late-nineteenth-century leaders' had. But when Du Bois moved to Atlanta in 1897 and confronted the ugly race relations of the South, he adopted a stronger commitment to protest. In 1899 he was horrified at the public burning near Atlanta of the corpse of a black farmer who had been lynched after he killed a white man in a debt dispute. In the course of a railroad journey in 1900, Du Bois was humiliated when he was refused a Pullman berth and had to sit up all night. Despite the fact that Booker Washington tried to get some redress from the railroad on his behalf, Du Bois apparently interpreted his experiences as evidence of the misguided nature of Washington's leadership.[28]

Part of the disaffection was purely personal. At the same time he was involved in the railroad dispute, Du Bois sought appointment as the head of black schools in Washington, D.C., but was passed over for the job. He blamed the Tuskegee principal, whose endorsement he sought and was

W. E. B. Du Bois. *Courtesy Library of Congress.*

promised and may have been given, for his failure to be appointed. By the end of 1900, his relationship with Booker Washington had turned cool. The next year he began privately to criticize Washington's philosophy and strategy. Du Bois's leading biographer concluded that his initial conflict with Washington had been "professional and then bitterly personal before it became ideological," and thus the ideological conflict was more a consequence than a cause of the rift.[29]

The ideological estrangement came clear in 1903 in Du Bois's *The Souls of Black Folk*. Objecting to what he perceived as Washington's acceptance of the denial of black voting rights, Du Bois argued that blacks had to insist on political rights if ever they were to protect themselves from white oppression. Washington, he wrote, "is striving nobly to make Negro artisans business men and property-owners; but it is utterly impossible, under modern competitive methods, for the workingmen and property-owners to defend their rights and exist without the right of suffrage." Du Bois believed that Washington's promotion of industrial education for blacks came at the expense of higher education in the arts and humanities. "He advocates common-school and industrial training, and depreciates institutions of higher learning; but neither the Negro common-schools, nor Tuskegee itself, could remain open a day were it not for teachers trained in Negro colleges." In Du Bois's eyes, Washington wanted to make the only black Americans worthy of note the local farmer or harness maker. Du Bois also faulted Washington for embracing conventional American values, because he believed that blacks should offer a contrary example to competitive individualism. They had a humane spirit that, if allowed to fill the world, might save it from the obsessions of status. "Negro blood" had a "message for the world" that soared above the commonplace preoccupations of white Americans. "We black men seem the sole oasis of simple faith and reverence in a dusty desert of dollars and smartness," he mused. Washington's program, on the other hand, "naturally takes on an economic cast, becoming a gospel of Work and Money to such an extent as apparently almost completely to overshadow the higher aims of life."[30]

It must have been a bitter irony to Booker Washington that his acceptance of competitive individualism made him enemies in two diametrically opposing camps. Just as Du Bois criticized his embrace of materialism, Tom Heflin exploited whites' hostility to Washington's strategy for blacks' advancement, which correctly presumed that as African Americans prepared themselves to compete with whites they sometimes would prevail in the contest for status. Thus black intellectuals and white-nationalist leaders hated Washington for essentially the same reason: the Tuskegee principal understood the white man's values all too well and was far too determined to master them.

In 1905 blacks' criticism of Washington resulted in the creation of a new African-American organization, later called the Niagara movement for the site of the first meeting. Du Bois and Trotter led thirty men united in their disaffection from Washington, which they voiced in a ringing dissent from his strategy. "We refuse," the Niagara participants declared, "to allow the impression to remain that the Negro American assents to inferiority" or that he "[is] submissive under oppression and apologetic before insults." Without calling his name, they had indicted Washington. "The Negro race in America...needs sympathy and receives criticism; needs help and is given hindrance, needs protection and is given mob-violence, needs justice and is given charity, needs leadership and is given cowardice and apology, needs bread and is given stone. This nation will never stand justified before God until these things are changed."[31]

The coincidence of the Niagara movement and the attacks from the white-nationalist leaders caused Booker Washington to lower his profile after 1905. His influence with Roosevelt waned, and then William Howard Taft disregarded his advice on federal appointments and implemented instead a "southern policy" of appointing whites to virtually all positions. When Roosevelt made a third-party challenge to Taft for the Presidency in 1912, Washington sat out the election, knowing but never

Public schools for black children in the South received a small fraction of the money of white childrens'. *Courtesy Library of Congress.*

saying that neither could be counted as a friend. Woodrow Wilson drew the support of Du Bois, who believed the Democrat would "treat black men and their interests with farsighted fairness." Soon Du Bois too would know the bitter taste of White House betrayal.[32]

After 1905, Washington gradually retired the "new and improved Negro" campaign in favor of a posture in which he publicly identified wrongs done to African Americans. In 1912 he wrote that blacks in the West Indies had a better chance to get an academic education than those in the United States. They also enjoyed more "protection of life and property and even-handed justice in the courts." Jamaica had "neither mobs, race riots, lynchings, nor burnings, such as disgrace our civilization." Southern states placed a higher monetary value on leased convicts—$46 per month—than they did on black schoolteachers, who earned only $30. "In the matter of education," Washington jibed, "the negro in the South has not had what Colonel Roosevelt calls a 'square deal,'" pointing to the Alabama county that spent $15 on each white child every year and 33 cents on each black student. In the northern states, African Americans had much better educational opportunities, but "from an economic point of view, the negro in the North, when compared with the white man, does not have a fair chance." His last statement on race relations, published posthumously in 1915, condemned residential segregation laws and went on to reject segregation in toto because it was "unjust...unnecessary...inconsistent...[and] administered in such a way as to embitter the Negro and harm more or less the moral fibre of the white man."[33]

Such criticism of American race relations marked a departure in tone and interpretation from Washington's earlier emphasis on the positive. He did not admit the failure of his "new and improved Negro" campaign, but he did begin to adopt what had become the consensus strategy among African Americans of protest against discrimination. The founding of the National Association for the Advancement of Colored People (NAACP) in 1909 had brought together various constituencies, including the failing Niagara movement, into an organization to protect black rights legally and agitate for them in various other ways. The founding of the NAACP, like the northern support for Tuskegee Institute, represented the persistence of a northern pro-black conscience that had been shaped by abolitionism and Abraham Lincoln, even as most of the northern public remained indifferent to exploitation of African Americans. Washington opposed the new organization because some of its founders were hostile to him, but the personal enmity at the time should not obscure the common concerns evident between the NAACP strategy and Washington's activities.

Washington had anticipated almost all of the NAACP's successful civil rights efforts. In the two decades prior to the NAACP's founding, he had made public protests against discrimination on railroads, lynching, unfair voting qualifications, and discriminatory funding in education. After 1909 he also spoke out against segregated housing legislation and discrimination by labor unions. Washington arranged and partly financed himself lawsuits challenging disfranchisement, jury discrimination, and peonage. And he campaigned constantly through his public statements and press releases against the pernicious images projected in the media and popular culture about blacks, as he would protest in 1915 the showing of *Birth of a Nation*, the motion-picture version of Dixon's novels. As early as 1903, Washington had seen the need for a national black newspaper in order to record African Americans' concerns and achievements in one periodical, and he attempted to make the *New York Age* that very thing.[34]

The NAACP would have the same concerns as Washington about segregated public accommodations, lynching and the criminal justice system, and economic discrimination, and it would bring legal challenges to protect blacks' right to vote, get an education, and have fair access to housing. It would also condemn regularly the ugly stereotypes prevalent in American life. One of the NAACP's, and Du Bois's, greatest successes was the establishment of the magazine *Crisis* in 1910 to report on civil rights issues to a national black audience. *Crisis* accomplished much of what Washington had in mind with a nationwide black publication.

Washington thus had anticipated virtually all of the NAACP's later successful protest agenda. In fact, a consensus of what needed to be done to protect black rights had been identified as early as 1900, and he and the NAACP had in turn pursued it. By 1910 there was little debate among African Americans about the necessity for direct challenges to discrimination.

But there were important ideological differences between Du Bois and Washington. In the early 1900s, Du Bois was becoming a black ethnic nationalist. To be sure, he would be much more than an ethnic nationalist: he advanced understandings of both democratic socialism in the United States and cultural cosmopolitanism in a transatlantic context. But he did in fact believe in essential differences between blacks and whites—that people of African descent were born with a kind of second sight or sensibility superior to whites'. Washington, on the other hand, assumed that blacks and whites were innately alike and that history and environment accounted for the differences in group behavior. He wanted blacks to have a stronger positive identity as a group—hence his emphasis on improving communication—but not as a people with a special racial soul as Du Bois imagined. Washington thought first of black people in competition with Dixon, Vardaman, and Tillman and their followers. The conflict with Du Bois and Trotter represented to him a vexing and unnecessary distraction from his real challenges in the South.

Washington had faith that democratic values, as defined by Abraham Lincoln, provided the ideological foundation most likely to enable black uplift. Du Bois had less faith in the American nation and its creed. He saw African Americans providing a foil to dominant American values, which he believed were materialism and excessive competitiveness. Finally, Du Bois thought mainly in terms of advancing the educated elite of blacks, while Washington's strategy more nearly encompassed the ambitions of all African Americans. Indeed, the similarities between the two men have been obscured and the differences often misunderstood.

III

While race leaders engaged in ideological battles, the dynamic of racial competition for urban space, economic opportunity, and political influence became ever more apparent. The white line drawn first on railroads set a pattern of separate and inferior treatment that would be applied to successive new forms of public transportation in the early twentieth century. Streetcars became the location of racial conflict between 1900 and 1906 as most southern cities passed laws to separate passengers by race. Streetcar companies opposed the laws, because they were expensive and difficult to administer, and the companies were vulnerable to the economic pressure of blacks, who usually composed a large share of the riders. In place after place, angry black riders boycotted the streetcars when the laws went into effect. But the companies had to listen to strident white demands for separation, because they were subject to the oversight of state and city governments in which white voters had the controlling influence. Segregation always prevailed. But streetcars remained an arena for racial conflict because of frequent confusion about the location of the line between the races. "White people will seat from front of car toward the back and colored people from rear toward front," read the sign passen-

Streetcars were segregated in the South despite many black protests. *Courtesy Birmingham Public Library.*

gers saw upon boarding a streetcar in turn-of-the-century Atlanta. "The color line is drawn, but neither race knows just where it is," one observer wrote. "Indeed it can hardly be drawn...because it is changing."[35]

Racial competition for jobs increased in the South as more farmers moved to town. It grew intense on southern railroads after 1900, when the lines began to replace white unionized firemen with lower-paid, nonunion blacks. The Georgia Railroad had been adding black firemen for several years when in 1909 the Brotherhood of Locomotive Firemen struck the line and began to whip up the white public's racial feelings. "Will the people of Georgia back their own men," the union leader asked in a public letter, "or will they back the Georgia railroad in trying to ram negro supremacy down the throats of its white firemen?" Soon white mobs were pulling black firemen from trains and beating them. The violence ultimately brought a compromise that allowed the railroad to continue to use black firemen but required it to pay them at the same rate as whites, an agreement that took away the railroads' incentive to use black labor. Over the next few years, white railroad workers across the South campaigned against the use of black firemen, and the number of black men working on the railroad began an inexorable slide downward.[36]

For African Americans in the North, job discrimination continued to pervade industry and trades after 1900. "All men know," *Crisis* reported in 1912, "that under ordinary circumstances no black artisan" worked in any of twenty-three listed trades from baker to upholsterer "unless he works as a 'scab.'" In trades where blacks had enjoyed a strong presence in the nineteenth century, competition from white immigrants often drove them out of jobs after 1900. The number of black barbers and waiters in Cleveland fell so sharply in the early 1900s that by the 1920s almost no black rendered those services to whites—and this became increasingly the case in all the American cities that received substantial numbers of immigrants from southern Europe after 1890. African Americans were almost entirely excluded from the new jobs that emerged around the turn of the century—electrician, streetcar conductor, telephone operator, and department store clerk, to name a few.[37]

Strikebreaking afforded the best opportunities for higher-paying jobs for African Americans. In Chicago blacks worked as replacements in the 1904 stockyard strike and the 1905 teamsters strike, and in both instances they endured violent attacks from striking whites, including one instance in which five thousand whites stoned two hundred blacks outside a meat-packing plant. Although many whites also worked as strikebreakers in Chicago, only blacks acquired the reputation of being a "scab race." After the strikes were defeated, blacks typically lost their new jobs, but rein-stated white workers neither forgave nor forgot the strike experience. "It was the niggers that whipped you in line," Ben Tillman told a large gath-ering of defeated Chicago packinghouse workers in 1904. "They were the club with which your brains were beaten out."[38]

Race violence was becoming much more real than the white-nation-alist leader's symbolic language. A series of riots in northern cities and towns starting in 1900 revealed the potential seriousness of racial conflict. In New York City in 1900; Evansville, Indiana, in 1903; Springfield, Ohio, in 1904 and 1906; and Greenburg, Indiana, in 1906, white mobs pursued African Americans in black neighborhoods, assaulted many, and killed a few—and destroyed much property.[39]

The most noteworthy riot of the period occurred in 1908 in Spring-field, Illinois. Angry at the safe removal from the Springfield jail of two African Americans, one charged with rape and the other with murdering the rape victim's father, a mob destroyed twenty-one black-owned busi-nesses and lynched two black businessmen, one an eighty-year-old shoe-maker. The mob burned the houses of forty poor black families and then ransacked those of well-to-do blacks throughout Springfield. A high pro-portion of the rioters were working men who clearly meant to run all blacks out of the city and to force the city's elite to go along with it. The rioters singled out the town's wealthiest blacks for the worst violence—and death. Visiting Springfield just after the riot, one journalist found the most common explanation for the violence among Springfield whites to be "the niggers came to think they were as good as we are!" The rioters saw Springfield's blacks as a threat to "their sense of dignity and status," one historian has observed. "Any signs of black success, power, and upward mobility may have angered them."[40]

Competition for urban space intensified after 1900 as African Americans continued a slow but steady move to the large eastern cities, and more began going to "border" cities such as Baltimore, Kansas City, Louisville, and St. Louis. Between 1900 and 1910, a half million African Americans moved to southern cities, more than during any previous time. Responding to the fears of white residents of McCulloh Street when a Yale-educated black lawyer moved his family into a home there, the city of Baltimore in 1910 made it illegal for citizens to occupy a house on a street that currently was populated entirely by people of another race. While the NAACP challenged the Baltimore law as a violation of property rights, whites bombarded the black homes on McCulloh Street. In Kansas City, a two-block area of formerly all-white housing experienced five separate bombings after two African-American families moved there. Such violence only convinced more cities that they needed segregation laws. Between 1911 and 1914, Atlanta, Norfolk, Richmond, Birmingham, New Orleans, and many smaller cities passed such ordinances.[41]

African Americans also lost in the competition for political opportunities, especially with the return of a Democrat to the White House. Their bitter disappointment with Roosevelt and Taft having turned them to Woodrow Wilson, Du Bois and many African-American voters were shocked by the new president's policies. Within a few months of taking the White House, Wilson had ordered segregated toilets, lunchrooms, and work areas in the Treasury and Post Office departments. For the first time, photographs began to be required on applications for federal civil-service jobs. Wilson replaced all African Americans in the attorney general's office and the Navy Department with whites. African Americans received the clear message that the national government—formerly their friend and protector—had become belligerently hostile to their interests.[42]

IV

Even after Booker Washington had given up his "new and improved Negro" campaign, there remained a great need to address the ugly stereotypes and vicious images that most whites held about blacks. In

1915, African Americans' concerns about racial stereotyping in American popular culture reached new heights with the release of David W. Griffith's film *Birth of a Nation*. Griffith used such new cinematic techniques as the close-up and the flashback to tell a story of the Civil War and Reconstruction based on Thomas Dixon's novels. The film recounted the experience of two families, one southern and one northern, joined by marriage, who moved from the carefree and peaceful antebellum time through the tragedy of war and then into the chaos of emancipation and Reconstruction. African Americans were portrayed in the antebellum years as happy and loyal servants, but then after the war mainly as dangerous beasts intent on sexual exploitation of white women and thwarted only by the emergence of multitudes of mounted Ku Klux Klansmen. Its most evocative scenes showed a lustful "renegade Negro" chasing a southern white woman until he drove her to suicide.[43]

After its premiere showing in Los Angeles, the NAACP responded quickly with protests and demands for censoring the racist portrayals. In the face of the NAACP protests, however, Thomas Dixon took the film to the White House and screened it for his friend Woodrow Wilson. "It's like writing history with lightning," the president reportedly said. "My only regret is that it is all so terribly true." With Wilson's endorsement, the film opened two days later in New York City, and despite the presence of many protestors, three million people would see it there during the next year. This powerful new medium made old images more horrible than ever, and against that influence African Americans' consistent protests seemed powerless. When *Birth of a Nation* was screened in Atlanta, the streets near the theater were filled with white Georgians mounted on horseback wearing full Ku Klux Klan regalia.[44]

These same years brought the first notable example of Americans' race anxieties revealed in sporting contests. Boxing commanded wide popular interest in the early twentieth century, and its champions were well-known celebrities. When in 1905 boxing's longtime heavyweight champion Jim Jeffries retired, the sport's popularity began to wane, and in order to bring back some fans, the new champion in 1908 agreed to fight Jack Johnson, a powerful black boxer. This represented a break with the practice of white boxers' refusing to enter the ring with African

Americans. Given the one chance, Johnson knocked out the champion and took the title, an act that, according to the *Chicago Tribune*, made black residents of that city jubilant: "It was too good to be true.... It was purely pride of race that made them joyful." In the next year Jack Johnson met five white opponents and defeated them all. Almost immediately a campaign emerged to ban boxing, but there was more support for finding a "white hope" to beat Johnson, who compounded his challenge to white supremacy by taking a white wife.[45]

"A naygur prizefighter havin' baten a white prize-fighter," observed the satirist Peter Finlay Dunne in the character of Mr. Dooley, "an almost univarsal demand arose from all classes f'r th' renowned James J. Jeffries to issue fr'm th' seculusion iv his saloon an' put a head on th' Sengam-byan." Many whites assumed that the former champion would settle once and for all the issue of white supremacy, but the *Chicago Daily News* expressed some Darwinian doubts about who was the fittest: "Could even Herbert Spencer extract comfort from so dread a situation?" the editors wondered, assuming that the chief proponent of "social" Darwinism would share their fear that Anglo-Saxon civilization was in real jeopardy

Jack Johnson. *Courtesy AP/Wideworld Photos.*

in the contest with the "gifted but non-Caucasian Mr. Johnson." A few days before the fight, Jeffries tried to reassure white America: "That portion of the white race that has been looking to me to defend its athletic superiority may feel assured that I am fit to do my very best." The *New York Times* reported that Americans had seen nothing for years like the anticipation of the Johnson-Jeffries fight, on which rode much more than the purse: "If the black man wins, thousands of his ignorant brothers will interpret his victory as justifying claims to much more than mere physical equality with their white neighbors."[46]

A chorus of "All Coons Look Alike to Me" thundered from the 20,000 spectators gathered in Reno as Jack Johnson entered the ring on July 4, 1910. Another 30,000 stood in New York's Times Square reading tape reports of the match, and 10,000 waited outside an Atlanta newspaper office for any word. It was clear from round one who was the fitter, though Johnson, laughing and taunting, allowed Jeffries to survive for fourteen rounds before knocking him out in the fifteenth. As the news flashed around the country, racial violence broke out in northern cities and small towns in the South. Three thousand whites attacked blacks in midtown Manhattan, and three African-American supporters of Johnson died in a gunfight in Uvaldia, Georgia. In communities throughout the United States, blacks revised the lyrics of an old spiritual:

> *Amazin' Grace, how sweet it sounds,*
> *Jack Johnson knocked Jim Jeffries down.*
> *Jim Jeffries jumped up an' hit Jack on the chin.*
> *An' then Jack knocked him down agin.*
> And a new ditty was heard in black neighborhoods:
> *The Yankees hold the play,*
> *The white man pull the trigger;*
> *Make no difference what the white man say,*
> *The world champion's still a nigger.*[47]

Apparently invincible in the ring, Johnson proved vulnerable outside it when in late 1912 he was charged with abducting a young white woman and taking her across a state line for immoral purposes. The law was

intended to stop prostitution, and though Johnson's liaisons were all con-
sensual, the U.S. government prosecuted him relentlessly and won a conviction in 1913. "This negro, in the eyes of many, has been persecuted,"
the prosecutor announced after the conviction. "Perhaps as an individual
he was. But it was his misfortune to be the foremost example of the evil
in permitting the intermarriage of whites and blacks." Johnson fled to
Europe, and in 1915, showing the ill effects of the persecution and exile,
finally lost the title to a "white hope." In 1920 he returned to the United
States, served a year's prison sentence for his conviction, and prepared at
age forty-two to reclaim his title, only to have the current champion Jack
Dempsey announce that he would fight only white boxers. Johnson's
boxing career was over.[48]

The fate of Jack Johnson and the triumph of *Birth of a Nation* demonstrated that American race conflicts in the twentieth century would be
dramatized in symbolic conflicts watched by the popular masses. Each
revealed the intense racial competition for status in American
society—among whites insisting on enforcing supremacy in every place
and among blacks struggling to achieve equality, or at least some fairness,
in the areas where it was warranted. Furthermore, both the fall of Jack
Johnson and the plot of *Birth of a Nation* turned on whites' hysterical
opposition to black men's sexual desire for white women, whether real
(Johnson's) or imagined (Dixon's and Griffith's). Black men had to be
stopped from consorting with white women, because doing so seemed
to afford them equal power to white men. Rarely, however, would the
growing millions of Americans who watched racial competition in the
popular culture achieve a deep or complex understanding of what was
happening. Most of the time, they would just root for their man to win.

V

The first decade and a half of the twentieth century had witnessed the
emergence of compelling race leaders who pushed their followers to
keener racial consciousness in order to advance their group's status in

American society. The white-nationalist leaders exploited every means to elevate whites over blacks. They especially relished the example of Booker Washington, whose efforts to help blacks rise were used to instruct whites to be aggressive, even brutal, in the defense of whites' superior status. Washington, on the other hand, understood the nature of the racial competition for status, and he developed an artful, if finally unsuccessful, strategy to defuse white hostility. He developed ideological appeals to challenge the ideas used to keep blacks down—race degeneracy, ethnic enmity, sectional hatred—and he promoted with vigor his more positive views of black progress, interracial affection, sectional reconciliation, and American patriotism. Washington showed other African Americans the kind of action that would be necessary to overcome the oppression they endured. His rival Du Bois would advance a similar strategy after Washington's death in 1915 in a more open manner than Washington thought possible for himself. Over the course of the next two generations, the protest strategy would succeed.

For Washington and the white-nationalist leaders who hated him, race competition occurred entirely within the southern context. But after 1915 much of the discussion of race relations in the United States took place in the North, where whites lacked the power and the will to dominate blacks as completely as they did in the South. There African Americans would demonstrate a more aggressive pursuit of new opportunities and more determination to resist violence against them. Getting out of the South generated much new hope for fulfillment of Abraham Lincoln's promise of democratic values to blacks. Indeed, the North in the years ahead would become for many southern blacks the "land of hope." In strange places, at a time when the world seemed in flux, African Americans would find great opportunities to create for themselves a new and improved Negro.

CHAPTER 3

THE SYNCOPATED RHYTHM

ON A SUMMER AFTERNOON in 1916, a neatly dressed African-American man ambled casually through a group of black people standing near a street in a Mississippi town. No one there knew him, but as he walked he spoke in a low, measured voice, without ever stopping. "Anybody want to go to Chicago, see me." He said it over and over until he passed out of the group, at which point he continued his leisurely walk in the direction of the train station. The man was a labor recruiter, and many like him were circulating through the Deep South in 1916 searching for workers to take the jobs in northern industries that European immigrants had filled before the outbreak of war in Europe in August 1914 stopped the flow of immigrants to the United States. That spring agents from Pennsylvania industries had recruited African-American workers in Georgia and Florida, and in July the Pennsylvania Railroad Company brought more than 13,000 black workers northward to work on track maintenance. During 1916 and 1917, a mass of African Americans, estimated to number between 300,000 and 400,000, moved to northern cities. States in the Deep South experienced population losses as high as 100,000 during those two years. Between 1910 and 1920, Chicago's black population more than doubled, Cleveland's quadrupled, Detroit's multiplied seven times, and many smaller cities experienced black population growth of similar proportions.[1]

The labor agents in most cases gave only the final nudge to African Americans who already knew they wanted to go north. Most migrants in fact paid their own fare, which they took from savings or raised by selling furniture and other personal items. Often a young man in the family went north first and worked to save enough earnings to purchase fares for the remainder of the family. The opportunity for much higher wages provided the powerful first reason to migrate. "We are forced to go," wrote a prospective migrant. "When one [thinks] of a grown man wages is only fifty to seventy five cents per day . . . , he is compelled to go where there is better wages and sociable conditions." Their numerous and deep-seated grievances against the white South provided the more fundamental motive for leaving. "I am in the darkness of the south," one who hoped to leave Birmingham wrote to a northern newspaper. "I am counted no more thin a dog." Calling her Mobile, Alabama, home "not fit to live in," a woman wrote that "I am the mother of 8 children 25 years old and I want to get out of this dog hold because I don't know what I am raising them up for in this place and I want to get to Chicago where I know they will be raised and my husband [is] crazy to get there because he know he can get more to raise his children." Asked why African Americans were leaving Mississippi, one man was expansive: "Just a few months ago they hung Widow Baggage's husband from Hirshbery bridge because he talked back to a white man. He was a prosperous Farmer owning about 80 acres. They killed another man because he dared to sell his cotton 'off his place.' These things have got us sore." Many sources cited the boll weevil's eastward expansion and the heavy spring rains in the Deep South in 1916 that actually prevented the planting of crops in some areas. Both the insect and the rain dislocated share-croppers and gave an additional push out of the South.[2]

The pull forces from the North got suddenly stronger in 1916 when the insistent voice of Robert Abbott, editor of the *Chicago Defender*, was spread across the South. Published in the Windy City but widely available in barber shops and churches in the South, the *Defender* had since

1905 reported realistically—and sometimes sensationally—about whites' mistreatment of blacks in the South. "When the Mob Comes and You Must Die Take at Least One with You" ran one headline after a Georgia lynching. Starting in the summer of 1916, the *Defender* published many stories about the new demand for labor in the North, with headlines screaming "300 Leave for North" and "More Jobs than People to Fill Them." Abbott turned the migration into a crusade with news stories, editorials, photographs, and advertisements launching the "Great Northern Drive," the day—May 15, 1917—when masses of black southerners were to leave the South. In fact, many had already left before that day, and many more would leave afterward in what was coming to be called the Great Migration.[3]

The mass excitement notwithstanding, migration was a rational action of African Americans to increase their status and security in American society. Greater security came from getting away from southern lynch mobs and "Negro law," and improved status from better jobs and better schools. The prospect of sending their children to well-funded *white* schools in the North represented a powerful attraction to African Americans, who since emancipation had consistently expressed their faith in education as the avenue to higher status. Black newspapers declared in headlines, "Education Most Important Thing in Life," and editorialists insisted that "education is the secret of all successes."[4]

Black migrants also acted on ideological purposes. The North represented the possible fulfillment of Abraham Lincoln's definitions of democratic values. In the "land of hope," African Americans might realize democracy and equality. In Chicago or Detroit or New York, the very purpose of democratic institutions was not the enforcement of white supremacy, as it was in the South. There blacks would be away from the violence that denied the possibility of freedom in the South.

White southerners moved frantically to stop the northward movement. Policemen arrested 50 blacks at the train station in Americus, Georgia, and held them in custody pending "legal operations to stop the wholesale immigration north." In Macon the city council set the local license fee for labor recruiters at twenty-five thousand dollars and required each to have the endorsement of 10 local ministers, 10 local manufacturers, and 25 businessmen. But a few southern whites had to admit that African Americans were justified in leaving. A small-town Georgia editor owned up to the cost of white violence against blacks. "Whites have allowed Negroes to be lynched, five at a time, on nothing stronger than suspicion," and "to be whitecapped and their homes burned, with only the weakest and most spasmodic efforts to apprehend or punish those guilty—when any efforts were made at all." The *Montgomery Advertiser* acknowledged that whites' abuse of the criminal justice system was coming home to roost when it reported that local police raided poolrooms and charged all the blacks with vagrancy, only to find out the next morning that many had steady jobs. When released, the men left immediately for Cleveland, the paper noted, "where they don't arrest fifty niggers for what three of [them did]."[5]

In northern cities, the migrants discovered environments that were both strange and familiar. People in Chicago soon found the Hattiesburg Barber Shop, whose proprietor had lately operated an establishment of the same name in the Mississippi town. The strong migration "chains" from southern places to northern cities meant that migrants were surrounded by others of similar backgrounds going through the same assimilation process. But migrants encountered a physical environment altogether different from an isolated sharecropper's cabin in the rural South. One study of the arriving migrants in 1917 found "as many as four and five sleep in one bed, and that may be placed in the basement, dining-room or kitchen where there is neither adequate light nor air." Migrants discovered that rent for crowded, even unsanitary housing was astonishingly high—$25 per month almost anywhere and up to $40 in some places. Still, life seemed better in important ways: a recent migrant to Philadelphia wrote home to the South that he had not had "to mister every little white boy comes along," had not "heard a white man call a colored a nigger," but could ride on the streetcars "any where I get a seat."[6]

Jobs did prove to be plentiful. For the first time, the steel industry in the North hired black workers in significant numbers. In Chicago, two packinghouses alone employed four thousand African Americans during the war years, and thousands more took service jobs as waiters, porters, and janitors. Black women found that domestic work was easily available. In New York and Philadelphia, black men worked as stevedores and longshoremen, and many others as chauffeurs. Migrants were often astonished at the wages paid: people who had made no more than 75 cents a day chopping cotton or washing clothes in the South discovered that they could make that much *an hour* in the North. "It is tru the [black] men are making good," a Chicago migrant wrote home to Alabama. "Never pay less than $3.00 per day [for ten] hours—this is not promise . . . they do not hurry or drive you. Remember this the very lowest wages. Piece work men can make $6 to $8 per day."[7]

But for all the economic benefit, life in the northern cities reflected the harshest image of the competitive nature of race relations. New black migrants to East St. Louis, Illinois, were perceived as a threat to both the local dominance of the Democratic Party and the success of unionists in a strike at a local plant. In July 1917 whites attacked them, and when blacks retaliated, white workers and the police rampaged through black neighborhoods killing at will. Before the riot ended, six thousand blacks had been driven from their homes, and probably five hundred were killed. A congressional investigator reported that white mobs went to black homes, nailed "boards up over the doors and windows and then set fire and burn[ed] them up."[8]

The war that sparked the migration required vast new military manpower, and that too provided new opportunities for African Americans. The chance for black men to serve their country in uniform had resulted during the Civil War in radical changes in blacks' status, a fact not lost on African Americans in 1917. More than two million black men registered for the military draft, and about 367,000 of them served in the U.S. armed forces during the Great War, which represented about 13 percent of U.S. military personnel. The War Department, however, enlisted black troops with deep skepticism. The navy took blacks only as mess men. The army reluctantly trained black officers and then insisted on doing it at a segregated camp. When the War Department made the army give a command to its highest-ranking black officer, whites under him complained to a U.S. senator from the South, who prevailed upon President Wilson to have the officer removed. As they went through camps in 1917, black army trainees encountered intense prejudice and hostility. In Houston a group of black soldiers angry over the violent treatment they had received from city police broke into an ammunition storage area, armed themselves, and attacked a police station. They killed 21 whites, and six blacks died in the battle. The army secretly court-martialed the soldiers involved, hanged 19 of them without benefit of appeal, and sentenced many more to long prison terms.[9]

The Houston events shaped thereafter the experience of African Americans in the war. The War Department cut the number of black combat regiments from 16 to 4, and the remaining black combat troops trained very little in U.S. camps. In 1918 about two hundred thousand African Americans went to France as part of the American effort that helped the Allies finally win the war. Only one-fifth of the black soldiers in France were actually in combat units, the large majority working in such support roles as dockworker. Not trained as well as white troops in marksmanship or tactics, black combat soldiers in France sometimes performed poorly, though the French command was well pleased with the African-American infantrymen who fought under them. The American command stayed preoccupied with what it viewed as the overly friendly relationship between black soldiers and French women. "The kindly spirit which exists in France for the Negro," a French authority observed, "profoundly wounds Americans who consider it an infringement of their national dogmas."[10]

The surge of American nationalism accompanying the United States's participation in the Great War did little to broaden whites' understanding of democratic values—i.e., making the world safe for democracy created little desire to make Alabama or Mississippi safe for democracy. Despite Woodrow Wilson's rhetoric, American participation was not broadly interpreted in ideological terms, as had been the pro-Union position on the Civil War. World War I demonstrated that state nationalism could in fact have the opposite effect of what it had during the Civil War: during the Great War, nationalist fervor resulted in domestic conformity, a contraction of the meaning of freedom as limits were placed on freedom of speech and association. Moreover, events in 1919 would set off reactionary forces that narrowed even further most Americans' understanding of democratic values. Wilson lacked Abraham Lincoln's ability to direct the moral compass of his countrymen, and he had no inclination whatsoever to interpret the war's meaning to advance blacks' status. Nor apparently did any other prominent white American of the day.

But African Americans took the war to mean that, more than ever, they deserved better treatment. The Houston situation raised questions in the minds of many blacks about whether their support for the war effort was justified. Many were thus surprised in July 1918 when Du Bois published an editorial in *Crisis* supporting the war. Germany represented "death to the aspirations of Negroes and all the darker races for equality, freedom and democracy," he wrote. "Let us, while this war lasts, forget our special grievances and close our ranks shoulder to shoulder with our white fellow citizens." Du Bois understood that real jeopardy lay in blacks' appearing unpatriotic in the intensely conformist environment of 1918. Their contributions to the war effort left African Americans feeling ever more entitled to democracy and equality. The black chairman of the Liberty Bond Committee in Jackson, Mississippi, wrote that "if the Negro is called upon and furnishes his quota of fighters, man for man, he expects the ballot."[11]

Even more influential than the ideological stirring was the way the war opened for millions of southern blacks the possibilities for change in their status. If almost a half million had gone northward, a great many more thought about it, and some of them left the farm for a southern city or town. The urbanization of southern blacks freed African Americans from the intense scrutiny of rural white landlords, and it fostered the growth of autonomous black institutions—churches, fraternal orders, civic clubs—that would provide institutional bases for civil rights activism. Once in motion, African Americans kept moving: the migrations both to the North and to southern cities would continue at a similar pace in the 1920s. A black Mississippi newspaper editor later observed that prior to the Great War, "the Mississippi Negro seemed fully resigned to his condition," but the "shifting about of people" to other states and overseas "put him to thinking . . . on life and its meaning; thinking on possibilities." As the editor suggested, with mobility came contemplation of new attitudes. During the war years, a new spirit of resistance to oppression was seen—among the black soldiers in Houston, the new residents who fought the mob in East St. Louis, and the hundreds of thousands of black travelers who abandoned the "darkness of the South" for the light of new places outside it.[12]

The spirit of resistance during the war years was seen in the activism of the National Association for the Advancement of Colored People. The

Southern cities like Birmingham received many new black migrants during the war years, just as northern cities did. *Courtesy Birmingham Public Library.*

organization's magazine, *Crisis*, had become the authoritative voice for black protest through the writing and editing of Du Bois. By 1914 the NAACP already had organized legal challenges to the residential segregation laws, and its test of Oklahoma's grandfather clause resulted in a 1915 U.S. Supreme Court decision overturning that disfranchising mechanism. By 1916 the NAACP leadership had recognized the need to expand its membership base by recruiting new members in the South. Late that year, the NAACP leadership persuaded James Weldon Johnson to become its new field secretary. Johnson had been successful as a novelist, diplomat, and newspaper editorialist closely connected to Booker Washington. But his greatest fame had come as a song lyricist. He and his brother, the composer John Rosamond Johnson, wrote ragtime tunes for the musical stage. Some of James's early lyrics were coon songs that reinforced old stereotypes: "The best occupation is recreation; I ain't gwinter work no mo'." But the Johnsons soon abandoned the worst stereotypes and used their compositions to emphasize black characters' experiences of love and loneliness. They had already written the magisterial hymn "Lift Every Voice and Sing," later known as the Negro national anthem.

> *Lift every voice and sing*
> *Till earth and heaven ring,*
> *Ring with the harmonies of Liberty;*
> *Let our rejoicing rise*
> *High as the listening skies,*
> *Let it resound loud as the rolling sea.*[13]

In 1916, Johnson sensed that the prospects for changing African Americans' status were improving. "The great war in Europe, its recoil on America, the ferment in the United States," he wrote later, "all conspired to break up the stereotyped conception of the Negro's place that had been increasing in fixity for forty years, and to allow of new formations." What those new formations were, Johnson believed, would depend "largely upon what attitude and action the Negro himself and the white people willing to stand with him would take."[14]

Johnson transformed the organization's membership. When he came to the NAACP, there were 68 local branches in the United States, but only three of them were in the South. The organization had about nine thousand members, on whom it depended for most of its financial support. In early 1917, Johnson began a long tour through the Deep South to organize branches in southern cities, during which he formed 13 branches and signed up hundreds of new members. He later toured the upper South and Midwest with much the same effect, and in 1918 he made even more organizing tours. By the end of 1919, the NAACP had more than 300 branches and about 90,000 members, a tenfold increase in membership since 1916. "I was impressed with the fact that everywhere there was a rise in the level of the Negro's morale," Johnson later wrote. "The exodus of Negroes to the North ... was in full motion; the tremors of the war in Europe were shaking America with increasing intensity; circumstances were combining to put a higher premium on Negro muscle, Negro hands, and Negro brains than ever before; all these forces had a quickening effect that was running through the entire mass of the race."[15]

Johnson also organized NAACP protest activities. In 1917 he lobbied the War Department to train more black officers and pled unsuccessfully that they be trained with white officers. He watched NAACP lawyers argue the case of *Buchanan v. Warley*, a challenge to the residential segregation law in Louisville, Kentucky, that resulted in the U.S. Supreme Court's declaring such laws unconstitutional. On July 28, 1917, the NAACP staged a protest in New York City against the awful events in East St. Louis. Led by small children, ten thousand African Americans marched silently down Fifth Avenue, accompanied only by the sound of muffled drums and carrying such signs as "Treat Us So That We May Love Our Country" and "Mr. President, Why Not Make America Safe for Democracy?" Starting in 1918, Johnson lobbied the U.S. Congress for a national antilynching law, which would punish local governments and local officials that allowed a lynching to take place. The number of lynchings surged to 70 during the year after the armistice, and ten of the victims were wearing the uniform of the U.S. Army. In 1922 the bill passed the House, but southern senators' threatened filibuster kept it from a vote. Johnson found consolation from the decline in the number of lynchings during the 1920s, a sign that the campaign had changed some southerners' behavior if not the law.[16]

Johnson's effort represented an important strategic development for the cause of civil rights. Beginning with the campaign for antilynching legislation, race reformers in the twentieth century would regularly propose federal laws to put limits on southern states' denial of blacks' constitutional rights. In theory the national government had superior authority over the states, though since Reconstruction this authority had not been used to enforce equal rights for blacks. If that power could be invoked to fulfill the promise of democratic rights made to African Americans during the Civil War, race relations would be transformed in the United States.

Johnson had a cultural strategy to complement his political plan for race reform. In 1916 the editor and critic Henry L. Mencken told Johnson that black writers made a strategic error when they made "pleas for justice and mercy . . . when they argued to prove that they were as good as

James Weldon Johnson. *Courtesy Library of Congress.*

anybody else." What they should do, Mencken advised, was to "single out the strong points of the race and emphasize them over and over and over; asserting at least on these points, that they are *better* than anybody else." In the years ahead, Johnson promoted appreciation of blacks' contributions to American culture in the belief that African-American artistic achievement would open the door to equal treatment in the more pedestrian arenas of life.[17]

I

Rather than celebration and a sense of triumph, the aftermath of war brought chaos and fear to many white Americans. They felt even less secure after the war than they had during it. The postwar economy quickly contracted, bringing a sudden end to wartime prosperity and a rapid rise in unemployment, and setting off strikes across the country that in turn fueled a strong antilabor reaction among businessmen. At the same time, a series of anarchists' bombings provoked a fierce counterattack against radicals, a "Red Scare" that resulted in the imprisonment of several thousand socialists and anarchists. International events, especially the Russian Revolution and the campaign against colonial rule in India, further contributed to a sense that the traditional order of civilization was under siege.

In 1919 many American communities still were undergoing shock from the wartime changes. In the South, the urban population grew by 2.7 million people in the war decade, and more than five of every six new urbanites were whites going to industrial cities, mill villages, and mining camps. The big expansion of southern industrial jobs made the competition for economic opportunity more intense, mainly because so many white southerners went to town to get them. African Americans were locked out of the textile mills, but they did get jobs in Birmingham's mines and mills. At the Memphis railroad yards in 1919, white workers carried out a "wildcat" strike against several railroads for using African Americans as switchmen—an action in precisely the same ugly spirit as the Georgia railroad strike in 1909. The Memphis strike failed, but the white workers subsequently terrorized their fellow black workers on the Illinois Central. The all-white railway unions then negotiated changes in work rules that turned many train operator jobs, formerly black positions, into white jobs, a process that resulted in further decline in the number of black workers on American railroads.[18]

Violence still enforced whites' economic domination of rural African Americans. During the war the price of cotton rose to 40 cents per pound, higher than it had ever been, but landlords rarely shared the good times equitably with their tenants. In 1919 a black Arkansas sharecropper sold $3,500 of cotton, against which he borrowed only $23, but his landlord's statement to him showed an exact balance between income and expenses, and thus he got nothing. No longer willing to have their labor appropriated through such blatant fraud, black farmers joined a union of sharecroppers centered in Phillips County in southeastern Arkansas. In September 1919 whites attacked a union meeting and arrested the union's white lawyer, but in the process a white deputy sheriff was killed. For the next week whites from Arkansas and Mississippi conducted a reign of terror on black farmers in Phillips County. As with the riot at East St. Louis, blacks fought back against white terrorism. They killed five whites, which only intensified the white retribution. More than 200 black farmers were killed. Twelve were sentenced to death and 67 to long prison terms, though some of the sentences were later reduced or overturned. The wartime upheaval notwithstanding, violence remained the final authority for white supremacy.[19]

In 1919 African Americans in 25 cities and towns became the objects of rioting whites, each conflict evidence of the intensifying racial contest over economic opportunity, urban space, and political power. The biggest one erupted in Chicago in July 1919, the climax of conflict building since the black population began rising rapidly in 1916. During the next three years, whites complained that new black migrants were damaging property values, and 58 houses that had recently been occupied by blacks were bombed. What blew the mounting pressure in 1919 was a perceived black invasion of white space: a black swimmer accidentally came up on the "white" portion of the Lake Michigan beach. Whites beat the black swimmer to death, and after several days of rioting in which blacks fought back fiercely against attacking whites, 30 people were dead. The larger context of the Chicago riot, however, was formed by two strikes, among local meatpackers and steelworkers, in which black workers had crossed predominantly white picket lines. The close timing and physical proximity of the economic conflicts had made Chicago ripe for the 1919 explosion.[20]

The Chicago riot represented only the worst outcome of terrible housing shortages and overcrowding that blacks experienced in every large northern city. In Chicago's ghetto, 90,000 people lived in one square mile, whereas the contiguous white areas contained only 20,000 per square mile. Landlords gouged the migrants for high rents, which necessitated taking in borders, which in turn caused the deterioration of housing quality. In Detroit, realtors and landlords on the fringes of its large ghetto jacked up the rents on whites living in contiguous areas, and when the whites moved out, they escalated the rents even higher to blacks desperately seeking any accommodation. "Negro and white real estate sharks" were "preying upon homeless colored people," a local NAACP official reported, and as a result black renters usually put three or four families in each apartment, which meant "75% of the Negro homes have so many lodgers that they are really hotels."[21]

Whites living on the fringes of the black ghetto aggressively defended their turf against blacks who pressed against the boundaries. Even prior to the Great Migration, whites in the Hyde Park neighborhood of Chicago had created an "Improvement Protective Club" to keep blacks from moving into "their" blocks, and by coercing landlords and realtors and threatening and vandalizing black property owners, they had forced out and kept out most black residents. In the aftermath of the 1919 riot, whites in Chicago and cities across the United States embraced the "restrictive covenant," which was a private, contractual agreement between buyers and sellers of real estate to limit sales of property to particular racial or ethnic groups. Restrictive covenants blossomed everywhere, but nowhere were they applied with more vengeance than

around the burgeoning Black Belt of Chicago, where new property owners' associations organized to prevent all "colored encroachment."[22]

Often the most successful African Americans fought the hardest battles in the competition for space around the crowded ghettoes. In 1925,
Ossian Sweet, a young Detroit physician, bought a house on a formerly
all-white street, though other blacks lived only one street over. On his
second day in the house, a mob of two thousand whites surrounded the
home, pelted it with rocks, and shot at it. Sweet and his family fired back,
killing one white man and seriously injuring another in the crowd. The
young doctor was charged with murder. A highly publicized trial ended
in a hung jury, but Sweet was acquitted in a second trial. It proved to be a
pyrrhic victory: the Sweets were afraid to occupy the house, and it was
later partly destroyed by arsonists, something that happened time and
again to Detroit blacks who moved into previously all-white streets in the
late 1920s.[23]

The Sweet case dramatized the blacks' new determination not to
accept white violence passively. Starting with the East St. Louis riot and
the Houston soldiers rebellion in 1917, and continuing through the
Chicago riot and the Arkansas union rebellion in 1919 and the Sweet family's defense of their home in 1925, African Americans met violence with
violence in a more organized and sustained way than they had in the
past. This more militant spirit reflected a keener group consciousness
among blacks and more confidence that an aggressive response might
succeed. It also raised the possibility that race relations in the future
would be characterized by more violence, because now brutality seemed
to flow in both directions.[24]

As always schools served as a main racial battlefield. Throughout the
North in the 1920s, school systems moved to segregate black children in
ghetto schools. In Chicago, where prior to the Great Migration most
black students attended integrated schools and black teachers mainly
taught white children, whites pushed successfully for separate black
schools with the big increase of arrivals from the South. Through a
process of redrawing district boundaries, transferring whites, and building new schools in the Black Belt, the Chicago school system had by 1930

managed to get 82 percent of Chicago's black students into all-black schools. In Cleveland in the late 1920s and early 1930s, a similar process of rapid segregation took place by redistricting and transferring white students, this in a previously well-integrated school system in a city where the competition for residential space was not as severe as Chicago's. In Indianapolis and Gary, the few black students attending predominantly white schools were moved to all-black schools in the 1920s. Cincinnati and Philadelphia departed from the pattern only by operating both all-black and integrated schools in the interwar years.[25]

But even after the northern city began mirroring the Jim Crow South, it remained a powerful pole of attraction for southern blacks because of its job opportunities. In Detroit in 1919, the Ford Motor Company began hiring black workers in large numbers at its recently established five-dollar-a-day wage rate, and by 1926 it had added 10,000 African Americans. In the 1920s, Chicago's rapidly growing African-American population found new jobs for men in the packinghouses, foundries, coke works, and metal works and for women at sewing and lampshade factories. By 1928 an estimated 3,400 black Chicagoans had government jobs, mostly at post offices. In New York, by the late 1920s, about 2,000 black women worked in the "dress trade" as seamstresses, and more than that number, men and women, worked for the city of New York's schools, police department, and other municipal services.[26]

Even so, African Americans remained shut out of most white-collar positions. In New York City, Gimbel's department store and the Metropolitan Life Insurance Company refused to hire blacks, while the city subways and the gas and electric utilities offered only a few token positions. Chicago banks with many black depositors typically hired African Americans only as janitors. Drug, grocery, and department stores that served a mostly black clientele hired few if any black clerks. Although there were more low-status service jobs available to blacks, the new migration accelerated African Americans' loss of the higher-status service jobs that they had held prior to the Great Migration. In Pittsburgh and Cleveland, blacks were rapidly displaced from work as cooks, waiters, and barbers during and after World War I.[27]

The competition for jobs remained intense in the industrial workplaces, even as the opportunities for black employment continued. In Pittsburgh steel mills, blacks rarely were allowed to rise above unskilled labor performed in high heat. In Chicago, employers consciously set black workers against Mexican immigrants, who were brought to the city in the 1920s. The Mexican immigrants worked alongside blacks in the dirtiest and most dangerous jobs—or, in the case of packinghouses, in the coldest and most foul-smelling areas. "We have Negroes and Mexicans in a sort of competition with each other," a Chicago foundry supervisor admitted. "It is a dirty trick." African Americans typically were at a disadvantage because of the ethnic cohesion among European immigrants who had arrived in the plants much earlier. Black immigrants from the South experienced far greater difficulty in finding permanent jobs, especially those that yielded increased wages and status with long tenure in one position.[28]

In the North, African Americans regained some of the political power that disfranchisement in the South had taken from them. Chicago's Mayor "Big Bill" Thompson, a Republican machine politician with high tolerance for organized crime, promised black audiences in his 1915 election campaign that he would "give your people jobs, and any of you want to shoot craps go ahead and do it." Thompson gave blacks patronage, helped them get elected to office, told his policemen to treat blacks fairly, and made Chicago the only major American city where *Birth of a Nation* was not shown—all of which his Democratic opponents used against him in future elections. Except in the example of East St. Louis, political competition did not lead directly to violence, but the clear identification of blacks with the Republican Party and their growing voting strength provided another source of alienation from blue-collar white Democrats. African Americans made the most of their democratic rights: whereas only a third of Chicago's white ethnics voted in 1924, more than 50 percent of African Americans voted in the 1920s, and black participation climbed over 60 percent in the 1930s. Thompson helped Oscar De Priest, an African-American city alderman, build his own political network in the Black Belt, which in 1928 sent De Priest to Washington as a U.S. congressman.[29]

Thus even amid intense racial competition for housing and jobs in northern cities, African Americans could easily see that their lives held more promise there than they had in the South, where they could not vote, their schools were terrible, and jobs in the biggest industry, textiles, were strictly off limits to them. Many more African Americans moved north during the 1920s than had during the war years. It remained the land of hope to African Americans, and as such it fostered the building force for resistance and change.

I I

While many African Americans were building new lives in northern cities, new forms of ethnic nationalism were emerging in the United States. Whites refashioned the Ku Klux Klan and transformed it into a white *protestant* nationalist group that looked for a homogenous society domi-

The Ku Klux Klan spread to many parts of the United States during the early 1920s. *Courtesy Library of Congress.*

nated by white evangelicals. Its renewal began atop Stone Mountain near Atlanta in 1915, promoted by a huckster who timed the rebirth to follow the first showing of *Birth of a Nation* on Peachtree Street. The new Klan took off, however, only in the war's aftermath. The Red Scare, the post-war recession, and the race riots—all fertilized the field for rapid Klan growth starting in 1920. By 1924 the Klan was a powerful influence in all southern states, and it dominated the politics of Colorado and Indiana and of various far-flung cities. The Klan flourished where race competition was strong: In Pennsylvania it drew most of its support from white industrial workers in and around Pittsburgh, many of whom equated a black presence with strikebreaking. In 1923 the mayor of Johnstown ordered the removal of all blacks who had arrived since 1916, a throwback to the kind of race cleansing seen decades earlier in Indiana and Ohio.[30]

But the Klan's appeal was based heavily on the anti-Catholic, anti-Semitic, and nativist thinking that had been growing in the United States since the 1890s. One Klan wizard declared that "thousands of Mexicans, many of them communists, are waiting for a chance to cross the Rio Grande. . . . [O]n the Pacific Slope the yellow peril is a reality." Nativism and eugenics thrived during the war and postwar years, promoted by men like the amateur anthropologist Madison Grant, who argued that the United States could survive only if it upheld Anglo-Saxon racial superiority against the hordes of immigrants arriving from Europe. More immigration from southern Europe would result in mixing of the "higher types"—the Anglo-Saxons or Nordic people—with inferior races; and such a mixture would produce "a race reverting to the ancient . . . lower type." Grant was especially fearful of Jews, because "the cross" between the "European races and a Jew is a Jew." In response to such thinking, the U.S. government passed a literacy test for immigrants in 1917, and a limit on immigration in 1921, which was made permanent in 1924.[31]

Ultimately, however, the Klan failed to become the permanent institutional base for white nationalism. The economic upturn in 1923 no doubt undercut some of the fear to which the Klan appealed, just as the scandals that kept popping up among its leaders damaged the reputation of an organization making explicitly moral appeals. It ran into stiff political opposition from old elites. Many traditional Democrats in the South who opposed the Klan's prohibitionism or its Populist economic stances criticized the organization as a threat to white supremacy, a source of disunity that played into the hands of "black Republicans." In the North, the Klan's protestant nationalism drove into the enemy camp Irish, Polish, and Italian Catholic "ethnics" who otherwise embraced white supremacy but who worked to defeat the Klan's purposes.[32]

White protestant nationalism also assaulted one crucial definition of American freedom—religious toleration. Although many Americans disregarded such an understanding of democratic values in the postwar time of fear, the older tradition of tolerating different faiths resurfaced during the calmer time of the mid-1920s. The creation of the American Civil Liberties Union in response to the Red Scare marked another important new support for democratic values in the face of postwar actions to diminish them. White nationalism in the North lacked the alienation from the U.S. government that had given so much impetus to white nationalism in the South since the Civil War. The decline of the 1920s' KKK thus not only meant the end of the strongest institutional form of white nationalism to that point, but it also marked an awakening among many Americans about the dangers of ethnic nationalism. To be sure, a southern ethnic nationalism survived a while longer; it would take another, bigger war finally to undermine it.

Exactly coincident with the surge of white protestant nationalism was the growth of the strongest example of black ethnic nationalism yet to emerge in the United States. Marcus Garvey and his Universal Negro Improvement Association (UNIA) attracted hundreds of thousands, and perhaps millions, of members between 1917 and 1923. In 1921 his organization may well have had ten times as many members as the NAACP had after James Weldon Johnson's successful organizing. The UNIA's success reflected in part the desire of newly urbanized blacks for social connection in the midst of the strange and hostile new environment, but Garveyism found many adherents in the rural South, primarily among poor sharecroppers who embraced his message of race pride in the face of unrelenting white supremacy. "The Negro of the South is a new and diff-

erent man to what he was prior to the war," Garvey wrote as he promoted what he called "the New Negro Manhood Movement." Garvey
used the awful treatment of blacks during the war and postwar years to
justify a plan for the wholesale migration to Africa on his Black Star
steamship line. The United States was far too racist and undemocratic
ever to include blacks as equals, Garvey insisted. He denounced light-
skinned, integrationist blacks in the NAACP as being ashamed of their
black ancestry, asserting that "the N.A.A.C.P. wants us all to become
white by amalgamation," but its leaders lacked the honesty to admit it.
"To be a Negro is no disgrace, but an honor.... We love our race and
respect and adore our mothers."[33]

Garvey's pessimism about American race relations, however, belied
the hopefulness manifest in his movement. Few of his followers actually
intended to emigrate to Africa, but many responded to the movement's
promotion of race pride and its call to retake Africa from European colonialism. "Wake up Ethiopia! Wake up Africa!" Garvey frequently
exhorted. "Let us work toward the one glorious end of a free, redeemed
and mighty nation. Let Africa be a bright star among the constellations of
nations." Emphasizing black economic self-help, Garvey made the UNIA
a black-nationalist conglomerate, including a chain of grocery stores,
restaurants, and laundries. The UNIA created a fraternal order, "Empire
of Africa," that featured a hierarchy of knights, dukes, and other poten-
tates. Responding to his shout "Up, you mighty race!" Garvey's black
nation held parades that featured its paramilitary African Legion, followed by the UNIA's corps of Black Cross Nurses. Garvey even accommodated evangelical Christianity to black nationalism by portraying God
and Jesus as black. It worked: many of the UNIA's most devoted organizers in the South were Christian ministers.[34]

Virtually the entire establishment of black leadership denounced Garvey during his time of prominence, and no one with greater passion than
Du Bois, whose longstanding engagement with the meaning of the
African past was being overshadowed by a man he thought was a charla-
tan. In 1921 he called Garvey "without doubt, the most dangerous enemy
of the Negro race in America and the world" and "either a lunatic or a

traitor." The condemnation grew to a roar in 1922 when Garvey met with Ku Klux Klan leaders in Atlanta, with whom he shared the view that the United States would never become a peaceful, interracial society. Between the Klan and the "National Association for the Advancement of 'Certain' People," Garvey retorted, "give me the Klan for their honesty of purpose toward the Negro."[35]

His success as a black-nationalist leader ultimately raised the suspicions of the U.S. government, which took seriously rumors of armed Garveyites' preparing for race war. In 1923 he was charged with using the mail to defraud people of money raised for the Black Star Line, and his black enemies aided the prosecution. Foreshadowing subsequent expressions of anti-Semitism among black nationalists in the United States, Garvey blamed his conviction on the judge's being a Jew. Sent to prison in 1925, Garvey was pardoned in 1927 by President Calvin Coolidge and then deported. The UNIA went rapidly into decline in the late 1920s.[36]

Marcus Garvey. *Courtesy Library of Congress.*

Still, Garvey and his movement demonstrated the powerful appeal of ethnic nationalism to African Americans. For many Garveyites, the movement off the farm had raised the possibility of change at the same time that it forced confrontation with some of the harshest forms of white supremacy. For those left behind, Garveyism provided a means for hope amid awful agricultural poverty. Black-nationalist pride as promoted by the Garvey movement offered African Americans an active way—at once hopelessly romantic and harshly realistic—to deal with their circumstances.

III

During the same years, a new literary imagination also elevated African-American race pride. James Weldon Johnson followed H. L. Mencken's suggestion to advance the race's status by promoting black literary achievement. "The status of the Negro in the United States is more a question of national mental attitude toward the race than of actual conditions," Johnson wrote in introducing his 1922 anthology of black poetry. "And nothing will do more to change that mental attitude and raise his status than a demonstration of intellectual parity by the Negro through the production of literature and art." Through his focus on black aesthetics, Johnson was intent on discovering and promoting what the German sociologist Max Weber called "the hidden honor" that "pariah people" often embrace as a means for coping with their oppression. Like his old sponsor Booker Washington, Johnson wanted to encourage positive black images, and thus he drew attention to writers who "did not concern themselves with the sound of the old banjo and the singing round the cabin door; nor with the succession of the watermelon, possum, and sweet potato seasons."[37]

Johnson began promoting the artistic movement that would become known as the Harlem Renaissance. Du Bois did the same thing in *Crisis*, and Charles Spurgeon Johnson, editor of the National Urban League's publication *Opportunity*, also published the literature and editorialized on its behalf. The Renaissance comprised poets, essayists, and novelists, of which the most widely known were Langston Hughes, Countee Cullen, Claude McKay, Alain Locke, and Zora Neale Hurston. Through much of the writing ran a spirit of optimism, apropos the theme of rebirth, that celebrated African Americans' survival of a harsh past in the United States, their legacy of a rich cultural past on the African continent, and their expectation of better days ahead. The Renaissance shared the hopeful spirit of both Garveyite race nationalism and NAACP integrationism.[38]

The African-American musical forms connected more directly to American popular culture. Jazz emerged during the war era, an outgrowth of the ragtime music so popular on the minstrel and vaudeville stage. Ferdinand "Jelly Roll" Morton, King Oliver, Louis Armstrong, and a parade of similarly talented musicians brought "blues" from the South and integrated its themes with the syncopated rhythms and irregular melodies of ragtime. Syncopation was emblematic of the African-Ameri-

The writer Zora Neale Hurston. *Courtesy Library of Congress.*

can influence on popular culture: it provided a new tone on the unaccented beat of aesthetic expression in the United States, and the sound it created marked the most distinctive cultural achievement of the society to date. "Syncopation is the soul of every American," the composer Irving Berlin declared in 1916, just as he and other, mostly Jewish-immigrant composers were transforming Tin Pan Alley's popular music offerings into a blended product based heavily on ragtime tunes. Ira and George Gershwin borrowed not only the syncopated beat but the message in their "Fascinatin' Rhythm" (1924) and "I Got Rhythm" (1930).[39]

The power of the syncopated, syncretized sound was hugely magnified in the 1920s with the rapid growth of sound records and the emergence of radio to send the sound everywhere. With upwards of ten million radios playing records in the United States in the 1920s, two powerful cultural phenomena resulted: black jazz artists—Armstrong, Oliver, Duke Ellington, Bessie Smith, Fats Waller, and dozens of others—became known to and appreciated by average white Americans, and white musicians adapted their cultural expressions to the black influences. The musical convergence began to undermine the great barrier that existed, at least in the minds of most whites, between the races.[40]

At the same time, James Weldon and Rosamond Johnson set out to recognize the other great African-American musical contribution—the Negro spiritual—with the publication of two collections of traditional songs. Earlier James Weldon had offered a paean to the spiritual in a poem, "O Black and Unknown Bards."

> O black slave singers, gone forgot, unfamed,
> You—you alone, of all the long, long line
> Of those who've sung untaught, unknown, unnamed,
> Have stretched out upward, seeking the divine.

Johnson believed that the spirituals were "purely and solely the creation of the American Negro," expressions that "although seemingly miraculous" came naturally because "the Negro brought with him from Africa his native musical instinct and talent." The spirituals, Johnson insisted, demonstrated that "the great majority of Africans are in no sense 'savages'; that they possess a civilization and a culture."[41]

In yet another effort to preserve distinctive African-American cultural traditions, Johnson in 1927 published a collection of "folk sermons" of the traditional African-American preacher. Covering central themes of Christianity—the Creation, salvation, and the Resurrection—Johnson's sermons mimicked the oral poetry of generations of black people in America. *God's Trombones* also rehabilitated the reputation of the black preacher, the object of much scorn in American popular culture. According to Johnson, the "old time Negro preacher" had been "portrayed only as a semi-comic figure," but to blacks he was "an important figure, and at bottom a vital factor." It was through the African-American preacher that "the people of diverse languages and customs who were brought here from diverse parts of Africa and thrown into slavery were given their first sense of unity and solidarity." The old-time preacher had provided "the mainspring of hope and inspiration for the Negro in America."[42]

If the efforts of Johnson and others lifted the spirits of African Americans, they did nothing to quell the appetite of most white Americans for the old, degrading black stereotypes. In the late 1920s radio began to sate that desire when two white vaudeville actors created a nightly serial for a Chicago radio station about a pair of southern blacks in the North. They mimicked and exaggerated "black" speech—misusing grammar and adding malapropisms—in the way that white minstrels in blackface had done. By 1930 an estimated forty million Americans tuned in for 15 minutes each night as Amos, the shifty, dishonest, and usually unsuccessful Zip Coon figure, manipulated the simple and slow Andy, the Jim Crow character. The program remained wildly popular into the 1940s. Mass-circulation magazines in the 1920s featured short fiction that lampooned black life using the familiar images. Lengthy and illustrated stories in the *Saturday Evening Post* and *Collier's* promoted an image of blacks as innately immoral, ignorant, lazy, and prone to violence. The NAACP protested the stories, but whites imbibed them happily into the 1930s.[43]

White filmmakers also relied heavily on the minstrel stereotypes in the 1920s and 1930s. The addition of sound to movies greatly enhanced the medium's ability to communicate black inferiority by using exaggerated Negro dialect. *The Jazz Singer*, the first "talkie," was about a blackface entertainer. Hollywood issued many films in the 1930s featuring Jim Crow and Mammy characters acting foolishly, but with great loyalty, toward such stars as Will Rogers and Shirley Temple. The actor Stepinfetchit rendered Jim Crow many times to the great hilarity of whites throughout the 1930s. The silver screen took the stereotypes to new heights of influence as Americans tried to escape from the hard times.[44]

"Amos 'n' Andy," racist short fiction, and Stepinfetchit all based their humor on the cultural backwardness of black characters, emphasizing the same superstitiousness, proclivity for gambling, and ignorance of how the world really works that the minstrel shows and vaudeville blackface acts had used. The underlying message was that African Americans were far outside the cultural mainstream in America. The strong continuity between the negative stereotypes created for the minstrel stage in the nineteenth century and those used in new media in the twentieth century revealed the strength of the dominant white culture's commitment to the icons that bolstered its sense of cultural superiority. But what was different in the 1920s was that those cultural expressions were now contested by images of black achievement and competence. The more positive images were not, to be sure, as widely disseminated and appreciated as the negative ones, but now African Americans and many whites could find in their culture something honorable about the pariah's experience in the United States.

IV

The waves of fear that washed over American society as the Great Depression took hold after 1929 made people seek security with even greater intensity than they did in normal times, and the desperate search yielded ruthless competition for jobs and money that blacks were destined almost always to lose. As cotton fell to five cents a pound in 1932, southern landlords told large numbers of sharecroppers—by no means

The Great Depression left many blacks and whites in desperate circumstances.
Courtesy Library of Congress.

all of them black—to vacate their simple shacks and fend for themselves because cotton was simply too cheap for them to have any hope of breaking even on another crop. African Americans in the South rapidly lost many of the positions they had gained in southern industry during World War I. In Birmingham white foremen gave so much preference to white workers during the cycles of layoffs and callbacks that black industrial employment fell drastically. Black railroad workers, long under attack from whites to take their jobs, were besieged during the Depression years by angry whites. In Mississippi between 1931 and 1934, whites shot and killed several black trainmen as they worked in order to take their jobs. In Atlanta in 1930, a vigilante organization called the Black Shirts attempted to drive blacks out of jobs, using the slogan "No Jobs for Niggers until Every White Man Has a Job!"[45]

It was not surprising, then, that about four hundred thousand African Americans migrated to northern cities during the 1930s, following the migration chains of family and neighbors to the "land of hope." Northern cities offered better and more equitable relief but very few jobs. At a time when national unemployment rates were 25 percent, African-American unemployment hovered around 50 percent in New York, Philadelphia, Chicago, and Detroit. Even the most fortunate blacks, the ones who kept their jobs, saw their incomes fall precipitously. A survey of two thousand skilled workers in Harlem discovered that in 1932 they earned just half of what they had made in 1929.[46]

The Depression accelerated the trend toward segregation and discrimination in northern cities. Northern schools, on which the southern migrants had placed so much hope, increasingly in the 1930s mimicked the discriminatory character of southern education. In Chicago, as African-American school attendance went up 50 percent during the 1930s, the quality of the education fell sharply. With more black children to educate and fewer tax dollars to do it, the Chicago school system put most black schools on double sessions, which meant that children attended school for only half the day. A half day of school often meant a half day on the street; during the 1930s street gangs of idle teenagers menaced Chicago's Black Belt schools with theft, vandalism, and fighting, thus exacerbating the already high tendency to crime in the area. Black students were denied admission to its one technical high school where white students learned trades. The pattern was repeated elsewhere: in Cleveland's all-black high schools in the 1930s, foreign languages were dropped, mathematics was not taught to more than half the tenth graders, and industrial classes were focused on sewing, cooking, and laundry work.[47]

As race competition and discrimination were getting worse, the 1930s revealed a new determination among African Americans to protest directly against the wrongs done to them. This surely reflected both the growing independence of thought that had been encouraged by the NAACP, Garveyism, and the cultural flowering in the 1920s and the rapid urbanization of African Americans. The more broadly based spirit of protest also resulted from the desperation in northern cities growing out of the Depression and from the radicalism that the Depression encouraged in many quarters of American society. Starting in Chicago in 1929, blacks initiated a "Don't buy where you can't work" campaign, which involved boycotts of chain retail stores. During the next few years, these boycotts spread to 35 cities, and in some instances the boycotts succeeded in getting significant numbers of African Americans hired as clerks. Meanwhile African Americans in a dozen northern cities organized boycotts against school systems that were discriminating against their children.[48]

Many African Americans in the 1930s protested against the treatment of the nine young black men known as the "Scottsboro Boys." Two white women riding on a freight train falsely accused them of rape, and they were initially convicted in Scottsboro, Alabama, in 1931. Successful appeals resulted in several retrials and more convictions through the early 1930s. Although there had been literally hundreds of miscarriages of justice against blacks in the South brought to the attention of Americans, the Scottsboro case received more public attention than any other up to that time. The notoriety of the case owed much to the involvement of the American Communist Party, whose International Labor Defense wrested control of the defense of the Scottsboro boys from the NAACP. In 1928 the party had focused on southern blacks as a body of potential recruits, but while its efforts had turned only a few blacks into communists, the interest had led them to the propaganda bonanza of the Scottsboro case. The party's constant national promotion of the Scottsboro atrocity encouraged both mass protest action and intense focus of African Americans on legal injustices. The irony of the situation was lost on most Americans: Russian-inspired radicalism was pricking American sensibilities about the denial of democratic rights in the United States.[49]

The Communist Party also played a part in pushing a revitalized labor movement toward greater racial equality than it had shown in the past. When the National Labor Relations Act of 1935 sparked the creation of company-wide industrial unions, Communist Party members agitated for inclusion of black members on an equal basis with whites. New unions of steelworkers, autoworkers, and rubber workers did indeed declare their commitment to racial justice, though they often failed to live up to their promises. The very existence of a large segment of organized labor at least nominally committed to racial fairness marked a break with the past and was a cause for optimism about the future.[50]

Franklin D. Roosevelt and his New Deal helped to change the course of race relations in the United States, though initially the administration seemed to care little for African Americans. The National Recovery Administration (NRA) demonstrated such indifference to black suffering that African Americans often said the acronym stood for "Negroes Rarely Allowed." The Works Progress Administration (WPA) and the Federal Emergency Relief Administration discriminated against African Americans in both relief payments and opportunities to work on projects. The Agricultural Adjustment Administration, administered mainly at the local level by rich farmers, rarely made landowners share subsidy payments with their black tenants. Then, starting in 1934, the Roosevelt administration began to exhibit real concern for blacks, led by the First Lady Eleanor Roosevelt. At that time Mrs. Roosevelt began making public statements that demonstrated a genuine empathy for the conditions of

Eleanor Roosevelt. *Courtesy Library of Congress.*

African Americans. Walter White of the NAACP led her to the new sensitivity, and Mary McLeod Bethune, who presided over the "black cabinet" of African Americans serving the New Deal, educated the First Lady about African-American conditions. Mrs. Roosevelt's advocacy for "fair play and equal opportunity for Negro citizens" became a media fascination, something she capitalized on with her "My Day" column in many Americans newspapers. "Do We Really Live in the 'Land of the Free'?" she asked in one column. "Are you free if you cannot vote, if you cannot be sure that the same justice will be meted out to you as to your neighbor; if you are expected to live on a lower level than your neighbor and to work for lower wages; if you are barred from certain places and from certain opportunities?" Eleanor Roosevelt's willingness to ask publicly such questions inspired hope that race relations could change.[51]

At the same time, Franklin Roosevelt, who avoided discussions of black rights out of fear of alienating southerners in Congress, began to address Americans' ideological commitments in order to build support

Franklin Delano Roosevelt. *Courtesy Library of Congress.*

for expanding federal power over the economy. He worked to revise Americans' understanding of freedom when he discussed it in terms of the deep economic insecurity the Depression had caused. In 1934 in his second radio "fireside chat," the president defined liberty as "greater security for the average man." He was already acting on calls from unionists and intellectuals for the national government to provide jobs as the underpinning to American freedom. Citizens had as much right to work and live securely as they did to vote, it was argued, and thus it was the responsibility of the government to protect them from "economic slavery," just as it defended their political freedom. In 1938 the president declared that if Americans were not able to "sustain an acceptable standard of living," they were unlikely to uphold liberty in a democracy.[52]

Redefining freedom as an economic responsibility of government represented a 180-degree turn in the common use of the word up to the 1930s, because its prevailing application had been liberty *from* government intervention in the economy. Such discussion of basic values and the consequent redefinition of fundamental ideological understandings gave the powerful impression that the rules of American society were in flux, that change was afoot, or at least quite possible. For African Americans, the 1930s thus inspired hope, even amid suffering.

The sense that the Roosevelt administration was changing American society helped him win a large majority of African-American voters in 1936, a reversal of their 1932 support for the Republican Herbert Hoover. To signal to blacks that times were changing in the Democratic Party, Roosevelt's organizers asked an African-American minister to give the 1936 Democratic convention's invocation. During the prayer, South Carolina's Senator "Cotton Ed" Smith charged out of the hall and declared: "By God, he's as black as melted midnight! . . . This mongrel meeting ain't no place for a white man!" Not since 1860, *Time* magazine reported, had politicians been so "Negro-minded," the result of one million black voters' now being concentrated in nine northern states. At Roosevelt's behest in 1936, the Democratic Party changed its requirement of a two-thirds majority to nominate candidates, a rule that traditionally had given the South veto power in the choice of party nominees. As Roosevelt expanded the base of the Democratic Party to include many immigrants as well as northern blacks, the South lost its dominant influence over the party. White southern Democrats were fearful that the loss would undermine their control over race relations, and with good reason.[53]

In an even more structural sense, the New Deal enabled changes in American race relations by shifting the location of power away from states to the federal government. The Great Depression precipitated a rapid expansion of the national government's authority over the economy when the New Deal attempted to bring about economic recovery and reform. The central government began to overwhelm the states on those matters that it chose to rule. Civil rights did not immediately become such a matter, but the stage was set for the national government to override the southern states' autonomy in the area of race relations.

When the framers of the U.S. Constitution separated the powers of the three branches of the national government, they created another structural reality that was about to become important to race reform. Each branch maintained some independence, and one branch could commit to a policy that another branch opposed. That meant the Congress could cancel a president's initiative, or vice versa. The judiciary could pursue policies entirely independent of the Congress and the president, indeed in opposition to the elected representatives of the people. And, while the federal courts had been powerful and independent since the time of John Marshall, the broad construction of the Constitution that resulted from the New Deal's response to the Depression only served to enhance their power further. The independent power of the federal judiciary held the potential to alter the course of American race relations.

IV

For many African Americans, the years since 1915 had brought much hope that their lives were going to change, that new possibilities now existed. The approximately two million who had gone north between

1916 and 1937 had grasped good job opportunities, at least compared with what had existed for them in the South. They exercised the right to vote, and they sent their children to schools that were far better than what they had in the South—even if they were not as good as the ones white children attended. They partook of the flowering of black culture that had begun in the 1920s. They had far more freedom to express their own views and even to protest if they chose. Even those blacks who remained in the South began to think more positively about change, as the Great Migration, Garveyism, and the black cultural expressions stirred all African Americans.

African Americans witnessed the political and ideological flux of the 1930s. To the most optimistic, it seemed that history was about to reverse its course. Democracy had been the instrument of white supremacy and southern white nationalism since Reconstruction, and it still was in the 1930s. But the actions of the Roosevelt administration, and the ideology that it invoked to justify its works, gave hope that democratic institutions could be turned to protect those Americans now denied their rightful freedom and equality.

The year 1938 would usher in a new era in American race relations, a time of protest and change. A convergence of national and international events would sharpen Americans' ideological thinking and make the people more conscious of their values than they were during normal times. Indeed, the crisis of the Great Depression had already done that to a great extent. Intense focus on the meaning of democracy and freedom gave immediate inspiration to African Americans' call to protest against segregation and all forms of white supremacy. The persistent response to that call began in 1938, and it would continue with few pauses until victory could be legitimately claimed in 1965. At the end of the period, a prophet of the protest movement would declare that "the arc of the moral universe is long, but it bends toward justice." Indeed by then it had bent toward justice at the behest of millions who demanded that it do so.

PART TWO

THE ARC OF THE
MORAL UNIVERSE, 1938–1965

CHAPTER 4

THE FOUR FREEDOMS
AND THE FOUR EQUALITIES

ON THE NIGHT of June 22, 1938, seventy thousand people jammed into Yankee Stadium to see the fight for the heavyweight championship of the world between Max Schmeling, who held the title, and his challenger, Joe Louis. It was a return match: two years before in this same stadium, Schmeling had knocked Louis out in the twelfth round to become the champion, a triumph that earned him the gratitude of his nation's leader, Adolf Hitler, and its press, which reported that Schmeling had "saved the prestige of the white race." This 1938 rematch held even greater political importance, because the balance of race prestige had swung back the other way after the first fight when a group of African-American athletes led by Jesse Owens had dominated the Germans at the 1936 Berlin Olympic games. The outraged führer refused to honor the victorious Americans, and German propagandists dismissed the U.S. Olympic success as being based on unscrupulous deployment of the "black auxiliary force." The 1938 "Fight of the Century" was the next level in the escalating war of race and nation status, and few in Yankee Stadium or among the many millions listening on the radio missed the political symbolism at work.

The bell for the first round had barely rung before it was clear how this race-and-nation contest was going to come out. The "Brown

Bomber" charged Schmeling, assaulted him relentlessly, and knocked him down three times in less than three minutes as the multitude in Yankee Stadium roared their support. The German threw only four punches before he gave up.[1]

American honor and black status soared together with the triumph of Joe Louis that night. The fact that they could rise together reflected both the changing circumstances in the United States and the particular way that Joe Louis presented himself to the American people. By 1938 many Americans realized that the rise of fascism in Europe and Asia presented some danger to the United States, though no one could yet imagine how it would disrupt lives. Joe Louis made it easy for white Americans to embrace him as a countersymbol to the Nazi threat, even though up to that time whites had never accepted a black person as a thoroughly American icon. Consciously or not, Louis projected an image entirely different from Jack Johnson. Whereas Johnson was a spendthrift who associated only with white women, the barely literate Louis was quiet and humble, devoted to his black wife, generous to charities and his family, but otherwise frugal with his money. If Johnson had appeared to conform to the stereotype of Zip Coon or the dangerous "bad nigger" of Thomas Dixon's fiction, Louis matched none of those negative characteristics. Louis clearly benefited from a national press that liked him and from what he symbolized in the emerging international conflict. Never the victim of any political or racial persecution as Jack Johnson had been, Louis was unashamedly patriotic. He would join the army within weeks of Pearl Harbor, and at an early rally for military support at Madison Square Garden, Private Louis inspired a throng of nervous Americans with his one and only line: "We'll win because we're on God's side."[2]

At precisely the time that Joe Louis was emerging as a symbol of powerful Americanism, the United States Supreme Court was beginning to strengthen the meaning of democratic values. The separate and independent power of the federal judiciary was about to become the main protector of blacks' rights, especially after the arrival of Franklin Roosevelt's new judges on the Supreme Court. Starting with Hugo Black in 1937 and continuing with the appointments of four more justices in the ensuing years, the court took positions far more sympathetic to the inter-

Joe Louis knocked out Max Schmeling in the first round of their 1938 fight. *Courtesy AP/ Wideworld Photos.*

ests of minorities than it had ever done before. It was, however, Calvin Coolidge's appointee Justice Harlan Fiske Stone who provided the first powerful justification for expanding the court's protection of blacks' rights. In *United States v. Carolene Products* in 1938, a case that upheld the power of the Congress to make laws regulating commerce without undue judicial interference, Justice Stone commented that the courts were still justified in overturning any laws aimed specifically at racial, ethnic, or religious groups. Stone no doubt had seen reports throughout 1937 and 1938 that Japanese mistreatment of the Chinese and Nazi persecution of Jews were intensifying, and clearly he connected those injustices to the treatment of minorities at home. "Prejudice against discrete and insular minorities," Justice Stone wrote in his *Carolene Products* opinion, especially when reflected in laws that undermine a minority group's political power, justify close scrutiny, and probably rejection, by federal courts. In a private letter written on the day after the opinion was announced, he explained to a colleague that he had become "deeply concerned about the increasing racial and religious intolerance which seems to bedevil the world, and which I greatly fear may be augmented in this country." Stone had seen clearly the evils that democratic majorities in Germany had visited on racial minorities, and knowing that such wrongs could exist in the United States, he established a justification for judicial activism in defense of minorities.[3]

Consistently with Justice Stone's call for judicial activism, the Supreme Court rendered other decisions in 1938 that advanced the efforts that African Americans had already made in challenging racial discrimination. The court upheld the right of individuals to picket at businesses against job discrimination in the "Don't Buy Where You Can't Work" boycotts, and black protestors began new boycotts in several northern cities. The court ruled that the state of Missouri had to admit Lloyd Gaines, a black student, to its only state-run law school. Until then, Missouri had provided scholarships for a few black citizens to attend law school in another state, a common practice among southern and border states. The *Gaines* decision became the first in a series of cases over the next 15 years in which the courts made ever stricter the enforcement of the "equal" standard of the "separate but equal" *Plessy* doctrine.[4]

By 1938 many arms of the United States government were making contributions to the improvement of African-American conditions. That year the Works Progress Administration, through its many projects, provided a wage to one million black families. Most jobs were in construction, but the WPA also created work for black writers and artists. Under the New Deal, the number of black federal civil service employees rose to 150,000, which represented fully 10 percent of the total. The Civilian Conservation Corps corrected its discriminatory practices, and it became a major provider of adult literacy for African Americans. The National Youth Administration underwrote the expenses of thousands of black college students, and by 1938 its minority director Mary McLeod Bethune had turned optimistic: "These are times of a great awakening and new opportunities for all; the spirit of democracy is being galvanized into realistic action."[5]

A public event in 1939 surely awakened some to the tension between the spirit of democracy and American race practices. The Daughters of the American Revolution (DAR) denied permission for the use of Constitution Hall in Washington for a concert by the contralto Marian Anderson, an African-American woman then recognized as one of the great opera singers in the world. In response, Eleanor Roosevelt immediately resigned from the DAR, and the NAACP quickly organized a concert at the Lincoln Memorial for Easter Sunday afternoon. Seventy-five thousand Americans, black and white, listened as Anderson sang a series of patriotic hymns and spirituals. The concert demonstrated an emerging sophistication among African Americans about symbolic politics in America, especially the ways to dramatize the contradictions in American values. The image of the pretty black woman, standing alone before the giant sculpture of the Great Emancipator, captured the essence of equality's triumph over white supremacy.[6]

At the same time that Joe Louis and Marian Anderson were altering the African-American image in national public life, black people in southern towns and cities were organizing challenges to white supremacy. They reflected new optimism that politics in the age of Roosevelt might provide opportunities to expand rights. "Roosevelt has done more for colored people than any other president," a black man in South Carolina declared. "He give us our first school—a three-room WPA school. . . . He give us food when we was hungry and our children hot WPA lunches in school." In Birmingham in 1938, a group of black industrial workers and employees of the WPA formed the Right to Vote Club to push voter registration efforts among African Americans. The next year several new neighborhood political organizations—led variously by a tailor, a barber, and a railroad employee—merged to form a county Negro Democratic Club that marshaled black voting strength in local and state elections. Starting in 1939, Birmingham's only black lawyer filed suit after suit against the county board of registrars for failing to register black applicants. Between 1935 and 1939, similar political organizations arose in Selma, Montgomery, Mobile, Gadsden, Tuscaloosa, and Tuskegee. They were often led by businessmen and govern-

Marian Anderson. *Courtesy Library of Congress.*

ment workers, though professionals and blue-collar workers collabo-
rated fully in nearly all groups.[7]

The Alabama developments were mirrored in urban areas in every
southern state. Local civic organizations similar to the one in Birmingham became intensely active between 1936 and 1939 in Petersburg and
Richmond, Virginia; Durham and Reidsville, North Carolina; Greenville,
South Carolina; Atlanta and Savannah, Georgia; Tampa and Jacksonville,
Florida; Vicksburg, Mississippi; New Orleans, Louisiana; Tulsa, Oklahoma; Little Rock, Arkansas; and Dallas and San Antonio, Texas. All the
civic leagues focused on getting the right to vote and using it strategi-
cally. To be sure, the NAACP branches and the Garvey chapters had been
antecedents of the voting clubs, and black political organizations had
been formed earlier, but few had lasted. Clearly, however, the immediate
impetus was the widespread feeling that the New Deal had made racial
change more possible, even in the South. The voting leagues created in
the late 1930s would last in most cases well into the 1960s, and they typically evolved into larger civil rights organizations.[8]

The emergence of voting leagues in so many towns and cities in the

late 1930s marked the beginning of a "civil rights movement"—overt challenges, sustained over many years, to white supremacy in at least one of
its main forms. Until the mid-1950s, the black activists would aim mainly
at the denial of voting rights. Unlike the activism in northern cities in the
1930s, there was little picketing or marching in southern communities in
the 1930s and 1940s, because southern whites' propensity for violence still
made it too dangerous. But the processes of organizing African Americans to go before hostile boards of registrars, study for and take literacy
tests, pay their poll tax, and sue boards in court over unfair denial—all
represented acts of defiance to one of the central pillars of white
supremacy, the disfranchisement of black voters. Relatively little public
or media attention accompanied the many voting struggles that were
taking place by 1939, and thus the simultaneous development of activism
in so many communities was often overlooked. But in each community, a
cadre of African Americans had made an ideological decision to act
against white supremacy and then pursued their course for many years.

Black activists found some white allies in the South in 1938 when an
interracial group of labor activists, radicals, and politicians came together
to form the Southern Conference for Human Welfare (SCHW) to pursue
political and social reform. Prominent New Dealers, including Eleanor
Roosevelt, attended the SCHW's organizational meeting in Birmingham,
which called for an end to the poll tax. This device prevented most poor
southerners from voting and thus accounted, SCHW members believed,
for the failure of southern states to provide decent education and welfare. Although little was said openly about the implications for African-
Americans rights, both supporters and enemies of the SCHW
understood that an end to the poll tax would be a long step toward liber-
ating southern blacks from disfranchisement.[9]

Thus events in 1938 and 1939 marked a sharp turn in the history of
American race relations, though few whites recognized it as a pivotal
time. Some of the events were more symbolic than substantive, but in a
society becoming ever more connected through mass communications,
symbolic action shaped ideology, which in turn directed other events. But
the court decisions were very real, and they directly affected the course
of subsequent policies. The creation of local civil rights groups and a

regional interracial organization demonstrated that the commitments to changing race relations had found institutional bases to mount a struggle. No one knew how long it would take, but many blacks saw that a struggle had begun.

I

Those watershed events in 1938 and 1939 all connected in some way to the sharpening focus on national ideology, which the war in Europe helped to prompt. Like Woodrow Wilson, in whose administration he had served during the Great War, Franklin Roosevelt defined American commitment to the war in terms of democratic values. In calling for full-scale rearmament in 1941, he said that Americans' responsibility was to a "moral order" in which were guaranteed four freedoms—freedom of speech and of religion, and freedom from want and from fear. Roosevelt believed that every American was entitled to these freedoms, and he wanted his nation to help guarantee them everywhere. The content of the four freedoms, especially the concern about want and fear, recognized the growing desire of Americans for security. This basic need, which operated at an even more fundamental level than the yearning for status, had emerged most clearly during the devastation of the Great Depression. Prior to this time, most Americans had viewed security as something elusive, not really attainable on this earth. But security had begun to seem more achievable as Americans expanded their government to address the crises of the 1930s. Franklin Roosevelt knew that the coming war would test vigorously Americans' ability to keep themselves secure, and he enunciated that goal in the four freedoms so that Americans would be thinking about what was at stake.

That same year, Eleanor Roosevelt did her part to proclaim an expanded definition of equality. "There must be equality before the law, equality of education, equal opportunity to obtain a job according to one's ability and training, and equality of participation in self-government," she wrote in *Ladies Home Journal* in 1941. Over the next few years, Mrs. Roosevelt would constantly reiterate the four equalities in magazine and newspaper articles and speeches, just as the press and the federal government's propaganda machinery repeated the president's four freedoms time and again. She had done two things: She had reminded whites that blacks were in no way extended equality in American life, and she had given blacks the ideological bases for rejecting white supremacy. Although many African Americans hardly needed to be told, the First Lady's endorsement of their view of equality's meaning was powerful support.[10]

The year 1941 brought still another forceful interpretation of national values, this one from Henry Luce, the Republican publisher of *Time*, *Life*, and *Fortune* magazines. In a *Life* essay entitled "The American Century," Luce argued that in the twentieth century the United States had become the most powerful nation in the world, but Americans had not accepted that reality "spiritually and practically." Americans' failure, he believed, had been disastrous for the world, now increasingly victimized by imperial fascism and communism. We live, he wrote, in a paradoxical century, one unmatched both in human progress and in the scale of "pain and anguish and bitter death," one with the "biggest wars in the midst of the most widespread, the deepest and the most articulate hatred of war in all history." Luce offered his prescription: "The cure is this: to accept wholeheartedly our duty and our opportunity as the most powerful and vital nation in the world and in consequence to exert upon the world the full impact of our influence, for such purposes as we see fit and by such means as we see fit." Americans were specially suited to shape international affairs because "we have some things in the country which are infinitely precious and especially American—a love of freedom, a feeling for the equality of opportunity, a tradition of self-reliance and independence" and also because "we are the inheritors of all the great principles of Western civilization—above all Justice, the love of Truth, the ideal of Charity." Luce believed that so much virtue was reinforced by the special gift for capitalist enterprise, which Americans should apply to overcoming hunger and want in the world. Recognizing Americans' peculiar gifts and accepting commensurate responsibility to the world would make the age of Roosevelt—and Luce—what it should be, the American century.[11]

"The American Century" would prove to be one of the most influential assertions of American nationalism ever made, though it would more often be condemned for its triumphalism than appreciated for its realistic view of the powers and the perils of the time. Through the war years, Luce's understanding of U.S. responsibility shaped Americans' attitudes toward their circumstances and reinforced Franklin and Eleanor Roosevelt's ideological explanations of America's mission. As the nation's power expanded, so would the importance of how its people acted.

On the eve of what they perceived would be a great American mission in the world, Luce and the Roosevelts imagined a broader definition of democratic values than their countrymen had embraced in recent decades. Together their conception of the nation and its meaning reclaimed the broad understanding that Abraham Lincoln had put forward in the course of the Civil War. The Lincoln revision of American values had not been forgotten, but its hold on national ideology had weakened over three generations. Consciously or not, the president, the First Lady, and the most influential man in mass communications had revived the Great Emancipator's definition of the American nation.

Coming as the country still suffered from the Great Depression, their expanded notions of freedom, equality, and national honor also reflected Americans' growing preoccupations with security—or to be more precise, the profound insecurity many had suffered for more than a decade. Security in the midst of the most horrific war in history would be elusive if not impossible, but Americans would reach for it by insisting that after the war their nation must protect individual rights more jealously than it had in the past. The war would inspire a "rights revolution," and while many Americans still would not have their full rights during wartime, the beginnings of a more nearly free and equal society came with the attack on Pearl Harbor.

II

During 1939 and 1940, as the likelihood grew of American involvement in the crises in Europe and Asia, African Americans maintained a deep skepticism about their participation in a future war. Already the irony of blacks' fighting racism in Europe and Asia weighed on the minds of many. They remembered both their mistreatment in the armed services during the Great War and the extremes of violence and intolerance after the war. Starting in 1937 the *Pittsburgh Courier*, by then the most widely circulated black newspaper in the country, began a campaign to end segregation in the armed services. Its editor Robert Vann argued steadily for the next few years that blacks should make up 10 percent of the *fighting* force. The 1940 Republican presidential nominee Wendell Wilkie offered a strong civil rights plank in the realistic understanding that African-American voters might hold the balance of power in several large electoral states. In response President Roosevelt appointed the army's first black general and committed to giving blacks access to all military occupations, including flying. In December 1940, *Crisis* told its readers, "This is no fight merely to wear a uniform" but a "struggle for status, a struggle to take democracy off of parchment and give it life."[12]

With the promise of fair treatment, black leaders began to call for full African-American commitment to the war effort, arguing that if blacks let the white man fight the war, then whites would have the right to do as they pleased to blacks after the war. After Pearl Harbor, the prevailing attitude emerged as a commitment to fight for democracy on two fronts—at home *and* abroad—and this would later be captured in the "double-V" slogan. Still, not everyone easily grasped the logic, including the southern sharecropper who on December 8 chattily said to his landlord, "By the way, Captain, I hear the Japs done declared war on you white folks!" The *Courier's* columnist George Schuyler wrote that "our war is not against Hitler in Europe, but against the Hitlers in America." A government survey taken in Harlem in the spring of 1942 discovered that most black residents believed that they would be as well or better off if the Japanese won the war.[13]

African Americans' skepticism about fair treatment in the military proved to be wholly warranted. Still convinced that blacks had not performed well in World War I, the U.S. military command assumed that black men lacked courage and leadership ability. Although the army had

Black soldiers were typically segregated at southern training camps. *Courtesy Library of Congress.*

agreed to unrestricted use of black troops, it never treated black soldiers equally, and some commanders simply refused to accept black combat troops. In one of the major race-policy battles of the war, the army agreed to let African Americans in the air corps, but it insisted on segregated training. Through the early war years, African Americans felt bitter about their participation in the U.S. war effort. Black soldiers commonly joked that their epitaph would read: "Here lies a black man killed fighting a yellow man for the glory of a white man."[14]

Much black anger about the military's treatment originated in their experience at training bases in the South. In early 1941, as the first draftees were arriving at camps, a black private was found hanging from a tree at Fort Benning, Georgia, his hands and feet tied. Responsibility for the act was never determined, but the lynching set a tone of fear among black soldiers who would train in the South. In 1941 black soldiers in North Carolina fought with white civilians and military policemen in bars and on buses. In 1943 race relations reached their low point when angry black soldiers at three southern camps took up arms against whites. "I would just as soon die fightin' for democracy right here in Georgia," one black soldier said. "Kill a cracker in Mississippi or Germany, what's the difference!" In the end, the army's best solution was to ship black soldiers overseas as quickly as possible.[15]

The experience of African-American soldiers and sailors improved during the last two years of the war. The navy, which originally used blacks only as cooks and dockworkers, integrated some crews in 1944 and 1945. African Americans made up half the transportation corps in Europe, and several black combat units saw some action. During the Battle of the Bulge in early 1945, about 2,500 blacks from supply divisions were integrated into previously all-white ground combat units, and they fought valiantly through the invasion of Germany. By early 1945 black soldiers were writing home from Europe that race relations in the army were better.[16]

However fraught with conflict and indignity, the participation of African Americans in the military advanced their broad-based commitment to civil rights that had emerged in the 1930s. One million blacks put on uniforms and served their country, action that gave them full claim to the privileges of American citizenship. Polls reported that their participation in the war effort had "speeded up the long-time growth of consciousness" among the African-American population that "this is a free country, that they have rights and are not getting them."[17]

Next to fairness in military participation, African Americans' primary concern was getting to participate in the wartime economic boom. In early 1941, A. Philip Randolph, head of the Brotherhood of Sleeping Car Porters and the nation's leading black unionist, organized a protest effort, the march on Washington movement, to bring pressure on the Roosevelt administration to hire African Americans in war industries. Randolph planned to bring thousands of people to the Lincoln Memorial to create the kind of symbolic demonstration that the Marian Anderson concert had been. But unlike the Anderson concert, this action was strongly opposed by the Roosevelt administration , and to prevent its taking place, the president issued Executive Order 8802 establishing a Fair Employment Practices Committee (FEPC) to investigate and identify cases of employment discrimination. The march on Washington movement accomplished two things: It showed black activists that merely the threat of mass protest had brought a new response from the national government, and it prompted the FEPC to keep the issue of fair play in the economic sphere on the public's mind through the war years, even though the FEPC lacked the authority to enforce fair hiring on resistant employers.[18]

Many major employers discriminated thoroughly. Boeing Aircraft in Seattle, which had not one African American among its 41,000 employees, tried to shift blame, announcing that "only those of the Caucasian Race" were acceptable to the machinists' union. Among the other five major aircraft manufacturers, which in 1942 employed more than 100,000 workers, about 100 African Americans were on the payrolls. Shipyards were almost as bad, especially those organized by the Brotherhood of Boilermakers, which vigorously discriminated against African- and Mexican-American workers, regardless of the manpower shortages. In 1941 only 100 of 8,500 shipyard workers in Los Angeles were black. In Mobile, Alabama, where much of the nearby available labor supply was black, one shipyard employing 10,000 workers in 1943 had hired exactly 22 African Americans, 11 of them as porters. Various industries in Chicago, Milwaukee, Cincinnati, and the New York area claimed that African Americans lacked needed training or that white workers and their unions would not tolerate their being hired. In 1942, General Electric had 16 blacks on its payroll of 6,500, Sperry Gyroscope 21 of its 11,212.[19]

Such discrimination meant that most African Americans had to wait until the supply of available white labor was completely exhausted before they could get hired in many war industries. Blacks largely missed the early war-industry jobs, and thus the war emergency failed to yield the kind of economic progress that could have been possible with fair hiring. Late in 1942, however, labor shortages began to hurt war industries throughout the nation, forcing many employers to hire black workers in order to maintain production. Whereas blacks composed only 3 percent of U.S. war workers in the summer of 1942, they would make up 8 percent in 1945. To get the war-industry jobs, about 1.5 million blacks left the South for industrial cities in the Midwest and Northeast. About 75,000 migrated to Pacific Coast cities, especially Los Angeles, San Francisco, and Portland, to work on docks and at shipyards. In the South, the impact of migration was felt mainly in coastal cities where shipbuilding was located—Houston, New Orleans, Mobile, Charleston, Norfolk, and Baltimore.[20]

Many African Americans who were hired faced intense union discrimination. In closed-shop shipyards, black workers paid dues to the Boilermakers but were not allowed to participate in union deliberations or get the benefit of union protection of seniority or promotion and grievance rights. In the scores of steel mills, tire factories, and auto plants organized since 1937, Congress of Industrial Organizations (CIO) unions publicly supported fair employment but used their newly acquired shop-floor power to negotiate work rules that created segregated lines of promotion. Black workers with long seniority were put on promotion ladders that went no higher than unskilled "helper" positions. In 1942 the National War Labor Board ordered companies that were producing for the war effort—which included all CIO-organized plants—to maintain the union membership of their employees in exchange for the unions' commitment not to strike. The maintenance-of-membership order bound blacks to their union regardless of how they were treated.[21]

Once plants hired blacks, they were subject to hate strikes by white workers. In 1943 whites at Packard in Detroit, Bethlehem Steel in Baltimore, and Sun Shipbuilding near Philadelphia struck against black employment. That year in Mobile, 20,000 white shipbuilders refused to accept 12 blacks as welder trainees, rioted against the blacks, and then boycotted their own jobs. The War Department reached a compromise with the company to create segregated shipways where black skilled workers could be deployed, while most of the massive installation remained the exclusive preserve of white skilled labor. Whites' recalcitrance carried right through the victory celebrations in 1945, when war-industry plants in Ohio, Illinois, and Missouri were found to have virtually no black employees, because white workers violently rejected the prospect and their unions used their expanding power to enforce black lockouts.[22]

The hate strikes and the blatant defiance of fair-employment standards revealed the intense racial competition for economic opportunity that had always been a fundamental reality of race relations in America. Coming when the American economy was still depressed, the war had created jobs that whites aggressively sought and protected for their exclusive benefit. Perhaps whites' insecurity accounted for their lack of awareness about their discriminatory ways. A poll taken in late 1944 found that 55 percent of Americans—and 66 percent of southerners—responded affirmatively when asked "Do you think Negroes have the same chance as white people to make a good living in this country?"[23]

But even with pervasive discrimination, the war provided a remarkable surge in opportunities for African Americans. There were a million more blacks employed in civilian jobs in 1944 than there had been in 1940, and most of those jobs yielded a much higher income than the average black worker had earned at the start of the war. For many of them, the war enabled a move off the farm, which usually represented a journey

Black war workers in Alabama stopped to sing at a Fourth of July celebration. *Courtesy Library of Congress.*

from desperate poverty to a dependable, and often decent, wage. African-American women found fewer war-industry positions than white women, but a high proportion of them moved from low-wage agriculture or low-paying domestic work to much higher earnings in service jobs in restaurants, laundries, beauty shops, and hotels. At any time during the war, more than a half million African Americans were in uniform, earning government pay and often additional support for families. By the end of the war, a million black veterans had earned benefits for education, housing, and health care that would make the future more promising economically.

The wartime employment improved African Americans' economic position. Before the war, the average income of black men in the United States had been 41 percent of white men's, but by 1949 it had increased to 48 percent. Black women's income as a portion of white women's during the same period went from 36 to 46 percent, a remarkable gain. Although the racial discrepancy remained great, African Americans enjoyed more economic progress in the 1940s than at any time since emancipation.[24]

The experience of war at home and abroad escalated the protests of African Americans. Incidents of conflict on public transportation, usually arising when segregation was enforced on overcrowded streetcars and buses, convinced whites in dozens of southern cities that something had changed about blacks. Fights between bus drivers and rebellious black passengers were routine in southern cities throughout the war. In the year after Pearl Harbor, the Birmingham transit authority dealt with 88 cases of blacks' occupying "white" space on streetcars and buses, 55 of which were open acts of defiance in which blacks refused to give up their seats.[25]

Continuing what had begun with the voting leagues in the late 1930s, African Americans congregated at boards of registrars at the local courthouses during the war years to demand the right to vote. Some of the determination arose from the Supreme Court's 1944 ruling in *Smith v. Allwright*, which outlawed the white primary. This meant that African Americans who were registered could now vote in the election that really mattered in the one-party South—the Democratic primary. Large numbers of blacks appeared at voter registration boards in Birmingham,

African Americans attempted to register to vote in Birmingham in 1944.
Courtesy Birmingham Public Library.

Atlanta, and other cities and towns during the summer and fall of 1944. During the war years, the number of NAACP local branches trebled, and its membership increased ninefold, to almost a half million by 1946, with most of the growth occurring in the South. At the instigation of its rapidly expanding membership, the NAACP sponsored lawsuits against discrimination in voting and teacher salaries. Progress was clear: in the 1940s, the number of African-American registered voters across the South rose dramatically, and local school boards largely equalized the pay of black teachers to white teachers.[26]

New protests against economic discrimination spread across the country. The "Don't Buy Where You Can't Work" pickets continued in several cities. In San Francisco, Detroit, and many war-industry cities, African-American workers created new groups to fight industry and union discrimination. In an attempt to open hiring, Cleveland's Future Outlook League picketed Bell Telephone in 1941 and then followed the street protests with a massive "dial-in" in which thousands of women simultaneously dialed "o" and jammed the switchboards. A Birmingham locomotive fireman forced from his job by the white brotherhood's exclusionary tactics sued on behalf of all African Americans who had lost their jobs. Harlan Stone, now chief justice, wrote an opinion in *Steele v. L&N* in 1944 that echoed his *Carolene Products* decision in its concern that minorities be able to protect themselves from oppressive majorities: if a labor union that was supposed to represent all members of a craft conspired to take away blacks' jobs, Justice Stone declared, then "the minority would be left with no means of protecting their interests or, indeed, their right to earn a livelihood." The court held both the union and the railroad responsible for unconstitutional denial of rights and ordered that the blacks be rehired.[27]

The black protest spirit caught the attention of many observers. A government investigator traveling through the rural South in 1942 found that African Americans were "becoming more fearless and ready to state what they believe to be the basic rights of the group." The black church provided "the means here and there for encouraging Negroes to resist the controls which the landlord has held over them." The investigator reported that "ideas about 'rights' are being introduced in a few instances to Negro sharecroppers through Negro preachers and their educated white and Negro friends." A black sociologist surmised that "each increment in education, each rise in status" had exposed for African Americans the discrepancy between democratic values and white supremacy, and that this had "heightened the racial consciousness of the group as a whole and produced frustration, cynicism, and bitterness in many individuals." A pollster who surveyed black opinion concluded that the "draft and war industry migration have greatly speeded up the long-time growth of consciousness among Negroes that this is a free country, that they have rights and are not getting them."[28]

III

The emerging civil rights movement alarmed white southerners, many of whom were already worried by the New Deal's incursions on their domi-

nance of southern society. Since Reconstruction, wealthy whites had usually controlled southern governments, which given their disproportionate
influence in the U.S. Congress, had secured for these whites dominance in
race and class relations in the South. But under the New Deal, the
national government had taken power from the states, and Franklin Roosevelt's popularity among new ethnic and black voters in the North
largely canceled southerners' control of the Democratic Party. The FEPC
was viewed as dangerous federal interference in race relations. The war
buildup provoked white hysteria about the presence of black soldiers in
the camps and even demands that they all be removed from the South.
White planters were angry about the loss of cheap labor. "The trouble is,
one nigger'll get a job and the whole crowd of them will live off that one
and won't raise a hand to do anything," an Alabama planter announced,
referring to the impact of a nearby army base on his labor supply. "We
never paid them more than $1 a day around here and now they're making
$4. ... They'll buy automobiles and radios and won't work for hell."[29]

By mid-1942 rumors of race upheaval flashed through the South.
Whites whispered that black men assumed that "when white men go to
the Army, the Negro men will have the white women." Blacks were
"buying up ice picks to attack the whites," went one irrepressible story.
Black domestic servants allegedly had vowed to put "a white woman in
every kitchen by 1943." Black women in fact were leaving domestic service for better-paying jobs elsewhere, but they were not, as imagined, join-
ing "Eleanor Clubs," a backhanded tribute to the First Lady's concern for
blacks' rights. White southerners believed in the Eleanor Clubs because,
they said, "she goes around telling the Negroes they are as good as anyone else." Wherever Mrs. Roosevelt has spoken, they told one sociologist, "Negroes always act like they are white folks."[30]

Such views represented only the extreme of the strongly white
supremacist opinion that prevailed nationally in 1942. A poll that year
revealed that when white Americans were asked if they thought Negroes
were as intelligent as white people, 48 percent said no, 42 percent yes. Only
21 percent of white southerners answered yes. When asked if they thought
that whites and blacks should go to the same school, 66 percent of white

adults said no, 30 percent yes. Should there be separate sections for blacks on streetcars and buses? Fifty-one percent said yes, 44 no. Would it bother you if a Negro of similar education and income to yours moved onto your block? Yes, answered 62 percent. Two years later, the question was posed, "Would it make any difference to you if a Negro family moved in next door to you?" and 69 percent answered in the affirmative. In 1942 a clear majority of white Americans—and no doubt an overwhelming majority of white southerners—believed that segregation was correct.[31]

When tested by war-generated fear, whites' racial instincts resulted in a revival of hostility to Asians and the nation's worst mass act of racial bigotry in the twentieth century, the Japanese internment. In 1942, U.S. military authorities, worried about possible attacks on the West Coast, recommended that all persons of Japanese descent, including those who were American-born and U.S. citizens, be held in prison camps. Radio and newspaper commentators promoted anti-Japanese hysteria. One newspaper dismissed the possibility that American-born Japanese could be loyal: "A viper is nonetheless a viper wherever the egg is hatched." Competitors of Japanese farmers promoted their removal for nakedly selfish reasons. The U.S. attorney general found no security reasons to remove the Japanese, but President Roosevelt acceded to the West Coast hysteria, and 110,000 Japanese Americans spent the war years behind fences in camps scattered across the country.[32]

Meanwhile, white race fears were seen in the intense competition for space that came with the rapid movement of blacks to cities. Still tightly circumscribed in a small area of Chicago, the 60,000 new black migrants to the city during the war years often jammed ten persons to a room in rapidly deteriorating housing. In Los Angeles and San Francisco, which were receiving their first large African-American in-migration, the housing situation for blacks would have been much worse but for the homes vacated by the interned Japanese Americans. Shortages resulted in harsh conflicts over public housing in Dearborn, Detroit, Chicago, Baltimore, and New York City. Each antiblack action drew loud protests from African Americans, but there was little relief. Conflicts over housing and protests against discrimination never abated during the war years.[33]

The wartime tensions finally exploded during the summer of 1943, first in Los Angeles when white soldiers and sailors entered movie theaters and dragged young Mexican-American and African-American men into the street and beat them. The *Los Angeles Times* and the *Los Angeles Daily News* had recently reported, with much exaggeration, a crime wave by Mexican-American men, and when criticized for racial profiling, they began substituting the term "zoot suits" for the racial identification—alongside pictures of Mexican-American men in broad-rimmed hats and trousers flared at the knees and tight at the ankles. In fact, very few Mexican Americans were so dressed. The newspapers wrongly reported that soldiers and sailors acted in self-defense: "Zoot-Suit Gangsters Plan War on Navy" was a typical headline.[34]

A few days later, the worst violence of the war years occurred in Detroit. During the war the city would receive about 50,000 black immigrants but many more whites, a high proportion of them from the South. The wartime arrival of white-supremacist preachers from the South escalated the antiblack extremism in America's "Arsenal of Democracy." After a year of intensive in-migration, a conflict at an amusement park on a hot Sunday afternoon boiled over into a race war. Rumors of racial attacks—that a black man had raped and killed a white woman, that a white man had thrown a black baby off a bridge—fueled the violence. Detroit policemen probably were responsible for most of the blacks' deaths, but large mobs of whites entered the black ghetto to hunt for victims. By the time U.S. government troops belatedly restored order, 34 people had been killed and hundreds injured.[35]

The deadliness of the Detroit riot, coming in the aftermath of the disturbances in Los Angeles and of another in Beaumont, Texas, frightened the entire nation, and the fear was reinforced two months later when rumors of a police killing provoked a riot in Harlem. The Harlem disturbance was distinctly different from the other riots in that it was characterized not by whites' attacking blacks but by blacks' destroying white-owned property. It was, however, similar to one in Harlem in 1935, when blacks looted only white-owned businesses. A young writer named Ralph Ellison described the 1943 riot as a "naïve, peasant-like act of revenge." "I don't have to do this," Ellison heard one man say as he threw a trashcan through a white-owned business's window. "I make a fair salary as a longshoreman. I'm doing this for revenge." The object of this revenge was not clear, though Ellison observed, "I get the impression that they were giving way to resentment over the price of food and other necessities, police brutality and the general indignities borne by Negro soldiers." The unspecified anger that justified wholesale theft in Harlem in 1943 portended large difficulties for American cities in the future.[36]

The 1943 riots, which coincided with well-publicized racial conflicts at southern army camps, dampened some civil rights activism. The NAACP and African-American newspaper editors cautioned blacks to restrain protests or risk more violence. Northerners blamed the violence on recent white southern migrants and Axis subversives, but white southerners answered that the failure to segregate blacks outside the South was the cause of the riots. "It is blood on your hands, Mrs. Eleanor Roosevelt," a Mississippi editor wrote. "More than any other person, you are morally responsible for those race riots in Detroit.... You have been personally proclaiming and practicing social equality at the White House and wherever you go."[37]

IV

"The way to change an ideology is to get a new point of view," the black sociologist Charles S. Johnson wrote in 1943. Race ideology in the United States reached a fork in the road at precisely the time Joe Louis's symbolism of black competence and civic idealism dawned on the American public. In 1938 the anthropologist Franz Boas published a new edition of his nonracialist interpretation of culture, *The Mind of Primitive Man*. As early as 1906, Boas had argued that environment was more important than heredity in shaping behavior, and that blacks in similar environmental circumstances had moral and intellectual capacities essentially equal to whites'. Washington and Du Bois had embraced his positions, but few whites listened to Boas in the 1910s and 1920s. After the Nazis came to power in 1933, Boas, who was Jewish, worked more intently to counter racist thinking. His goal was to demonstrate that "while we may find that certain characteristic traits are inherited in a family, the race is altogether too complex to infer that racial characteristics as such are inherited." Much of Boas's influence came through his students, especially Ruth Benedict and Margaret Mead, who found among primitive peoples social and cultural practices that reflected equal abilities to more advanced civilizations. Although it would take American participation in a war against Japanese and German racism to persuade a clear majority of American intellectuals to adopt an antiracist position, Boas and his followers had laid a firm intellectual foundation by the late 1930s.[38]

American intellectuals, who during the 1930s had been preoccupied with the class divisions in American society, gained a new appreciation for democratic values during the war years. The theologian Reinhold Niebuhr wrote in 1944 that "man's capacity for justice makes democracy possible, but man's inclination to injustice makes democracy necessary." Gunnar Myrdal's instantly influential 1944 work *An American Dilemma* ratified the wartime discussion about the dangerous hypocrisy between America's announced values and its treatment of black citizens. A Swedish economist, Myrdal identified an "American Creed of liberty, equality, justice, and fair opportunity for everybody." The great contradiction to these values, he wrote, was the "Negro problem." It was an "anomaly in the very structure of American society," the source of "moral uneasiness," and "a problem in the heart of the American."[39]

The outlets of mass communication promulgated the ideology of democracy. In 1938 and 1939, the American media had begun to show greater sensitivity to racial minorities. *Life* magazine, created by Henry Luce and the *Time* interests, began publication in 1936 with references to African Americans as "darkies" or even "bad niggers" who manifested "barbaric" behavior. But in 1938 such bigotry largely disappeared, and emphasis instead was placed on black achievements, especially artistic ones. The *Saturday Evening Post*, long the home of racist short fiction, began about 1937 to tone down the illustrations that accompanied "darky" literature, and then in the early 1940s it abandoned racist fiction in favor of nonfiction pieces that empathized with the experience of American minority groups. *Reader's Digest*, the most widely read magazine in the United States, had regularly run "darky" stories in dialect, but after April 1943 such entries suddenly stopped.

Just as important, magazines that previously had little to say about race relations began running articles encouraging racial and ethnic tolerance. In 1942, *Ladies' Home Journal* for the first time gave an intimate profile of a black family. *Look, Collier's, Life, Time,* and *Fortune* featured stories that emphasized the democratic responsibility for fairness to blacks, Jews, and other minority groups. *Glamour, Mademoiselle, Harper's Bazaar,* and *Seventeen* all ran articles promoting racial tolerance. Margaret Mead told *Mademoiselle*'s young readers that in the past people had upheld their status by discriminating against those of different color, religion, or nationality. "To believe that a man's character was somehow related to the color of his skin or the way his hair was laid on his head was not an evil belief as long as there was no knowledge to refute it," Mead wrote. "But these beliefs were tested and found false—to still cherish them is to close one's ears to the truth." In 1945, *Look* admonished its readers: "Nail the lies. Refute the moth-eaten labels, libels and wornout club-car jokes about members of minority groups.... The Negro's achievement in the arts and science, in industry and on the fighting front, blast the myth that he 'can't do skilled work.'"[40]

In 1942 the first popular national magazine for African Americans, *Negro Digest,* appeared, and it immediately found a large audience just as black economic and geographic mobility was accelerating. Modeled after *Reader's Digest,* it reprinted journalism of interest about African Americans, drawing from black newspapers and some white sources. *Negro Digest* began to nurture a stronger sense of connection among African Americans nationally, thus enhancing further the communal sense among blacks that the war was fostering.

Radio for the first time provided programming that gave in-depth analysis of cultural diversity in the United States and exposed some racial wrongs. The U.S. Office of Education sponsored the development of such multipart series as *Americans All, Immigrants All,* an interpretation of American history emphasizing the contributions of various ethnic groups, and *Freedom's People,* which told the story of black history and culture in the United States. *America's Town Meeting of the Air,* a continuing public-affairs discussion program, addressed such questions as "Are we solving America's race problem?" These series and others like them ran on the major commercial networks. Radio brought to a mass audience a sense that African Americans and other minority groups had an important place in American life and that their grievances were legitimate. A medium that had previously only lampooned and demeaned—and still presented "Amos 'n' Andy" once a week—was now exposing injustice.[41]

The Office of War Information (OWI) was concerned especially with the negative images in film, in part because of the propaganda power that Josef Goebbels and the Nazis had already proved film had. The government sponsored the making of many propaganda films, including *The Negro Soldier*, which promoted the contributions of black servicemen and women to the war effort but disappointed many African-American viewers because of its failure to recognize the many wrongs done to blacks in uniform. Simultaneously, the NAACP campaigned in Hollywood to end racial stereotyping of blacks, and it received promises from movie executives to cooperate. But the industry did not turn around quickly: a study of American movies during 1943 and 1944 found that of 100 films reviewed with black characterizations, 85 were found to project negative stereotypes. In 1943 OWI had to abandon its efforts in Hollywood because of the attacks made against the agency by southern congressmen upset over its challenges to white-supremacist image making. Still, if the NAACP and OWI lost most of their battles during the war, their positions won in peacetime Hollywood. The stereotypes of incompetent blacks that characterized virtually all of Hollywood films from the 1920s into the early 1940s quickly disappeared in the postwar period.[42]

By the end of the war, American public opinion about race had already shifted significantly. A 1946 poll found that on the question of intelligence, 53 percent of whites now said that blacks were as smart as whites, up from 42 percent in 1942. For the first time in American history, most whites professed to believe in blacks' equal potential. Clearly, many white Americans were thinking in new ways.[43]

The war provoked people everywhere to think more critically about the use of violence. At least six million Jews and probably more Russians had died at the hands of the German government, and the Japanese had killed a comparably unfathomable number of Chinese. The explosion of two atomic bombs in Japan at the end of the war gave the world a taste of the U.S. military's destructive capacity. The horrors of the war experience made people in the West far more fearful of violence. Peace movements became even stronger than they had been after World War I. Support for universal human rights surged throughout the world.

Americans, known for a casual attitude toward gunplay and the cultural celebration of brutal heroes, recognized that violence was the antithesis of security. Within the construct of American democratic values, freedom came to be understood in part as the absence of violence. The war made Americans' concern for security far more pressing, as massive death counts only could do. More than three hundred thousand Americans had died in the war, with many others having suffered wounds and contemplated death. Survivors of the war grasped for means to prevent future violence. In the face of the new "Cold War" with the Soviet Union, the United States built by far the strongest peacetime military establishment it had ever maintained—in the hope of preventing more violence. The desire for security also caused Americans to expand domestic programs. If the United States did not create as comprehensive a public system of social welfare as western European nations did, it built a much larger system of government benefits for housing, health care, and old-age pensions than had existed before. Private insurance and pension programs grew rapidly as Americans sought lifelong security.

The discovery of massive death camps in 1945 forced Americans to see the extreme end to which racism could go. The pictures of the Holocaust and the reports of the unimaginable scale of murder so repulsed thinking people that any and all suggestions of racial prejudice were called into question. Americans' historic casual acceptance of anti-Semitism quickly was reversed. In the United States, the Holocaust confirmed the correctness of the wartime emphasis on racial and ethnic toleration among government propagandists, intellectuals, the media, and popular culture. The German atrocities created a pole from which decent people were repelled, and subsequent behavior was expected to demonstrate that repulsion completely.

As a consequence of the war, whites in the South began to abandon the southern ethnic nationalism they had embraced since the late 1860s. Any form of ethnic nationalism that could be likened to that of Germany or Japan now was called into question. Many southern whites had made great sacrifices to defend the American nation, and the old sense of the United States as an oppressor of white southerners largely disappeared. The myths and romances of the Civil War era no longer seemed relevant compared to what many had been through in recent years. To be sure, most southern whites held on to the ideology of white supremacy, but it was now based far less on the distinctly southern experience and more exclusively on the belief in blacks' cultural and moral inferiority. The demise of white nationalism as an ideological underpinning for racial attitudes was not complete or immediately apparent, but its weakened claim on southerners' thinking would become clear when they faced a full-scale assault on segregation in the 1960s.

V

In 1946 many white southerners already felt besieged by the intensified commitment to voter registration among African Americans. That year black activists, many of them returning veterans, founded the Mississippi Progressive Voters' League and immediately enlisted 5,000 members amid the worst white-supremacist oppression. In Birmingham 100 black war veterans marched in uniform, carrying their discharge papers, to the voter registrar's office, where they refused to "interpret" the U.S. Constitution when asked, because state law only required that they be able to read it. At the same time in Atlanta, the United Negro Veterans marched by the hundreds to demand the appointment of black policemen. In Savannah 12,000 new black voters registered in 17 days. Statewide the number of black voters in Georgia went from 20,000 in 1945 to 135,000 by the end of 1946. African Americans in the South, a black activist observed in the mid-1940s, were a "politically inspired people."[44]

The federal courts continued to advance the cause of civil rights, usually at the instigation of NAACP lawyers. Between 1946 and 1950, the NAACP won major decisions that outlawed restrictive covenants and segregation on interstate transportation. Having largely achieved the equalization of teachers' salaries, the NAACP decided to stop challenging unequal educational situations and instead sued only for integration of schools. By 1948 the Supreme Court had spent a decade removing the pillars on which white supremacy stood—disfranchisement, job discrimination, housing segregation, and educational disparity. By no means were all the supports gone, but this one branch of the national government clearly and consistently had acted to protect the rights of minorities, as it had promised it would do in *Carolene Products* in 1938.[45]

Segregation was dealt its most severe symbolic blow in the spring of 1947, when major-league baseball accepted its first black player of the twentieth century, Jackie Robinson of the Brooklyn Dodgers. Not only a gifted athlete but also a fierce defender of civil rights, Robinson had been court-martialed during the war for refusing to move to the back of a military bus. He proved to be an excellent choice for breaking down the race barrier, because he endured racist slurs from both opponents and fans without a visible reaction and managed to play superbly on the field. Robinson earned the admiration of his Dodger teammates, several of whom were southerners, and the mass enthusiasm of African Americans. "How did Jackie do today?" was the most common query in black households during the summer of 1947. Robinson suggested to whites the inevitable demise of segregation and a powerful precedent for believing that it could end without much difficulty. Like Joe Louis, Robinson had become an American popular hero, universally so to blacks but also to many whites.[46]

Unseen changes worked in the 1940s to undermine white supremacy. In 1950 there were half as many black sharecroppers in the South as there had been in 1930, and in another ten years, two-thirds of those would have left the farm. The demise of sharecropping took African Americans away from the direct control of landlords, who since emancipation had been the most powerful white-supremacist authority. During the 1940s the portion of African Americans acquiring a high-school education in the South shot upward, a reflection of both rising black prosperity and heavy increases in southern states' spending on black schools—done in an effort to thwart desegregation. The number of African Americans attending college grew 150 percent during the 1940s. The big changes in the black educational profile increased the number of people with the confidence and wherewithal to demand their rights. The full impact of the economic and educational changes would not be felt until the 1950s and 1960s, but African Americans had accumulated many new resources during the war decade.[47]

Blacks' improving economic position spurred renewed racial competition for space, which yielded more violence in the postwar years. In Atlanta there were 30 bombings of houses recently occupied by blacks in

Jackie Robinson in 1947. *Courtesy AP/Wideworld Photos.*

formerly all-white neighborhoods. Birmingham witnessed so many explosions on streets where blacks were beginning to move that it earned the name "Bombingham." In Chicago the battle along the frontiers of the Black Belt became even more intense than it had been during the war. During 1945 and 1946 whites repeatedly attacked—29 times with bombs—houses recently occupied by blacks. For several nights during the summer of 1947, thousands of whites attacked police protecting black veterans who had moved into a new public-housing project in Fernwood Park that whites wanted reserved for them. Marauding white gangs, reminiscent of the 1919 riot, attacked African Americans in Chicago's black neighborhoods.[48]

Battles over school integration always accompanied the competition for space. At the same time that blacks were boycotting segregated schools, white students in several cities struck against attempts at integration. In Gary, Indiana, one thousand white students abandoned Froebel High School in the fall of 1945 when two hundred black students were accepted. Gary attracted the attention of the singer Frank Sinatra, who saw the white boycott as an opportunity to apply his influence for racial tolerance. Sinatra had developed a keen sensitivity to ethnic prejudice during his youth in a tough neighborhood in Hoboken, New Jersey. In 1945 he starred in an Academy Award–winning short film to promote tolerance. In *The House I Live In*, Sinatra tells a street gang that racial and religious differences "make no difference except to a Nazi or somebody who's stupid." He also crooned the film's theme song:

> *What is America to me*
> *A name, a map, or a flag I see*
> *A certain word, democracy*
> *What is America to me*
>
> *The house I live in*
> *A plot of earth, a street*
> *The grocer and the butcher*
> *Or the people that I meet . . .*

The howdy and the handshake
The air a feeling free
And the right to speak your mind out
That's America to me. . . .

The children in the playground
The faces that I see
All races and religions
That's America to me

"Believe me, I know something about the business of racial intolerance," Sinatra told 5,000 people at the Froebel High auditorium. "At eleven I was called a 'dirty guinea.' . . . We've all done it. We've all used the words nigger or kike or mick or polack or dago. Cut it out, kids." He sang "The House I Live In" and then asked the students to say a pledge of tolerance. "We will strive to work together to prove that the American way is the only fair and democratic way of life." The Gary boycott soon ended.[49]

Tolerance was in short supply in the South in 1946. That year two of the most belligerent white supremacists, Governor Eugene Talmadge of Georgia and Senator Theodore Bilbo of Mississippi, ran successfully for reelection using ugly racial appeals. Talmadge exhorted white voting officials to purge their rolls of the one hundred thousand African Americans who had been added in the past few months. On the day before the election, Bilbo called on "every red-blooded American who believes in the superiority and integrity of the white race to get out and see that no nigger votes," and he hinted that the best time to prevent black voting was the night before the election. Whites did indeed attack black Mississippians, some of them war veterans, as they went to the polls. Other acts of racial terrorism in 1946 lacked any political purpose. In South Carolina a policeman billy clubbed and blinded a uniformed black soldier who had argued with a bus driver. In Walton County, Georgia, a white mob executed two African-American couples after one of the black men had argued with a local white man. Just a few days later, a mob in Minden, Louisiana, dismembered and burned an African-American veteran who had complained that advantage had being taken of his sharecropper grandfather.[50]

Responding to these atrocities, President Harry Truman appointed a Committee on Civil Rights to investigate the causes of racial violence. At the same time, Truman was advised that many black voters would probably vote Republican in 1948 or perhaps embrace the third-party candidacy of former vice president Henry Wallace, a strong advocate for civil rights. African-American voters could determine who won several large northern states and California. "New and real" efforts for civil rights, the advisor, Clark Clifford, insisted, were necessary to keep African Americans in the Democratic column. Truman responded by proposing legislation to end segregation in public transportation, outlaw poll taxes, reduce employment discrimination, and make lynching a federal crime. In July 1948 he ordered the desegregation of the armed forces.[51]

Truman had made a far stronger commitment of the executive branch to civil rights than any president since Lincoln. He in effect had aligned the executive branch with the judiciary, which for a decade had been expanding the meaning of equality. If the president could persuade Congress to get in line and pass his civil rights legislation, American race relations would be transformed.

The white South responded hysterically to Truman's civil rights commitments. The president was trying to "Harlemize" the whole country, Senator James Eastland of Mississippi declared. Having defeated every effort for antilynching, anti–poll tax, and pro-FEPC legislation over the years, the southerners in Congress killed Truman's civil rights bills. Even so, many southerners took Truman's efforts as the signal to leave the Democratic Party. A new States' Rights Party, known popularly as the Dixiecrats, soon convened and chose Governor Strom Thurmond of South Carolina as its presidential candidate. Truman's civil rights program, one Dixiecrat pronounced, would "reduce us to the status of a mongrel, inferior race, mixed in blood, our Anglo-Saxon heritage a mockery."[52] The Dixiecrats took four southern states, but Truman's pro–civil rights electoral strategy worked when black voters helped him win enough large states to carry the election.

The 1948 presidential election exposed the political crosscurrents about race that would characterize postwar America. Black political influence was now sufficient to elicit civil rights support from both political parties, and the presidency had been pushed to embrace a comprehensive race-reform agenda. But the pressure for civil rights caused a powerful white-supremacist reaction seen clearly in the Congress, which remained virtually as committed to white supremacy as it had been when Tom Heflin and Ben Tillman walked its halls. The Congress would have to change before the branches could be aligned to mandate an end to segregation.

VI

By 1948 the Cold War provided a new language for expressing white-supremacist opposition to civil rights activism. Since the late 1930s, white supremacists in the South had accused labor and civil rights activists of communist connections. After World War II, white southerners habitually accused anyone advocating the end of segregation of being a communist. The notion of integration was so radical in the view of most whites that they believed it had to originate from a foreign ideology, and communism was the alien dogma on everyone's mind in postwar America.

The first victims of redbaiting in the South were labor and civil rights activists. Already under pressure from antilabor forces exploiting Cold War fears, the CIO began its 1946 campaign to organize southern workers by renouncing any involvement by communists, which included, the campaign director noted pointedly, participation by the Southern Conference for Human Welfare. That year the Southern Conference, the interracial organization created in 1938 to pursue a liberal political agenda for the South, lost many of its high-profile members because of the perception that its leadership was tied too closely to communists. Indeed, some of its leaders were, or had been, members of the Communist Party, though by no means had most of its original membership been communists. But the House Un-American Activities Committee (HUAC) condemned SCHW as a "most deviously camouflaged Communist-front organization." In 1948 the organization went out of business, a victim mainly of the anticommunist assault.[53]

The U.S. government had encouraged the association of communism with civil rights activism. The attorney general came up with a list of subversive groups that included several race-reform organizations. The FBI led investigations into the loyalty of government employees with such questions as "Do you ever entertain Negroes in your home?" and "Did you ever write a letter to the Red Cross about the segregation of blood?" J. Edgar Hoover, the FBI director, apparently equated membership in either the NAACP or unions with radicalism, a belief that resulted in the firing of a number of black government workers.[54]

The anticommunist hysteria focused on celebrities who had criticized American race policies. "How do you explain the fact that you have an album of Paul Robeson records in your home?" was a favorite FBI question to test for loyalty—referring to the black opera singer known also for

Frank Sinatra in 1945. *Courtesy AP/Wideworld Photos.*

his radical politics. Even before he received his Academy Award for *The House I Live In*, Frank Sinatra had been condemned by right-wing commentators as a "front" for communist organizations and, remarkably, called "Mrs. Roosevelt in pants." The head of the California state senate's committee on un-American activities branded him a communist. Sinatra publicly defended Albert Maltz, the screenwriter for *The House I Live In* and his friend, who was blacklisted in 1947. After Sinatra slugged one of its columnists, the Hearst newspapers ran a story headlined "Sinatra Faces Probe on Red Ties" and another reporting that HUAC regarded Sinatra as "one of Hollywood's leading travelers on the road of Red fascism." The Hearst columnist pledged to "continue to fight the promotion of class struggle or foreign isms posing as entertainment"—such as *The House I Live In.*[55]

Sinatra was at first resolute against the redbaiting. "Once they get the movies throttled, how long will it be before the committee gets to work on freedom of the air? How long will it be before we're told what we can say and cannot say into a radio microphone? If you make a pitch on a nationwide radio network for a square deal for the underdog, will they call you a commie?" He soon got answers to those questions: his record label, his movie studio, his radio program, and his agent all fired him. As his career sank into a five-year depression, Sinatra recognized that his way had to be the anticommunist way: "I don't like Communists and I have nothing to do with any organization except the Knights of Columbus," he said.[56]

VII

The Cold War reversed the influence of nationalism on efforts to reform American race practices. The commitment that Henry Luce and the Roosevelts had made in 1941 to expand the meaning and reach of democratic values had provided great authority to extend freedom and equality to African Americans. Now nationalism in the Cold War era had the opposite effect on American freedom: it demanded conformity to a narrow

definition of Americanism and punished severely those who dared to criticize American institutions. Without Hitler to give it an antiracist commitment, nationalism only encouraged orthodoxy of thought and action at
home. White-supremacist southerners co-opted the anticommunist hysteria to defend segregation against all who dared to challenge it. In the late
1940s, Cold War nationalism canceled the simple faith of *The House I Live
In* and mocked entirely "the right to speak your mind out."

But the Cold War and anticommunism, big obstacles that they were,
did not stop the movement for civil rights that had begun in 1938 and
gathered momentum into 1946. Progress slowed—to a crawl at times—
but the commitment to change among African Americans and some crucial white allies remained strong. During the 1940s black people had
gained resources to support their movement, and their understanding of
the promise of democratic values was unchanged by the Cold War hysteria. If the Cold War presented a strong ideological obstacle to race
progress, other influences on American thinking still worked to the benefit of civil rights. The revulsion caused by the war against racist thought
and violence actually became more intense as the war's meaning was
contemplated in the 1950s. Popular culture and mass communications
became evermore insistent in promoting racial equality, at the same
time, paradoxically, that they advanced Cold War fears. The 1950s would
see both intense pressure of anti-communist conformity on race reform
and powerful new expressions of cultural integration and democratic
idealism. From a distance, that time looks like a period of preparation for
great change.

CHAPTER 5

THE BORROWING TIME

ONE NIGHT IN 1949, a 24-year-old white war veteran named Dewey Phillips went to radio station WHBQ in Memphis and set fire to a trashcan. The smoke drew the on-air disc jockey out of the studio, whereupon Phillips sneaked in and began playing records and talking nonstop. Some WHBQ listeners already knew of Phillips because he managed the record department at a local five-and-dime, where he was famous for shouting over the store intercom about tunes he liked. He was determined to be a disc jockey after another Memphis station, WDIA, had become the first radio station in the United States to design programming to suit a black audience. Phillips wanted Memphians to hear at night the same kind of good music that WDIA played until sundown—thus his stunt with the trashcan. Aware of the black programming success at WDIA and the crowds known to stand around the five-and-dime just to listen to Phillips, the management of WHBQ gave Phillips a late-night time slot. He immediately discarded the "pop" music of Perry Como and Gene Autry that his predecessor had played and began spinning an eclectic mix. In a two-hour show, he might play the blues of Muddy Waters, the pop of Frank Sinatra and Nat King Cole, the gospel of Sister Rosetta Sharpe, and the country of Hank Williams. If

Dewey really liked a song, he would play it over and over—like the night he played the bluesman Otis Jackson's "Tell Me Why You Like Roosevelt" 20 times in a row.

> *Tell me why you like Roosevelt? Wasn't no kin.*
> *Huh, God Almighty; was a poor man's friend.*

People loved Phillips's rebellious spirit. He typically received 50 telegrams a night. After reading ads, which he often bungled, he always shouted, "Tell 'em Phillips sent ya!" Soon people on Beale Street were greeting one another with "Phillips sent me, man!" and one woman, having gotten the best of her husband with a knife in a domestic dispute, instructed the ambulance driver to "carry [him] to the hospital and tell 'em Phillips sent 'im."[1]

Dewey Phillips's arrival reflected a fundamental shift taking place in American popular culture. As realized from its inception, radio was a "broadcast" medium that had influence across social divisions, and thus it could undermine the old compartments of culture that had served to support white supremacy, just as it had reinforced the traditional race images with such programs as *Amos 'n' Andy*. In fact, Phillips's audience was known to be much wider and to include many whites, especially teenagers and young adults. At about the same time, disc jockeys with similar bents emerged in Houston, St. Louis, Washington, Baltimore, Cleveland, and New York City. All the programs promoted more eclecticism and rebellion. Rhythm and blues and black gospel were heard before and after country music and some kinds of pop—singers like Nat King Cole, Frank Sinatra, and Johnny Ray, who melded some blues or jazz with more conventional "white" style.[2]

Simultaneously, all-black-format radio was nurturing African Americans' race consciousness. Although almost all of the new black stations were white owned—they switched to black format mainly because television had undermined traditional listening patterns—and though they rarely offered news reporting that explicitly addressed civil rights, they validated black culture to blacks. "Simply by airing black music, speaking in the distinctive argot of the black streets and fields," one historian has written, and by "reporting on the achievements of black leaders, athletes and celebrities, and announcing the latest black community and national news, black radio helped to define what was distinctive about black American culture and to legitimize it as something unique and valuable."[3]

At the moment that Dewey Phillips was revolutionizing Memphis radio, Sam Phillips, no relation, was nearby developing a recording studio that would also advance cross-cultural sharing among blacks and whites in the United States. "Negro artists in the South who wanted to make a record just had no place to go," he explained later, so in 1950 Sam Phillips set up a recording studio, later known as Sun Records, to record B. B. King, Ike Turner, Howlin' Wolf, and other Memphis-area rhythm-and-blues talents. His records immediately made their way onto Dewey's show and those of disc jockeys around the country playing "black music." Sam realized early that white teenagers and young adults composed much of the audience for rhythm and blues, but he also saw that the race divide would prevent many whites from becoming more than secret admirers of the sound. It appealed to white youth, he later explained, but they often resisted buying this music. "The Southern ones especially felt a resistance that even they probably didn't quite understand. They liked the music, but they weren't sure whether they ought to like it or not." Now, "if I could find a white boy who could sing like a nigger," Sam Phillips is reputed to have said, "I could make a million dollars."[4]

Sam Phillips found what he was looking for in 1954 when he recorded a Memphis teenager named Elvis Presley singing "That's All Right," an old blues number. Sam played it for Dewey, who immediately put it on the turntable at WBHQ—and kept it there. He played it 14 times the first night, seven times in a row. In the midst of his joyful exclamations about the song, Dewey summoned Elvis for an on-air interview. "I asked him where he went to high school," Dewey later reported about the interview, "and he said, 'Humes,'" referring to the all-white school from which Elvis had recently graduated. "I wanted to get that out, because a lot of people listening had thought he was colored."[5]

Sam Phillips soon began promoting other "crossover" white singers, including Carl Perkins ("Blue Suede Shoes") and Jerry Lee Lewis ("Great Balls of Fire"). By 1956 rhythm and blues, at least that part consumed by white youth, had been renamed "rock and roll," and its sources of creation had moved far beyond Memphis and included many African-American performers. A major contributor, the piano-playing baritone Fats Domino, came from New Orleans, and a wide assortment of "doo-wop" singers came from northern ghettoes, many of them growing out of street gangs.[6]

The rage for rock and roll naturally sent its popularizers to television, the new mass-communications medium that was transforming American culture in the early 1950s. In 1956, Dewey Phillips's *Pop Shop* and similar afternoon rock-and-roll television shows appeared in cities across the country, mostly to be displaced when Dick Clark's nationally broadcast *American Bandstand* debuted in 1957. But even though Clark lacked altogether the rebellious nature of Dewey Phillips, *American Bandstand*

Elvis Presley. *Courtesy Library of Congress.*

proved to be a nationwide purveyor of the transracial cultural phenomenon. Rock and roll's appeal was overtaken in the 1960s by the "Motown"
and "soul" sounds, but by then white youth in the United States had shed
all inhibitions about embracing black music.[7]

Many people believed that rock and roll represented a revolutionary
challenge to white-dominated popular culture, though clearly the best of
American music since the turn of the century had been shaped by
African-American influences. By the summer of 1956, city governments
across the country were debating whether to allow rock-and-roll concerts
to take place within their borders. The opposition was transparently
racist: a Connecticut psychiatrist declared the music "tribalistic and canni-
balistic" and even called it a "communicable disease," and a Boston bishop
pontificated that "rock and roll inflames and excites youth like jungle tom-
toms." Rock and roll departed from rhythm and blues by toning down,
but not quite eliminating, the sexual content of lyrics, and thus many
older Americans assumed it was leading the younger generation into
immorality. The most violent reaction came in the Deep South, where
rock and roll became a fixation of the emerging White Citizens' Councils.
Asa Carter, a council leader in Alabama, explained that rock and roll was
the "basic heavy heat of Negroes" which "appeals to the very base of
man, [and] brings out the animalism and vulgarity." In March 1956 several
of Carter's associates attacked Nat King Cole onstage during a concert in
Birmingham, an act that, given the variance between Cole's style of
music and the emerging rock-and-roll genre, exposed the crudely racial
nature of the white-supremacist reaction. In a nonviolent protest a few
weeks later against performances by such genuine rock-and-rollers as
Clyde McPhatter and Bill Haley, Carter's people chanted such messages as
"NAACP says integration, rock & roll, rock & roll," "Jungle Music promotes integration," and "Be-bop promotes Communism."[8]

During the same years, other forms of popular culture also began to
bridge the gulf that had separated blacks from whites. Hollywood continued on its path away from the consistent denigration of blacks toward
more positive presentations. In 1947, *Gentleman's Agreement* had reflected
Americans' heightened postwar sensitivity to anti-Semitism, and that

concern carried over to a new, general commitment against prejudice in
movie themes. Three 1949 films dealt more realistically with race issues
than perhaps any one movie up to that time. *Pinky* and *Lost Boundaries*
explored race issues from the perspective of a light-skinned African
American moving from North to South. In *Home of the Brave,* the producer Stanley Kramer told the story of a troubled black soldier who had
suffered from racial prejudice while serving in the army. From the end of
the war on, Hollywood rejected the old stereotypes almost as completely
as it had embraced them up to that time. It was a stunning reversal.[9]

Television programming, which developed from about 1948 forward,
emerged in a time of greater tolerance and thus never really had to reject
the old racial presumptions. During 1949 and 1950, two black entertain-
ers, Hazel Scott and Bob Howard, each hosted a musical variety show,
and Columbia Broadcasting System (CBS) aired an all-black variety series
called *Sugar Hill Times.* In 1956, Nat King Cole debuted his own variety
program, which won positive reviews and many viewers but failed to
attract a major sponsor. In 1951, CBS adapted *Amos 'n' Andy* for television
in a weekly half-hour show with consistently funny scripts and a brilliant
all-black cast. The NAACP attacked the show for portraying black doctors as "quacks and thieves," black lawyers as "slippery cowards," and
black women as "cackling, screaming shrews." After such criticism and
threats of boycotts, CBS in 1953 cancelled the program.[10]

The demise of *Amos 'n' Andy* ended American popular culture's open
acceptance of the pernicious black stereotypes that emerged in American
culture in the nineteenth century and were adapted from the minstrel
stage to vaudeville and burlesque to radio and the movies. With Jim
Crow, Zip Coon, and Mammy largely gone from active media, the perpetuation of the stereotypes became more difficult, and their influence
on American ideology gradually weakened. That is not to say that American popular culture suddenly became egalitarian in the overarching
racial message it delivered. Certainly it did not, but the removal of old
symbols of black inferiority began to dissipate white-supremacist and
white-nationalist ideologies and to make room in the culture for new
symbols of black competence and equality. By the early 1950s, far more

Amos 'n' Andy ran on television for only three years
in the early 1950s. Spencer Brown, Tim Moore,
and Alvin Childress starred in the TV production.
Courtesy AP/Wideworld Photos.

positive black icons—Jackie Robinson in sports and Nat Cole, Louis Armstrong, and Duke Ellington in music—had taken the center stage of
American popular culture.

Television, it should be noted, was very slow to offer replacement
black images in its entertainment programming. "Colored, colored on
Channel Two," people shouted throughout Henry Louis Gates's small-
town neighborhood in West Virginia in the 1950s on the rare occasions
that an African American appeared on television. The end of *Amos 'n'
Andy* was one of the saddest days in Gates's neighborhood. *"Everybody
loved Amos and Andy,"* the literary critic Gates later wrote in a memoir,
because "their world was *all* colored, just like ours." But, he added, *"they
had their colored judges and lawyers and doctors and nurses, which we
could only dream about having, or becoming." No all-black cast
appeared on television for almost twenty years.[11]

Television news developed slowly in the early 1950s, but from its inception the medium's power to broadcast sound and pictures together multiplied exponentially its influence. In 1951, when Senator Estes Kefauver opened his hearings on organized crime to television cameras, he inaugurated a change in how Americans followed public events. The Army-McCarthy hearings in 1954 demonstrated how television coverage could shape events: seeing Senator Joseph McCarthy's behavior caused many Americans to recoil in disgust from him and to question his anticommunist crusade. The networks offered nightly fifteen-minute broadcasts of national and international news, enhanced by moving pictures. Even with limited airtime for news and a general paucity of filmed events to broadcast, television soon became the most influential medium for reporting racial issues. The networks covered the major civil rights events of the 1950s—especially the Montgomery bus boycott in 1956 and the Little Rock school crisis in 1957. Henry Louis Gates wrote that in his hometown the civil rights movement arrived late in terms of local protests, but "it came early to our television set," which he called "the ritual arena for the drama of race."[12]

An important new development in mass communication was the black-oriented magazines created by the Chicago publisher John H. Johnson, who began *Negro Digest* in 1942, *Ebony* in 1945, and *Jet* in 1951. *Ebony*, a black version of *Life*, focused on the lives of black celebrities but also covered civil rights activities. *Ebony*'s circulation began at almost a half million and grew steadily from there. *Jet*, a weekly pocket-sized newsmagazine, immediately attracted a circulation of three hundred thousand and became to many African Americans the most regular and authoritative source for news about themselves. Newspapers, magazines, and television were inundating Americans with images, and blacks "were going places we had never been before and doing things we'd never done before, and we wanted to see that," Johnson later observed. He assumed that his publications had a larger social impact: "You have to change images before you can change acts and institutions." By the early 1950s, Johnson's magazines nurtured among millions of African Americans a sense of common interests and concerns, including the growing demand for civil rights. Johnson's publications advanced a communal sense among all African Americans, and they did so with the publisher's clear understanding of the status desires of all Americans, blacks included. He proceeded on the same assumption that Booker Washington had acted: the image of African Americans, among both whites and blacks themselves, had to change in order to alter more fundamental realities of race relations.[13]

And indeed it was changing: By 1956, when white Americans were asked if they believed blacks were as intelligent as whites, 78 percent said yes, whereas in 1942 only 42 percent had answered affirmatively. To the question of whether they thought that whites and blacks should go to the same school, 49 percent of white adults now said yes as compared with only 30 percent in 1942. Should blacks and whites be separated on public transportation? In 1942, 51 percent had said yes, but now 60 percent said no, although only 19 percent of southern whites accepted integrated travel. On the question about accepting African Americans of similar education and income as neighbors, 52 percent of whites now answered that they would not mind having black neighbors, whereas in 1942, 62 percent had said they would. A large shift in white opinion had taken place toward acceptance of equal status for African Americans.[14]

Developments in popular culture and mass communications, it must be understood, helped *make possible* changes in race relations, rather than *causing* the changes. The expansion of civil rights resulted directly from the efforts of blacks themselves, but the new developments in culture and communications made African Americans more cohesive as a group and whites more accepting of a different status for blacks.

I

Anticommunism dominated American domestic politics with Joseph McCarthy's rise to national prominence in 1950. McCarthyism commanded an unquestioning acceptance of the righteousness of the American way and tolerated no self-criticism of the kind that had recognized

American hypocrisy and encouraged racial reforms during World War II. The FBI appears to have viewed any civil rights advocate as a potential communist, and thus leading national figures like Mary McLeod Bethune as well as hundreds of local black activists were investigated. The Cold War and McCarthyism took a lasting toll on the black voices most critical of American race relations, the same ones that were most critical of American foreign policy. In 1949 the singer and actor Paul Robeson came under fire after he was reported to have told an international meeting that it was "unthinkable that American Negroes would go to war on behalf of those who have oppressed us for generations against the Soviet Union which in one generation has raised our people to full human dignity." The U.S. government took away his passport, and the constant criticism of Robeson's politics kept people from attending his concerts. Robeson was not alone: in 1951 the 82-year-old W. E. B. Du Bois was arrested and jailed, charged with being an "agent of a foreign power" for his sympathies with communist governments. The charges were soon dismissed, but Du Bois also was made to surrender his U.S. passport, and

Supporters of Paul Robeson published this pamphlet in 1951 to protest the State Department's cancellation of his passport for his alleged anti-American actions.

when the passport was returned seven years later, he promptly moved to Ghana and renounced his U.S. citizenship.[15]

Blacks' staunchest white allies often fell victim to anticommunism. Among the strongest voices for civil rights had been unions led by communists and socialists. In 1949 the CIO expelled 11 unions for failing to comply with government regulations requiring them to guarantee that no communists held office in their organizations. Virtually all the "red" unions soon disappeared, and with them went much of the pro–civil rights commitment that the labor movement had earlier manifested.

Anticommunism bolstered white southerners' arguments for upholding the status quo. Communist influence provided them with an explanation for why some blacks were challenging segregation, and at the same time it allowed whites to hold fast to their belief that all sensible southern blacks knew that segregation was the proper order of society. The belief that the "nigger trouble" was being caused by outside agitators manipulated by communists provided so much psychic comfort that it was repeated with the same regularity as grace was said in southern homes before supper. Politicians of every sort, preachers of every denomination, and editorialists in most newspapers constantly reiterated the claim of radical incitement to integration.

It then followed that the NAACP was a communist organization, and whenever the organization's lawyers won a case against segregation, accusations of un-American radicalism flew all over the South. Starting in 1950, the NAACP purged itself of communists, instructing local branches to remove radicals or dissolve the branch itself. The executive director Walter White condemned communism and attempted to stifle criticism of U.S. race relations by African Americans outside the country. But the more anticommunist its public pronouncements became, the more insistent were the accusations that the organization was a communist front. In the aftermath of *Brown v. Board of Education,* the 1954 decision that made segregated schools unconstitutional, the red-baiting rose to new heights, and the NAACP was forced out of operation in some southern states.[16]

McCarthyism dampened the activism of white southerners who

opposed segregation. They had already witnessed how fears of communism had destroyed the Southern Conference for Human Welfare in 1948. The Southern Regional Council (SRC), an Atlanta-based interracial organization, announced its official rejection of segregation in 1951, whereupon it drew hot fire from segregationists who insisted that the council was a communist-front group. In 1954, Governor Herman Talmadge's newspaper mouthpiece declared that the SRC "espouses ideologies completely foreign to the South." Even though the council's leaders were in fact staunch Cold Warriors themselves, the constant allegations of communism and an investigation by the Georgia attorney general forced the council to require a loyalty oath from its staff. In 1956 the Hearst newspapers reported that virtually the entire roster of the council's leadership were communists or fellow travelers. The reports clearly were libelous, but to sue the newspapers meant creating more publicity about the communist allegations and making even more precarious the existence of the few white integrationists in the South.[17]

At the same time, some Americans recognized that racial discrimination in the United States gave the Soviet Union a powerful propaganda weapon in the Cold War. The State Department and President Truman insisted that better treatment of blacks was necessary to win the propaganda battle. African-American activists often reiterated the point, and the argument even made its way into court briefs against segregation. But the nation's leading Cold Warriors of the 1950s, President Dwight Eisenhower and his secretary of state John Foster Dulles, rarely used their influence to assist the cause of civil rights. White southerners, who were for the most part strong supporters of U.S. Cold-War policy, typically scorned the notion of changing race relations in order to improve the country's image among the Russians, the enemy. "One of the more grossly fraudulent clichés of the segregation controversy," one southern editor wrote in 1956, "is that we've got to integrate and even honeybunch the colored man because the Communists will make capital of it in Asia." By that logic, he declared, "to disarm Communist propaganda we would have to . . . raze Wall Street buildings, socialize medicine . . . level and sow Hollywood with salt." In the 1950s such narrow views of American interests abroad overrode the pro–civil rights impulses engendered by the Cold War.[18]

II

Despite the chill that the Cold War put on civil rights activism, there were signs of progress in black life. A noteworthy indication was the virtual end of lynchings after 1946. Tuskegee Institute announced that 1952 was the first year since it had begun keeping records on lynching in the early twentieth century that not one was recorded in the United States. As the ultimate enforcement of white supremacy, the ritual killing of a black person represented the total power of whites and the profound insecurity of blacks. If such unrestrained violence had really ended, African Americans had indeed moved into an age when white power over them was restrained.

Local movements for civil rights continued in communities across the South. In 1951 in Greensboro, a group of black professionals led a successful effort to put one of their own on the city council, and two years later the black city councilman arranged the appointment of the first black member of the city's board of education. In Tuskegee, a group of college professors and federal employees, who believed that they had lived up to Booker Washington's directive to acquire economic independence and that now they deserved political rights, led a determined effort to register voters, against a county board of registrars that often refused to convene rather than add blacks to the voting rolls. Even so, the four hundred black voters began to determine the outcome of close contests between whites and to entertain the possibility of running a black person for a county board. Even in Mississippi, extensive activism emerged in the early 1950s, including the establishment in 1951 of the Regional Council of Negro Leadership, which held annual mass meetings where thousands of black Mississippians learned voter-registration procedures. As a result, the number of African-American voters in Mississippi rose steadily from 1946 to 1954, by which time there were more than 20,000 blacks registered in the state. The Mississippi NAACP grew during these years, propelled in part by such remarkable activists as Aaron Henry, a pharmacist; Amzie Moore, a postal worker; and Medgar Evers, an insurance agent—all of them young war veterans determined to impose some democracy on their home state.[19]

Black schools in the South rapidly improved in the early 1950s, as southern state governments spent heavily in a belated attempt to "equalize" black schools. Louisiana increased the amount it spent on each black child from $16 in 1940 to $116 in 1950, which brought it up almost to the level of spending on a white child. Black literacy and the number of blacks attending high school in the South rose rapidly in the early 1950s. The desegregation of higher education in the South had in fact begun quietly and proceeded steadily in the early 1950s. More than 40 private "white" colleges accepted black students in the immediate postwar years.[20]

Thurgood Marshall led the NAACP's legal assault on segregation. *Courtesy Library of Congress.*

The federal judiciary continued to broaden the meaning of equality. Since the *Carolene Products* and *Gaines* decisions in 1938, the U.S. Supreme Court had regularly shown African Americans that progress was being made. In 1950 the court ruled that a hastily established Jim Crow law school in Texas could not be used to circumvent the dictates of the *Gaines* decision. The court also forced the University of Oklahoma to provide the full range of student services to a black student who had been admitted but denied access to such amenities as the campus cafeteria. Even as black educational opportunities were improving through the court's equalization decisions, NAACP lawyers were challenging the fundamental policy of segregation in five separate cases working their way through the courts in the early 1950s.[21]

But the other branches of the national government did little to uphold the values of liberty and equality. The election of Dwight Eisenhower as president in 1952 ensured that the executive branch would make minimal effort to aid civil rights in the 1950s, a sharp turn away from the concern for black rights that Harry Truman had voiced. Conservative by instinct and shaped by a long career in the segregated army, Eisenhower believed that attempts to force changes in black-white relations would backfire. His administration did not increase black employment in the federal government, nor did it use its authority to enforce fair hiring among defense or federal highway contractors. The National Labor Relations Board failed to punish unions that discriminated against minorities. Perhaps most important, Eisenhower gave no moral or administrative support to school desegregation.[22]

Control of the legislative branch of the national government remained firmly in the hands of southern senators and congressmen, who used their seniority and mastery of institutional rules and traditions to continue to protect white supremacy. Since the early 1920s, they had defeated efforts to institute antilynching, fair-employment, and anti–poll tax laws, including Harry Truman's proposals from 1948 through 1952. The most influential legislator in the early 1950s was Senator Richard Russell, a Georgia Democrat respected and even feared for his dominance in the upper chamber. Seeing the growing preoccupation with civil rights legislation, Russell in 1949 found an opportunity to get Senate rules altered to make it all but impossible to stop filibusters, traditionally the southerners' final barrier against legislation they opposed.[23]

With Russell dominating the Senate and Eisenhower in the White House, there was little possibility that the separate powers would unite on civil rights. But the judicial branch followed its own lights, which gave hope to civil rights activists in the often bleak times of the early 1950s. Through those years the U.S. Supreme Court was very carefully deliberating over a decision that would forever alter race relations in the United States.

III

Most Americans in the early 1950s were more concerned with partaking of the good economic times than settling issues of communism or civil rights. Postwar prosperity enabled a housing boom, which met the pent-up demands for more and better housing left by the Depression and the war. The U.S. government supported new housing by subsidizing loans to buy homes, sponsoring public housing, and building highways that facilitated suburbanization. Inevitably, however, housing led back to race issues. Because of the Supreme Court's 1948 decision that outlawed restrictive covenants, most of the postwar boom might have taken place in an atmosphere of open housing that could have allowed blacks and other minorities equal opportunities to find good homes. Having realized big economic gains in the 1940s, many black families had the resources to afford better housing. But few opportunities for fair housing actually emerged. The real estate industry remained largely committed to protecting the status quo, including honoring now-illegal restrictive covenants. Realtors, developers, and builders could discriminate in a hundred private ways to protect whites' privileges in the housing market, and they could justify them as a business necessity for maintaining the favor of white homeowners.[24]

Government agencies that backed most postwar housing loans usually acted to preserve segregation. The Home Owners Loan Corporation (HOLC) made policies about real estate appraising that virtually ensured race-based divisions of housing quality. On its urban "security" maps used by banks and insurers, HOLC divided metropolitan areas into color-coded sections ranging from the most desirable and credit-worthy—coded green, as in *money*—to the least desirable and least worthy of credit—coded red, as in *Danger!* The green areas contained new and homogenous housing inhabited by "American business and professional men," as opposed to immigrants and ethnic minorities, who were more likely to be found in the less attractive blue or "definitely declining" yellow areas. The red areas contained old, usually center-city housing that was deemed to have declined already because it was occupied mainly by African Americans—regardless of the socioeconomic position of the black residents or the actual condition of the housing. The federal housing agencies paid close attention to the movements of black populations in order to know what areas of a city were "declining." Thus originated the practice of "redlining," which would be used for the remainder of the twentieth century to discriminate against minorities in the issuance of loans and of insurance on houses, automobiles, and lives. The impact of such appraising policies was to create economic incentives for new housing and thus encourage suburbanization and discourage the rehabilitation of older, inner-city housing, supporting urban housing's decline.[25]

Suburban tract housing built in the 1950s conformed entirely to existing segregationist tendencies. The various "Levittowns" in the Northeast rarely included any African-American homeowners. Levittown on New York's Long Island had grown to 82,000 residents by 1960, not one of whom was black. "We can solve a housing problem or we can try to solve a racial problem," William Levitt self-servingly responded to critics, "but we cannot combine the two." He reflected the attitudes of most who bought his houses: a black family who moved into Levittown, Pennsylvania, faced verbal and physical abuse from white residents, one of whom conceded that the black owner was "probably a nice guy, but every time I look at him I see two thousand dollars drop off the value of my house."[26]

At the same time, American cities began to clear their slums and build public housing. Slum clearance in the early 1950s forced hundreds of thousands of African Americans to look for new places to live, and many ended up in formerly all-white neighborhoods. A vast expansion of highways in and around American cities in the 1950s further aggravated housing problems, because many new roads were routed through slums, which displaced thousands of black residents at a time. The United States Housing Authority, which subsidized public-housing projects when corresponding units of slum housing were destroyed, allowed local governments to decide where to place new projects. As literally millions of public-housing units were created in the two decades after the war, nearly all conformed to existing patterns of racial segregation—i.e., projects identified as black went up in existing black ghettoes and those viewed as white were built in white areas. With heavy federal subsidies, the Chicago Housing Authority built a string of 25 high-rise public-housing projects along State Street in the Black Belt, perhaps the highest-density segregated housing in the United States but generally suggestive of what was happening in cities across the country in the 1950s.[27]

A suburban town could, and usually did, simply decline to build public housing, thus keeping away the poor and minority people who could not afford the private housing market. In Dearborn near Detroit, the longtime mayor Orville Hubbard always made good on his promise to keep his town white. "Housing the Negroes is Detroit's problem," Hubbard declared. "When you remove garbage from your backyard, you don't dump it in your neighbor's."[28]

Racial competition for housing still existed in older industrial cities, and it intensified on the nation's southern perimeter. In Birmingham the active opposition to the expansion of black neighborhoods came mainly from Klan bombers. In Chicago the opposition was based in neighborhood organizations and federations of neighborhood groups, such as the White Circle League, founded in 1949 to "keep white neighborhoods free of negroes." Detroit witnessed a proliferation of white neighborhood organizations in the postwar years and continuous harassment of blacks who moved into formerly all-white areas. In Miami, conflict over blacks' occupation of a public-housing project resulted in bombings in 1951. Slum clearance in Dallas in the early 1950s resulted in several years of bombings and intense antiblack agitation by neighborhood-defense activists. Los Angeles, which saw a large influx of African Americans in the late war years continue through the 1950s, underwent the same pattern of white defensive associations, violent border conflict, and finally rapid racial transition in the area south of the city's downtown and in nearby Compton.[29]

The story of Chicago's housing conflict captures much of what was happening throughout postwar America. The city experienced a housing deficit immediately after the war of an estimated 200,000 units, and new suburban development alleviated the stress for whites but did little to help blacks. In 1948 in the city's Black Belt, 375,000 African Americans crowded into an area large enough safely to house 110,000, but the situation only got worse during the 1950s as migrants kept coming from the South. The border conflicts that had marked Chicago neighborhoods during the 1930s were repeated after the war as the outward pressure from the Black Belt increased. Significant numbers of units changed from white to black occupancy, but there was never enough decent housing. Continuing the pattern of mobbing seen in the 1947 Fernwood riot, 10,000 whites in the Englewood neighborhood in 1949 attacked an arriving black family. In 1951 a similar scene occurred in the suburban town of Cicero when several thousand whites attacked an apartment building into which a black family had moved. The building was burned and looted, and it took the National Guard to restore order. In 1953 the largest riot yet occurred in Trumbull Park, where thousands of neighborhood whites attacked a new public-housing project occupied by African Americans. After the Trumbull Park riot ended, local whites carried on for another decade with bombings, harassment of blacks, and street demonstrations against any black presence.[30]

The housing riots in Chicago were family and community affairs. Young white males from the immediate neighborhood usually performed the violent acts but with the full support of their fathers, wives, mothers, and sisters. As the young men threw rocks and bricks at black "invaders," their families and neighborhood friends would gather on a nearby lawn to scream insults at new arrivals. The housing mobs were composed heavily of blue-collar "ethnic" Americans—Irish, Poles, Czechs, Bohemians—those who had been unable or unwilling to flee to the suburbs in the postwar housing expansion. The threat of racial integration sharpened the white ethnics' identities: "The foreigners...built this country," one community newspaper declared. "They are not tearing down—they raise families, buy homes, beautify their little neighborhood. Can the Negro compare with that?"[31]

For many ethnics in Chicago and other northern cities, homeownership represented the height of self-fulfillment, a symbol of sacrifice and achievement that they rarely earned in industrial work. In their view, any black presence in their neighborhood undermined much of what they had accomplished. Why did they think that? Blacks were "hypersexed, immoral, and dangerous," a Chicago neighborhood newspaper explained, and they would bring the "savage, lustful, immoral standards of the southern Negro" into whites' cohesive, orderly communities. This racist assumption reflected, of course, their image of the overcrowded, mostly-poor Black Belt nearby, where indeed violence and crime were far higher than in the surrounding white enclaves. But white attitudes also revealed the continuing authority of the ugly black stereotypes in American culture, even as those images were being undermined in the 1950s.[32]

Chicago's postwar housing conflicts also dramatized intensifying status conflict. As African Americans' socioeconomic conditions improved and as they acted on their growing confidence to demand better living conditions, blue-collar whites felt besieged, their tenuous hold on their own status and security threatened. The leader of Trumbull Park whites expressed his pride that in 1955 people everywhere were "astounded that a community so small has dared to fight" the powerful forces arrayed against the neighborhood defending its racial purity. Among the enemies he listed were the NAACP, the Urban League, the Anti-Defamation League of B'nai B'rith, and the Catholic Interracial Council.[33]

Even with violent riots occurring at least every other year in the post-war decade, relatively few people outside these Chicago neighborhoods were aware of the rioting. Chicago's newspapers largely ignored the conflicts, at least until a local television station reported the 1951 Cicero riot and forced the newspapers to acknowledge some of what was happening. Even so, the continuous and violent conflict in Chicago did not significantly enter that city's, or the nation's, racial consciousness in the 1950s. Similarly, the Detroit news media suppressed news of violent housing disputes until 1956, leaving anyone outside the immediate area of conflict unaware of the continuous violence visited on blacks. "Race news is news only if it occurs under a magnolia tree," a Detroit reporter observed. A study of newspaper coverage in the mid-1950s concluded that the *New York Times* and *Detroit Free Press* usually suggested that racial problems in their midst had been solved and that the *Chicago Tribune* mostly ignored local racial conflict altogether. This deficit of knowledge misled many northerners to believe that American race problems were confined to the South, and it would cause them to be shocked at the violence in their own cities when racial conflicts in the 1960s received intense coverage.[34]

At a time when much of the nation was focused on school desegregation in the South, northern school systems continued to segregate blacks from whites and to practice the racial disparity in resources that had emerged in the 1930s. In 1954 white ethnics in Chicago took a dim view of the *Brown* decision because they thought it would bring pressure for housing integration and continue to push the "whole white race . . . downhill." More than 80 percent of black children in Chicago's elementary schools in 1958 endured double-shift classes, which meant that their school day was shortened and the teaching time much reduced, whereas only about 2 percent of white schools operated on more than one shift. A few years later, a study found that white schools had 50 percent more operating funds and spent 18 percent more on teachers' salaries than black schools.[35]

The competition for space often shaped urban politics in the postwar years. In Detroit in 1949, a liberal Democratic candidate for mayor had the strong backing of the United Auto Workers and other CIO unions in the nation's most unionized city but lost to the conservative Republican Albert Cobo, who carried many blue-collar neighborhoods. The UAW's support of integrated public housing alienated many of its home-owning members, who voted for Cobo in the belief that they were protecting the value of their property and the racial integrity of their neighborhoods. Later, Thomas Poindexter, a Democratic lawyer, organized petition campaigns for homeowners' rights ordinances in Detroit, a movement that got him elected to the city council and kept city politics centered on race conflict for space. Big-city Democratic Party organizations like Richard Daley's in Chicago rarely allowed blacks political influence commensurate with their voting strength. By the time large numbers of black voters had accumulated in northern cities, most urban machines had matured to the point that representatives from a few large ethnic groups dominated the organizations' operations. Machine bosses typically gerrymandered ward lines to minimize black representation on city councils, and African-American operatives in machines usually took problems to, and directions from, the boss himself, rather than being integrated into the total workings of the machine. Blacks' influence thus was muted and dependent on white representatives who still listened mainly to other whites.[36]

Behind the conflict for space and political power inevitably lay the competition for economic opportunity. Black industrial employment grew very slowly after the war, and as automation ended thousands of jobs during the 1950s, African Americans did well to hold on to positions. Hiring prerogatives often remained in the hands of department heads and foremen, which in the absence of severe labor shortages usually meant that personal preferences and prejudices of low-level managers greatly affected who got hired. In Detroit, African Americans found some auto plants open to them and others almost completely off limits.

As black southerners continued to move to northern cities, industrial employers were going the other way, out of the big cities to newer plants in suburban and rural locations. Detroit alone lost 134,000 manufacturing jobs between 1947 and 1963. At new automobile plants in Dallas, Memphis, and Norfolk, exactly 53 of more than 6,000 jobs went to African Americans. At Ford's new Atlanta factory, only 21 blacks were hired. That was because, one plant manager admitted, "we agreed to abide by local custom and not hire Negroes for production work."[37]

Those African Americans who did hold jobs found an intense competition for the better jobs in industrial plants, even where CIO unions had fully organized the workplace. The unions in steel, automobiles, rubber, paper, tobacco, oil, and chemicals typically negotiated work rules that counted seniority by the tenure on a single job, rather than by time spent in the department or the plant. This meant that a black worker who had begun as a laborer in one part of a plant had little chance of "bidding" up to more skilled, higher-paying jobs in other parts of the plant. In fact, black workers' "seniority rights" usually applied only within their all-black "yard labor" or maintenance department. In 1960 only 91 of 18,550 skilled workers at Chrysler and General Motors in Detroit were black, less than one-half of 1 percent, when about 23 percent of auto workers overall were black.[38]

African Americans remained shut out of important segments of the economy. The building trades in Detroit let only a handful of African Americans into apprenticeship programs. During the 1950s in New York state, the percentage of blacks allowed into apprenticeship programs of the building trades rose from 1.5 to exactly 2 percent. At the seven major newspapers in New York City in the 1950s, less than 1 percent of printers were African American. Blacks remained drastically underrepresented in the aircraft and aerospace industries, which kept high levels of employment through most of the postwar years and which might have been opened up through federal fair-hiring mandates. In the southern textile industry, which in 1960 employed 122,000 people, less than 5 percent of workers were black. Oil companies in Louisiana and Texas, with major assistance from their labor unions, refused to hire more than token numbers of African Americans.[39]

The industrial changes and continuing discrimination caused the level of unemployment among African Americans to climb in the late 1950s. As early as 1954, the ratio of black-to-white unemployment reached two to one, where it generally remained for the rest of the twentieth century. Among teenage black males, the unemployment rate nationally exceeded 20 percent in 1958, and in northern cities that were still receiving tens of thousands of black migrants from the South each year during the 1950s, the rates were even higher. The movement of southern blacks off farms all too often represented a move to unemployment in a northern city.[40]

African Americans' status largely stood still during the 1950s, a decade when millions of whites entered the world of homeownership and enjoyed more power to consume than ever before. Between 1949 and 1959, black men's incomes as a percentage of white men's actually fell from 48 to 47 percent. In the five largest southern cities, the incomes of black men had been 56 percent of whites in 1949; in 1959 it was down to 52. During the same period, black women's incomes as a portion of white women's went from 46 to 62 percent, a gain revealing a divergence in economic prospects between black men and women that would continue for the rest of the twentieth century. Housing in southern cities ended the decade of the 1950s more segregated than ever, and while most cities in the North and West were static or improved slightly, the Chicago area became even more divided spatially by race. For blacks the optimism of the 1940s had given way to increasing frustration in the 1950s and a growing determination to do something more to improve their circumstances.[41]

IV

On May 17, 1954, the U.S. Supreme Court delivered the long-awaited school decision *Brown v. the Board of Education of Topeka*, wherein it overturned the 1896 *Plessy* decision and declared segregated education inherently unequal and thus unconstitutional. The immediate unanswered question became what the decision would mean for American race relations, especially because the court delayed for a year its implementation order. When that order did appear, it called for desegregation "with all deliberate speed," a guideline ambiguous enough to encourage both integrationists and segregationists. But *Brown* gave a great boost to black expectations and a sense to many whites that equality was now inevitable. It provided a powerful precedent for ending school segregation for those southern federal judges willing to defy white opposition and for others who applied the ruling to end segregation on buses, airplanes, and taxis and in transportation terminals, public parks, ballparks, and golf courses. It clarified the definition of equality in the United States by deciding formally that it could have no racial content. As one barrier after another fell in adherence to the *Brown* precedent, the sense of segregation's inevitable demise grew stronger.

But the implementation order failed actually to desegregate southern schools, and it did propel a powerful white resistance to black efforts to end segregation. The massive resistance of white southerners to *Brown* ultimately redounded to the benefit of civil rights, however, because it effectively taught the rest of the nation that the white South would have to be forced to conform to American standards of freedom and equality. With school integration no longer debatable in the eyes of many Americans, and yet with white southerners flouting what was now the law of the land, the cause for action against segregation became ever clearer.[42]

The national office of the NAACP responded to the *Brown* implementation order as if the court had ordered "full speed ahead." In the summer of 1955, the NAACP sent out word to its southern branches to petition local school boards to desegregate, and as a result 170 school boards in 17 states received transfer requests from black parents asking that their children be sent to currently all-white schools. The petitions ignited fierce responses in the Deep South. Whites responded first with economic coercion typically organized by local White Citizens Councils, prosegregation groups founded in the aftermath of *Brown*. In Yazoo City,

Mississippi, the names of the 53 African Americans who signed petitions appeared in the local newspaper, setting off retributions serious enough to drive many signers away from Mississippi altogether. In Selma, Alabama, 16 of the 29 blacks who petitioned the city school board were immediately fired from their jobs, and others quickly begged to have their names removed from the petition. "The white population in this county controls the money and this is an advantage that the Council will use in a fight to legally maintain complete segregation of the races," the Selma Council announced. "We intend to make it difficult, if not impossible, for any Negro who advocates de-segregation to find and hold a job, get credit or renew a mortgage."[43]

Southern states moved to put the NAACP out of business altogether. In 1956 an Alabama judge used a law governing "foreign corporations" to order the organization to provide a list of its members to the state's attorney general. When the organization refused, knowing the harassment that would come to members named, the NAACP could not legally function in Alabama, and the Alabama state courts managed through delays and obstruction to keep it shut down until 1964. Although no other state succeeded so completely as Alabama did, the NAACP by 1957 was fighting in courts to stay alive in eight other southern states.[44]

The challenges to segregated schools fired the passions of the South's white workingmen. "I am a Southerner, an American, and a Union man, in the order listed," an American Federation of Labor leader in Alabama declared in 1956. "We will fight at every turn if the Negro race seeks to mongrelize the white race." Throughout the South, white workers threatened to leave the newly merged AFL-CIO rather than honor its announced support for civil rights. More than four hundred steelworkers from one Birmingham mill wrote to the federation's president George Meany in early 1956 to say that the NAACP "had upset the most harmonious white and black race relationship on earth," and their white brothers at a nearby mill made their loyalties equally clear: "If we have to choose between staying in the union [or] see[ing] our segregated way of life being destroyed, we will pull out and form our own union."[45]

The reaction to the *Brown* decision brought the resumption of terror-ism in the South. In 1955 and 1956, Klan bombings and beatings plagued black activists in Alabama—much of the violence done by industrial workers in Birmingham and Tuscaloosa and building-trades unionists in Montgomery. In Mississippi in 1955, several leading activists were shot, one was killed, and several fled the state to save their lives. In Money, Mississippi, a 14-year-old Chicago boy named Emmett Till, who was visit-ing family members for the summer, was lynched. On the way out of a country store in which he made a small purchase, Till apparently said something that Carolyn Bryant, the young white clerk, interpreted as sexually suggestive. Bryant reported whatever it was to her husband, and several nights later Roy Bryant and his brother abducted Till, beat him to death, and dumped his body in the Tallahatchie River. They were arrested, brought to trial, and quickly acquitted.[46]

The ability of southerners to enforce white supremacy with violence, however, had reached a turning point with the Till case. Because his mother wanted "the world [to] see what they did to my boy," she held an open-casket viewing of his mutilated body for three days in Chicago, and an estimated 50,000 people filed past. *Jet* ran pictures of Till in the casket, photographs that made a huge impression on an entire generation of young Americans. The boxer Muhammad Ali, the singer Bob Dylan, the writer Maya Angelou, and dozens of 1960s activists have testified to the startling effect the Till pictures had on their awareness of race violence in the South. The trial of Till's murderers brought to Mississippi reporters from the leading national magazines and newspapers, and it attracted extensive radio and television coverage. The Mississippi activist Amzie Moore said it was "the best advertised lynching that I had ever heard [of]." Several months after the trial, *Look* magazine published an article in which Bryant and his brother, having been paid four thousand dollars, revealed how they had killed Till.[47]

The Till murder came after lynching had all but stopped in the South, and yet it appears to have shocked far more people than any other lynch-ing in American history to that time. That was the result of more exten-sive and repetitive reporting of the event, especially from *Jet* and radio and television. It was due also to the lower tolerance for violence after World War II, when Americans had felt overexposed to the atrocities of war and genocide. The Till lynching came at a crucial moment, when both black activism and white resistance were rising and racial conflicts were looming. It would shape the understanding of those watching subsequent events in the South, because it had taught that white southerners perpetrated murder of children for the sake of maintaining white supremacy. People who could do that, many observers deduced, had no understanding of American liberty, and as a result they would have to have the correct national morality forced upon them. The murder of Emmett Till thus shaped an important dynamic of the national movement for civil rights.

V

When on December 1, 1955, Rosa Parks refused to relinquish her seat on a Montgomery city bus to a white person, she sparked a protest that had been many years in the making. Civil rights activism had begun there in the late 1930s when Edgar D. Nixon, local head of the Brotherhood of Sleeping Car Porters, began encouraging black voter registration. Nixon led the local branch of the NAACP, whose activities were also coordinated by Rosa Parks. In 1943 several African Americans sued the board of registrars for denying their right to vote. During the next dozen years, the number of black voters rose slowly but steadily until it had reached about 1,700—enough voters to influence the outcome of most local elections. Along the way the black community had strengthened economically with more spending on black education, at the local state college and at the two new black high schools. The Women's Political Council, created in 1949 when black professors were denied membership in the local League of Women Voters, further strengthened the local commitment to civil rights and political activism. The appearance in 1953 of a black newspaper and the city's first all-black radio station resulted in greater social and political cohesion in the Montgomery black community.[48]

Then in 1953 a white candidate for the three-person city commission asked local black leaders for their votes in exchange for his support on matters of their concern. Having witnessed the creation recently of the first black library branch, Montgomery's African Americans were optimistic in 1953 that their political influence might cause the city to hire black policemen. The candidate promised to support that, and he was elected. At the time of Rosa Parks's arrest, African-American leaders had come to believe that they could elicit improvements, including better treatment on city buses, by appealing to the new, more flexible city government.[49]

The Montgomery bus boycott shaped the course of history in large part because of the ugly white reaction to it. A boycott similar to the one that emerged in Montgomery had developed in Baton Rouge in 1953. There African Americans organized a bus boycott and a substitute, private transportation system to take its place—which was exactly what would happen in Montgomery. But after only a few days in Baton Rouge, the white authorities capitulated to black protestors. With the boycott over so quickly, the events received very little attention outside Baton Rouge. In Montgomery, city officials condemned the boycott in the local media even before it began, thus helping to promote black awareness of the forthcoming protest. Once the boycott was underway, the blacks' initial solution to the bus problem was a fixed seating arrangement, with whites at the front, blacks in the back, and no requirement that blacks relinquish seats to whites. This proposal amounted to a reform that *preserved* segregation, but white authorities rejected it: "If we granted the Negroes these demands," the attorney for the bus company declared, "they would go about boasting of a victory that they had won over the white people, and this we will not stand for." For whites in Montgomery, the issue was less segregation than maintaining total white dominance over blacks. Whites began to say that "the Negroes are laughing at white people behind their backs"—a reflection of how the boycott had threatened their status.[50]

Whites' anxiety about their control brought violence and more recalcitrance. The home of the boycott leader, Martin Luther King, Jr., was bombed, and then the local district attorney indicted almost a hundred black leaders for breaking an old antilabor law against boycotts. The bombing and the mass indictments brought much national media exposure to the Montgomery events from the *New York Times*, the newsmagazines, and the television networks. A few weeks after the indictments, King's conviction for breaking the antiboycott law brought more front-page news in publications around the United States, each with confirmations from Montgomery's protestors that the boycott would continue. Four and a half months after the boycott began, the U.S. Supreme Court struck down segregation on a South Carolina bus line, but Montgomery officials immediately announced that they would still enforce segregation. When in November 1956 the U.S. Supreme Court ordered the desegregation of Montgomery's buses and the boycott ended, the worst violence yet ensued. Buses were shot into, and the homes of boycott leaders and four churches were bombed—all events that received extensive national news coverage.

The boycott dramatized the strength and solidarity of southern blacks, something that the national media interpreted as new and unusual, as well as the persistent racism and violence of southern whites, on which journalists from outside the South focused heavily. Together the good Negroes and the bad southern racists created an irresistible melodrama for a mushrooming number of reporters. Magazine coverage of civil rights issues in 1956 tripled over what it had been in 1955; *Life* ran 35 stories in 1956, as compared with the one it had offered the previous year. The *New York Times* increased its already-strong coverage by about 150 percent.[51]

The expanded national coverage in 1956 altered African Americans' thinking about protest. Heretofore, blacks rarely heard much about direct-action protests in other cities. White-owned newspapers tended to ignore protest activities outside their own area of readership. Streetcar boycotts in the early 1900s, "Don't buy where you can't work" pickets in the 1930s, school boycotts in the 1940s, and voter registration campaigns in the late 1930s and 1940s usually had happened in a virtual vacuum of information. Thus many African Americans were surprised when they repeatedly received reports in the leading national magazines and on television that all of Montgomery's 50,000 blacks joined in a sustained and successful protest. It was powerful validation that something "new" had begun.[52]

The boycott introduced to the nation the 27-year-old Baptist minister Martin Luther King, Jr., who would shape the ideological understandings of American race relations for the remainder of the twentieth century. Subsequent events would suggest that no American since Abraham Lincoln had better understood the nature of national values and the inherent conflicts within them. One historian has observed that King realized in Montgomery the necessity of showing both blacks and whites the evil of segregation and then devoted his career to arranging other demonstrations of that reality. One might say that during the boycott King learned how to exhibit the incompatibility between liberty and white supremacy and then how to persuade Americans to expand the meaning of liberty sufficiently that white supremacy might be overturned.[53]

He did this with constant, eloquent appeals to American democratic values. We are here, he told the first mass meeting to support the boycott, "because first and foremost we are American citizens and we are determined to apply our citizenship to the fullness of its meaning." Yes, that was right, the crowd replied. "We are here also because of our love for democracy, because of our deep-seated belief that democracy transformed from thin paper to thick action is the greatest form of government on earth. . . . If we were incarcerated behind the iron curtains of a Communistic nation we couldn't do this. . . . But the great glory of American democracy is the right to protest for right." With such words King appealed to the Lincoln understanding of democratic values, a faith to which African Americans almost universally held. But it was also an ideology that the young preacher sensed would connect the Montgomery protestors to many whites who subscribed to the Great Emancipator's values, even if they rarely acted to uphold freedom and equality for blacks.[54]

In that first speech, King revealed the remarkable power he exercised with the use of language, which for him often carried the symbolic action of suffering but also of hope. "We, the disinherited of this land, we who have been oppressed so long, are tired of going through the long

night of captivity. And now we are reaching out for the daybreak of freedom and justice and equality." King connected the particular events just
unfolding to great moral authority: "We are not wrong in what we are
doing. If we are wrong, the Supreme Court of this nation is wrong. If we
are wrong, the Constitution of the United States is wrong. If we are
wrong, God Almighty is wrong." At a later mass meeting: "We have been
plunged into the abyss of oppression. And we decided to rise up only
with the weapon of protest.... If we are arrested every day, if we are
exploited every day, if we are trampled over every day, don't ever let anyone pull you so low as to hate them. We must use the weapon of love."
In King's language, African Americans acted in powerful, symbolic ways:
They "reached" for freedom, "rose up" after being "plunged" into
oppression, and loved those who "trampled over" them. Indeed they
fought their oppression with a great symbolic "weapon," love.[55]

Martin Luther King, Jr. *Courtesy Birmingham Public Library.*

King's ideological influence has often been placed in the context of his philosophical commitment to nonviolence. One scholar has shown that King actually had little commitment to nonviolence and knew little about Gandhian thinking prior to the bus boycott. But he immediately saw that nonviolence was a way to symbolize blacks' moral superiority over whites and to emphasize the centrality of violence to white supremacy. When his home was bombed a few weeks into the boycott, King spoke from his porch to an angry crowd of blacks, many of them vowing to get revenge. "We cannot solve this problem through retaliatory violence," he told the group. "Remember the words of Jesus: 'He who lives by the sword will perish by the sword.'" Please go home, he pleaded with the crowd, as Montgomery's white-supremacist mayor and chief of police stood silently beside him. "We must love our white brothers no matter what they do to us. . . . We must meet hate with love." The crowd did disperse, and King's three-minute "sermon on the porch" set forth the strategy, and the justification, for what would be an almost irresistible ideological appeal.[56]

King did begin to invoke the philosophy of Mahatma Gandhi to suggest both the commitment to nonviolence and the successful example of colored people throwing off their oppressor. Within weeks after the boycott began, he told reporters that African Americans in Montgomery were among "the oppressed people of the world" who were "rising up . . . against colonialism, imperialism and other systems of oppression."[57]

But the most fundamental influence on King's ideology was the religious values of the traditional African-American church, which came to him naturally as the son and grandson of preachers. Biblicism held the highest authority among African Americans, whose deep commitment to evangelical Christianity had made the religious experience of the black church the most affirming aspect of African-American culture. The "sermon on the porch" demonstrated King's embrace of the New Testament theology of love. But he relied even more on such Old Testament prophets as Isaiah and Amos to warn of destruction unless change was forthcoming. The prophetic King also invoked constantly the imagery of deliverance from the stories of the Israelites' captivities in Egypt and Babylon, which for generations had supplied the message of hope for African Americans. The figure of Moses was central to the message, and African Americans soon drew the analogy of King to the Israelite leader. "In every crisis God raises up a Moses," the famous Detroit minister C. L. Franklin preached. "His name may not be Moses but the character of the role that he plays is always the same. . . . His name may be Joshua or his name may be David, or his name, you understand, may be Abraham Lincoln or Frederick Douglass or George Washington Carver, but in every crisis God raises up a Moses, especially where the destiny of his people is concerned."[58]

Even before the end of the Montgomery boycott, as the young preacher traveled the United States promoting support for the boycott before groups and through the media, many Americans believed the new Moses' name was Martin Luther King, Jr. Whether prophet or messiah, King by 1957 had become the voice that might unite all African Americans into a cohesive community demanding change.

King's ideological influence went far beyond black Americans to affect the thinking of the millions of whites whose support was needed to force changes in race relations. King developed an influential following among white, northern Protestants through his preaching and writing. Almost as soon as he became the leader of the boycott, he began making fundraising trips to New York, Chicago, Detroit, and Los Angeles, where he filled the pulpits of large and wealthy churches. He would regularly return to those churches over the rest of his life. There he gave sermons in which he often had borrowed language and ideas from white preachers already well-known among liberal Protestants. They included Harry Emerson Fosdick, George Buttrick, and J. Wallace Hamilton, all of whom preached often on the radio and published prolifically.[59]

King applied one idea emphasized by Fosdick and the others to important effect, the notion that each person has the capacity for both great good and great evil. Over and over King would preach that whites who were oppressing blacks needed only to find their goodness, and they could redeem themselves and American society. Indeed, the American nation was itself the "prodigal son" who strayed into the evil of racial oppression, but it too could be saved and brought to goodness. If the message of deliverance provided the ideological thrust to blacks for increased protest, the "intertextual" King had found an ideological appeal that built support for civil rights among influential whites outside the South.[60]

Much later some would characterize King's borrowing as plagiarism, but in fact it was a common practice among preachers, especially for the large majority who never published their sermons. His borrowing of prominent white preachers' ideas represented an ideological analog to the cross-cultural sharing that was taking place simultaneously in American popular music. There whites "borrowed" black rhythm and blues to create the common cultural ground of rock and roll. King discovered a theological territory to share with whites whose support blacks needed. The lowered barriers of thought and taste enabled more and more whites to bridge the racial divide, something necessary for fundamental changes to take place in American race relations.[61]

By the end of the bus boycott, Martin Luther King had embraced a national strategy to end segregation. To implement it, he had acquired shrewd advisers such as Bayard Rustin, a longtime civil rights activist, and Stanley Levison, who had extensive connections among New York radicals and northern Jews sympathetic to civil rights. Levison became King's most consistent adviser on strategy, the main fundraiser to support his actions, and the point man for connecting King to liberal, wealthy Jews. In 1957, King formed the Southern Christian Leadership Conference (SCLC) to pursue direct-action protests that would be aimed at eliciting national laws against segregation and disfranchisement. In a sense it was a continuation of the NAACP effort begun after World War I to get federal antilynching legislation, except the SCLC planned to use street protests to dramatize the hopeless immorality of southern whites. Little was accomplished to that end in the late 1950s, but it was a strategy that ultimately proved to be remarkably successful.[62]

VI

For most southern whites in the late 1950s, the end of segregation still remained unthinkable. In July 1954, when asked if they would object to their children's going to an integrated school, 15 percent of white southerners said they would not object; by 1959 that number had fallen to 8 percent. Indeed, whites in Virginia had moved resolutely to abolish public schools in several counties. If a protest movement had been agitating for the end of private property, it would have seemed no more radical to most whites in Alabama and Mississippi than the civil rights activities in their midst. In Montgomery, even as the buses operated on an integrated basis, voter registration had stopped, any white moderation had been stifled, and bellicose segregationists controlled the city commission. Montgomery's segregationist leaders believed they were winning because almost no whites had broken ranks with white supremacists. "When the history of the second reconstruction is written," the local White Citizens Council predicted in 1959, Montgomery would be reported as the place where "integration efforts were stopped cold."[63]

In nearby Tuskegee, where a black boycott of white businesses followed the 1957 gerrymander of the city limits that removed virtually all black voters from the city, whites insisted that the blacks' action was explained simply—"they want what we have." A young Tuskegee housewife told a white interviewer that "the Negroes want complete control and they will do anything to get it," a characterization that bore no resemblance to what blacks had asked for but that in fact reflected exactly the behavior of whites in Tuskegee. "They will go to any extreme to get equal with the white," a Tuskegee businessman said of his black neighbors. "When they get equal with the white, then they will want to be better than the white man." In the late 1950s most white southerners still viewed any breach in the wall of white supremacy as a catastrophic threat to their status.[64]

They saw, however, that holes were appearing in that wall. When "massive resistance" caught fire in early 1956, almost all southerners in Congress signed a "Southern Manifesto" against the *Brown* decision. They

called it a "clear abuse of judicial power" and a "derogation of the authority of Congress," and they demanded legislation to repeal it. But their
clamor got far less attention than the efforts of a growing pro–civil rights
coalition in Congress led by Senator Hubert Humphrey of Minnesota.
The coalition replied to the manifesto with calls for legislation to protect
black voting rights and housing opportunities. The manifesto exposed one
crucial break in segregation's defensive wall: The Senate majority leader
Lyndon Johnson of Texas did not sign it, excused by his mentor Richard
Russell, an author of the manifesto, because Russell wanted the Texan to
be president and he knew from his own failed run for the Democratic
nomination in 1952 that no southern segregationist could be elected.[65]

Johnson then pushed through the Senate the Civil Rights Act of 1957
and thus began establishing his *bona fides* as a supporter of civil rights.
The first civil rights legislation passed by the Congress in more than 75
years, the 1957 act provided some weak protection for voting rights and
established the U.S. Commission on Civil Rights to investigate denials of
rights. One civil rights advocate said the new law put him in mind of
Abraham Lincoln's homeopathic soup—"thin as the soup made from the
shadow of a crow that has starved to death"—but Johnson maintained it
was an important first step, and the wily and willful Democrat later
proved exactly what that meant. The act began the process of pulling the
legislative branch into alignment with the judiciary to expand the meaning of equality for African Americans.[66]

The depth of white resistance to change in the 1950s was finally dramatized at the unlikely location of Little Rock. The desegregation of Central High School in 1957 forced into the open what had mostly been
implicit in the simmering racial feelings since the *Brown* decision was
announced—that established national law flatly contradicted the social
system that nearly all white southerners believed was the right one. The
issue came to a head in Little Rock primarily because the state's governor,
Orval Faubus, had determined that his best chance for reelection in 1958
lay with becoming the strongest segregationist in the race. Having seen
the intensity of the resistance build in 1956, many southern politicians

came to the same conclusion, but it was Faubus, formerly a racial moderate, who confronted a clear order to desegregate and defied it. His reluctant hand now forced, Dwight Eisenhower sent army troops to escort the nine black students into Central High. The army's presence immediately connected the 1957 event to white southerners' mythic understanding of Reconstruction and called forth their old ethnic-nationalist resentments in full force. Crowds of whites gathered outside Central High to harass the well-dressed, serious black students as they entered the school. Elizabeth Eckford, 15 years old, approached the school by herself. "Here comes one of the niggers!" someone shouted. "Lynch her! Lynch her!" came another voice. "Go home, you bastard of a black bitch!"[67]

As they screamed epithets, 250 reporters—and a similar complement of photographers—captured it all. *Life* magazine delivered stark renderings of the faces of hate in the Little Rock crowd—men, women, and teenagers—though the police at one point threw all of the *Life* photographers in the Little Rock jail. Some later believed the most influential reporter was the 30-year-old John Chancellor of the National Broadcasting Company (NBC), who stood amid the mob to show his burgeoning national audience the ugliness of Little Rock each day. A newspaper reporter who covered Little Rock later acknowledged that television coverage "gave that story a color and attraction and emphasis that newspapers couldn't do." Even with no commentary, the newspaperman added, "a shot of a big white man spitting and cursing at black children did more to open up the national intellect than my stories ever could." In West Virginia, young Henry Louis Gates and his family were riveted by scenes from Little Rock on their television: "All of us watched it," Gates later wrote. "I don't mean Mama and Daddy and [my brother]. I mean *all* the colored people in America watched it, together, with one set of eyes."[68]

In fact none of the black students was killed, though their experience at Central was miserable, and Orval Faubus closed all city high schools the next year rather than comply with desegregation orders. The crowd did beat up black reporters and threatened death to the education editor of the *New York Times*. The Little Rock events set important patterns for the way that civil rights events in the South would be communicated to the nation: Violence, even the symbolic attack of shouted epithets, became the centerpiece of coverage. White southerners' hostility toward the media ensured that the sympathies of reporters and photographers lay entirely with the main objects of violence, African Americans seeking equality. In the decade ahead, the images of protest and violence would shape the character of the nation's great movement for civil rights.

CHAPTER 6

THE HIGHWAY UP FROM DARKNESS

IN THE EVENING OF March 7, 1965, George and Lillie Leonard settled in front of the television in their San Francisco home to watch the news. An editor for *Look* magazine, George Leonard had seen much of the world and moved in the company of well-informed people, but he was not prepared for the images that appeared before him now. "The TV screen showed a column of Negroes striding along a highway," Leonard later recounted of events that had occurred that afternoon in Selma, Alabama, but "a force of Alabama state troopers blocked their way" just after they crossed a bridge on Highway 80. When the marchers stopped, a trooper captain ordered them to turn around, but the marchers stood still for a long minute. "There was a lurching movement on the left side of the screen," Leonard remembered. "A heavy phalanx of troopers charged straight into the column, bowling the marchers over." He heard a "shrill cry of terror" as the troopers clubbed their way forward. "The scene cut to charging horses, their hoofs flashing over the fallen," and then appeared an image of tear gas enveloping the highway. Leonard realized that Lillie was crying. "I can't look any more," she said. "Sermons have been preached, crusades launched, books on ethics written, systems of morality devised, with no mention whatsoever of how American

Negroes are treated," George Leonard later explained about his moment of revelation. "When the senses lie, the conscience is sure to sleep."

His senses shocked and his conscience now more awake than it had ever been, George Leonard knew he had to place himself "alongside the Negroes" in Alabama, and thus he went directly to the San Francisco airport to begin an all-night journey to Selma. He soon began to meet others who had the same visceral reaction to the television scenes: a severely handicapped Episcopal priest who had witnessed firsthand the Nazi terrorism of Jews in Germany in 1938; the student radical Mario Savio, who had started the free-speech movement at Berkeley the previous fall, along with his girlfriend in high heels; and the theatrical agent William Morris and his wife, who were having a distracted dinner at their Malibu Beach home after seeing the pictures from Selma when at the same moment each had asked, "Why are we sitting here?" Arriving in Selma the next day, Leonard and the other pilgrims met civil rights leaders, including Martin Luther King, Jr. "Now we have a problem here in Alabama," King told the new arrivals. "Perhaps the worst sin in life is to know right and not to do it."

On Tuesday morning Leonard and the others followed King out of the Brown Chapel church and along the route on Highway 80 that the beaten marchers had gone the previous Sunday. But a judge had enjoined further marching, and they turned back. Still, it was the cathartic experience of George Leonard's life. "America's conscience has been sleeping, but it is waking up," he wrote a few weeks later. "A trip to Alabama is a small thing, but out of many such acts, let us hope, may come a new America."[1]

George Leonard's journey to Alabama suggests several crucial truths for understanding why a powerful movement for change happened in American society between 1960 and 1965. It demonstrated, first and foremost, that many Americans were acting to uphold Abraham Lincoln's now century-old definitions of liberty and equality. If the Lincoln revision had been allowed to lie dormant, asleep within the American conscience for the past century, it was now vibrant and moving in the nation, and the likes of George Leonard were demonstrating that.

His journey also showed what had first come clear in the Montgomery bus boycott: protests against segregation elicited violence from southern whites. "Bloody Sunday" revealed again that such violence drew compelling media attention to American race problems. And as a result of the images of violence flashed around the country, many Americans acquired a new sensitivity that they interpreted as a call to action against white supremacy. By 1965 an important theme running through American thinking was a growing fear about the violent nature of society. Violence threatened Americans' security. White southerners, on the other hand, were generally more comfortable with violence than other Americans were, and some remained ready still to use it, as they always had, to enforce white supremacy. During the early 1960s white southerners came to be seen as the source of much brutality in American life, and finally public policymakers acted against them.

Bloody Sunday marked the climax of an intricately connected sequence of events that had begun five years earlier with the first sit-in in Greensboro, North Carolina. The two events may serve as the bound-

Bloody Sunday in Selma, March 1965. *Courtesy AP/Wideworld Photos.*

aries to the historical period in which the most tangible changes took place. This was the time of direct-action protest, an era that has captured our historical imagination ever since. The lunch counter sit-ins of 1960; the Freedom Rides of 1961; the protests at Albany, Georgia, in 1961 and 1962; the Birmingham demonstrations in 1963; the long, violent Mississippi summer of 1964; the Selma march of 1965—all worked to dramatize the incompatibility between white supremacy and the values of liberty, equality, and democracy. One protest after another, coming in steady succession, acted to push the conflict in values to the forefront of American consciousness.

When on February 1, 1960, four black students at North Carolina Agricultural and Technical College asked to be served at the all-white lunch counter of a Greensboro five-and-dime store, they set off a seemingly spontaneous eruption of protests. Within a week sit-ins had spread across North Carolina and within a month to Virginia, South Carolina, Florida, Alabama, and Tennessee. The sit-ins startled many Americans with proof that southern blacks simply refused any longer to acquiesce in the Jim Crow system. Executed mostly by college students in towns and cities where a black college existed, sit-ins created a scene of clear moral distinction. The black students, dressed as if going to church, sat politely at the lunch counter, the Bible or a schoolbook resting on the counter before them. Denied service, the students used the time to study. Their polite behavior often contrasted with that of the rowdy onlookers, usually white males with sneering lips and nasty tongues. Many times the hecklers poured catsup on the protestors or pressed a lighted cigarette against them. Rarely did a protestor retaliate. When the police arrested them for breaking the local segregation ordinance, the students assumed the posture of passive resistance. Their limp bodies had to be carried away from the lunch counters.[2]

This scene, enacted hundreds of times in scores of places during 1960, became part of an ongoing drama of good and evil. To most white observers from outside, and to most blacks everywhere, it was easy to conclude that justice was on the side of the clean-cut college students, who only wanted a hamburger to sustain them in pursuit of an education. The sit-ins were typically portrayed in 1960 as something entirely new, but as with so much black protest, there were all-but-forgotten precedents to this kind of action. In 1942 activists in Chicago had organized a sit-in at a coffee house, and the next year students at Howard University sat in at Washington, D.C., restaurants. In 1958 and 1959 there had been sit-ins in various states.[3]

But the 1960 sit-ins were reported as a new tactic representative of a new militancy on the part of young African Americans, and as would be the case in the years ahead, the medium played an important role in shaping the sit-ins' message. In 1958 the *New York Times*, which had kept a full-time correspondent in the South since 1947, assigned a young Georgian, Claude Sitton, to cover full-time the civil rights developments in the South. A man of remarkable energy and endurance, Sitton would lead the national media in a frenetic race from one hot spot to another for the next six years. Soon *Newsweek* and the *Washington Post* made similar commitments to the civil rights story, and the television reporters were never far behind. By 1960 television news was beginning to acquire the enter-

A sit-in in Raleigh. *Courtesy North Carolina State Archives.*

tainment value that so characterizes it today—the maximum amount of filmed action on the evening news and regular, longer features on issues and events. The civil rights movement would provide television with violence, emotion, and pathos. Television especially advanced the sit-in movement by communicating its development instantaneously to African Americans all over the South. Soon segregationists were charging that television crews were conspiring with black students to stage sit-ins. Before long, city officials in Montgomery and Birmingham had sued the *Times* for libel, a none-too-subtle attempt to keep Sitton and his colleagues from exposing the face of white supremacy.[4]

The sit-ins put intense pressure on downtown merchants throughout the South, and they began to yield results. Within a year lunch counters in more than a hundred cities had been desegregated. "Somewhere along the way, the movement became a vehicle for the Negro's opposition to segregation in all its forms," Sitton wrote in the *Times* in March 1960. Sit-ins were organized at theaters, hotels, and parks, and boycotts often followed. Exasperated by the tension from constant sit-ins in downtown Atlanta, Ivan Allen, president of the chamber of commerce and the future mayor, admitted that "the national publicity was running us crazy," and that the downtown merchants wanted a compromise "even if it means desegregating the stores." The Southern Regional Council announced that the sit-ins showed that segregation could not be maintained "short of continuous coercion and the intolerable social order which would result."[5]

The sit-ins advanced all activism by establishing once and for all the efficacy of direct-action protest. The Southern Christian Leadership Conference, having floundered somewhat since its creation in 1957, suddenly found that enthusiasm was rising for its protest plans. Fundraising at the SCLC and NAACP improved greatly starting in 1960, as did membership in the NAACP and the Congress of Racial Equality (CORE). But the sit-ins also raised questions about the established pattern of civil rights leadership. In April 1960 a group of college students formed the Student Nonviolent Coordinating Committee (SNCC) to conduct protests in communities across the South. Members of SNCC were oriented more to community organizing than to Martin Luther King's national political strategy, and relatively few of them shared his intensive religious orientation. Instead SNCC workers were dedicated to day-to-day resistance to white supremacy in communities where there was little protection for activists.[6]

King spent much of 1960 attempting to advance his strategy for federal civil rights action in the presidential election. He was focused on getting an executive order ending all segregation—a kind of "Emancipation Proclamation" from Jim Crow. Both candidates in 1960 seemed more likely to help than President Eisenhower had been. As vice president, the Republican nominee Richard Nixon had listened to King's concerns. Senator John Kennedy of Massachusetts, the Democrat, had taken a cool posture toward civil rights in the Senate. King counseled African Americans to watch carefully what the candidates and the party platforms said. During the campaign Kennedy criticized the outgoing administration for not doing more on civil rights, saying at several points that Eisenhower could have relieved much housing discrimination with executive orders. Still, black voters seemed closely divided until near the end of the campaign, when Kennedy made a gesture of concern to King's wife Coretta after the civil rights leader had been put in a Georgia prison on a minor charge. Kennedy received 68 percent of the black vote in 1960, as compared with the 61 percent that the Democrat got in the 1956 election. Many observers believed that Kennedy's call to Mrs. King and the resulting gratitude from black voters provided the margin of victory in a close race.[7]

The civil rights leadership immediately proposed that Kennedy issue an executive order ending discrimination among employers with federal contracts and in the administration of all federally aided programs. The latter change would have attacked segregation in schools, welfare programs, and national guard units in the South. Kennedy and his advisors responded that such a strong order would doom his administration with the southerners in Congress. He did issue Executive Order 10925, which called on all federal contractors to take "affirmative action" to employ minorities. The order established a Committee on Equal Employment Opportunity, chaired by Vice President Lyndon Johnson, but this committee did little more than get pledges from contractors to do better. Johnson would not coerce businessmen, and no one else in the administration forced the issue. Within months of having very high hopes about the new administration, civil rights leaders believed that Kennedy had broken his promises.[8]

I

But it was a time when African Americans were willing to force issues, and the Freedom Rides of 1961 demonstrated that perfectly. The Congress of Racial Equality resolved to get enforcement of a 1947 ruling that had ordered the desegregation of bus terminals in interstate transportation but that had never been enforced in the South. In May 1961, CORE leaders assembled a group of blacks and whites, members of their organization and SNCC, and put them on buses heading southward from Washington, D.C. "We planned the Freedom Ride with the specific intention of creating a crisis," James Farmer of CORE later explained. "We were counting on the bigots in the South to do our work for us." Farmer assumed that violence against the Freedom Riders would elicit a

A Freedom Rider bus was burned in Anniston, Alabama. *Courtesy AP/Wideworld Photos.*

response from the Kennedy administration. "We figured that the government would have to respond if we created a situation that was headline news all over the world, and affected the nation's image abroad. An international crisis, that was our strategy."[9]

The Freedom Rides created three incidents of violence that became widely influential for revealing the ugliness of white supremacy. At Anniston, Alabama, Ku Klux Klansmen threw an incendiary bomb into the riders' bus and almost kept them from escaping it. Other riders arrived a while later in Birmingham, where they were set upon by another Klan mob. Although the bus station sat within the shadow of City Hall, no Birmingham policeman was there to protect them. The Klansmen beat the riders, two reporters, and a newspaper photographer. A CBS reporter who happened to be in Birmingham on another assignment witnessed the bus station beatings and described them for his television audience: "When the bus arrived, the toughs grabbed the passengers into alleys and corridors, pounding them with pipes, with key rings, and with fists." Virtually the same scene occurred in Montgomery a few days later, except that the beatings of the riders and the newsmen were worse, and the Kennedy Justice Department's representative on the scene was knocked unconscious near the bus station. The mob also moved to cripple the media by attacking an NBC television reporter, his crew, and two *Life* photographers.[10]

In the aftermath of the Montgomery riot, Martin Luther King announced that "the Deep South will not impose limits upon itself" and that unless the federal government acted "forthrightly in the South to assure every citizen his constitutional rights, we will be plunged into a dark abyss of chaos." Attorney General Robert F. Kennedy was learning King's lesson on the fly: Alabama's Governor John Patterson, a Kennedy supporter in the 1960 election, had promised protection of the Freedom Riders in Montgomery but reneged, thus tacitly allowing the violence. Against pleas from the Kennedy administration not to go on, the Freedom Rides did continue to Jackson, Mississippi, where replacement riders were gently arrested for breaking segregation laws. Refusing bail, some spent the summer in the state's Parchman penitentiary.[11]

The violence provoked by the Freedom Rides horrified all who saw it, and in an even more visceral fashion it reinforced the impact of the sit-ins for demonstrating segregation's evil. Photographs of the burning bus in Anniston, the Klansmen bent over Freedom Riders in the Birmingham station, and the bloody faces of riders and reporters in Montgomery decorated the front pages and television broadcasts around the world. White southerners had flaunted violent means to defend segregation, and people everywhere recoiled from their inhumane behavior.

But the Freedom Rides had a transforming effect on some whites in Birmingham and Montgomery. All desegregation in Montgomery had stopped after the decision ending bus segregation in November 1956, and the few whites who favored compromise with blacks on any issue had been shunned and persecuted. In 1959 the city commission had closed the city parks rather than obey a desegregation order. In 1960 the president of the Montgomery Chamber of Commerce had said the sit-in protests were a "coldly deliberate, calculated move on the part of the agitators to goad and provoke the Southern white man to the very limits of his patience and endurance." But the mayhem of the Freedom Rides led some local businessmen to demand that city officials stop such lawlessness. These white "moderates" took something crucial from segregationists—the assumption that whites held one and only one view on race relations.[12]

In Birmingham the dynamic was similar. A white business group had worked on in an interracial committee for compromise with black interests in the early 1950s, but the angry reaction to *Brown* had quashed that, and a long silence of any moderate white opinion then followed. In 1958 a liberal white minister, Robert Hughes, became so frustrated at the failure to address local problems that he began contacting national media outlets to encourage them to do exposés on Birmingham. His efforts hit the jackpot in April 1960, when in the midst of sit-in demonstrations, the *New York Times* reporter Harrison Salisbury wrote a startling description of the Alabama city: "Every channel of communication, every medium of mutual interest, every reasoned approach, every inch of middle ground has been fragmented by the emotional dynamite of racism, reinforced by the whip, the razor, the gun, the bomb, the torch, the club, the knife, the mob, the police and many branches of the state's apparatus."[13]

Such exposure of Birmingham's violence forced some moderate whites into the open. Within weeks of the Freedom Rider beatings in Birmingham, a group of progressive lawyers and businessmen began to focus on a way to rid the city of its police commissioner, Eugene "Bull" Connor, a man who had made a long political career of agitating white racial feelings to his own benefit. They landed on a plan to change the form of city government from a three-person commission to mayor and council, which would do away with Connor's office. Connor and his allies did not go quietly, denouncing enemies who "for another dollar in the till, or for another industry in our city, or for fear of the printed or broadcast tongue-lashings . . . would yield to this cacophony of intimidation." To the surprise of many observers, the referendum changing the government passed. White progressives and their black allies, who were also mainly businessmen and professionals, believed that Birmingham was about to be delivered from its ugliness.[14]

Birmingham's Eugene "Bull" Connor. *Courtesy Birmingham Public Library.*

Throughout the South in 1960 and 1961, white businessmen were being forced to decide between segregation and the likely prospect of a troubled, stagnating business environment on the one hand, and a compromise with black protestors for the sake of peace and economic progress on the other. There were businessmen throughout the South whose status was shaped as much by membership in national elites as by their local standing, and those men disliked the external opprobrium they received for white-supremacist violence. The leading moderate in Montgomery was Winton M. Blount, owner of a construction company that built missile silos and rocket launch pads and a man with a growing network of friends among the nation's business elite. In Birmingham, Sidney Smyer, a real estate executive and one of the city's most vociferous segregationists in the 1950s, first confronted pictures of the Birmingham Freedom-Rider beatings while he was at a meeting of Rotary International in Tokyo in May 1961. Smyer spent much of the Tokyo meeting responding to fellow Rotarians' questions about how such things could happen in his city. He returned to Alabama resolved to prevent them from occurring again, and he became a leader in the change-of-government effort.[15]

Thus by 1961 new realities were dawning on southern whites. First, violence no longer had the effect of squelching civil rights activism. Burned and beaten and thrown behind bars, the Freedom Riders kept coming. Second, influential men made it clear that some things were in fact more important than segregation, namely peace and prosperity. With blacks no longer afraid and whites no longer united, segregation's demise had begun to seem possible by 1961.

The Freedom Rides brought home to the Kennedy administration the reality that black protestors had the power to create disorder beyond the federal government's ability to contain it. Such situations reflected badly on the current administration, making it look weak and ill prepared—the very impression that the Bay of Pigs invasion had left at about the same time. John Kennedy and his brother learned from the Freedom Rides that direct-action protests were a large liability to their political future, and accordingly they took steps to prevent future protests. At Robert Kennedy's behest, the Interstate Commerce Commission soon ordered segregation banned at all interstate transportation facilities. In 1961 and 1962 the Justice Department initiated discrimination suits against more than 50 individual boards of voter registrars in southern counties. The Kennedy administration tried to steer the civil rights leadership toward an emphasis on voting in the belief that when enough blacks were registered to vote, they would obtain fair treatment through the political process, rather than through street protests. Robert Kennedy helped arrange philanthropic support for the Voter Education Project, which supported activists working on voter registration in dozens of Deep South communities.[16]

But civil rights leaders deemed the Kennedy efforts insufficient. Where was the executive order on housing? Why was there no enforcement of fair hiring on federal contracts? In late 1961, Martin Luther King put these questions to the president, who answered that more action would cost too much politically with the southern-controlled Congress. Afterward King told a friend that while Kennedy had the understanding and political skill to be a great leader, he lacked the "moral passion." King wanted a president to help him make an ideological appeal to democratic values, to assist him in exposing the contradiction between white supremacy and freedom and equality. In the absence of that help, more pressure would have to be created.[17]

II

In late 1961 activists in Albany, a small city in southern Georgia, began a series of protests against its many forms of segregation, protests that they hoped would bring the city to an economic and political impasse and force powerful whites to compromise on segregation. African Americans marched, sat in, and picketed. To rally protestors and build enthusiasm broadly, the leaders convened nightly mass meetings, which featured strategy discussions, sermons, prayers, and singing that captivated all who heard it. The music of the Albany movement contained compelling language of symbolic action:

> *I know one thing we did right,*
> *Was the day we started to fight.*
> *Keep your eyes on the prize*
> *Hold on. Hold on.*
>
> *Albenny Georgia lives in race*
> *We're goin' to fight it from place to place.*
> *Keep your eyes on the prize.*
> *Hold on.*
>
> *I know what I think is right*
> *Freedom in the souls of black and white.*
> *Keep your eyes on the prize.*
> *Hold on.*
>
> *Singing and shouting is very well*
> *Get off your seat and go to jail.*
> *Keep your eyes on the prize.*
> *Hold on. Hold on.*
> *HOLD ON. HOLD ON.*
> *Keep your eyes on the prize*
> *Hold on. Hold on.*

"Hold On" was often followed by this song:

> *Ain't go' let nobody/Turn me 'round*
> *Turn me 'round/Turn me 'round*
> *Ain't go' let nobody/Turn me 'round*
> *Keep on a-walkin'/Keep on a-talkin'*
> *Marchin' on to Freedom Land.*

Several more songs followed, and then the mass meeting reached its climax with a long, continuous call of "Freedom, freedom, freedom." The chant suggested a willful surge of blacks toward the reality of freedom. Each rally ended with an old labor song, "We Shall Overcome," now becoming the anthem of the civil rights movement. From Albany on, the music of the civil rights movement was known as "freedom songs."[18]

But despite the soaring spirit of the freedom songs, Albany's civil rights leaders failed to create the standstill they wanted, and they called on SCLC to help them make city officials more responsive. King went to Albany and led protests, most of which were covered closely by the national media. Many protestors were arrested and jailed, but still the city refused to negotiate and instead closed down the bus system, shuttered the city parks, and repealed segregation ordinances but continued to enforce them. Albany's police chief enforced segregation without open brutality, and he arranged for surrounding counties to take prisoners when he made mass arrests. "We ran out of people before he ran out of jails," an activist later lamented.[19]

Soon the national media was interpreting the Albany protests as a defeat for black activists and a loss of face for King himself. Civil rights leaders in turn emphasized the Kennedy administration's failure to help the Albany movement. King privately faulted the Albany movement for not focusing on one specific goal—i.e., segregated lunch counters or buses—and for trying to force city officials to negotiate when concessions would more likely have come from downtown merchants. City officials were responsive to voters, few of whom were black, while merchants answered to shoppers, and in southern cities many of those were black. These were important lessons to take from Albany, but the experience there also confirmed in a negative way the larger strategy of SCLC and CORE: for direct action to elicit help from the national government, it had to provoke violence.[20]

By 1962 and 1963, as the tenth anniversary of the *Brown* decision approached, the refusal of southern schools to desegregate was a sore subject among activists and a few federal judges. A handful of black students entered New Orleans schools in 1960, an event that created more scenes of whites harassing black children—tiny elementary students abused as they walked to school every day. Some Georgia schools were desegregated in 1961, leaving only Alabama and Mississippi as the bastions of complete segregation. At the higher-education level, only the universities in those two states remained all white after 1961.

The desegregation of Ole Miss in the fall of 1962 tested again the Kennedy administration's ability to enforce national law. When a federal judge ordered that James Meredith be the first black student at the university, Governor Ross Barnett pandered to the defiant attitudes of white Mississippians by personally taking over the university's administration, refusing to register Meredith for classes, and physically stopping the university trustees from complying with the judge's order. All the while lawless whites were organizing armed resistance. John and Robert Kennedy alternately threatened and cajoled Barnett, who finally suggested that he could save face if federal marshals sneaked Meredith on the campus on a Sunday. He would tell his constituents that the federal government tricked him, but meanwhile, he promised, the state police would keep order. President Kennedy went on national television that Sunday night to announce that the situation was resolved, only to learn later that while he spoke a small force of federal marshals were holed up in an old administration building under siege by a shooting, fire-bombing mob. Finally the president ordered in the U.S. Army, but before they arrived on campus two men had been killed, one of them a reporter, and 166 marshals had been injured. Ole Miss was desegregated but at an awful cost.[21]

The Ole Miss situation delivered to the nation once again the powerful message that white southerners would resort to violence and death to deny African Americans rights that the federal judiciary had plainly said belonged to them. It again taught the Kennedy administration that southern politicians answered not to the Constitution nor to a sense of decency but to the prejudices of their white constituents. The Kennedys also saw once more how quickly events eluded their control and made them look ineffectual.

Their next challenge came in 1963 from Alabama's governor, George C. Wallace. In his 1962 campaign, Wallace had advertised himself as the

George Wallace speaking to avid followers in Alabama in the early 1960s. *Courtesy Birmingham Public Library.*

"fightin' little judge" who had "defied" federal Judge Frank M. Johnson when his old law school chum threatened to jail him if he did not turn over his county's voting records to the U.S. Commission on Civil Rights. In fact, Wallace had secretly capitulated to Johnson, but in his 1962 campaign he sent white Alabamians into convulsions of defiant yelling when he called Judge Johnson an "integrating, scalawagging, carpetbagging liar" and promised to "stand in the schoolhouse door" to prevent desegregation.[22]

Wallace represented a throwback to Tom Heflin and Ben Tillman, the white-nationalist leaders who had dominated southern politics earlier in the century. Political appeals to southern ethnic nationalism had abated after World War II, but the reaction to *Brown* had brought a resurgence of politicians, such as Orval Faubus, who focused entirely on defending white supremacy. Having himself started out as racial moderate and suffered defeat in the 1958 election for governor to a tougher segregationist, Wallace now embraced the southern nationalist's favorite myths. "Today I have stood where once Jefferson Davis stood," Wallace had announced in his inaugural address. "It is very appropriate then that from this Cradle of the Confederacy, this very Heart of the Great Anglo-Saxon Southland," the new governor continued, hitting all the mythic chords of southern memory, "that today we sound the drum for freedom as have our generations of forebears before us done, time and again down through history." Not only did he co-opt the fundamental democratic value, but he accomplished it with his own vivid deployment of language as symbolic action. "Let us rise to the call of freedom-loving blood that is in us," he exhorted his fellow Alabamians, and send "our answer to the tyranny that clanks its chains upon the South." Wallace taunted the forces of change: "In the name of the greatest people that have ever trod this earth, I draw the line in the dust and toss the gauntlet before the feet of tyranny. And I say segregation now, segregation tomorrow, segregation forever." He added a warning to the leaders of the national government: "From this day, from this hour, from this minute, we give the word of a race of honor that we will tolerate their boot in our face no longer."[23]

By the time Wallace made this speech, rational white southerners had recognized that the end of segregation was near, and Wallace was no doubt one who did. But he also knew that most white Alabamians—and many white Americans generally—wanted desperately to hold on to the privileges they enjoyed in a white-supremacist society. He further recognized that the people would reward leaders who gave hope of maintaining white supremacy, over and against the reason that indicated its inevitable demise. His was a perfect cynicism.

III

In 1963 much of the nation would be preoccupied with events in Birmingham. There deep divisions continued within both the black and white

communities, and the conflicts still buffeted any efforts to improve local
race relations. In early 1963 the white business progressives were working
to get white moderates elected to the new mayor and council offices.
Connor and his allies were trying just as hard to maintain segregationist
control in the new government. A group of black businessmen and professionals—led by the insurance executive Arthur G. Gaston, the lawyer
Arthur Shores, and the newspaper editor Emory Jackson—were allied
with the white progressives in the understanding that the new government would radically change race practices in Birmingham. But challenging the "middle-class" black leadership was the Alabama Christian
Movement for Human Rights, led by the Reverend Fred Shuttlesworth,
the city's fierce advocate for direct-action protest. Since the mid-1950s,
Shuttlesworth had been leading demonstrations and filing lawsuits
against segregation in Birmingham, and as a result he had been beaten,
bombed, and harassed for years. The threats on his life only made Shut-

The Rev. Fred Shuttlesworth led the Birmingham protests.
Courtesy Birmingham Public Library.

tlesworth more courageous, more convinced that God was protecting him, and more certain that his methods were correct. During the fall of 1962, he led marches and a boycott of downtown stores that resulted in a secret agreement to remove segregation signs in the stores. But when the agreement was revealed and segregationists began picketing the stores, the merchants put the signs back up. In early 1963, Shuttlesworth announced that he would lead more protests in the city, and that SCLC would help. His protests were scheduled for the precise time that moderate whites and blacks were campaigning to defeat Connor once and for all. The middle-class blacks wanted to give the political change a chance to work, and thus they opposed Shuttlesworth's plans.

King and the SCLC leadership misunderstood the nuances of the Birmingham situation when at Shuttlesworth's behest they agreed to come there to lead a protest drive. King's colleague Ralph Abernathy called the middle-class black leadership "Uncle Toms," and King himself described them as "a few Negroes in the middle class who, because of a degree of academic and economic security, and because at points they profit by segregation, have unconsciously become insensitive to the problems of the masses." The characterization was completely unfair, because within the anti-Shuttlesworth camp were African Americans like Arthur Shores and Emory Jackson who had been challenging white supremacy for 25 years. The reason King came to Birmingham was very simple. "The idea of facing Bull Connor was the thing," Shuttlesworth later explained, because SCLC knew they would have the "spotlight" with which "we might make a confrontation which would bring the nation to its conscience to recognize the injustice." They called the Birmingham operation Project C—for confrontation.[24]

King and the other SCLC leaders were usually less forthright about the provocative strategy that underlay the Birmingham effort. To overcome injustice, King explained, "you must expose them before the light of human conscience and the bar of public opinion, regardless of whatever tensions that exposure generates." He believed that protests in Birmingham would lead to the *"surfacing* of tensions already present," and that once a crisis was precipitated, "the pressure of public opinion becomes an ally in your just cause." Wyatt Tee Walker, the King aide organizing the Birmingham effort, was more straightforward, saying that he "didn't believe in provocation—unless the stakes were right." Demonstrations might be "peaceful and nonviolent," King did say, "but you make people inflict violence on you, so you precipitate violence."[25]

The SCLC leadership came to Birmingham intent on controlling the message that their protests delivered. They scheduled their protests to occur in time for the television reporters to get their film on the nightly news. Walker had morning press briefings where he announced and explained the day's actions. "Anticipating the needs of the press helped us to get our message out to the nation," Andrew Young, the SCLC staff person who worked most closely with the media, later explained. "We had to craft a concise and dramatic message that could be explained in just sixty seconds. That was our strategy." Again, Walker was more to the point: "There never was any more skillful manipulation of the news media than there was in Birmingham."[26]

Shuttlesworth and King agreed to delay the protests until the city election was settled, which meant they ended up waiting until the moderate candidate defeated Connor in the mayoral run-off at the beginning of April 1963. But even as the marches began, Connor and his allies were still challenging the legality of the change of government. Remarkably, both governments occupied City Hall while the appeal went forward. Connor thus maintained control of the Birmingham police and fire department. Good fortune had shined on SCLC leaders: they had deferred to the local moderates in delaying their protest, and though Connor appeared to be defeated, they still got to go against him in Project C.

Having learned the lessons of Albany, King and Shuttlesworth confined the effort to one main demand, desegregation of downtown stores, and aimed it at the merchants not the politicians. They began marches into the central business district, but for four weeks the Birmingham effort yielded little of the dramatic conflict between protestors and segregationists that SCLC desired. Connor's policemen acted with restraint, and the size of the marches remained small. Ten days into the campaign,

King and Abernathy went to the Birmingham jail for violating an injunction. While there King wrote his later famous "letter from the Birmingham Jail," a response to eight local white clergymen who had asked him to stop the protests. Mainly a justification of his strategy and a critique of the moral failings of white Christians, the letter was virtually ignored when it was distributed as he came out of jail. After almost a month of marches, the national media began to leave Birmingham.[27]

To get more troops, a King aide went into Birmingham's black schools and pressed students to join the marches. On May 2 and 3, thousands of schoolchildren of all ages poured into a downtown park singing "We Shall Overcome." The "children's crusade" made Bull Connor snap. Rather than allow the children to flood the central business district, he ordered his fire department to turn high-pressured water on the marchers, and his policemen used their big dogs to push protestors back. The scenes of black students pinned by torrents of water against buildings and chewed by police dogs flashed around the country and the world, the most powerful images yet of white-supremacist violence.[28]

On May 6 thousands more children marched into the park chanting "Freedom, Freedom, Freedom!" Connor's men again brought out the fire hoses and dogs, and the photographers captured the ensuing melee. As the demonstrations continued, a growing crowd of adult onlookers began to throw rocks and bottles at police and firemen. King admonished protestors to practice nonviolence: "The world is watching you," he said. Claude Sitton reported in the *New York Times* that on May 7 between 2,500 and 3,000 blacks "rampaged" through the central business district, having purposely slipped around Connor's troops amassed at the park. "A riot broke out," Sitton wrote, as the firemen raised the pressure on their hoses "so high that the water skinned bark off trees." As the riot was occurring, the leading downtown merchants, then in deliberation about what to do, suddenly agreed to desegregate their stores. A few days later an official settlement was announced, and the Birmingham demonstrations were hailed as a great victory for SCLC and Fred Shuttlesworth personally.[29]

The strategy had worked perfectly. The national media had exposed in Birmingham how whites used violence to enforce black subjugation.

White supremacy was no longer ugly in the abstract, but rather it now had a clear, two-dimensional shape. Because television viewers saw it in motion, with sound, white supremacy was all the more threatening. A newspaper reporter observed that while print photographers captured a realistic image of a big police dog, on television the dog snarled. John Kennedy said that the "shameful scenes" were "much more eloquently reported by the news camera than by any number of explanatory words." The president knew that for most Americans what was shown on television was perceived as reality, whether or not it truly represented it.[30]

By the day of the riot in the Birmingham business district, Martin Luther King had realized that more marching would damage his relations with the White House and thus jeopardize his national political strategy. Robert Kennedy had publicly criticized the use of children, but he also said that the refusal to grant equal rights to blacks in Birmingham made "increasing turmoil inevitable." The concern about violence went

The Birmingham police used dogs to try to stop demonstrators. *Courtesy Birmingham Public Library.*

well beyond Connor's behavior to a worry about the large collection of rock and bottle throwers in the onlooking crowd. The SCLC staff, the Kennedys, and many Birmingham businessmen could easily imagine a massive race riot. And a race riot did indeed materialize a few days later when the motel where the SCLC staff had stayed was bombed, spurring an angry black crowd to begin burning and looting.[31]

Robert Kennedy believed that the best way to keep the lid on racial turmoil was to submit a new, much stronger civil rights bill to Congress. Earlier in 1963, President Kennedy had promoted civil rights legislation focused mainly on easing voting restrictions, but the administration had not pushed it aggressively in the Congress. Now in the aftermath of Birmingham, the New York Times reported, the administration's goal was "to get the South's frustrated Negroes off the streets and into the courts." The president was also worried about the appeal of violence to African Americans and the possibility of leaders who advocated it emerging. "If King loses, worse leaders are going to take his place," he commented privately.[32]

The "worse leaders" referred no doubt to Malcolm X, the Harlem-based minister of the Nation of Islam, who by the spring of 1963 was drawing much attention from the media and the civil rights leadership. A self-educated ex-convict, Malcolm had been preaching black self-respect and hatred for whites on street corners in Harlem for more than ten years. The media had begun to seek out Malcolm, who proved to be a clever television personality. King himself had begun to speak in uncharacteristically harsh terms about the "Black Muslims" in public statements in 1963. Malcolm in turn dismissed all black leaders who attempted to get support from "corrupt" white leaders such as John Kennedy. Compared to Malcolm, King seemed eminently reasonable to the president.[33]

There was nothing reasonable about the governor of Alabama as far as the Kennedys were concerned. Within days of the Birmingham settlement, George Wallace made his "stand in the schoolhouse door" at the University of Alabama. The school had actually been desegregated briefly in 1956, but a mob had driven the lone black student from the campus. The university's board of trustees had for the next six years schemed to deny all subsequent efforts to desegregate, but that ended with a firm order to admit two black students in early 1963, by which time the administration and trustees were ready to accept the inevitable. Staging his stand before federalized Alabama guardsmen, a large contingent of reporters, and a huge national television audience, Wallace audaciously declared that "Alabama is winning this fight against Federal interference because we are awakening the people to the trend toward military dictatorship in this country." He then withdrew, and the desegregation proceeded as planned. Although many would condemn his grandstanding, Wallace knew that his action would endear him to whites fearful of racial change, even if he had done nothing to prevent the end of segregation. Wallace had found the key to electoral glory: Tell white southerners what they wanted to hear, say it belligerently, and then bask in their adoration.[34]

That evening John Kennedy told the nation in a televised address that in the civil rights cause Americans confronted a moral issue. "It is as old as the scriptures and as clear as the American Constitution," Kennedy declared, now delivering the ideological appeal that Martin Luther King had wanted from him. "If an American, because his skin is dark, cannot eat lunch in a restaurant open to the public, if he cannot send his children to the best public school available, if he cannot vote for the public officials who represent him, if, in short, he cannot enjoy the full and free life which all of us want, then who among us would be content to have the color of his skin changed and stand in his place?" The president announced that he was sending to the Congress a new civil rights bill. This legislation would give new powers to enforce voting rights and school desegregation, outlaw discrimination in federally assisted programs, and end segregation in public accommodations. If enacted, it would represent the most significant change in laws governing American race relations since the ratification of the Fourteenth Amendment.[35]

President John F. Kennedy. *Courtesy Library of Congress.*

John Kennedy had committed himself and the executive branch to the understanding of democratic values that the judicial branch had embraced for two decades. It was a significant historical moment, because it meant that large portions of political power were now arrayed against the institutions of white supremacy. Moreover, Kennedy had committed himself to changing the remaining bulwark of white supremacy, the United States Congress, into a supporter of black equality. If he accomplished that, then all three branches would be aligned to support the civil rights cause, and real change would follow.

But history had yet to proceed that far. While much of the nation was watching the president, a white man shot and killed Medgar Evers, the NAACP's field secretary in Mississippi, in front of his home in Jackson. Evers's small children ran to him as he lay dying. To a nation already preoccupied with racial trouble that day, Medgar Evers's assassination confirmed the message of unbridled white violence in the South.

IV

The Birmingham demonstrations seemed to trigger protests across the South. Within weeks direct-action campaigns had begun in Gadsden, Alabama; Savannah, Georgia; Cambridge, Maryland; and Farmville and Danville, Virginia. The protests brought results: in the weeks after the Birmingham demonstrations, the Justice Department reported that 143 cities had desegregated public accommodations. That year there were four times as many civil rights protests in the United States than there had been in 1962, and far more than in any year in American history before or since. The protests of 1963 persuaded at least half of all Americans that civil rights was the most pressing problem facing the nation. Prior to the Birmingham demonstrations, only about 5 percent of Americans believed that to be true. "In the summer of 1963," King later wrote, "the Negroes of America wrote an emancipation proclamation to themselves." The Negro was "shedding himself of his fear," King said privately, "and my real worry is how we will keep this fearlessness from rising to violent proportions." He was encountering "more bitterness because things haven't moved fast enough."[36]

The mounting spirit of protest achieved its most public expression in the march on Washington in late August. It resurrected A. Philip Randolph's aborted 1941 march for fair employment, and this march too was opposed by the president. John Kennedy feared that it might invite violence in the capital and alienate midwestern Republicans whose votes he needed for the civil rights bill. He argued to the civil rights leadership that they had moved into a new legislative phase that required new tactics, but he persuaded no one. In fact, the march delivered a message of peace, reconciliation, and deliverance from injustice. About two hundred thousand people came, the *New York Times* reported, "in the spirit of a church outing." There was not a hint of violence nor a note of discord in the ceremony, though intense pressure had been put on SNCC's spokesman not to criticize the Kennedy administration. The throng gathered at the Lincoln Memorial, the place most symbolic of freedom and equality to African Americans, where people had come to hear Marian Anderson in 1939. Various celebrities sang, and many civil rights leaders made remarks, but the main address was reserved for Martin Luther King, Jr., who delivered here his great sermon about his dream for America.[37]

He naturally cast it in the context of the promise of the nation's democratic values: When the founders of the republic created the Constitution and the Declaration of Independence, he declared, "they were signing a promissory note to which every American was to fall heir." His vision was that "one day this nation will rise up and live out the true meaning of its creed." He dreamt that "the sons of former slaves and the sons of former slaveowners will be able to sit down together at the table of brotherhood," that even Mississippi might be "transformed into an oasis of freedom and justice," and that his own children would "one day live in a nation where they will not be judged by the color of their skin but by the content of their character." He ended with the prophecy of deliverance: "With this faith we will be able to transform the jangling discords of our nation into a beautiful symphony of brotherhood.... Free at last, free at last; thank God Almighty, we are free at last."[38]

It was perhaps the most powerful language of symbolic action ever heard by Americans: people were to "rise up and live out" something good, and to "sit down together" in love and peace, and to "transform" their society and their thinking. Martin Luther King the prophet had wisely promised not only that blacks would soon have freedom and equality but also that whites would get something—peace and harmony.

King's message went far beyond the roaring throng in front of the Lincoln Memorial. Television networks carried the event live. The march on Washington coincided with a big increase in television news focus on African Americans and their special concerns. Five days later NBC cancelled its entertainment programming for a three-hour documentary on the civil rights movement, *The American Revolution of '63*, which was twice as long as any news documentary had been up to that time. "Television put Negro Americans into the living rooms of tens of millions of white Americans for the first time," the president of NBC later wrote. He might also have added that television put the civil rights movement into most black homes in the United States, thus spreading the message of protest—and deliverance—to all African Americans. Within a few weeks of the march, all the networks moved from a 15-minute to a 30-minute format, which required much more visual material. At the time of this change, the producer of NBC's nightly news wrote to his staff about how to meet the new challenge: "Every news story should, without any sacrifice of probity or responsibility, display the attributes of fiction, of drama. It should have structure and conflict, problem and denouement, rising action and falling action, a beginning, a middle and an end." At that moment the best news drama in the United States was the civil rights movement.[39]

Birmingham returned to center stage within days of the march on Washington. Several Alabama schools were due to desegregate in early September, and maintaining his cynical strategy of defiance, George Wallace wanted to prevent or delay school desegregation in Birmingham and three other Alabama cities. If integration happened peacefully, even in a token way, segregation as a political issue might be lost to him. He intended to show that desegregation was a threat to public order that he must stop, but he needed evidence of potential violence. With the encouragement of Wallace and his minions, segregationists in Birmingham organized rallies and pickets against desegregation throughout the summer of 1963. When the Birmingham school system and Alabama's federal judges stood firm against Wallace, the desegregation went off as planned without much violence. But the segregationists kept agitating in the days following the opening of school by organizing prosegregation motorcades of white students and marches on city hall. Racial tension was thus at a very high level when on the morning of September 15 several local Klansmen exploded a bomb at the Sixteenth Street Baptist Church, killing four black girls there for Sunday school.[40]

The murders in Birmingham represented the pinnacle of violence in a year of brutality. The scenes had come in rapid succession—fire hoses knocking people against walls, dogs chewing demonstrators, the bloody carport where Medgar Evers had died, and then the bombed-out church. Americans wanted the violence somehow to stop.

V

The violence gave John Kennedy a sense of urgency in the fall of 1963 about winning support for his civil rights bill. He strengthened it by adding a section outlawing employment discrimination, though he knew that provision stirred opposition among blue-collar whites in the North. Neither he nor his staff had been very effective in getting legislation through the Congress, and some in the White House seriously doubted that the civil rights bill would get out of the Senate. Even though polls showed that 60 percent of Americans favored the bill, loud objections were voiced about desegregating public accommodations. Not surprisingly their clearest articulation came from Richard Russell: "The use of federal power to force the owner of a dining hall or swimming pool to unwillingly accept those of a different race as guests creates a new and special right for Negroes in derogation of the property rights of all of our people to own and control the fruits of their labor and ingenuity." The civil rights bill was merely a calculated strategy for the 1964 presidential election, he insisted, to get Kennedy "all the big-city states where the negro vote is the balance of power." In fact, most of the president's political advisers thought the bill was electoral suicide and hoped that somehow compromises in the bill would save him.[41]

Russell planned to fight a protracted battle against the bill and hoped that black discontent and violence would ultimately dissipate the current public support for it. Because of the Senate's rules on cloture—a vote to stop debate on a measure—he needed only one-third of the Senate to tie up legislation, and up to this time, he had never lost a cloture vote on a civil rights bill. Between the southern Democratic bloc and the Republicans who went along when asked, he had easily found the necessary 34 votes. But the southern bloc had shrunk to 18 senators, and the support for civil rights among those from outside the South had risen sharply in the last few years. By late 1963, Senator Hubert Humphrey, the floor manager for the civil rights bill, counted 51 senators firmly committed to strong legislation.[42]

It was the climactic act of violence in 1963, John Kennedy's assassination, that provided the necessary force to push the bill through Congress. "No memorial oration or eulogy could more eloquently honor President Kennedy's memory," Lyndon Johnson declared in his first address to Congress as president, "than the earliest possible passage of the civil rights bill for which he fought so long." The necessary force was Johnson himself. Long before he entered the White House, Johnson had recognized that the civil rights issue mainly required moral leadership from the president. He had said privately that "what Negroes are really seeking is moral force and to be sure we're on their side." Although Johnson had been a segregationist early in his career, his closest associates insisted he was personally free of racial bigotry, a reflection, they said, of his deep empathy for the poor people of Texas. Johnson proved to be the most effective president since Franklin Roosevelt in using the presidential pulpit to articulate the larger meaning of American's democratic values, and the most committed since Abraham Lincoln to applying them to race reform. No president but the Great Emancipator demonstrated more clearly that he was "for" African Americans.[43]

Johnson advised civil rights advocates in Congress to push for the strongest bill possible, not to compromise away the coercive power needed to enforce real equality as he had done when he was Senate majority leader. Johnson knew that the votes were there to get a powerful bill if they could win a vote on cloture. He advised Humphrey to court the Senate minority leader, Everett Dirksen, to get enough Republican votes for cloture. Through the winter and spring of 1964, the Senate debated the bill. To get Dirksen's support, changes were made in Title VII, which covered employment discrimination. Sections were added explicitly stating that employers could continue to give an "ability test" and that no hiring quota could be imposed on an employer. Indeed, Humphrey stated in debate that Title VII did not "require an employer to achieve any sort of racial balance in his work force by giving preferential treatment to any individual." When Dirksen pronounced his backing, everyone knew that cloture was secure. In July, Lyndon Johnson signed the Civil Rights Act of 1964 into law.[44]

The largest share of credit for passage was due SCLC's campaign in

Birmingham. Its strategy of provocative protest had yielded the exposure of the violence inherent in white supremacy, and that brutality pushed American public opinion strongly to the side of laws to protect black rights. Martin Luther King's ability to advance the protest amid much conflict and controversy accounted for much of the success, as did his ability to project a powerful and consistent ideological message. John Kennedy came late to a moral position, but once there he moved forward forthrightly until the day he died. Lyndon Johnson translated Kennedy's martyrdom into the final reason for action on civil rights. His understanding of congressional politics assured that the legislative branch could be brought finally to the side of freedom and equality. With all three branches of the national government now lined up against white supremacy, American race relations began to change in ways that few had believed was possible.

VI

Even as national public opinion rallied to the cause of civil rights in 1963 and 1964, race competition for space and economic opportunity persisted. The housing battle continued in Chicago, with black protests resulting in violence during August 1963. At the same time, Thomas Poindexter, the Detroit city councilman who had long defended whites' rights to maintain all-white neighborhoods, was called to testify against the proposed civil rights bill. Claiming that "99 percent" of Detroit whites were opposed to Kennedy's bill, Poindexter insisted that housing integration always brought vice, prostitution, gambling, and drugs. The decline of moral standards led to "blight and decay" and for white residents "the loss of their homes and savings." Poindexter did not change many votes on the bill, but as the spokesman for Detroit's two hundred white neighborhood organizations, he revealed a large reservoir of white discontent.[45]

Taking advantage of the notoriety he earned at the schoolhouse door, George Wallace in the spring of 1964 entered several Democratic presidential primaries in which he appealed constantly to blue-collar whites' status concerns. He told a large crowd of white ethnics in Milwaukee that the civil rights bill about to pass would wreak havoc on their neighborhood schools, "destroy the union seniority system and impose racial quotas," and make it "impossible for a home owner to sell his home to whomever he chose." In Baltimore he informed a blue-collar audience that under the new law, the federal government would tell an employer who could be hired. "If a man's got 100 Japanese-Lutherans working for him and there's 100 Chinese-Baptists unemployed, he's got to let some of the Japanese-Lutherans go so he can make room for some of the Chinese-Baptists." What does that do to your seniority rights? he asked, answering with righteous anger: "It destroys them!" Wallace received 34 percent of the votes in Wisconsin's Democratic primary, 30 percent in Indiana, and 43 percent in Maryland—a show of strength that shocked most political observers.[46]

Wallace's strength reflected the rising racial tension in many northern cities in 1964. In 1963 and 1964 there were bitter conflicts over school desegregation and inadequate support for majority-black schools in New York, Chicago, and Cleveland. In July 1964 a large riot enveloped Harlem in New York City after a policeman shot a young African American during an arrest. Protests degenerated into a battle between blacks and the New York police, and then mobs burned and looted property and attacked whites for almost a week. The Harlem riot was to many northern whites the realization of the long-held fears about the growing black presence in their cities. It established a pattern for race disorder: An incident between police and a black man resulted in police violence, to which black residents responded with wholesale property destruction and theft. Police in turn meted out more violence. By the time calm was restored, dozens were dead or injured, millions of dollars of property was destroyed, and Americans were left wondering if their cities could be inhabited safely.[47]

Still, in 1964 most Americans thought of the South when contemplating racial violence. By then SNCC had been organizing voting efforts in Mississippi for three years, though it usually worked in collaboration with older activists. The organization's workers suffered regular beatings and harassment, but they set a powerful example of courage and determination in the South's most dangerous place to work for civil rights. They drew into the movement equally tough local farmers and domestic workers, many of them women, including Fannie Lou Hamer of Ruleville in the Delta. Originally a sharecropper, Hamer had advanced to timekeeper on a large plantation when she attended a SNCC meeting and was inspired to attempt to register to vote. Her employer told her either to withdraw the application to vote or be fired, whereupon Hamer replied: "I didn't go down there to register for you. I went down there to register for myself." She was fired and forced to move from the plantation, but as a result she became a mainstay of SNCC's efforts in the Delta.[48]

Activists with SNCC had grown frustrated at the indifference of those outside the Magnolia State to Mississippi's belligerent denial of black rights. National news coverage of civil rights issues in Mississippi focused on the big events such as the desegregation of Ole Miss and the

Fannie Lou Hamer. *Courtesy Library of Congress.*

murder of Medgar Evers, whereas SNCC workers organized day in and day out to develop autonomous institutions and independent thinking among black Mississippians. Newsmen almost never reported on these slow processes during the early 1960s.

Thus was conceived the Mississippi Summer Project of 1964, which brought a thousand northern white college students to the state. More important than their labor in the field was the national attention that their presence in the state would bring. "We knew that if we had brought in a thousand blacks," one of the project organizers later said, "the country would have watched them [be] slaughtered without doing anything about it." But if someone was going to die to expose the violence of Mississippi, "the death of a white college student would bring on more attention." The project had not quite begun when three of its participants disappeared from the Neshoba County jail. James Cheney, Michael Schwerner, and Andrew Goodman—a black Mississippian and two white northerners—had been arrested, released from jail, and then murdered by a group of Klansmen. The three were officially missing for many weeks as law enforcement officials, now including the FBI, hunted for their bodies, which were finally recovered in an earthen dam. The national media swarmed Mississippi throughout the summer of 1964, giving the state more attention than it had ever received and reinforcing the message of southern immorality. Again the movement strategy of creating a situation to invite white violence had worked, and again the nation's attention was focused on southern disregard for black rights.[49]

The Summer Project advanced the creation of the Mississippi Freedom Democratic Party (MFDP), founded to challenge the established Democratic Party that white supremacists dominated and used to maintain their racial control. The Freedom Democrats insisted that they were the only *democratic* party in Mississippi, because anyone, regardless of race, could join them. With that claim, the MFDP sent a delegation to the 1964 Democratic convention and demanded to be seated as the real Democrats from Mississippi. Testifying before the party's credentials committee, Fannie Lou Hamer riveted a national television audience with stories of the brutality she had been through as a SNCC worker. But the powers of the national Democratic Party, especially Lyndon

Johnson, did not want a divisive racial fight to mar the president's nomination. The MFDP was offered a token two seats in the convention. "We didn't come all this way for no two seats," Hamer answered with disgust, and the Freedom Democrats went home.[50]

The MFDP experience revealed how rapidly the civil rights agenda was evolving and what frustration new expectations could create. Within a few months, African Americans in Mississippi had moved from simply trying to get registered to vote without being killed to making legitimate claims for control of the state's most important political institution. With the Civil Rights Act, the national government had in effect recognized blacks' right to full equality in American life, and to activists in the MFDP that should have translated immediately into real power in the political sphere, especially because they were the only folks in Mississippi who respected democratic values. But change did not come *that* rapidly in 1964. The Freedom Democrats left the convention embittered about the political system.

The MFDP frustrations foreshadowed a fundamental disappointment that African Americans would know in the years ahead. By 1964 most black people understood their deprivations in terms of rights—to vote, to be served at a lunch counter, to go to a good school, to get justice in the courts. The civil rights movement had promoted the ideological bases for these rights through the constant discussion of freedom, equality, and democracy. But with the passage of the Civil Rights Act, the matter of blacks' having those rights was settled, at least formally. New advances would depend on finding sources other than ideology—political or economic power, for example—on which to base future progress. For blacks in the transformed South, that would prove to be a bigger challenge than anyone could imagine in 1964.

VII

There was work left to do in securing basic rights, especially the vote. Boards of registrars in southern counties still had the power to deny a black person's attempt to register simply by making the application process impossibly difficult. Nowhere was this truer than in Selma, Alabama. SNCC had begun to protest there in 1963, and local activists had continued in 1964 when a change of city government led them to believe that progress was possible. In early 1965, SCLC committed to help. The Selma movement would follow a similar pattern to the Freedom Rides and the Birmingham demonstrations: protests elicited violent behavior from local whites, which was communicated to a national audience and resulted in pressure for new national laws.[51]

The key to make the strategy work in Selma was Sheriff James Clark, known for his violence toward protestors. Clark captured the attention of reporters in January 1965 when he grabbed the leader of the Selma Voting League, the elderly Amelia Boynton, by the collar and pushed her a half block down a Selma street. Both the *New York Times* and the *Washington Post* ran photographs of this incident, as they did Clark's clubbing of another black woman a few days later. "I wish you would hit me, you scum," Annie Lee Cooper spat at Clark as he hovered above her, whereupon, according to the *Times*, the sheriff "brought his billy club down on her head with a whack that was heard throughout the crowd gathered in the street." Marches were aimed directly at Clark. By early February congressmen were commenting on the Selma protests. Soon 31 northern and western Republicans called for stronger voting legislation. The *Times* stated that media reports on Clark's treatment of blacks explained much of the new support.[52]

Protests spread to nearby towns, and at one, Alabama state troopers shot Jimmie Lee Jackson, a marcher. Someone sprayed black paint over the lens of NBC's camera and knocked its reporter Richard Valeriani unconscious. The next day Valeriani broadcast a report from his hospital bed with his head bandaged and his speech slurred. When Jackson died a few days later, protest leaders in Selma decided to march to Montgomery to deliver a set of grievances to Governor Wallace. It was this march that precipitated Bloody Sunday, which had brought George Leonard to Selma. Leonard had left Selma safely after the one foreshortened march, but another sojourner, a Boston Unitarian minister named James Reeb, was beaten severely by white men in Selma and died two days later, another martyr to southern violence.[53]

In the aftermath of Bloody Sunday, 50 members of the U.S. Congress condemned Alabama officials and demanded an immediate and forceful voting rights bill. The Justice Department prepared a new bill giving the federal government authority to take over registration processes in southern counties suspected of denying blacks the franchise. Lyndon Johnson announced the new bill to the Congress in a televised address in which he said that the Selma events represented "the effort of American Negroes to secure for themselves the full blessings of American life." Then in his slow Texas twang, Johnson made the moral case for the legislation. "Their cause must be our cause too. Because it is not just Negroes, but really it is all of us, who must overcome the crippling legacy of bigotry and injustice. And we shall overcome."[54]

Selma now riveted the nation's attention. There were sympathy protests in most American cities. Judge Frank Johnson had enjoined black leaders from further marches while he held almost two weeks of hear-

Marchers leaving Selma a second time, now with much federal protection. *Courtesy AP/ Wideworld Photos.*

ings on whether the protest should go forward. All the while support for action in Selma built. Thousands of Americans began the same pilgrimage that George Leonard had already made. When Johnson lifted his injunction, the march began again, and for five days a motley troop walked the 50 miles of Highway 80 to Montgomery. As they approached the state capitol, the marchers grew to a throng of 30,000 people.[55]

On March 25, 1965, the march came to a halt near the front of the Alabama state capitol, where just two years before, George Wallace had promised "Segregation forever!" There Martin Luther King gave what would prove to be the valedictory address, if not the benediction, of the civil rights movement. He reflected on the sequence of events that had brought them to that moment in history. Only ten years earlier here in Montgomery, he said, a "new philosophy was born of the Negro strug-gle," when for the first time an entire black community had confronted "its age-old oppressors." After Montgomery there had been conflicts in many places, but only when "the colossus of segregation" was attacked in Birmingham did "the conscience of America begin to bleed." And then came Selma: "There never was a moment in American history," he pronounced amid many cries of affirmation from the multitude before him, "more honorable and more inspiring than the pilgrimage of clergy-men and laymen of every race and faith pouring into Selma to face dan-ger at the side of its embattled Negroes." Over the past decade, the civil rights movement had gone "from Montgomery to Birmingham, from Birmingham to Selma, from Selma back to Montgomery, a trail wound in a circle long and often bloody, yet it has become a highway up from darkness."

Never had Martin Luther King waxed more prophetic than this day. He insisted that their work was not done, that they would have to keep marching against segregated housing and schools and against poverty. But people wanted to know how long it would be before the job was done. King ended with his most powerful assertion yet that moral right-eousness would prevail: "I come to say to you this afternoon however difficult the moment, however frustrating the hour, it will not be long, because truth crushed to earth will rise again. How long? Not long, because no lie can live forever. . . . How long? Not long, because the arc of the moral universe is long but it bends toward justice."[56]

The Voting Rights Act met relatively weak resistance in Congress— liberals were stronger, some younger southerners broke ranks to support it, and the old segregationists lacked the passion to stand for long against the right to vote. Lyndon Johnson signed it into law the following August. There was a straight line between the events at Selma and the new law. "Television made it possible," the Justice Department's civil rights chief later declared, citing the avalanche of letters to Washington that referred to the television images of Bloody Sunday. "Everybody in the business thought that."[57]

The passage of the Voting Rights Act signaled the official demise of white supremacy, the end of all legitimacy for the ideology of race in the United States. It and the Civil Rights Act represented huge achievements for Martin Luther King and the millions of African Americans who supported his drive to change their status in American life. In only five years on that "trail wound in a circle long and often bloody," African Americans had forced *their* nation to break with centuries of racial exploitation, to reclaim Abraham Lincoln's understanding of democratic values, and to revise again what they meant. So historic a change in the laws and ideas governing human relations was also a tribute to John Kennedy and, especially, Lyndon Johnson for enabling the civil rights movement to fulfill its purpose. They too had helped to redefine freedom, equality, and democracy.

No one could see it in 1965, but the triumph of the civil rights movement, and the official demise of white supremacy, opened fundamental questions about how Americans would understand their status. Indeed for most Americans, and virtually everyone in the South, race shaped their sense of honor and prestige more than any other social descriptor. Would that sense of race-based status simply go away in the absence of a legally and politically enforced white supremacy? Few people who had grown up in the racially prescribed society could imagine one where race did not matter, but then almost no one in January 1960 would have predicted the changes made in just five years. In the light of the prophet King's dream, the question could be entertained.

In fact, more people were thinking about the next step in the movement for race reform. Selma had taught activists again that changes in blacks' conditions came swiftly and completely when the federal government acted on their behalf. Unfortunately for them, that lesson would not generally apply after 1965. Americans' commitment to reform has historically been a limited one, and the ability to stay focused on injustices has always been inhibited by the inclination to self-righteousness. Americans' understandings of national values and racial problems would continue to evolve very rapidly in the tumultuous times of the late 1960s, and they would move in directions unfavorable to those who had led the long journey on the highway up from darkness.

PART THREE

THE MEANING OF EQUALITY, 1965–2000

CHAPTER 7

THE FEAR OF THE NEGRO

ON AUGUST 11, 1965, a hot night in the Watts section of Los Angeles, a highway patrolman stopped a young black man for speeding, discovered that he was drunk, and arrested him. A crowd appeared, including the mother of the man in custody, and the patrolman summoned help. A fight ensued between police and local residents, who threw rocks at passing cars. The next night more rock throwing occurred, much of it at storefronts. While reporting on the disorder, several newsmen were attacked by rock throwers, and one television soundman was beaten. The *Los Angeles Times*, which had no African-American reporters on its staff, sent Robert Richardson, a 24-year-old black advertising salesman, to report on Watts. "It was the most terrifying thing I've ever seen in my life," Richardson wrote in his first report. "It's a wonder anyone with white skin got out of there alive." He saw a white couple in their sixties pulled from their car and "beaten and kicked until their faces, hands and clothing were bloody," and "those not hitting and kicking the couple were standing there shouting 'Kill! Kill!'" Two white men were dragged from their wrecked car and beaten severely, and when black ministers came to their rescue the mob called them hypocrites. Black policemen who tried to disperse crowds "were jeered at, sworn at, called traitors and stoned."

Richardson wrote that "light-skinned Negroes such as myself were targets of rocks and bottles until someone standing nearby would shout, 'He's blood,' or 'He's a brother—lay off!'" After shots were fired at his car, he learned to shout "Burn, baby, burn!" It had been the exhortation of a local disc jockey about music he liked, but the rioters appropriated it as an oath of allegiance and a cheer for wanton destruction.

Then on the morning of August 13, a large crowd gathered in the Watts business district and began breaking windows and looting. Hundreds of women and children from nearby housing projects participated in the wholesale stealing. "Everybody got in the looting—children, grownups, old men and women," Richardson wrote. Looters were purposeful: They stripped only white businesses, because black businessmen put signs in their windows identifying themselves as "Soul Brother" or "Blood Brother." After looting, he reported, "everybody started drinking—even little kids 8 or 9 years old." That was when the cry went up, "Let's go where Whitey lives!" Local police tried for three days to control the disorder but failed. On the fourth day the National Guard moved into Watts and finally did end it. Six days of looting, arson, and sniping yielded 34 deaths and hundreds of injuries, four thousand arrests, and $35 million of property destroyed.[1]

Robert Richardson won a Pulitzer Prize for his reporting on Watts, in part because he was one of the few reporters with the courage to stay on the streets. In the face of such danger, one Los Angeles television station dispatched a helicopter to the riot. The newsman inflamed his report with spontaneous commentary and unconfirmed reports, and, according to one observer, he "repetitiously harangued his audience into a pitch of excitement almost unbearable." Competition among the city's seven television stations caused other reporters to ratchet up their coverage with breathless "this-is-war" accounts of uncontrolled violence. Images of chaos in Los Angeles spread across the country on television reports.[2]

The Watts riot came just five days after Lyndon Johnson had signed the Voting Rights Act into law, and only hours after the first federal voting referees moved into recalcitrant southern counties and began registering black voters by the hundred. Watts instantaneously altered the image that African Americans projected into the national media—from the long-suffering and peaceful southern Negroes to the thieving, fire-bombing black racists of urban Los Angeles. The violence, real and symbolic, now emanated from blacks and posed a direct threat to whites. The majority of Americans were consistent in this: They recoiled from the source of violence and sympathized with the object of it. What television and the rest of the media gave to the civil rights movement—the image of blacks' suffering from white violence—it could also take away. And it did, starting with Watts.

Watts canceled the expectation among sympathetic whites, and many African Americans too, that the great reforms of 1964 and 1965 would bring forth a time of racial harmony. Violence in the South had been punished with strong national action on the assumption, made by John Kennedy and others in 1963, that only real changes in blacks' conditions would prevent social disorder. Now whites' reward for having acted cor-

Rioters in Watts, 1965. *Courtesy AP/Wideworld Photos.*

rectly seemed to be black violence aimed at them. Whites felt far less secure after several years of addressing African Americans' grievances than they had before all the reform efforts began.

Why did they riot? Americans would ask this question for years, because Watts would prove to be only one point on a continuum of urban riots that had begun in Harlem in 1964 and that would last through 1968. Many whites believed at the time that radicals, perhaps foreign in origin, had instigated them. Certain structural realities were correctly identified as causes: poverty, discrimination, and bigoted police all made ghetto life hard. But they had existed for decades and never had anything quite like Watts occurred.

Robert Richardson asked Watts residents why they rioted and got one answer screamed at him: "We are going to put the fear of the Negro into these white people because they do not have the fear of God." Asked the same question, a black activist explained that Watts residents had seen all the concern about blacks in the South, but "there wasn't a damn soul paying one bit of attention to what was going on in Watts." So African Americans in Los Angeles "just spontaneously rose up one day and said: 'Fuck it! We're hungry. Our schools stink.'" They had tried seeking integration and gotten little attention. "Now we've got to go another way." Martin Luther King and Bayard Rustin toured the area in the riot's aftermath, and a young Watts resident told them, "We won!" Looking around at the destruction, an incredulous Rustin asked how he could believe that, to which the young man replied, "Because we made the whole world pay attention."[3]

The riots were a demand for the American public to pay attention to inner-city problems in the way that racial problems in the South had been highlighted in the previous few years. Bad housing and poor schools had existed in black ghettoes in American cities since World War I, but generally those problems had been ignored or covered up. They had gotten progressively worse, especially with the continued high levels of black migration into big cities throughout the 1950s and into the 1960s. Good job opportunities, especially the blue-collar positions requiring minimal education, had long since been exhausted in the inner cities, and as a result unemployment, especially among young adults, was extremely high. Prospects for finding high-wage work seemed dim. Frustration and anger naturally followed.

A later study showed that rioters tended to come not from the "riffraff" of the ghetto—the least-educated, least likely to work, disoriented recent southern arrivals—but from longtime residents who worked most of the time. As compared with those who had not rioted, self-identified looters and firebombers were more likely to believe that they deserved a better job but that discrimination kept them from having it; that whites deserved their hatred; that well-to-do Negroes were as bad as whites; and that the United States was not a country worth fighting for. These were not new opinions, because they were similar to what people had thought in Harlem, for example, in the 1930s and early 1940s. In his reporting on the 1943 Harlem riot, Ralph Ellison suggested that the basic motivation for rioting had been revenge, and that theory remained a plausible summary explanation for Watts.[4]

One explanation for the timing of the riots lay in the developments in mass communication that enabled the civil rights movement's successes in 1964 and 1965. The same television that brought the shocking images of white violence in the South also delivered the American consumer culture, with its constant flow of advertisements about what was needed for the good life. In the pre-electronic age, poor Americans had not had the 24-hour visual reminders of what material advantages they were missing, but by 1965, when virtually every American home, including ghetto flats, had the tube, they saw it every day. When combined with the message that something was being done about black conditions in the South, the disparity between ghetto reality and American material possibilities may have provoked some ghetto residents to act. Once the media had shown how people in Watts reacted to their plight, ghetto residents in dozens of American cities knew what they could do to demonstrate their own frustration in a way that got the nation's attention.

The riot came when Lyndon Johnson was moving into his next phase of legislative action to address race problems. In June 1965 he had announced that the next challenge was to ensure "equality as a fact and equality as a result." President Johnson argued that "you do not take a person who for years has been hobbled by chains and liberate him, bring him up to the starting line of a race and then say, you're free to compete with all the others, and justly believe that you have been completely fair." Johnson saw that, with segregation outlawed and political rights more nearly guaranteed, the real expansion of equality would come with greater economic power among minorities. Some effort to make up for past discrimination with remedial action was needed to overcome the burden of past discrimination.[5]

Johnson had already suggested some of his means for improving minorities' chances in his "War on Poverty." At the same time he was pushing for the 1964 Civil Rights Act, he had sponsored the most ambitious antipoverty legislation in U.S. history, again building on plans originated in the Kennedy administration. True equality of opportunity for the one-fifth of Americans who lived in poverty, Johnson believed, required more economic and educational assistance than they now received. The centerpiece was the Equal Opportunity Act of 1964, which established a cluster of new welfare initiatives, among them the Commu-

President Lyndon B. Johnson. *Courtesy Library of Congress.*

nity Action Program, which set up locally based agencies to plan and administer antipoverty projects; Head Start, a preschool program for poor children; and the Job Corps to train unemployed youth in schools. Now in 1965, Johnson prevailed on the Congress for new federal action in health care with the Medicare program, in education with the Elementary and Secondary School Act, and in environmental safety with antipollution acts. These measures represented the greatest volume of legislative action since Franklin Roosevelt's first administration.

At the same time Johnson was escalating American military engagement in Vietnam. Here Johnson's in-for-a-dime-in-for-a-dollar impulse was manifest, just as it was in his expansive domestic agenda. Eisenhower and Kennedy had supported American involvement in Southeast Asia as necessary to Cold War policy, but with limited military commitment. Johnson had grown pessimistic about the effectiveness of bombing campaigns on North Vietnam. In July 1965, just days before he signed the Voting Rights Act and the destruction in Watts occurred, Johnson ordered 50,000 additional ground troops sent to Vietnam, taking the number to 125,000. By the end of 1966, there would be 400,000 troops there.[6]

Johnson's rapid escalation in Vietnam reasserted American nationalism to the forefront of public consciousness. He put the nation's honor on the line in faraway jungles, and he clung to the belief that American security depended on a victorious outcome there. And he did not tolerate kindly persons who questioned the logic or level of his commitment, including prominent civil rights leaders. James Farmer of CORE declared that the United States could not fight poverty and bigotry at home while "pouring billions down the drain in a war against people in Viet Nam." Martin Luther King said "the war in Viet Nam must be stopped." Johnson took King's open disagreement as a personal betrayal from someone whose civil rights agenda he had personally pushed into American law. King believed that the war and civil rights both raised issues about whether people of color could enjoy freedom over the opposition of entrenched powers. Johnson insisted the concerns were completely separate: protecting blacks' civil rights bore no relation to stopping the spread of communism in Asia. Two men of equally strong resolve about their ability to know moral truth had reached an unfortunate impasse. Their disaffection personified the way competing values would undermine the civil rights movement.[7]

The rift between the civil rights leadership and Lyndon Johnson deepened just after the Watts riots with the release of a government study, *The Negro Family: The Case for National Action.* Daniel Patrick Moynihan, assistant secretary of labor, had prepared the report on black poverty in which he suggested that, despite the great gains of the civil rights movement, African Americans as a group were not progressing economically. Thinking about how to make equality a "fact" as the president had promised, Moynihan offered an astute assessment of the limits of Americans' understanding of equality. "The demand for Equality of Opportunity has been generally perceived by white Americans as a demand for liberty, a demand not to be excluded from the competitions of life—at the polling place, in the scholarship examinations, at the personnel office, on the housing market," Moynihan wrote. But by no means did liberty produce equality: "On the contrary, to the extent that winners imply losers, equality of opportunity almost insures inequality of results." Blacks were demanding equality in "group results" and "a distribution of achievements among Negroes roughly comparable to that among whites." Moynihan believed that "ethnic politics" in the United States had worked to distribute opportunities and outcomes about equally among ethnic groups, but most whites failed to see the importance of equal results. To ensure that blacks received a "distribution of success and failure" that was "roughly comparable to that within other groups," Moynihan called for an antipoverty effort to bolster the legislation passed that ended segregation and disfranchisement.[8]

The achievement of equal results presented a large challenge, Moynihan suggested, because the "Negro social structure, in particular the Negro family, battered and harassed by discrimination, injustice, and uprooting, is in the deepest trouble." Moynihan detailed problems of the African-American family: A black child was eight times more likely than a white to be born out of wedlock, and the disparity was growing; the number of children supported by federal welfare was rising rapidly, even as black male unemployment was trending downward; there were three times as many female-headed households among blacks as whites, and the difference was increasing. Moynihan laid out the historical circumstances—slavery, white supremacy, migration to cities—that accounted for most of the differences, but still he contended that the black family represented a "tangle of pathology capable of perpetuating itself without assistance from the white world." The problem of black family structure had to be addressed before hope for a reasonable equality of condition could be achieved, Moynihan argued, and that necessarily would come with an expanded social-welfare effort.[9]

The Moynihan report was released at the moment when looters and firebombers in Watts were reshaping the image of African Americans in the nation's media. But rather than seeing the connection between the sociological analysis and the awful current reality that suggested its accuracy, civil rights activists and social scientists responded with fury at Moynihan. James Farmer of CORE wrote that Moynihan had provided a "massive academic cop-out for the white conscience and clearly implied that Negroes in this nation will never secure a substantial measure of freedom until we learn to behave ourselves and stop buying Cadillacs instead of bread." A white psychologist denounced Moynihan for "blaming the victim" and used the phrase for the title of his book-length assault on the report. So incensed were 60 religious and civil rights organizations that they demanded that "the question of 'family stability' be stricken entirely" from future discussions of a civil rights agenda. Under fire, the White House postponed its planned conference to discuss how to achieve real social equality and began avoiding substantive debate. "Obviously one can no longer address oneself to the subject of the Negro family," Moynihan confided to a friend in the White House.[10]

The reaction to the report set the tone for how civil rights leaders and liberal academics would deal in the future with social problems among African Americans. Although several social scientists had already examined a "culture of poverty" among blacks and found that social pathologies were handed down, none had engendered the anger that Moynihan had. By the end of 1965, it was clear that some issues could not be broached without igniting intense emotions among many blacks and some white sympathizers. Thus was born an elephant in the living room of American race reform. The casualty of the controversy proved to be not Moynihan, who as a result of the controversy moved to the front rank of policy intellectuals in the United States, but frank discussion about how to achieve "equality as a fact." In the absence of honest consideration of social reality in the ghetto, people on the left and right often took rigid, polemical positions about the meaning of equality.[11]

It was astonishing how a few events, all taking place within a few weeks, had reordered priorities in American life far more swiftly than the civil rights movement had arranged them. Between Lyndon Johnson's pronouncement that "We *shall* overcome!" in March and the midsummer tumult of Vietnam escalation, Watts rioting, and Moynihan's report, the alignment of political power that had brought the official end of segregation had gone awry. There was emerging a furious disagreement over the meaning of equality but paradoxically a refusal in some quarters to discuss its competing definitions.

By late 1965 the argument about equality's meaning had attracted participants from across the political spectrum. One line of thought raised questions about whether compensatory policies such as Moynihan's proposed welfare expansion really helped poor people. Prompted by the fury over the Moynihan report, the New York intellectual Irving Kristol proclaimed his position in the title of a *New York Times Magazine* piece: "The Negro Today is Like the Immigrant Yesterday." Blacks were in about the same social condition that earlier immigrants to American cities had been when they arrived, Kristol insisted, and it would take time for African Americans to move up the socioeconomic ladder. What they needed was more education, and as educational levels rose over generations, blacks would rise in the socioeconomic order. But the emphasis on social pathologies seemed to be dictating massive new programs for people whom "antibourgeois" sociologists thought were especially disadvantaged. Kristol made a prediction: *"The more money we spend on public welfare, and the easier we make it for people to qualify for public welfare . . . the more people we can expect to find on welfare."*[12]

A related theme had already been explored by another New York intellectual, Norman Podhoretz, who in 1963 published a recollection of his Brooklyn youth, "My Negro Problem—and Ours," in which he told

of "being repeatedly beaten up, robbed, and in general hated, terrorized, and humiliated" by black boys in his integrated neighborhood.
Podhoretz expressed his resentment about the common assumption that
blacks were a persecuted minority: How could it be that "Negroes were
supposed to be persecuted when it was the Negroes who were doing the
only persecuting I knew about—and doing it, moreover, to *me*," he
asked. Podhoretz questioned what right blacks had to assign blame for
slavery on Americans like him in 1963: his Jewish family had been in Russia getting persecuted themselves during the time of American slavery.
He warned that white northerners were already nervous about the
racial integration that seemed imminent, and he predicted that many
whites would resist living next door to blacks or sending their children
to public schools—especially if their school district was redrawn solely
to integrate.[13]

Prior to the mid-1960s, Podhoretz and Kristol had been on the political left, but the questions they raised soon captured the attention of the
right. One interesting paradox about the United States was that it was the
most capitalistic, pietistic nation in the West, but that it had not produced
a strong movement of self-conscious conservative intellectuals. In fact,
since the 1940s, American conservatives had looked to a single book, Russell Kirk's *The Conservative Mind: From Burke to Santayana*, for ideological
guidance. Kirk argued for the existence of a natural hierarchy of intelligence and morality in society. Men were not born equal, and there were
no "natural" rights. "The only true equality is moral equality," he wrote.
The mid-1960s hardly seemed auspicious times for American conservatism. It had just suffered a devastating defeat when Barry Goldwater,
an ideological conservative in the way that Republican nominees rarely
had been, was trounced in the 1964 presidential election. Goldwater lost
in part because he stood foursquare for what the Right in the United
States traditionally advocated: free-market economics, limited government, the protection of private property, and anticommunism. His
defense of private property had dictated for him opposition to the Civil
Rights Act of 1964, which left him out of step with all but the white-
supremacist South.[14]

The Right's narrow view of equality had put it in opposition to the civil rights movement. This was true for the two leading conservative publicists, David Lawrence of *U.S. News and World Report* and William F. Buckley of the *National Review*. Buckley had called the *Brown* decision "one of the most brazen acts of judicial usurpation in our history, patently counter to the intent of the Constitution, [and] shoddy and illegal in analysis." He believed that southern whites were "entitled to take such measures as are necessary to prevail, politically and culturally," because they were "the advanced race." Lawrence asked about the Civil Rights Act of 1964, "Are we to use coercion to achieve conformity and thus destroy the constitutional concept of freedom of association?" The answer was no, of course, and Lawrence ended the editorial in smoldering contempt for equal rights. "Equality is a misnomer," he declared.[15]

The success of the civil rights movement had the ironic outcome of making irrelevant, and thus easily overlooked, the Right's legacy of racial bigotry and sympathy for "southern traditions." What was left of their social outlook was an antigovernment, anti-egalitarian, pronationalist view that had a growing number of adherents as American nationalism rose in the context of Vietnam, civil disorder seemed to threaten private property, and Lyndon Johnson expanded the welfare system.

I

Events in 1966 further propelled the image of civil rights activism away from peace and nonviolence. During a heated battle for control of SNCC, a group led by Stokely Carmichael, a 24-year-old veteran of the organization's Mississippi struggle, took it over and pointed it toward more aggressive, separatist tactics. For some time SNCC had been debating whether in fact whites could maintain a place in an organization whose purpose was the advance of African Americans, or whether power and responsibility should rest with blacks alone. After Carmichael's election, most whites either had left SNCC or were forced out. In June 1966 the entire civil rights leadership was drawn to Mississippi to continue a march that was begun by James Meredith but that had stopped when a sniper shot him. Martin Luther King and other leaders were taken aback when SNCC members began to exhort crowds with the shout, "We want Black Power!" Young people in the audience answered: "Black Power!" At one place Carmichael told a crowd, "We been saying freedom for six years and we ain't got nothin'. What we gonna start saying now is"—he paused and then shouted—"Black Power!" Sometimes "Black Power!" was followed by "We gonna get white blood!"[16]

Black Power gave the media a new theme. Reporters began portraying it as a new and radically different phase of the civil rights movement. The Black Power movement brought to television screens and the pages of magazines and newspapers the angry faces of young black men who seemed to reject the whole system of values on which the civil rights movement had been based.

But the sources of Black Power rested in the long-running debate about philosophy and tactics in the movement, a discussion that King had dominated with his emphasis on nonviolence and interracial brotherhood from 1956 through the Selma march. Members of SNCC had always been less committed than King to interracialism and nonviolence, and their frustrations at dealing with violent white supremacists over the years had pushed them even further away from King's ethos. The experience with the Mississippi Freedom Democratic Party in 1964 reinforced their alienation. Now Carmichael and others embraced and publicized a kind of black ethnic nationalism that had found its public name, Black Power. It was, Carmichael explained later, "a call for black people in this country to unite, to recognize their heritage, to build a sense of community . . . a call for black people to begin to define their goals, to lead their organizations and to support those organizations." Black Power rested on the premise that "before a group can enter the open society, it must first close ranks."[17]

Black Power also rejected integration and called for separatist black institutions and secular values. Integration was, according to Carmichael, a "subterfuge for the maintenance of white supremacy," and thus he swept away the presumption of black race-reform efforts for three generations. He and other SNCC activists began to express the sense of rage that Malcolm X had expressed toward the "blue-eyed devils" who con-

trolled the country. "If someone puts a hand on you," Malcolm commanded, "send him to the cemetery." On the matter of violence, Black
Power advocates also looked to the French anticolonial rebel Franz
Fanon, who had argued in his 1961 book *The Wretched of the Earth* that for
the oppressed person violence was therapeutic, a "cleansing force" that
freed him of his "inferiority complex and from his despair; it makes him
fearless and restores his self respect."[18]

The violence was only symbolic language at the beginning of the
summer of 1966, but it soon became real as the third straight year of riots
began. In Chicago black teenagers were angered when police shut off an
open fire hydrant in the midst of a summer heat wave, and three days of
looting, firebombing, and sniping ensued. A few days later Cleveland witnessed a similar phenomenon. In Atlanta, Carmichael exhorted African
Americans to violence after a police shooting, and he was later charged
with inciting the riot that followed. These were only the largest disorders
of 43 that occurred in the United States in 1966.[19]

Malcolm X. *Courtesy Library of Congress.*

Just days after the Chicago riot, Martin Luther King resumed a fair-housing campaign he had begun earlier in 1966. He led marches into several of the ethnic communities that since the 1930s had been fighting—through neighborhood organizations and bombings—to maintain their all-white character against black encroachment. The religious scholar Michael Novak, of Slovak heritage himself, would later offer a sympathetic rendering of the attitudes of European Americans he would characterize as the "unmeltable ethnics." Novak posited that the ethnics most wanted "communities of our own, attachment to family and relatives," whereas those of Anglo-Saxon heritage prized "atomic individual[ism] and high mobility." For ethnics "a home is almost fulfillment enough for one man's life." By the late 1960s these overwhelmingly blue-collar ethnics were fighting to maintain their cultural and social unity against the process of suburbanization—which represented an unacceptable dilution of their cultural strength. They also resisted the condescension they received from intellectual and governmental elites who disapproved of how they lived. Ethnics were convinced that elitist sympathy for blacks was phony, a pose they could assume because they had the luxury of being separated by class from competition with blacks. Novak maintained that ethnics often expressed these deep-seated feelings in racial terms because "the idiom of resentment in America is racist." However much their racial attitudes can be excused as the displacement of deeper frustrations, in 1966 white ethnics clearly saw blacks as the immediate threat to their cultural integrity and their status. According to Novak, white ethnics recognized the wrongs done to African Americans, but "their persistent question is why the gains of blacks should be made at *their* expense."[20]

Relatively few black Chicagoans joined King in the marches into ethnic neighborhoods, but large and ugly white crowds did. In Marquette Park, four thousand whites, some of them brandishing the Confederate battle flag and wearing Nazi helmets and others waving "George Wallace for President" signs, harassed King and his six hundred marchers. "We want Martin Luther Coon! Kill those niggers! Send them home!" they shouted. Throughout Marquette Park, whites sang a ditty to King as he passed.

I wish I were an Alabama trooper
That is what I would truly like to be;
I wish I were an Alabama trooper
'Cause then I could kill the niggers legally.

Catholic nuns and priests marching behind King were subjected to foul harassment, as were the Chicago policemen trying to protect the marchers. As King's group marched down a street of bungalows, whites sitting on stoops screamed, "Savages! Cannibals!" A rock thrown by one of them gashed King's head, knocking him to the ground. "I have never seen anything like it," King later said. "The people from Mississippi ought to come to Chicago to learn how to hate." He kept up the pressure, even announcing a larger march into all-white Cicero, a suburban town with a police force far too small to control antiblack mobs. Finally, Mayor Daley announced a pledge of fair housing, which King called a great victory. As soon as he had left the city, official Chicago ignored its promises and returned to segregation as usual.[21]

The crucial reality about Chicago, however, was that the violence of whites against civil rights marchers failed to elicit a fraction of the moral outrage that no more dangerous circumstances in Birmingham or Selma had caused. It was a different time, and more important, a different place. For all the ugliness white Chicagoans put on display, public opinion did not move toward sympathy with African Americans. In the immediate aftermath of the Selma march, Americans approved of blacks' demonstrating for their rights by more than two to one. By late 1966, 63 percent of whites said they *disapproved,* and the next year that number rose to 82 percent. When asked whether the Johnson administration was "pushing racial integration too fast," 30 percent of Americans had answered yes in February 1964, as the Civil Rights Act was being driven through the Congress. By November 1966, with no great legislative thrust for race reform impending, 53 percent responded in the affirmative. When whites were asked in November 1964 whether "Negroes have tried to move too fast," 34 percent had said yes. In October 1966, 85 percent answered that way.[22]

The Chicago struggles began to undermine King's positive image in the media. The two leading national newsmagazines, *Time* and *Newsweek*, had generally been positive about King's leadership through the Selma march, but when he turned northward, and against the Vietnam War, the highly interpretive news stories in these two widely read news outlets became hostile. They suggested that he had no business criticizing American foreign policy and little to contribute to the improvement of northern racial conditions. He was portrayed as the instigator of violence in Chicago. Your place is in the South, the newsmagazines as much as said to King. In the post-Selma period, he generally was treated favorably only as foil to the more radical, Black Power elements in the civil rights movement.[23]

A growing economic insecurity among blue-collar white men fueled some of the anger about housing protests. Within the large, unionized industries, groups of black workers had organized in the early 1960s to challenge job discrimination. Relatively little progress had been made prior to 1965, when Title VII of the Civil Rights Act, making employment discrimination illegal, went into force. This provision had worried white workers all along, a concern that George Wallace had exploited in 1964 with his illustration of "Japanese Lutherans" being fired to make room for "Chinese Baptists." Starting in 1965, thousands of black workers brought their labor unions and employers before the Equal Employment Opportunity Commission (EEOC) for maintaining job discrimination, and in some instances the unions and the companies allied to fight changes and preserve current seniority systems. Often unwilling to accept EEOC fairness rulings, unions and companies in many instances had to be sued to change work and seniority rules and to pay the lost wages of black workers. By 1966 many white workers justifiably believed that black workers threatened their jobs.[24]

The competition for housing and good jobs was inevitably felt in politics. In the fall elections of 1966, a white backlash against civil rights was apparent. "Go into Chicago today in any bar, any home, any barber shop," Roman Pucinski, a Democratic congressman from Chicago, observed in September 1966, "and you will find people are not talking about Viet Nam or rising prices or prosperity." What they were talking about was "Martin Luther King and how they are moving in on us and what's going to happen to our neighborhoods." Challenged by a Republican who made what was becoming a popular appeal in 1966 against "riots in the street," Pucinski was feeling "white backlash." He had introduced legislation to limit demonstrations. "The demonstrations may be intended to be nonviolent," he argued, "but can the organizers truly be nonviolent, knowing in their hearts and minds that their conduct will assuredly precipitate violence in others?" The House minority leader Gerald R. Ford put the Republican position forward: "How long are we going to abdicate law and order—the backbone of any civilization—in favor of a soft social theory that the man who throws a brick through your window or tosses a fire bomb into your car is simply the misunderstood and underprivileged product of a broken home?" Ford had found the symbolic language for restoration of white authority—"law and order"—that would be deployed in the political discourse for the remainder of the century.[25]

On Election Day 1966, angry white voters helped to unseat 47 Democratic congressmen and three senators. Ethnics in Chicago were largely responsible for the defeat of Senator Paul Douglas, a strong advocate of open-housing legislation. The election of Ronald Reagan as governor of California owed much to hostility to open housing and to insecurity arising from the Watts riot. "Whether we like it or not," Reagan's Democratic opponent said in the election's aftermath, "the people want separation of the races."[26]

The backlash election of 1966 revealed that many Americans were turning away from the liberal agenda that had been so extensively enacted during the past two years. Lyndon Johnson heeded the signal: he relaxed his pressure for more reform programs and asked for much less spending on poverty than the civil rights leadership wanted. Republicans showed much stronger resistance to proposed open-housing and equal-hiring legislation in 1966 than they had to the Voting Rights Act in 1965. The opposition to reform reflected in some measure an honest belief that enough had been done. But many Americans, both black and white, would understand the growing opposition to government action in racial terms. White backlash signaled that race competition for economic opportunity, space, and political power would continue, even with the legal bases for white supremacy now undermined.

II

Opposition to the Vietnam War had grown in lockstep with the troop call-ups through 1966, and by 1967 Lyndon Johnson's domestic-policy achievements were far more often questioned than celebrated. Doubts about his foreign-policy leadership colored everything about his presidency. The war in Southeast Asia represented the climax of Cold War nationalism, the logical extreme of defending American honor against communism. At the same time, however, the anti–Vietnam War movement put American nationalism under its sharpest scrutiny since the 1930s. While Cold Warriors argued for the necessity of stopping Ho Chi Minh, peace activists insisted that the United States had no interest in fighting a nationalist movement in Southeast Asia. By 1967 their protests became a primary focus of domestic affairs. College students who had recently been singing "We Shall Overcome" and shouting "Freedom!" were now chanting "Hey, Hey, LBJ, how many boys did you kill today?" Both friends and foes of the Vietnam War agreed that American nationalism was the overriding issue after 1965.

After the negative reactions he received for his criticism of the American war effort in July 1965, Martin Luther King had kept mostly quiet about Vietnam until April 1967, but then he offered his harshest denunciation yet of American involvement. "I knew that I could never again raise my voice against the violence of the oppressed in the ghettos," he told three thousand clergymen and antiwar activists at Riverside Church in New York City, "without having first spoken clearly to the greatest purveyor of violence in the world today—my own government." He compared Americans' use of weaponry on the Vietnamese people to the Germans' "new medicines and new tortures in the concentration camps of Europe." He predicted that "a nation that continues year after year to spend more money on military defense than on programs of social uplift is approaching spiritual death." A few days later, he told an even larger crowd at the University of California at Berkeley that "the clouds of a third world war are hovering mighty low" and that the U.S. government "will have to take the chief responsibility for making this a reality."[27]

At the same time, King announced that the civil rights movement was becoming "a struggle for *genuine* equality." He called for a "radical redistribution of economic and political power." He wanted a "reconstruction of the entire society, a revolution in values." Americans needed to see that "the evils of racism, economic exploitation, and militarism are all tied together, and you really can't get rid of one without getting rid of the others." But he recognized that "America's problem in restructuring is that she is a conservative nation . . . a hypocritical nation" that "must set her own house in order."[28]

Martin Luther King, Jr., spoke out strongly against the Vietnam War. *Courtesy Library of Congress.*

Such sweeping condemnations of the United States represented a kind of bridge burning for King and his strategy. He had based his appeal for civil rights reforms on democratic values that most white Americans associated with their national identity. It had worked because King had idealized what the United States was supposed to mean, and he left the strong impression in his speaking and writing that he believed that Americans wanted to live up to freedom and equality. But with such harsh indictments of American morality in 1967, King effectively abandoned further appeals to "American" ideology. How could he legitimately ask a "spiritually dead" nation to expand its ideological commitment to equality? In 1965 one acute observer had concluded that King's success as the symbolic leader of African Americans rested heavily on his image as a man who compromised with reasonable white leaders, listened to presidents, and held the "vital center" among civil rights activists. King had always made clear that there were good whites who helped African Americans. By 1967 it appeared that he had abandoned his centrist, conciliatory posture.[29]

Some activists believed that King was forsaking civil rights. His anti-war positions undermined his call for radical restructuring of wealth in society. King was "diverting energy and attention from the basic problems of poverty and discrimination," one black activist said. "And how are you going to denounce Lyndon Johnson one day and ask him the next for money for poverty, schools, housing?" The war was dividing the civil rights community, just as it was so many other American institutions in 1967.[30]

The summer of 1967 brought another awful season of riots. Major disorders occurred in Tampa and Cincinnati before a massive conflagration took place in Newark in July. The pattern of how violence had unfolded elsewhere held in the New Jersey city: Anger at police brutality resulted in protests, which degenerated into looting. In their effort to control looting, policemen shot innocent blacks, which precipitated black sniping. Then came huge amounts of police and national guard power. Before the Newark riot was over, 23 people lay dead. A few days later, perhaps the worst rioting yet seen in the United States enveloped

Detroit, leaving 43 people dead and at least $50 million of property destroyed. The 1967 riots spurred President Johnson to appoint a Commission on Civil Disorders, which reported that, whereas the public believed that riot cities were paralyzed by sniper fire, in fact most sniping incidents were gunfire from police or national guardsmen. Although the riots were racial in character, they mainly involved blacks' attacking symbols of white authority and white property rather than white people. The commission fixed blame for misconceptions on the media, which gave the false impression that the riots were "confrontations between Negroes and whites rather than responses by Negroes to underlying slum problems."[31]

The commission failed to see how much the riots escalated Americans' fear of crime. An earlier government study on crime detailed a big jump in murders and assaults, and it placed blame for the increase mainly on "the young and the poor in the urban slums." Crime did indeed skyrocket during the 1960s: homicides went up 71 percent. The murder rate among blacks was about ten times that of whites, and blacks were much more likely to commit aggravated assault and robbery. These statistics were frequently reported between 1966 and 1968, and the causes of the crime increase in the 1960s were much debated. One explanation was demographic: young men between 15 and 24 commit most violent crimes, and there were many more young men in the population at that time than at others. Another theory centered on the rebellious spirit of the 1960s: the African-American writer James Baldwin suggested in 1966 that to respect the law "in the context in which the Negro finds himself" meant surrendering self-respect, whereas being a law-breaking "bad nigger" reflected to other blacks an admirable rebellion. Whatever the cause, crime reached scary proportions, and the rise was largely understood as a racial phenomenon.[32]

The explosion of crime resonated with the old stereotypes of the violent, criminal Negro. Although now largely removed from popular culture's renderings of African Americans, prejudices still existed in remnant form among older whites, and now the outlets of mass communications carried forth the stereotypes of the immoral and lazy black person in their news reports on poverty and crime in the United States. One scholar has found that the news media began in the mid-1960s to misrepresent the racial proportions of poverty, greatly exaggerating in their depictions what part of the poor in the United States was black. To be sure, blacks constituted a highly disproportionate share of the nation's poor people, but they never constituted the 80 percent that news stories suggested in their choice of photographs of poor people. News reporters often separated the poor into those who were "deserving" and those who were not, and almost always the examples of indolence were black and those thrown only accidentally into poverty were white. Once established, these tendencies characterized reporting through the 1970s and 1980s, thus over-racializing the media representation of poverty for the rest of the twentieth century.[33]

It can be no more an accident that this awful development began when American cities were burning than was the focus on spiraling black crime. Americans wanted explanations for the disorder, reasons for their sudden surge of insecurity. The racialization of crime and poverty may have been the worst outcome of the riots, though it has been a largely unrecognized one. Order would be restored and the cities rebuilt long before the image of blacks was rehabilitated.

The idea that blacks were the perpetrators rather than the victims of violence also characterized reporting about southern African Americans' efforts to defend themselves from racial violence. In 1965 and 1966 the media played up the emergence in Louisiana of an organization called the Deacons for Defense and Justice, which openly armed itself to fight against Klan terrorism. In fact, armed self-defense among blacks was as common as it was among whites. But the highly public use of nonviolent tactics seemed to many in the media to make black self-defense especially newsworthy, a kind of "man-bites-dog" story. However inconsistent and ahistorical this reporting, it contributed to the sense among white Americans that blacks had turned to violence.

During the summer of 1967, the Black Power movement became startlingly violent in its presentation to the American public. Damning all "honkies," Carmichael told black audiences, "To hell with the laws of the United States." In Cuba he described the fight for liberation of blacks in the United States as a struggle of "total revolution in which we propose to change the imperialist, capitalist and racialist structure of the United States which oppresses you outside and us within." His plan for revolution, announced on the soil of the nation's chief enemy in the Western Hemisphere, was widely reported in the American media. Notwithstanding the immediate condemnations that came from the civil rights leadership, Carmichael reinforced the impression that Martin Luther King had left in his 1967 speeches—that the dominant black leaders were not patriotic Americans.[34]

When Carmichael resigned as head of SNCC, H. Rap Brown took his place and projected an even more menacing persona. During the summer of 1967, the 23-year-old Brown traveled from city to city as riots occurred, and he left the strong suspicion that he promoted looting, firebombing, and sniping wherever he went. Officials in at least three cities blamed either Brown or Carmichael for riots. Brown gave a speech in Cambridge, Maryland, in which he was widely reported to have said: "If America don't come around, we going to burn it down. The white man talks about black people looting. Hell, he the biggest looter in the world. He looted us from Africa. He looted America from the Indians. . . . [Y]ou can't steal from a thief. . . . Look what the brothers did in Plainfield. They stomped a cop to death. Good. He's dead. . . . Detroit exploded, Newark exploded, Harlem exploded! It is time for Cambridge to explode, baby. . . . If America don't come around, we're going to burn America down, brother." To a crowd in Jacksonville, Florida, Brown advised: "If you are gonna loot, brother, loot a gun store. Don't be running around here looting no liquor, 'cause liquor's just for celebrating. We ain't got nothing to celebrate about. You better get yourselves some guns, baby."[35]

Black Power alienated much of the strongest white support for civil rights. By all measures the most consistently liberal portion of the American population, Jews had historically provided a large share of the financial support for black colleges and the NAACP, and during the 1960s they gave much financial support to all civil rights organizations. But they increasingly faced anti-Semitism during the 1960s. In 1964 polling data began to show a sharp increase in anti-Semitism among young African

H. Rap Brown. *Courtesy Library of Congress.*

Americans, and soon thereafter the hostility between blacks and Jews broke into the open. In 1966 a black CORE activist, speaking during a heated debate over a school desegregation plan in Westchester County, New York, shouted at his mostly Jewish opposition, "Hitler made a mistake when he didn't kill enough of you." The organization immediately issued apologies and disavowals, but the statement confirmed for many Jews that some blacks had a special hatred for them, regardless of the sympathies they had shown. Malcolm X had connected the Nation of Islam's anti-Semitism to the Middle East: "The Jews . . . with the help of Christians in America and Europe drove our Muslim brothers (i.e., the Arabs) out of their homeland, where they had been settled for centuries and took over the land for themselves," he said. In June 1967, when Egypt attacked Israel to begin the Six-Day War, both the Nation of Islam and SNCC proclaimed their support for their Muslim "brothers" against their "Zionist aggressors." At that point, many American Jews washed their hands of the civil rights movement.[36]

Black-Jewish relations deteriorated even further during a public-school controversy in New York in 1967 and 1968. It centered on an attempt to give the poor, mostly black citizens in the Ocean Hill–Brownsville section of Brooklyn more control over schools. The experiment soon erupted into an ugly conflict between Black Power advocates, on one side, and Jewish teachers and their union leader, Albert Shanker, on the other. Shanker had supported the local-control experiment, but when the Black Power leader Sonny Carson engineered the firing of 27 white teachers, Shanker resisted and ultimately took all city public-school teachers out on strike for much of the fall of 1968. Carson called Shanker a "great big honky" and told white teachers that "the Germans did not do a good enough job with you Jews." He informed blacks that "the Weinsteins [and] the Goldbergs are wasting our kids' time on other people's cultures." In the end most New Yorkers supported Shanker and the teachers, who were reinstated. The Ocean Hill–Brownsville crisis fueled mounting ethnic conflict in the city, though many black leaders insisted that black anti-Semitism was being exaggerated. When Black Power advocates say "Jew," James Baldwin explained, "they mean 'white.'" Such disavowals were cold comfort to Jews watching the New York school situation, and black-Jewish relations were forever altered among those who witnessed the events.[37]

The riots, the rising crime rates, and the encouragement of racial disorder sent Americans' fears of violence to new heights by the end of the summer of 1967. In their crude way, Carmichael and Brown expressed what another SNCC member suggested with more sophistication: "History has proved that any meaningful social change has come through a bloody revolution." Or as the African-American psychologist Kenneth Clark put it, violence was "the cutting edge of justice." Few white Americans accepted any of these justifications for violence. But neither could many separate out the disparate sources of danger and the fear they felt. The Vietnam War was becoming a daily dose of violence on the evening news. Mounting war casualties, rising crime rates, and widespread death and destruction in American cities worked together to make Americans feel more insecure than ever.[38]

III

The widespread anger of African Americans perplexed southern whites, who saw all around them in the late 1960s evidence that conditions for African Americans were improving rapidly. Blacks now voted in large numbers, and some were running for office. Most public accommodations operated peacefully on an integrated basis. In 1970 the U.S. Commission on Civil Rights reported that a "swift and almost total end" to discrimination and segregation in southern hospitals had occurred. Many aspects of white attitudes were going through a sea change. Polls showed that whites were becoming much more accepting of integrated transportation, schools, and social interaction than they had been as late as 1963. By 1970 almost half of all Americans accepted interracial marriage, at least in theory. That year even a majority of southerners said they accepted integrated public accommodations. Good things happened once segregation ended: the city of Atlanta attracted professional baseball, for example, and it built on that base to become a major city for sports in the United States. The commercial renderings of American society were becoming integrated on a daily basis: African Americans began to appear in advertising with much greater frequency than they had before the mid-1960s, and typically they were portrayed as just another segment of middle-class America. The only issue on which whites' attitudes did not become more liberal in the late 1960s was housing, an exception that boded ill for the future.[39]

Many whites presumed that life was much better for African Americans because such great improvements had occurred in the South. Indeed, the region in the late 1960s seemed at odds with the rest of the country because it appeared to be progressing toward a more peaceful coexistence. The white South adjusted far more easily than it had ever imagined it could to many of the changes brought by the civil rights movement. If integrating public accommodations had seemed unthinkable in 1964 to most whites, it had become natural, or at least unremarkable, within the first few years of implementation. Token school integration took place with relatively little trouble in 1966 and 1967.

Although there were minor riots in some southern cities, nothing like the death and destruction of Watts or Detroit occurred.

The Voting Rights Act facilitated the registration of about three million new black voters in the South in the late 1960s, and again the white South made a complete about-face with far less conflict than most had imagined. To be sure, some resistance to black registration had to be overcome in 1965 and 1966, but by 1968 whites generally assumed that blacks who wanted to were going to vote. The most obvious reflection of the change was in the tone of electoral politics in the Deep South: gone were the race baiters and white-race nationalists making open declaration of white supremacy, and arising instead were white politicians who spoke in more conciliatory phrases about political and social issues.

One unexpected consequence of the civil rights movement was a large expansion in the number of new white voters, which greatly exceeded the number of new black voters. The end of the poll tax, the rising educational and economic levels among southern whites, the migration of 1.8 million whites into the region during the 1960s—the first net in-migration into the South since the Civil War—all contributed to the increase of whites on the voting rolls. So too did the competitive sense among blue-collar whites that if blacks were becoming politically potent, they had to become more active themselves. The enfranchisement of whites largely offset the expected liberalization of southern politics from blacks, because the mass of new white voters was overwhelmingly suspicious of state action and generally hostile to taxation.[40]

In the late 1960s, the focus of civil rights activism turned back to the local communities, and issues of economic opportunity and relief from poverty took the center stage of local politics. In many places, whites co-opted the increased federal involvement in welfare, housing, and education wherever they could, just as they historically had controlled local administration of agricultural subsidy programs. As more and more blacks became politically active, and as they confronted the intransigence of white power in communities after having high expectations for how access to democracy would improve their lives, bitter conflicts frequently arose. Protracted disputes over the administration of poverty programs marked post-1965 community politics in many Deep South places.

Thus the late 1960s surprised both black and white southerners. Whites experienced a much easier time of transition than they had expected to have after so much change had been forced on them. Blacks had expected that with the vote, the opportunity to send their children to a "white" school, and the right to be treated respectfully in public places would come peace and prosperity in their lives. In that, the times often disappointed them. One side was too relieved and the other too disappointed to appreciate the irony of their separate but equally unexpected results from the civil rights "revolution."[41]

Blacks experienced real economic progress in the 1960s, improvement on the scale of what they enjoyed in the 1940s. The portion of African Americans living in poverty had declined from 55 percent in 1959 to about 34 percent at the end of the 1960s. In 1959 the average income of black men in the United States had been 47 percent of white men's, lower than what it had been ten years earlier, but in 1969 the ratio had grown to 58 percent. During the same period, black women's incomes as a portion of white women's jumped from 62 to 84 percent, a phenomenal gain.[42]

The income gains among black men resulted in part from the federal government's equal-employment pressure in skilled and semiskilled industrial jobs. Industries that had long relegated blacks to separate lines of promotion—steel, automobiles, rubber, and paper—now quickly opened up skilled opportunities for black workers with long tenure. In the aftermath of the 1967 Detroit riot, the big automakers forsook traditional personnel practices to hire blacks with poor education and even criminal records, and succeeded in increasing substantially the black presence in their plants. Under pressure to keep federal contracts and to fill slots in a tight labor market in the mid-1960s, the textile industry in the South ended its historic lockout of black workers, and the percentage of black textile workers tripled in the 1960s. By the end of the 1970s, it had risen to the point that blacks composed a portion of southern textile workers roughly commensurate with their numbers in the population. Major income gains among African Americans came from big increases in professional and managerial jobs. Black women gained many new managerial jobs, but their larger overall increase in income came from clerical work, where they more than doubled their presence.[43]

While fear and violence grew in the streets, American popular culture became increasingly committed to American democratic ideology, including the acceptance of racial integration. In the mid-1960s television and the movies had moved forward in the promotion of integrationist ideals. Television had finally cast African Americans as real people. In 1965, Bill Cosby starred in *I Spy,* the first program in which a black actor played a main role in a dramatic series. Blacks took important roles in *Star Trek* starting in 1966, and in 1968 Diahann Carroll would play the central role in the series *Julia*. Sidney Poitier, who became the first African American to win an Academy Award for best actor, in *Lilies of the Field* in 1963, had leading roles in two powerful and controversial films in 1967. In the crime drama *In the Heat of the Night*, Poitier played a northern policeman investigating a murder in the South, during which he earned the respect of a bigoted white cop and sparked fear in a southern aristocrat, whom he slapped in retaliation for having hit him. In *Guess Who's Coming to Dinner*, Poitier played an educated Negro who must deal with the worries of both his parents and his white fiancé's parents. By the time the film appeared in late 1967, however, interracial marriage of a black man to a white woman did not represent progress to black nationalists, and Poitier came under personal attack for such modern-day "Uncle-Tomism."[44]

Mainstream popular culture did not, however, show much tolerance in the late 1960s for values that were not integrationist. As with the experience of Joe Louis in 1938 and Jackie Robinson in 1947, sports in 1967 exposed the nerves of American race relations. If Louis and Robinson became national heroes by standing with the flag, black nationalism and American nationalism came into open conflict in 1967 in the person of the boxer Muhammad Ali. Born Cassius Clay, the 23-year-old Kentuckian declared that he was a member of the Nation of Islam on the day after he won the heavyweight title in 1964. In 1965 he was called to his draft board, where he sought exemption from the draft as a conscientious objector and minister of his faith. "I will not disgrace my religion, my people or myself by becoming a tool to enslave those who are fighting for justice, equality and freedom," Ali announced, referring to the North Vietnamese. When he was indeed drafted in the spring of 1967, Ali refused induction into the U.S. Army. He was convicted of draft evasion

and spent four years appealing it, during which he was denied the opportunity to box. Along the way, Ali became a major symbol of black-nationalist anti-Americanism. Much of the mainstream media insisted on
calling him Cassius Clay for years after he had renamed himself, reflecting the powerful bias against black ethnic nationalism in general, and the
"Black Muslims" in particular.[45]

IV

Although it would have seemed impossible that American society could
get more volatile than it had been during 1966 and 1967, the year 1968
brought even more stunning violence and greater fear. In January and

Muhammad Ali embraced the Nation of Islam once he became heavyweight boxing
champion. *Courtesy AP/Wideworld Photos.*

February, Ho Chi Minh's guerrilla forces executed the Tet Offensive in South Vietnam, a concerted attack that brought few lasting military gains but that alienated many Americans from the war. By the end of March 1968, Lyndon Johnson had withdrawn from that year's presidential race, and he had ceased the bombing of North Vietnam. But he stopped short of any more substantial reversal of American policy, and thus the war was the dominant issue during the Democratic primaries. Senator Eugene McCarthy, a Minnesota Democrat, had rallied the antiwar movement when he challenged Johnson in the early primaries, and then Senator Robert Kennedy of New York entered the race as a peace candidate. Vice President Hubert Humphrey also sought the Democratic nomination, but he did so in the harness of Johnson's Vietnam policies.

Black nationalism continued to capture the astonished attention of many Americans. In 1967 a small group of young African-American men in Oakland calling themselves the Black Panthers organized a heavily armed self-defense effort to oppose "racist" police brutality. Led by Huey P. Newton, a 24-year-old petty criminal, the Panthers got instant notoriety when 30 of them, fully armed, pushed past guards to go onto the floor of the California Assembly in opposition to a gun-control law. "Only with the power of the gun can the Black masses halt the terror and brutality perpetuated against them by the armed racist power structure," Newton declared. The Panthers' battle cry became "Off the Pig!"—Kill the police. According to some, that was exactly what Newton and some Panthers did to an Oakland officer in a shootout in late 1967. Newton also took a bullet and then was jailed for murder. Now shouting "Free Huey!" the tiny Panther cell turned for leadership to Eldridge Cleaver, a career criminal who considered rape of white women a revolutionary act. Cleaver soon found himself in a shootout with Oakland police, and facing charges from it, he fled the country. Gunfights continued through 1968 and 1969, and true to their stated mission, the Panthers killed more police than they themselves lost.[46]

The Black Panthers thus symbolized to many whites the worsening threat of black violence in the United States. Although there were obviously two sides to the conflict between the Panthers and the police, whites generally perceived it as a direct challenge to law and order—and thus to their own security. The Panthers reinforced the impression made earlier by Stokely Carmichael and Rap Brown that violent, immature young men had grasped control of black interests in the United States.

In late 1967 and early 1968, Martin Luther King devoted much of his energy to promoting programs to improve economic conditions for minorities. SCLC organized a massive demonstration of poor people to take place in the spring of 1968 to dramatize the economic issues and to bring pressure on the national government for increased spending for welfare and jobs programs. The Poor People's Campaign was controversial from the beginning, because some in the civil rights leadership believed that it misperceived the political environment of 1968 as being receptive to mass protest in the way it in fact had been in 1964 and 1965. The riots had exhausted white Americans' tolerance for disorder, which was expected to come with the campaign. Still, the planning proceeded. Two things undermined King's pressure for broader government action to address the problems of the poor in America: his war stance had undermined his ability to appeal to American democratic values as the basis for helping blacks, and the racialization of poverty had hardened many whites to welfare expansion. The Poor People's Campaign confirmed for many whites the mainstream media's now-frequent judgment that King was a special pleader.[47]

That was his prevailing reputation among whites when in early 1968 he was asked to help black garbage workers in Memphis who had struck against poor pay and working conditions. King visited the city several times to rally support, and on one such trip, on April 4, 1968, he was assassinated. A white-supremacist drifter was later convicted of his murder.

The death of Martin Luther King removed from American life the most influential moral leader of the second half of the twentieth century. Indeed, his ability to shape how Americans understood democratic values ranks with Abraham Lincoln's and Franklin Roosevelt's. Although his authority over what whites thought had waned after mid-1965, the nation would never know how King, still only 39 years old in 1968, might have directed public discourse on the crucial matters of national existence had he lived out a normal life.

The King assassination ratified the sense that the United States was a nation being consumed by violence. Robert Kennedy reported King's death to a shocked audience on the streets of an Indianapolis ghetto neighborhood and then acknowledged that it was understandable if black people were "filled with bitterness, with hatred, and a desire for revenge." Americans could go in that direction, "or we can make an effort, as Martin Luther King did, to understand and to comprehend, and to replace that violence, that stain of bloodshed that has spread across our land, with an effort to understand with compassion and love." The evidence sadly reveals that many Americans took the first of Kennedy's choices. The assassination instantly sparked rioting in 125 U.S. cities. Army troops were called to bring order in Baltimore and Chicago, where Mayor Daley had told his policemen to "shoot to kill" arsonists.[48]

The King assassination and its violent aftermath did move the U.S. Congress to provide the first real protection against racial discrimination in housing. The Fair Housing Act of 1968 made it illegal to discriminate in buying, selling, and renting in all transactions except those offered by one private individual to another. This would be the final significant piece of civil rights legislation of the 1960s, and it represented a posthumous tribute to Martin Luther King in the area he had tried so hard to reform in the last few years of his life.[49]

In June the assassination of Robert Kennedy provided further confirmation to many Americans that their society had fallen into an uncontrolled downward spiral of lawlessness and violence. Kennedy's death removed from the presidential race a candidate who might have appealed across the racial divide, because despite his liberal social agenda, he had projected the personal toughness to deal with the disorder that seemed rampant. Hubert Humphrey, a man of even longer commitment to equality, now by default became the Democratic nominee, but he was too tainted by the war to appeal strongly to many on the left and too liberal to gain many blue-collar whites' support. Any hope that the Democratic Party might overcome its divisions and save the liberal agenda was

Robert F. Kennedy. *Courtesy Library of Congress.*

lost in its Chicago convention in 1968. While peace advocates argued loudly with traditional party powers inside the convention hall, outside antiwar demonstrators fought with the Chicago police, who beat and arrested hundreds of them. All the images from Chicago confirmed the familiar sense of 1968 that American society was in chaos.

Because events had determined that the presidential election of 1968 could not serve as a referendum on Vietnam, it became in many ways a vote about race issues. George Wallace, running as a third-party candidate, deftly exploited the multiple fears and resentments that Americans felt in 1968. He appealed to whites' sense of lost status not by advocating segregation as he had done in Alabama but by calling for the return of authority to the states from federal bureaucrats and judges. He developed a coded language for maintaining white domination—"control for local communities," "law and order," and "the return to constitutional government." He worked on the resentment that blue-collar whites held for intellectuals, who knew so little of real value that they could not "park a bicycle straight," but who assumed they could tell working people how to live. He appealed intensely to American nationalism, calling for an end to foreign aid and to "this academic freedom talk that allows people to call for Communist victory" while American soldiers were dying to defeat communism abroad. The antiwar movement provided him with the perfect foil to demonstrate his bellicose defense of both American nationalism and law and order. When antiwar protestors heckled him at his rallies, he asked his audience, "Why do the leaders of the two national parties kowtow to these anarchists?" The way to deal with them, Wallace suggested, was with his own brand of violence. He often reminded his audience that protestors had lain in front of President Johnson's car at one point. "I tell you," he shouted to large crowds, "the first time they lie down in front of my limousine it'll be the last one they'll ever lay down in front of; their day is *over!*"[50]

Wallace prompted the Republican nominee Richard Nixon's embrace of "law and order." Nixon chose as his running mate Governor Spiro T. Agnew of Maryland. In the aftermath of the King assassination, Agnew had condemned "Hanoi-visiting, riot-inciting, burn-America-down"

Wallace supporters in 1968. *Courtesy Birmingham Public Library.*

black leaders, and his role in the Republican campaign was to make the "bad cop" appeal to white voters. Nixon's television commercials exploited the surging fears of violence, apparently to great effect: one ad featured scenes of burning cities, antiwar protestors, and armed troops over which played Nixon's voice: "The first civil right of every American is to be free from domestic violence, so I pledge to you: We shall have order in the United States."[51]

Keenly conscious of the way black voters had made the difference against Republican presidential candidates, himself included, Nixon avoided anything that might be interpreted as a direct racial appeal until late in the campaign, when he began to criticize the federal judiciary's "forced busing" orders to desegregate schools. Here he exploited what Wallace had taught voters—that damning the federal judiciary was a coded way to oppose black interests. Nixon said he preferred "freedom-of-choice" plans that his audiences knew meant only token desegregation. At the same time, Nixon's campaign began to warn voters that a vote for Wallace would help to elect Humphrey. The Democrat came on strong at the end, but as he did, Wallace faded when many southern and border-state voters took what they believed was the more practical route to "law and order" by voting for Nixon, who won.[52]

Thus began a long swing back to the right in American politics, though Nixon himself would hardly prove to be a consistent conservative. In some ways it was only the natural turn in the cycle from the activist state back to a more limited one. But it also reflected Americans' deep fears about the disorder of their society and the real frustration about how to stop violence and end the erosion of American honor.

The three years between the Watts riot in August 1965 and the Democratic convention in August 1968 had smashed the faith that Americans built up in the early 1960s that they should broaden the definitions of liberty and equality. Many Americans believed that Lincoln's idealism had been applied sufficiently in 1964 and 1965. The violence and disorder of the late 1960s threatened Americans' security and pushed their ideological positions toward narrower understandings of democratic values. The Vietnam War intensified discourse about American nationalism, and both pro- and antiwar positions undermined the advancement of civil rights: Supporters of the war wanted conformity to patriotism, and thus they resisted the kind of criticism of American institutions that underlay more race reform, while opponents of the war were so preoccupied with foreign policy that they neglected or even disparaged domestic reform. The civil rights leadership got caught up in hostility to American nationalism and lost the advantage that the appeal to national honor had given them in their movement to broaden democratic values. Even worse, the memory of troubled years in the late 1960s would set strict limits on how much of that faith could be recovered in the time ahead. After 1968 the violence in the streets would subside, but in its place would come a bitter, dispiriting struggle over the "genuine" equality called for by Martin Luther King.

CHAPTER 8

THE ZERO-SUM SOCIETY

ON "PARENTS' WEEKEND" at Cornell University in Ithaca, New York, in April 1969, 110 of the school's 250 African-American students seized control of the student union building. They went armed with rifles, shotguns, and homemade spears. The immediate cause for their takeover was the university's disciplinary action against five black students. But they were also angry over the "middle-class, white, racist" curriculum and the university's resistance to establishing a separate black college focused on the ghetto experience. Tension had been building through the school term over black student protests and white retaliatory actions, most recently a cross burned on the steps of some black students' residence. Taking over the campus radio station, the students warned that "Cornell has three hours to live" and that "racists" on the faculty "would be dealt with." Sympathetic white members of the Students for a Democratic Society (SDS) set up a "defense line" around the building in order that whites could receive, according to one SDS defender, "the lumps [blacks] have taken for 300 years." The university administration signed an amnesty agreement with the students, absolving them of any discipline. At the end of the weekend, the students surrendered the building. Pictures of the rifle-bearing black students exiting their stronghold appeared on the cover of newsmagazines and on television throughout the country.

Cornell's administrators justified their capitulation on the grounds that they avoided the mayhem that would have resulted if the campus had been invaded by state police and national guardsmen. The Cornell faculty rejected the amnesty, which sent the black students into a new fury. "In the past it has been the black people who have done all the dying," the black student spokesman announced. "Now the time has come when the pigs are going to die too." The faculty quickly reconsidered. "We couldn't conceive of watching troops and students battling," an English professor explained. "We felt we had to draw back from the abyss of chaos." The black students were given final and total amnesty and allowed to keep their guns. A minority of Cornell faculty members did object to the university's decisions, including the classicist Allan Bloom. "The resemblance on all levels to the first states of a totalitarian take-over are almost unbelievable."[1]

The Cornell events were part of a larger student revolt that had begun on campuses across the country in 1968 as students protested massively against the Vietnam War. Throughout the turmoil, African-American students had pushed forward racial issues. When SDS occupied buildings at Columbia University in the spring of 1968, black members summarily ejected their white colleagues, announced that the "the black community is taking over," and invited into their new fortress people from the streets of nearby Harlem. The winter and spring of 1969 brought Black Power protests in which African-American students blockaded or occupied buildings on campuses across the country. They demanded more black students and faculty, centers for black culture, and more study of African culture and African-American history. Institutions scrambled to establish departments and appoint faculty to meet the need. In the aftermath of the Cornell takeover, the Harvard faculty voted to give black students the power to choose professors and set curriculum in their new black studies program, a redistribution of authority without precedent in the history of the nation's most prestigious institution of higher education. At universities across the country, African-American students and faculty established autonomous black studies programs that rejected the scholarship of white academics, because, as a historian later explained, "although whites continued to pose as experts in the field, their studies seemed biased and misleading" to black students at the time. The editor of the journal *Black Scholar* declared in 1969 that "a black-studies program which is not revolutionary and nationalistic is, accordingly, quite profoundly irrelevant."[2]

The campus protests in 1968 and 1969 reinforced a strong sense among many Americans—nurtured by the urban riots, Black Power radicals, and the Black Panthers—that the younger generation of African Americans preferred violence to peace, disruption to order, and separation to integration. They seemed to have no respect for fundamental institutions of society—not the police, not the U.S. government, and not even the most liberal havens of the "establishment," the universities. The campus protests also led to the unavoidable conclusion that young blacks had rejected the achievements of the civil rights movement. Integration and the quest to realize American democratic values were now deemed misguided goals, their pursuit the work of activists duped by entrenched powers. The vast majority of white Americans held virtually opposite views about established institutions, the effect of the civil rights movement, and the significance of democratic values. Although much of the alienation between viewpoints also applied to white college students, the gulf between black nationalism and mainstream America in the late 1960s kept racial tensions in the society much higher than most whites thought was necessary or acceptable. Deep racial suspicions thus carried over into the 1970s.

By 1970 armed student uprisings had given way to a broader black-nationalist political agenda insisting on racial unity and rejecting integration emphatically. At a meeting of the Congress of African People in Atlanta that year, the favorite slogans were "black unity," "black nationalism," "pan-Africanism," and "nation building." Jesse Jackson of SCLC declared that integration was not the opposite of segregation: "The mixing of races is not a political process, but a biological process that was done by the racist rapist. The time for integration is past." CORE endorsed the strategy of desegregation without integration. Integration would doom blacks to be "perpetually in the minority," the organization's head announced, because whites wanted to "integrate blacks and control them."[3]

"Empowerment" became the political goal of black nationalism. In 1967 black candidates had won the mayoralty in Gary and Cleveland, and more such black empowerment was expected because America's largest cities experienced marked demographic transformations during the 1960s as blacks continued to move in and whites moved out at an even faster pace. New York lost 617,000 whites and gained 579,000 blacks. In Chicago there were almost 300,000 more blacks in 1970 than a decade earlier and a half million fewer whites. Detroit took in 177,000 new blacks but lost almost twice that many whites. By 1970 four large American cities—Washington, Newark, Gary, and Atlanta—had black majorities, and St.

Jesse Jackson of the Southern Christian Leadership Conference. *Courtesy Library of Congress.*

Louis, Baltimore, New Orleans, and Detroit had black populations of more than 40 percent.[4]

The empowerment of black-nationalist attitudes in urban politics meant that African Americans could do something about their longstanding grievances against urban police forces. In Atlanta, Maynard Jackson, a young African American elected mayor in 1973, immediately took control of the police department, installing his own black chief. The new chief constantly faced corruption charges and crime soared in the city, but blacks' anti-police feeling overrode concerns about dishonesty and disorder. The same year in Detroit, Coleman Young, a former labor organizer with a strong racial appeal in Detroit's black neighborhoods, won a mayor's race focused heavily on the behavior of the city's police force. "Criminals on the streets," Young proclaimed, "were seriously rivaled by the ones in squad cars." He told a black group that everyone knew that "law and order is a code word for 'Keep the niggers in their place.'" Crime was a problem, he admitted, in a city where two people were murdered every day in 1974, "but not *the* problem.... [T]he police are the major threat" to blacks. By 1976, Detroit had earned a national reputation for its lawlessness, and suburbanites avoided going into the city. Young in turn blamed the suburbs for Detroit's problems and demanded financial help from them. Whites could not "stand for black folks to run a damn thing," Young declared, "and if we do, they're going to destroy it." Whites believed that Young was trying to drive them from Detroit, and many of the ones still there left during his early years in office. As they departed, Young became invincible in city politics, getting reelected four times. When charged with corruption in the 1980s, the mayor denounced his critics confidently: "To attack Coleman Young is to attack Detroit—and to attack Detroit is to attack black."[5]

The success of black-nationalist politicians in the 1970s and 1980s fostered continuing racial alienation. As Young's rhetoric suggested, those men sometimes promoted black solidarity through explicitly racial appeals. Black empowerment meant that whites had lost some ground in the longstanding racial competition for political power. They had literally relinquished control of physical space in many American cities as blacks became majorities in those places. Whites often pointed to the rise of crime, violence, and corruption as the consequence of black empowerment—usually without much rigor in comparing the behavior of new black leaders with that of the old white regimes. Whites' resentments were often more latent than overt, frequently resting silently in the suburbs, but they nevertheless shaped racial attitudes in the post-1968 years.

Opinion polls among African Americans revealed that, while most rejected the violence, and many even the political objectives of Black Power, a majority believed that studying African culture and celebrating the African past were good things. By 1968 black ethnic nationalism was popularly represented in the wearing of natural "Afro" hair and dashikis; the rapid replacement of "Negro" with "black" as the accepted racial designation; and the creation of black holidays such as Kwanzaa, a harvest celebration created partly as an African-American alternative to Christmas. Black nationalism provided much new psychic satisfaction for African Americans. "We became aware of ourselves," a Detroit autoworker later told a reporter. "'Black is beautiful, black is power.' We had a unity there. You passed somebody on the street and you were 'sister,' you were 'brother.'" Black cultural nationalism nurtured the emotional engagement of African Americans with their history, as they not only discovered black culture and achievement in the past but also fully exposed the ways they had suffered throughout history, through the brutal exploitation of the people and environment of Africa, the slave trade, the sexual abuse of black women, lynching, and segregation.[6]

Black-nationalist thinking in the late 1960s presumed that African Americans needed to separate from whites in order to survive amid the dominant white culture. Survival depended on creating a group consciousness and a sense of black collective responsibility. In fact, an ethnic consciousness had long since been established among African Americans: an ethnic communal sense had evolved among blacks since the 1920s and had reached maturity between about 1955 and 1963. What Black Power and black nationalism more nearly intended was to reorient that communal sense toward an ethnic consciousness defined intensively by opposition to the dominant white authority in the United States. At least theoretically, black nationalists rejected integration with whites as submission to white control, whereas the earlier communal consciousness had assumed that the goal was to integrate into the American mainstream. Like all movements for ethnic nationalism, black nationalism also depended heavily on the creation of myths about the past to enhance the group's sense of its uniqueness and special mission.[7]

Black Power and black consciousness represented an ethnic nationalism that was not acceptable to most whites. Since the World War II experience with Nazi and Japanese racism, Americans had generally been hostile to ethnic or racial nationalism. That feeling largely accounted for the demise of southern nationalism after the war. Rightly or not, many Americans associated ethnic nationalism with a questionable loyalty to country. Like southerners who had held too tightly to their southern ethnic identity after World War II, African Americans who placed too high a value on their black identity were suspect to most whites. Whites typically perceived that black politicians such as Maynard Jackson and Coleman Young who openly cultivated black solidarity were exploiting racial feeling for their own gain. Thus black nationalism contributed, along with the perception of rampant black violence, to the continuing racial alienation in American society after 1968.

But white hostility to black ethnic nationalism was moderated by the emergence of group consciousness in many other forms. The women's movement in the late 1960s effected huge changes in behavior and expectations in women's rights and gender roles. At about the same time, a gay liberation movement resulted in both more openness about sexual preference than had ever existed in the United States and firmer commitment against prejudice toward homosexuals. Other ethnic groups, but especially Hispanics, organized to protect their rights and promote group consciousness in much the same fashion as African Americans were doing. The various "consciousness" movements resulted in a broader tolerance toward cultural difference in the United States, which defused much of the potential hostility to black ethnic nationalism. As more Americans confronted more groups experiencing consciousness-raising efforts, they became rather quickly more tolerant of ethnic and cultural difference, even when expressed in nationalistic tones.

Thus black nationalism, while aggravating the dominant culture's hostility to ethnic nationalism, was tolerated, especially after the militant, anti-American rhetoric was mostly replaced with a softer cultural consciousness. The intense criticism of American state nationalism that came with the antiwar movement but that was accepted far beyond the protestors also facilitated the acceptance of black nationalism. As state nationalism became less legitimate in the eyes of many Americans, tolerance for ethnic nationalism could rise.

American popular culture helped to make room for black nationalism as part of a broader cultural tolerance in the early 1970s, the result mainly of the expanding rights movements among women, homosexuals, and Hispanics. Evidence of the growing tolerance of black nationalism lay in the way that in the 1970s most white Americans began to accept the boxer Muhammad Ali, including his Muslim religion and name, as one of the twentieth century's greatest athletes. The themes of Black Power and autonomy suddenly were more prominent in American popular culture. Beginning with *Sweet Sweetback's Baadasssss Song* in 1971, white audiences began to pay some attention to black-made films, especially the "blaxploitation" efforts of the actor-director Melvin Van Peebles in which tough, black-nationalist characters freely visited mayhem on white enemies. *Shaft*, a 1971 Hollywood movie directed by the black artist Gordon Parks, centered the action on a strong-willed and sexually accomplished black detective who inhabits a mostly black and racially tense New York. *Shaft* raised a black hero who feared no one and made no accommodation to the white world. White-directed Hollywood films continued the move to greater realism about race: the 1972 film *Sounder* provided one of Hollywood's first and clearest indictments of racial exploitation in the South; and *Lady Sings the Blues*, also in 1972, celebrated the art of the jazz singer Billie Holliday at the same time that it dealt honestly with her life.[8]

Television made great strides in promoting both ethnic tolerance and social realism in the early 1970s, and it relied almost entirely on comedy that had racial content. In 1970 the black comedian Flip Wilson hosted his own variety show in which he lampooned black characters in a good-natured way. In 1971 the white producer Norman Lear introduced *All in the Family*, a satire in which the character Archie Bunker voiced racial and ethnic bigotry, in opposition to his left-wing son-in-law and his equally bigoted black neighbor. In 1972, Lear produced *Sanford and Son*, the story of black father-and-son junk dealers in Watts, the first all-black-cast television program since *Amos 'n' Andy* went off the air in 1953. For five years, the comedian Redd Foxx brilliantly portrayed the bigoted, unscrupulous Fred Sanford, the first black television character since the Kingfish in *Amos 'n' Andy* to reveal abundant human flaws. Lear went on in the 1970s to produce other situation comedies in which black characters experienced poverty, race discrimination, and interracial marriage—all subjects that television had avoided entirely up to the 1970s.[9]

The single most important popular-culture development for race relations in the 1970s was *Roots*, Alex Haley's 1976 book about his family's history. Haley traced his origins to a village in Africa whence came his ancestor Kunte Kinte, who was sold into American slavery, and then Haley followed subsequent generations of family members through slavery and into freedom. *Roots* commanded a huge readership of both blacks and whites. It was made into an eight-part television dramatization that riveted much of the nation's attention in early 1977. Both the book and the television series offered a harsher view of slavery and segregation than had been shown the American public in any popular genre. It effectively challenged and overturned the still-influential interpretation of slavery offered by Hollywood in *Gone with the Wind*. *Roots* satisfied the black-nationalist agenda on several points: it connected African Americans with their experience on the mother continent in a way that celebrated their origins; it dramatized the evils of slavery and of whites' general inhumanity to blacks for hundreds of years; and it offered a powerful narrative of black triumph over oppression. Haley's research would subsequently be questioned, and some scholars concluded that *Roots* was more fiction than fact in places. But ultimately it mattered little whether *Roots* was myth or history, because its impact on Americans' thinking about the black past was unquestionably profound.[10]

Thus popular culture in the late 1960s and 1970s functioned to soften the hard edges of political life at the time. It achieved far greater realism about white bigotry and discrimination, etched with a finer hand black

attitudes, and promoted more honest humor about American race relations than any popular entertainment had before. Popular renderings of
black nationalism created cultural space for its existence in a society in
which the dominant ethos was generally very hostile to such ideology. As
it had done in the 1950s, popular culture in the post–civil rights years
served the function of finding common ground amid racial conflict—and
at times even obscuring the deep divisions that persisted.

I

Compared with Lyndon Johnson or John Kennedy in his last year, or
even Barry Goldwater, at the other end of the ideological spectrum,
Richard Nixon lacked ideological passion that shaped his racial views as
president. According to his aide John Erlichman, Nixon thought blacks
were genetically inferior, but such views never came to public light. His
advisers later commented on his lack of interest in domestic politics and
his willingness to accept without much deliberation policy initiatives put
forward by others. When one administration official complained that a
proposed new welfare program was a direct contradiction of Nixon's philosophy, Erlichman replied, "Don't you realize the president doesn't have
a philosophy?" The electoral calculus most clearly shaped Nixon's racial
positions. He could not bring himself simply to write off black votes,
having gotten 32 percent of the black vote in 1960 and knowing the deci-
sive influence black voters often had in large states, but he apparently
reckoned that his appeal was limited to about 30 percent of the black
vote, and only 12 percent of nonwhites had actually voted for him in
1968. Thus there was ample incentive to try to cultivate black support,
but there was a gamble as well: if blacks had become too solidly Democratic to entertain a Republican candidate, more was to be gained by
exploiting white racial hostility in order to capture white voters from the
Democrats than by taking positions to win blacks' favor. As Nixon was
coming into office, the political scientist Kevin Phillips announced that
the New Deal coalition of the Democratic Party was breaking up, the

main reasons for this being "the Negro socioeconomic revolution" and the Great Society programs that had aligned the Democratic Party with "many Negro demands." Alienated whites promised to form what Phillips called the "emerging Republican majority."[11]

Nixon did exploit white backlash, especially in his handling of school integration and his appointment of judges, but his administration took some bold steps in expanding the authority of the federal government over race relations. Daniel Patrick Moynihan, now Nixon's chief domestic-policy adviser, suggested to Nixon in 1970 that "the time may have come when the issue of race could benefit from a period of 'benign neglect.'" Although this was interpreted by liberals at the time as Nixon's opposition to further progress on civil rights, racial policies under Nixon were neither benign nor neglected. His administration enforced compensatory measures for African Americans with greater determination than the Johnson administration had done after the summer of 1965. That fit the larger pattern of his domestic-policy impact: his administration was responsible for some of the most far-reaching government expansions of the late twentieth century—most notably, the new regulatory authority imposed by the Environmental Protection Agency and the Occupational Safety and Health Administration. Nixon's legacy on race relations thus comprised a cynical accommodation to both residual white-supremacist impulses and demands for extensive race-based compensation. His inconsistency contributed to a broader societal confusion about race policies and goals in the 1970s.[12]

Nixon and Moynihan believed that Lyndon Johnson's War on Poverty represented a political opportunity for the new administration. Welfare policy remained racially charged with two rigidly opposing positions. Moynihan now believed that most of the War on Poverty had been misguided, and he sold Nixon on the idea of a guaranteed annual income as a simplified antipoverty effort. Moynihan thought direct cash payments to the poor were the best way to address poverty, and his plan had the advantage of cutting out many of the black welfare bureaucrats who Moynihan believed were among his and Nixon's enemies. Although subsequent developments demonstrated that his 1965 report on the black

family had been prescient, Moynihan in 1969 was still persona non grata
to many on the left who supported the Johnson programs. Most social
scientists and civil rights activists insisted that the antipoverty programs
were going to alter the ghetto so much that black family problems would
be overcome and replaced with new behaviors and values. This view
became less a prediction or hypothesis than a faith that social science had
to uphold. By 1970 it was clear, one black sociologist later wrote, that
studies of ghetto pathologies were no longer acceptable. The only
research on poor blacks that could avoid ideological attack from the left
was that "conducted by minority scholars on the strengths, not the weak-
nesses, of inner-city families and communities."[13]

Nixon's guaranteed income plan failed to pass the Democrat-con-
trolled Congress, and the Johnson programs lived well past Nixon's time
in the White House. Indeed, during the early 1970s Congress took the initiative to expand the welfare benefits, and Nixon made no real effort to
stop them. Welfare spending calmed the nation, Nixon believed, and
domestic peace worked to his political benefit. The Congress made Food
Stamps a federally administered program with broader eligibility and
raised its benefits. It also increased benefits for Aid to Families with
Dependent Children (AFDC). These changes precipitated a welfare
explosion: Food Stamps, which had 400,000 recipients in 1965, grew to 4.3
million recipients in 1970 and then to 17.1 million in 1975. The number of
people benefiting from AFDC grew from 3.1 million in 1960 to 11.1 million
in 1980. The monthly benefit per recipient rose by 28 percent, and in 1981,
44 percent of those recipients were black—almost four times their proportion of the population.[14]

Nixon's impact on federal employment discrimination policy proved
to be large and lasting in an area where very little change had come
despite decades of national discussion about fair hiring. The change originated in the construction industry, a sector in which the federal government had few options to use in enforcing fair employment because
federal construction funding was typically awarded to local governments,
not directly to construction contractors. There was no directly coercive
path to force hiring of minorities. In response to Lyndon Johnson's 1965

Executive Order 11246 to end discrimination in federal contracts, the Labor Department had developed the "Philadelphia Plan," a way to force contractors on federal projects to hire greater numbers of minorities through the contract-compliance process. But bureaucratic opponents in the Johnson administration kept the plan from being implemented. George Shultz, Nixon's secretary of labor, adopted the Philadelphia Plan as the policy of the Office of Federal Contract Compliance (OFCC). Shultz insisted that under his direction the Philadelphia Plan would impose not quotas but "ranges" of minority employment in particular crafts, though in time there proved to be no difference between the two. "Affirmative action" in its original use in John Kennedy's 1961 executive order on federal contractors' hiring had suggested only making extra effort to recruit minority applicants, not the application of quotas. Title VII of the 1964 Civil Rights Act had specifically forbidden quotas. Lyndon Johnson's 1965 fair-employment order had a similar meaning, but his imperative to make "equality as a fact and equality as a result" was potential justification for quotas.[15]

Shultz and Nixon had good political reasons to address hiring practices. During the summer of 1969, there were violent conflicts over job discrimination in the building trades in Pittsburgh and Seattle, and job protests in several major cities. Following the logic of successful protests of the 1960s, civil rights leaders believed that confrontations might bring federal action on jobs. By the same logic, the administration justified reform action as a means to keep domestic peace. But there was also gain from vexing Nixon's enemies. Shultz had shown "great style," Erlichman later wrote, in taking a position that placed two of the administration's most powerful opponents, organized labor and the NAACP, in opposition to each other. "Before long, the AFL-CIO and the NAACP were locked in combat," Erlichman wrote, over hiring quotas, and the Nixon administration "was located in the sweet and reasonable middle."[16]

Then in 1970 the Labor Department applied the Philadelphia Plan's model of proportional representation by race to all activities by federal contractors, not just construction contracts. Critics argued that the new rules did away with "ranges" for employment levels and replaced them with "flat quotas," but the public paid relatively little attention as a quota system went into effect. Nixon coalesced with congressional Democrats behind new legislation that gave the Equal Employment Opportunity Commission (EEOC) authority to initiate court proceedings against employment discrimination. Between 1968 and 1972 the budget of the EEOC more than doubled and its staff more than quadrupled, and the agency would continue to grow rapidly in the ensuing years. In January 1973, American Telephone & Telegraph, under threat of court action by the EEOC, reached a settlement to give millions of dollars in back pay to minority and women employees and to implement high goals for hiring and upgrading both women and minorities. At that point, hiring quotas were established as the broad policy of the national government and were on the way to being settled expectations for American business.[17]

The use of quotas in hiring was advanced with the U.S. Supreme Court's 1971 ruling in *Griggs v. Duke Power Co.*, which found that testing for job qualification, even when applied fairly, was not acceptable if the tests resulted in a disparate racial impact. The *Griggs* decision pleased civil rights advocates, who by 1971 were committed to "results" measurements of whether discrimination was at work. The head of the EEOC announced that *Griggs* "redefined discrimination in terms of consequences rather than motive, effect rather than purpose."[18]

The loudest complaints about Nixon's employment policies came from Jews, long the victims of quotas. Just after World War I, eastern universities had sharply reduced the number of Jews accepted. Columbia cut its Jewish enrollment from 40 to 22 percent. At Harvard in 1922, President A. Lawrence Lowell, alarmed that 21 percent of his entering class were Jews, instituted a Jewish quota of 15 percent for future admissions, and similar quotas were soon imposed at other Ivy League institutions. Jewish quotas were enforced through much of American higher education until after World War II, when most were abolished. American Jews thus understood that the application of quotas limited their opportunities and represented an affront to their individual rights. In 1963, when quotas were recommended to the United States Commission on Civil

Rights as a means to correct discrimination in housing and employment, the American Jewish Committee declared that the "imposition of a quota simply cannot be squared with the requirement of equal protection of the laws guaranteed by the Fourteenth Amendment." Civil rights "are individual, not group rights," the committee said. In 1971 the sociologist Nathan Glazer criticized the Commission on Civil Rights for shifting its goals from equal opportunity to "*full equality* of achievement for minority groups." The measure of civil rights conditions, Glazer observed, was no longer "Are members of minority groups discriminated against?" but rather "Are they found in employment, at every level, in numbers equal to their proportion in the population?"[19]

During the 1972 presidential campaign, leaders of Jewish organizations complained about quotas, and Nixon declared his total opposition to them, notwithstanding his administration's role in implementing their use. Nixon made his opposition to quotas such an issue in the campaign that his Democratic opponent George McGovern declared that "the way to end discrimination against some is not to begin discrimination against others." McGovern flatly rejected quotas "as detrimental to American society."[20]

Such lip service against quotas mattered little, because the arena for setting and implementing civil rights policies had shifted. Martin Luther King had arranged demonstrations of the evil of segregation in order to get the president and the Congress to act against segregation, but now decisions were made elsewhere. The triumph of the Philadelphia Plan and the expansion of the power of such new agencies as the OFCC and EEOC represented a victory for the regulatory "subgovernment" of Washington. This subgovernment was composed of the OFCC and the EEOC, which enforced Title VII of the Civil Rights Act; the Commission on Civil Rights, which frequently reported on the efforts, and especially the failures, to enforce civil rights laws; the Civil Rights Division of the Justice Department, which enforced the Voting Rights Act of 1965; the Office of Civil Rights within the Department of Health, Education, and Welfare (HEW), which implemented school desegregation; and the corresponding offices for civil rights in the Defense Department, in Housing and Urban Development, and soon in all eleven cabinet departments. Outside the executive branch but monitoring and working with the civil rights subgovernment were two other concentrations of power. One was the civil rights organizations that represented constituents to be protected by the agencies—the NAACP; the Urban League; and the Leadership Conference on Civil Rights, which was a broad consortium of groups that included organized labor and foundations. The other concentration existed in Congress. It included congressional oversight and funding subcommittees such as the House Judiciary Subcommittee on Civil Rights. In 1971 the Congressional Black Caucus was formed.[21]

By 1972 a triangle of power connected executive agencies that ran programs and enforced policies to congressional committees and caucuses that oversaw and funded them, and to constituent groups that benefited from the policies and campaigned for their continuation and expansion. Civil rights policies would largely be made inside the lines of this three-sided political form, away from the direct influence of democratic majorities. As a result, Richard Nixon could exploit popular hostility to such remedial policies as affirmative action at the same time that he advanced their application. Such cynicism accounted for much of the public confusion about the meaning of equality in the 1970s.[22]

The growing bureaucratic commitment to quotas in the early 1970s reflected the belief that discrimination was so deeply entrenched in the minds of whites that only direct and coercive remedies would end it. Of course, any African American or woman attempting to join the Birmingham Fire Department or the Steamfitters' Union in Philadelphia in the early 1970s—or any minority trying to get into a work group characterized by a "brotherhood" mentality—could most assuredly draw the conclusion that quotas were the only practical remedy to persistent discrimination. But the use of quotas over time had the effect of defining equality as proportional representation, of using the census to decide what was discrimination. Its adherents would insist that affirmative action represented the broadest definition of equality, but soon others would argue, just as vehemently, that it was so narrow that it was un-American.[23]

II

Nixon viewed school desegregation as far more dangerous politically than welfare or fair employment, and he tried to shape policy to preserve the status quo. Although little school desegregation had taken place in the South prior to 1969, court decisions had put a faster desegregation process in motion. In 1965, HEW had developed guidelines for implementing the Civil Rights Act on school desegregation, using as the stick to enforce desegregation the withdrawal of federal funds. The following year an appeals court had ordered that HEW guidelines be put into force to "undo the harm" of an Alabama school system's segregationist past. This signaled the end of the judiciary's acceptance of a gradual, token approach and demanded a wholesale transformation of practice in southern education. In a Virginia case in 1968, the Supreme Court rejected "freedom of choice" desegregation plans once and for all and demanded that the segregated system come forward with a plan that "promises realistically to work *now*." Alarmed that whites would blame Nixon for pushing integration, Attorney General John Mitchell ordered HEW to stop making desegregation plans and to leave the orders to the courts. The outcome was little changed, because the federal judiciary was now fully committed to enforcing desegregation. When HEW withdrew its approval of a plan to desegregate 33 Mississippi school districts in late 1969, the Supreme Court ordered the districts to stop "at once" the operation of dual systems and to operate "now and hereafter" unitary school systems.[24]

At that point the desegregation process began to move rapidly in the South. In the summer of 1970, school desegregation suits were filed against 57 southern school districts, and the Internal Revenue Service cut off tax exemptions to all-white private schools. Between 1968 and 1972 the portion of southern black children in all-black schools fell from 68 percent to 8 percent. Much was accomplished by closing schools and redrawing zones, but often desegregation orders required busing students, both black and white. "The school bus was the carrier of the disease of segregation," one scholar wrote, "as Negroes were carried past

white schools to black ones." Now courts prescribed the big yellow vehi-
cles to cure that disease.[25]

Busing was necessary because of the continuing reality of segregated
housing. In 1972 the Commission on Civil Rights reported that black students attended schools that were more than half black at least 90 percent
of the time in Los Angeles, Chicago, Philadelphia, and Detroit. The
largest cities had actually become more segregated overall during the
1960s. Blacks were more separated from whites than any other ethnic
group in the country, including Asians, Mexican Americans, and Puerto
Ricans. In Los Angeles in 1980, 81 percent of blacks lived in blocks that
were overwhelmingly black, whereas only 57 percent of Hispanics
resided mainly among Hispanics and 47 percent of Asians dwelt among
Asians. Residential segregation could not be explained fairly by economic
difference, especially since the number of affluent African Americans had
begun to grow rapidly in the 1960s. Poor whites and blacks typically did
not reside side by side, and neither did wealthy people of different colors.
Residential desegregation faced not only the longstanding prosegregation bias of the federal-housing and lending establishments but also the
psychological obstacles among both blacks and whites. Sociologists discovered that both blacks and whites had a "mental map" of where each
belonged in a particular urban geography, and the willingness of either
to move to "alien" territory was highly limited. In intensive studies done
in the Detroit area in the 1970s, one sociologist developed flash cards
depicting various levels of racial mixing that were used to find the subject's ideal neighborhood. He discovered that for whites the ideal was a
neighborhood with only a few blacks—but not all white—and for blacks it
was a neighborhood that was about equally black and white. The reality
was, of course, that each race was uncomfortable with, and thus unac-
cepting of, the other race's ideal, which explained much about the failure
of housing integration.[26]

Opposition to busing flared everywhere it was imposed, but anger
exploded after the Supreme Court in early 1971 ruled unanimously in
Swann v. Charlotte-Mecklenburg that busing to achieve a racial balance was
constitutional. Realtors in cities under court order began to advertise

busing-free areas, and parents worked up bus-dodging schemes. As the new school term approached in the fall of 1971, George Wallace ordered three Alabama school districts to defy federal court orders to bus. Meanwhile, parents in Augusta, Georgia, organized a school boycott against a busing order, and Governor Jimmy Carter declared that he would endorse a statewide boycott if no other remedy was found. In San Francisco, Chinese-American parents objected to busing their children away from Chinatown. A movement sprang up for a constitutional amendment to outlaw compulsory busing. The Gallup Poll reported in November that 76 percent of Americans opposed busing from one district to another.[27]

The antibusing sentiment quickly took the form of a popular movement in places where orders were being implemented. In Pontiac, Michigan, which became one of the first northern cities ordered to bus children, Irene McCabe led an anti-busing crusade in the early 1970s. A homemaker, mother of three, and self-described member of the "blue-collar working class," McCabe made herself the spokesperson for the threatened white suburbanites in the Detroit area. Her group of housewives emphasized that their concern was for the safety of their children. "A mother is a mother," one of their leaflets read, "no matter what her color, creed or ethnic background." "Her first concern is her child, who she wants to be near." McCabe feared the place where her daughter was being bussed. "It's an area of town the fire department won't even go to unless accompanied by armed guards." McCabe and other housewives organized a school boycott and picketed the very General Motors (GM) plants where their husbands worked, including one where school buses were manufactured. More than half of GM workers refused to cross the anti-busing picket line. In the midst of the furor, bombs destroyed ten buses.[28]

Anger about busing reverberated through suburban Detroit in early 1972 with the decision in the NAACP's case challenging school segregation in the Detroit area. Judge Stephen Roth had studied a massive amount of evidence about residential discrimination in the suburbs and unequal treatment of blacks in the city schools. Roth found that what most people had believed was de facto segregation resulting from residential separation was instead de jure segregation based on government decisions about housing, roads, and schools. He ruled that Detroit and its surrounding suburbs had to integrate their schools, the first urban-suburban consolidation order in the North. Roth's implementation order affected Detroit and 53 suburbs, including Pontiac, and it meant bus rides of up to 90 minutes each day for almost half the 780,000 children involved. The decision escalated white parents' fears about their children's security. Detroit was coming to be known as "Murder Capital, U.S.A.," with an average of two killings per day, double the next-worst American city. Its schools had long had a reputation for poor achievement and violence in the halls. An observer in sympathy with suburban parents wrote: "There is a great deal of emotional power and reasonability to the cry of a mother asking, 'What gives some judge the right to send my child to a violent, deteriorating school in the inner city?'"[29]

In early 1972, as the election year began, politicians reckoned with the political dynamite that busing represented. Nixon promised to try to find a way to limit busing, though the means—constitutional amendment, federal law, or executive action—was unclear. The busing stakes got much higher with the Detroit decision and one just before it that had found that the predominantly black Richmond school system and its contiguous, mostly white suburban systems had been created and maintained by racial motives and thus had to be addressed with a cross-district merger plan. In the wake of the Detroit decision, George Wallace brought his campaign for the Democratic presidential nomination to Michigan and delivered fiery condemnations of federal judges, their "asinine busing decisions," and the "briefcase-carrying bureaucrats who are trying to run your lives." Wallace won a majority in the Michigan primary. Immediately the Congress reached a compromise on legislation aimed at curbing busing, and much of the support came from liberals and moderates from outside the South.[30]

In those places where it was tried extensively, busing usually succeeded or failed on matters of demography and geography. Busing worked in Charlotte, North Carolina, which had a large county-wide school system with the city centered geographically, making it difficult for whites to flee to suburbs in another district. The district had a relatively small black minority of 29 percent. No Charlotte schools reached the "tipping" point of 40 percent black, the proportion at which all whites usually left the school. Still, almost immediately more than 20 private schools were established in Charlotte, which together enrolled about 10,000 students, or about every sixth child in the county. But in 1973 support for the system under *Swann* built among whites, and by 1974 there was a significant decline in racial incidents in schools. Richmond's busing plan, on the other hand, foundered because the system was 65 percent black in 1970 when busing began, and because two almost all-white systems were contiguous to the city. Half the whites left the Richmond system, pushing the white percentage down below 20 percent by 1976.[31]

Boston proved to be the most notoriously anti-busing northern city, a sad irony for the home of abolitionism. In 1974 more than half of Boston's black students attended schools that were at least 90 percent black when a federal judge ruled that the school system had "knowingly carried out a systematic program of segregation." When a desegregation order was enforced, the only real trouble came at South Boston High, which sat in an all-Irish blue-collar neighborhood that had been "paired" with all-black Roxbury. Nearly all whites boycotted the school, and furious parents screamed epithets and threw rocks at the buses bringing the black children. Louise Day Hicks, a school board member from South Boston, joined with five thousand angry neighborhood residents in marches, and she helped form an anti-busing organization, Restore Our Alienated Rights, or ROAR. The conflict continued for several years as South Boston's whites roared their refusal to concede. In the end they did not have to give in, in part because anti-busing whites held a voting majority in the city of Boston and thus could use their control of the local political apparatus to back up their defiance. Nevertheless, by the end of the 1970s, almost half of Boston's white children had abandoned the city for suburban schools.[32]

An unintended consequence of the Boston situation, however, was to give vivid form to white bigotry in the North. Many white southerners enjoyed the discomfort that the television-news scenes of cursing, rock-throwing women in Boston in 1974 caused for northern whites who had fixed blame for American race problems on the South. Those images ended once and for all any regional self-righteousness about racial bigotry in the United States. Broader recognition that white bigotry was a national problem did not increase acceptance of busing, but it may have created more support for other compensatory efforts.

Within a year of the *Swann* decision, some courts began to undermine it. In June 1972 an appeals court said that the Richmond cross-district order had exceeded the judge's authority. Then in 1974 the Supreme Court overturned the Detroit desegregation order in *Milliken v. Bradley*. The majority of justices found that the suburbs had not *caused* housing segregation in the Detroit metropolitan area, and thus they did not have to participate in integrating the schools. The court majority discounted Judge Roth's findings that governments at all levels had cooperated with banks and realtors to establish residential segregation throughout the metropolitan area. "No single tradition in public education is more deeply rooted than local control over the operation of schools," Chief Justice Warren Burger wrote in the majority opinion in *Milliken*. "Local autonomy has long been thought essential both to the maintenance of community concern and support for public schools and the quality of the education process." Justice Thurgood Marshall answered that "desegregation is not and was never expected to be an easy task," but constitutional principle should not defer to white anger. "Today's holding, I fear, is more a reflection of a perceived public mood that we have gone far enough in enforcing the Constitution's guarantee of equal justice than it is the product of neutral principles of law."[33]

The *Milliken* decision reflected a turning point for the federal judiciary on racial matters. Since *Carolene Products* in 1938, the judiciary had consistently expanded the definition of equality to protect minority rights, and the Supreme Court had made broadly protective rulings as late as 1971 in the *Swann* and *Griggs* decisions. But Nixon's appointees Warren Burger, Lewis Powell, and William Rehnquist had by 1974 pointed the court back toward a narrower definition. The change in direction was gradual and not always straight, but it soon became clear that protections for minorities would not expand as they had for the past 35 years.

Thus the public school, long the arena where status competition was settled in the United States, remained the source of much anger and anxiety. The Supreme Court's unwillingness in *Milliken* to unravel the racial origins of housing segregation gave authority to subsequent decisions in lower courts to avoid altogether the impact of past actions in considering future remedies. In 1979 a federal district judge, presented with thousands of pages of evidence of Atlanta's history of enforcing residential segregation, declared that "there is just so much baggage a school case can carry." He ruled that, because a fair-housing law was on the books now, housing discrimination would not be considered in establishing a school desegregation order in Atlanta. The Supreme Court upheld the decision. Atlanta's black community had, however, already accepted the end of strenuous efforts to desegregate the schools. As early as 1973 black teachers and administrators had acquiesced in the status quo of school boundaries in exchange for their control of the inner-city system. Empowerment had trumped integration.[34]

In the absence of more successful school desegregation, blacks seemed locked in the old inferiority. Schools were a main way Americans handed down status to their children. For whites in the suburbs, that meant high status. "Neighborhood schools symbolize, above all else, the effort of America's vast middle class to transmit shared values and aspirations to its children," one scholar concluded, but to inner-city blacks, neighborhood schools meant perpetuation of the lowest status in American society and "a slow suffocation in the dankness of the ghetto."[35]

III

As the busing controversy unfolded in 1972 and 1973, the Watergate scandal broke, and in 1974, Richard Nixon was forced to resign the presidency. His successor, Gerald R. Ford, condemned "forced busing" but otherwise did not interfere with the growing welfare programs or the implementation of affirmative action through the regulatory agencies. Watergate boosted the Georgia Democrat Jimmy Carter to the White House in 1976. Despite much romanticism attached to the arrival of a reformed southern segregationist in the Oval Office, and corresponding high hopes among race reformers for new initiatives especially in the economic area, Carter mostly embraced policies on affirmative action, welfare, and school desegregation that had been set under Nixon.[36]

More important for the evolution of race relations was the end in 1973 of the American economy's long period of growth that had begun in 1941 and continued with only a few dips for more than 30 years. Starting in 1973 and continuing for about a decade, inflation and recessions caused a decline in real income for the average American. During these years, the labor force was growing faster than employment, in part because of the entry into the labor market of the huge postwar "baby boom" generation. More people were chasing fewer jobs. At the same time, the American economy was undergoing a rapid structural change from a predominantly industrial economy to one more dependent on services for economic growth. The "deindustrialization of America" meant that there were fewer high-paying manufacturing jobs and that those that did materialize had high educational or skill requirements for entry.

For the first time in more than three decades, the real incomes of American families stopped growing. Median family income had risen by almost 50 percent between 1960 and 1973, but it fell by 3.5 percent in 1974 and 2.6 percent in 1975. In 1973 hourly earnings went down for the first time since 1951, and it kept going down for the next two years. Weekly earnings, reflecting the lower number of hours worked in the recessionary economy of 1973–75, fell even more. During the long period of steadily increasing prosperity from 1941 to 1973, Americans had accepted a rising tax burden without strong political reaction. Between 1953 and 1976, the average tax burden on the median family income in the United States had gone up 92 percent, with most of the increase coming in state and local taxes. At the federal level, Social Security contributions had increased by 473 percent between 1960 and 1975, a rate about two-and-a-half times faster than incomes were rising. The United States was ripe for a tax revolt.[37]

Many white Americans thus lost ground economically at the same time that they perceived, correctly, that African Americans continued to gain. As the wages of whites declined or stagnated during the 1970s, blacks' held steady or rose. Black males' average income, which had been 58 percent of white men's in 1969, rose to 63 percent by 1979, while black females' income went from 84 to 92 percent of white women's. For many whites, the continuing large disparity overall between blacks' and whites' incomes was far less important than the reality that African Americans were improving economically, and they were not.[38]

White Americans had always believed that there would be winners and losers in the competition for opportunities. They had assumed this as a fact of economic life even when rapid economic growth would have meant that most people were winners in a fair contest—as during the massive industrial growth of the late nineteenth century and during the early World War II years. In 1980 the economist Lester Thurow reported that in fact Americans did now live in a "zero-sum" economy: for one to gain, another had to lose. In order to create a truly equal-opportunity society, Thurow argued, whites would have to accept losses, while blacks gained. To keep from perpetuating the effects of past discrimination into the present and the future, whites would have to accept some discrimination to end the effects of past discrimination. Most whites suffering a loss of status in the sluggish economy of the 1970s understood the unhappy logic of the zero-sum economy. But that did not mean that they accepted with resignation the policy conclusion. They would resist, though the means did not emerge immediately.[39]

Thus it is surprising that, at the time when blue-collar whites were less secure than they had been since the Great Depression, direct economic competition between blacks and whites for job opportunities seemed to dissipate. The dynamic that had shaped so much about American race relations all but disappeared in the 1970s. The absence of job competition reflected the reality that white workers rarely could control workplaces as they had in the past. Unions had been taught their lesson about discrimination and were fairer toward minorities. The structure of the labor market now offered fewer blue-collar jobs for which to compete. Perhaps most important, the federal regulatory authority prevented the discriminatory tactics whites had used in the past.

The best arena left for the expression of conflict between blacks and whites was politics, and not surprisingly political action retained much racial content in the 1970s. Whites' doubts about welfare, school desegregation, and affirmative action would solidify in the late 1970s and 1980s into implacable opposition. Some of that hardening of white political attitudes, it should be understood, resulted from the frustration of economic ambitions. Political contests often served as proxies for economic conflict that had been stifled.

The most pressing political issues carried racial implications. When asked during the 1970s to name their greatest concern, Americans most consistently answered crime. The rates of murder, assault, and rape became ever more intrusive on Americans' consciousness as they spiraled upward between 1964 and 1974. There had been a general expectation that crime would go down once American society became more egalitarian, but in fact the opposite had occurred: crime went up while incomes of African Americans were rising and rights were being secured. Blacks continued to commit a disproportionate share of violent crimes, though whites' rates of crime had risen too. Whites living in big cities experienced the crime explosion personally, if not as victims then as spectators in the never-ending reporting of murder, assault, and robbery. Most Americans embraced more punitive measures for fighting crime, and popular hostility mounted against the federal courts' protections of the rights of the accused. In the mid-1970s, about two-thirds of Americans believed the country was spending too little on "halting the rising crime rate."[40]

About three-fifths of the people thought *too much* was being spent on welfare. Many whites understood their sense of declining status as the result of the expansion of government aid to African Americans. The rapid growth of Food Stamps, AFDC, and employment quotas gave clear evidence of the public sources of rising black status. Much of the employment gains among middle-class blacks came in government jobs. Great Society programs generated two million new government jobs, and a disproportionate share of these jobs went to blacks—about 850,000 of them between 1960 and 1976. In 1970, 57 percent of black male college graduates and 72 percent black female college graduates worked for governments. Government employment among African Americans accounted for much of the tripling in size of the black middle class between 1960 and 1976.[41]

Blacks and whites had decidedly different attitudes about government's role in their lives, even as both groups now broadly subscribed to democratic values and both rejected white supremacy. During the 1970s and early 1980s, almost three-fourths of blue-collar African Americans believed that it was government's responsibility to provide for citizens' economic well-being, whereas almost half of blue-collar whites said that the responsibility rested entirely with the individual. This suggested that most blacks still subscribed to Franklin Roosevelt's expansion of liberty to mean freedom from want, while half of whites now rejected that definition. One study concluded that "what most blacks want from the federal government goes far beyond what most working-class whites support for themselves, much less for blacks." Whites were much more likely to challenge and resist the intervention of government in their lives, and that instinct became racial because blacks were perceived as the special beneficiaries of expanded government. What often would be called racial politics was then in fact "regular politics"—a debate over how much government Americans should have. One political scientist has called it a "deep and disfiguring mistake" to remove race issues from regular politics, "to suppose that the clash of interests and ideas over issues of race is unique, independent of the differences that divide Americans over a range of issues." But it did happen very often in the 1970s and subsequent years that debates over the role of government were interpreted as disagreements over supporting or opposing a particular racial interest.[42]

In this context in the mid-1970s, the largest popular conservative political movement in American history was born. The 1973 decision in *Roe v.*

Wade sparked a new mass political movement of evangelical Christians opposed to abortion. The movement's institutional base resided in such organizations as the Moral Majority and the National Conservative Political Action Committee. For the most part Christian conservatives opposed segregation and racial discrimination, but they also lent much force to the growing doubts about the welfare system and the effectiveness of public education. As moral absolutists, they rejected the ambiguity of affirmative-action policies, and they made a connection between ambiguous racial policies and the moral and cultural relativism that they viewed as the fundamental problem of modern society. How could it be, they in effect asked, that racial discrimination was wrong at some times and not at others?

During the same years, a powerful critique of liberal positions on race emerged from a group of intellectuals who in 1976 began to be known as "neoconservatives." They were new conservatives because they had been committed to civil rights, and thus had been aligned with liberals on racial issues up to 1965, as opposed to "paleoconservatives" such as William F. Buckley, who had consistently opposed the civil rights movement. Most neoconservatives were Jewish—though by no means did most Jews become neoconservatives—and thus they were connected by tradition and culture to the most staunchly pro–civil rights portion of white Americans. In the late 1960s, however, the anti-Semitism of the ghetto and the Black Power movement combined with the New Left's anti–Vietnam War radicalism and such campus disruptions as those at Columbia in 1968 and Cornell in 1969 to push neoconservatives away from their longstanding place on the left. Opposition to affirmative action solidified the neoconservative perspective as quotas were applied widely. Two high-profile public intellectuals who had begun gravitating to the right in the mid-1960s now led the neoconservatives: Norman Podhoretz, editor of *Commentary*, the monthly publication of the American Jewish Committee, which aggressively opposed campus radicalism, Black Power, and race and gender quotas; and Irving Kristol, editor of the *Public Interest*, who addressed most of the same issues. One critic of the movement estimated in the late 1970s that one-fourth of the American intellectual elite were neoconservatives. They were centered in New York, the home base for the American media and publishing. Especially adept at influencing the media, Kristol defined a neoconservative as "a liberal who has been mugged by reality."[43]

Neoconservatives insisted that current policies on busing, hiring quotas, and welfare expansion were demanding change at a disruptive and unnatural pace. "We had seen many groups become part of the United States through immigration," Nathan Glazer wrote in 1975, "and we had seen each in turn overcoming some degree of discrimination to become integrated into American society." Blacks had been "lifted through the success of the civil rights struggle, and one could expect the economic and educational advancement of blacks that had been evident in the 1960s to continue." With that expectation, why was there a need for quotas and other remedial action? By the mid-1970s blacks were getting many government jobs, and Glazer did not see "how different [this was] from Irish domination of police forces in the past, or Jewish concentration in small business."[44]

The neoconservatives' lasting contribution to the equality debate lay in their articulation of the implications of race-based remedies on democratic values. They formulated the argument that affirmative action in its various shapes was an affront to the ideal of equality. What America stands for, they said, is equality before the law, or equality of opportunity, not equality of condition or equal results—which is the objective of affirmative action. They popularized the term "reverse discrimination," arguing that the civil rights establishment in the post-1965 years was demanding not equality but preferential treatment for African Americans. They insisted that theirs was the true, broad definition of equality, whereas the Left's definition had become so narrow as to be discriminatory. The neoconservatives thus showed the Right how to make equality *their* issue.

The Left's response to the neoconservatives was essentially what Lyndon Johnson and Daniel Patrick Moynihan had argued in 1965. For equality to have real meaning to people who have experienced generations of oppression, it must contain a strong measure of economic and political parity with whites—that is, *equal results*. The burden of past discrimination would simply weigh too heavily and too long unless some remedial action was taken to lighten the load. Hiring quotas and school busing were small compensation, liberals argued, for the long exploitation of blacks. Indeed, to deny such remediation was to perpetuate past wrongs.

The neoconservatives intensely resisted affirmative action in higher education, an issue that came to a head in the late 1970s. In the late 1960s, universities and professional schools began to give preferential treatment in admissions to minority groups who were underrepresented in their student populations. Because standardized tests were universally used as the objective criteria for admission, it was easy to show that blacks received favoritism over whites. Thus the tables were now turned. The irony was immediately apparent, especially to those whites refused admission to a school even though their test scores were higher than blacks admitted. In 1978, in the case of *Bakke v. University of California*, an unsuccessful applicant to a California medical school showed that the school's quota for blacks and Hispanics prevented him from getting his rightful place. In a five-to-four decision, the Supreme Court declared that racial quotas for school admission were unconstitutional and that the plaintiff had to be admitted. "The guarantee of equal protection cannot mean one thing when applied to one individual and something else when applied to a person of another color," Justice Lewis Powell wrote in the majority opinion. "If both are not accorded the same protection, then it is not equal." But a slim court majority also approved of a school's prerogative to give special consideration to minority applicants in order to create a heterogeneous student body. "In order to get beyond racism," Justice Harry Blackmun argued, "we must first take account of race." There was "no other way."[45]

The federal judiciary thus maintained its commitment to broadening the definition of equality, even as it confronted the apparent contradiction represented by quotas. In 1979 the court upheld racial quotas in job-training programs, and in 1980 it ruled in favor of quotas, or "set-asides," for minority contractors seeking government work. Although it came down on the side of African Americans as it had almost always done since 1938, the decisions were becoming more divided and sometimes less emphatic in their meaning. Affirmative-action policies perpetuated group rights, whereas American jurisprudence, one constitutional scholar argued, was characterized by "a political and legal culture of individualism that defines a problem exclusively in terms of the rights of individuals, not of groups." As long as the courts discovered that the individual liberties of blacks were denied, they consistently ruled for blacks. But when the question became whether blacks should be recognized as a group in order to remedy past inequalities of opportunity—as was the issue in the *Bakke* case and subsequent affirmative-action controversies—the judiciary hesitated, and some judges halted entirely, unable to require individuals to sacrifice rights in order to bestow them on a group.[46]

Affirmative action persisted as a highly symbolic civil rights issue for the remainder of the twentieth century. Many schools continued to use quota-type mechanisms in their admission processes, and thus the issue resurfaced regularly in the years ahead. Conservatives argued that affirmative action had become the entitlement of well-to-do black people, something that functioned mostly for their benefit. It secured for them many government jobs, places in higher education, and a fair share of white-collar jobs in corporations. Liberals held on to affirmative action as *the* crucial civil rights policy after its ambiguity had been exposed to ridicule by conservatives. They asked hard questions of conservatives: How else could past wrongs be promptly corrected? Why object to a policy that costs today's society so little if you truly favor black equality? For many African Americans, acceptance of affirmative action was the litmus test to determine whether or not, as Lyndon Johnson had earlier put it, whites were "for" blacks. That certainly was a natural human instinct, especially given how recently many whites had demonstrated their inability to be for blacks.

But the commitment to affirmative action surely limited the thinking of civil rights advocates about a reform agenda, perhaps preventing the pursuit of policies less ambiguous in their values implications and with more potential for broader white support. The single-minded commitment to affirmative action later prompted one commentator to remember the psychologist Abraham Maslow's warning: "When the only tool you own is a hammer, every problem begins to resemble a nail."[47]

IV

At the end of the 1970s, many Americans despaired at the condition of race relations. Indeed, there was a strong predisposition to see the glass half empty at the end of the decade. Many of the remarkable achievements in human relations since 1964 had quickly been taken for granted. Both whites and blacks were disappointed that so many places had failed to integrate. Who was to blame? African Americans were far less interested in integration in 1975 than they had been in 1965 or 1955, if it meant any reduction or postponement of their deserved empowerment. White suburbanites were clearly afraid of integration if it meant insecurity for them and their children. Many of them had bitterly washed their hands of the inner city, dismissing it as the home of crime, corruption, and welfare dependency. "When will they be satisfied?" was the question of whites angry at the persistent black claims about "rights" denied.

For many African Americans, such appeals revealed disappointment that came mainly from unfulfilled expectations. Most had expected the end of segregation to lead to significant material improvements in their lives. Most blacks had indeed enjoyed substantial economic improvements over the previous two decades. But the continuing great disparity between black and white levels of wealth was evidence to many African Americans with "middle-class" incomes that there was no real equality in the United States. At least one-third of blacks remained poor, and for those people the acquisition of civil and political rights meant far less than their continuing material deprivation. As the African-American political leader of a mostly black, very poor Alabama county put it, "Until people become economically strong, political power alone won't do."[48]

Just as politics provided the main arena for whites to act on their sense of status competition with blacks, it was also the place for African Americans' group action. During the 1970s civil rights organizations had lost much of their claim on the attention and emotions of African Americans. Protest marches and sit-ins never seemed to yield the results that they had in the 1960s. Both SNCC and CORE had disappeared, SCLC was doing little, and the Urban League and the NAACP had much lower national profiles. In their place, most African Americans engaged with a local political organization, usually the descendant of one of the voting leagues created in the late 1930s, or a new one started by a charismatic politician such as Maynard Jackson or Coleman Young. They elected many blacks to local and state offices in the 1970s. Without question there remained a racial character to politics. The Democratic Party clearly was understood to be the party of African Americans, and the Republican Party was the home for whites. Accordingly, in the South in the 1970s, many whites forsook their traditional home in the Democratic Party. On the one hand, this racial division of party preserved the traditional race conflicts among Americans. On the other, if one looked inside the Democratic Party, there were clear signs that race mattered less because African Americans coalesced successfully with whites in most places.

Both blacks and whites were disappointed that their communities remained tense, if not openly in racial conflict, when many of both races had expected the end of white supremacy to inaugurate an era of interracial consensus. This had been an unrealistic, if understandable expectation, given the sweeping changes that most communities, South and North, had undergone in the 1960s. Having largely entered national civic life with the idealistic phrases of Martin Luther King still ringing, African Americans were ill prepared for the messy, indefinite nature of the political arena. Politics continued to be what it had always been, the field for interest-group conflict and compromise, only now many more of the combatants were black. Inevitably many blacks were disappointed in the nonideological, compromised nature of decisions made in the political sphere. It was easy to find evidence of old, bad habits being carried forward.

By the late 1970s, much of the division on racial matters came down to one's position on the extent of change in American society. Most people on the right were struck by how the world had changed, because they themselves had altered their views significantly. Neoconservatives found evidence in the social sciences that showed how different current realities were for blacks from what they had been less than a generation earlier. Paleoconservatives surely knew how much change had come, because they had been forced to accept things they had fought to stop. Southern whites daily confronted the evidence that the society in which they had grown up had been turned on its head. Thus the insistence by black radicals, civil rights leaders, and liberal academics that little had changed was not only counterintuitive and easily contradicted by facts, it was suspiciously political and present-minded and probably an interpretation tailored to promote particular policies. On the left, people suspected that resistance to more change in the form of remedial policies such as busing and affirmative action only masked residual racism. Poor African Americans found too little evidence of change in their lives—too few new opportunities and too many old barriers. More affluent blacks frequently pointed to the continued white domination of the sources of power in the United States as confirmation that little of significance had been altered.

Much of the late 1970s' pessimism reflected Americans' discomfort with ambiguity. Americans are addicted to universal panaceas, one sociologist has suggested, though they are deeply divided about what the one solution is. People on the left tend to see greater equality as the cure-all, and those on the right often believe that the free market solves most problems. It was simply "easier to remember and promote a single universal formula than many ad hoc ones." Similarly, Americans tended to be mono-causationists about continuing racial problems. Those on the left blamed current problems on continuing white racism, while those on the right put it to a black culture of poverty and dependence on the welfare state. In time more textured and complex understandings might emerge about the United States's continuing concern with race relations. Surely there were many paradoxes to explain and knots to unravel. But out of the despair of the 1970s Americans turned not to the contemplation of ambiguity and contradiction but to an affirmation of plain definitions and absolute applications of their national values.[49]

CHAPTER 9

THE CONTENT
OF THEIR CHARACTER

IN 1980, Ronald Reagan startled many on the left of American politics when he won that year's presidential election in a convincing manner. Reagan had taken positions on the right wing of the Republican Party from 1964 when he first came to national political prominence, and to most Democrats and even many centrist Republicans, his presidential ambitions had seemed far-fetched—that is, until 1979 and 1980 when the price of gasoline reached one dollar per gallon, inflation went over 10 percent, and Islamic radicals in Iran took people in the American embassy hostage. In response, Reagan the candidate called for restoration of American strength and status in the world and for respect for the American taxpayer. He tapped the antigovernment anger that had been building since 1973, as, for example, when he compared government to a baby—"an alimentary canal with a big appetite at one end and no responsibility at the other." Reagan's antigovernment attitude resonated far better than most political observers had imagined, but then not since the Great Depression had so many Americans been as anxious about their status.[1]

Although always insulted by any suggestion that he was a bigot, Reagan played to whites' racial resentments. Some of it exploited white southerners' old sectional grudge: he declared that the Voting Rights Act was "humiliating to the South." But more of his message was aimed at hostility to welfare recipients, which could be justified as a legitimate critique of government but which also, with the racialization of poverty in the public's mind, carried a coded race meaning. In 1972, George Wallace had won big cheers in Detroit when he told a rally about "one woman collecting six welfare checks—that's paid for with your tax dollars." During his unsuccessful 1976 campaign for president, Reagan had consistently played to resentments about welfare with a story, based on news reports in the mid-1970s, about a "Chicago welfare queen" who had many aliases and fraudulently collected large amounts of government money—and the totals seemed to escalate each time Reagan told the story.[2]

Reagan worked to revive Americans' sense of national honor so damaged by the Iranian hostage experience and the Vietnam War. He recast the United States's international posture into a holy war against the Soviet

President Ronald Reagan. *Courtesy Library of Congress.*

Union's "evil empire" around the globe. He clothed all his positions with patriotic feeling, and for the most part his strategy worked. Once again, rising nationalism in the Cold War context limited the possibilities for more race reform. Reagan denied that he or his supporters bore any responsibility or guilt for the wrongs done to previous generations of blacks. Any further acknowledgement of past wrongs undermined the impulse to reclaim American greatness. Much of Reagan's popularity, a leading intellectual of the right would observe, lay in his ability "to offer mainstream America a vision of itself as innocent and entitled (unlike Jimmy Carter, who seemed to offer only guilt and obligation)."[3]

In Reagan's view of American nationhood, the United States was supposed to be free of racial distinction, and now it had become that. Because he believed himself to be "color-blind," so in fact was the nation he personified. Reagan popularized the notion that the political right was working to build a color-blind society, including one free of the racial preferences that had come into force in the 1970s. He succeeded in contrasting his own concern with the status of individual Americans with that of the Democratic Party, which he claimed "sees people only as members of groups." Any policy based on recognition of groups was wrong, even un-American, he believed.[4]

Reagan defeated Jimmy Carter in large part because he took away from the Democrats two major parts of the New Deal coalition, white southerners and blue-collar northerners. Even running against a white southern Baptist, Reagan captured the votes of a large majority of southern white men. He also won easily in blue-collar neighborhoods in northern cities where busing had been a main concern and many jobs had been lost. Twenty-two percent of Democrats voted for Reagan, and the defection of Democrats was even greater among those opposed to special government aid to minorities. A Democratic Party analysis of the loss of blue-collar voters dwelt heavily on the racial motives for changing party allegiance. "The white Democratic defectors express a profound distaste for blacks, a sentiment that pervades almost everything they think about government and politics," the analyst concluded after extensive interviews of disaffected Democrats in the Detroit area. They blamed blacks "for almost everything that has gone wrong in their lives." African Americans served as a negative reference for how blue-collar whites defined a good life: "Not being black is what constitutes being middle class; not living with blacks is what makes a neighborhood a decent place to live." All efforts to help blacks overcome past discrimination were viewed as obstacles to whites' opportunities. "Discrimination against whites has become a well-assimilated and ready explanation for their status, vulnerability and failures," the study found. As opposed to the Democratic Party's weakness, passivity, and failure to "speak for the average person," Ronald Reagan "represented a determined consistency and an aspiration to unity and pride."[5]

Reagan thus served in part as a means for whites to act in opposition to the force of black empowerment that had been felt in American society since the late 1960s. Blacks may have captured control of many big cities, many whites reasoned, but a hard-nosed, truth-telling conservative had taken over the White House. In a way that no national politician had done effectively in the 1970s, Reagan challenged openly the affirmative-action and welfare policies that many whites opposed. He did so without acknowledging or accepting any racial motive. His insistence on the "color blindness" of his positions left his followers guilt-free at the same time that it dismissed out of hand the view generally held by blacks that race still mattered in America.

Liberals would insist that Reagan and his followers were engaged in "color-blind racism," a cynical and willful denial of the continuing reality of racial discrimination against blacks and other minorities. Evidence abounded that opportunities were not equal for minorities, whether the limits were consciously imposed by whites or were remnants of past discrimination. In the 1980s and 1990s, tests of housing and employment opportunities using subjects of equal qualifications but different race virtually always turned up significant white preferences for other whites over blacks. To the left, those who maintained that American society had achieved an acceptable level of "color blindness" were only protecting their own color privilege. Whites professing color blindness typically asserted that "the past is past" and "if the Asians have made it, why can't the blacks?" Liberals dismissed such points as misleading and self-serving, as "whitewashing race."[6]

Whether race still mattered served as the central question in the "politics of memory" in the 1980s and 1990s. Martin Luther King was memorialized with a national holiday after contentious debate in some places. But at about the same time, the right appropriated his memory as the ideological authority for color blindness. Conservatives frequently recalled that King had dreamed that his children might be judged by the "content of their character" rather than the color of their skin. The civil rights leader Julian Bond declared that conservatives did not honor King "the critic of capitalism, or the pacifist who declared all wars evil, or the man of God who argued that a nation that chose guns over butter would starve its people and kill itself," but instead they made him "an antiseptic hero" to justify their own agenda.[7]

The trend of blue-collar abandonment of the Democrats, and a more general defection of white southerners to the Republicans, escalated in the 1984 election when Reagan won a landslide victory over Walter Mondale. By then, Reagan hardly had to use coded messages like the welfare queen to remind white voters of their threatened status. The growth of "Reagan Democrats" became a stampede of northern whites. Mondale's campaign manager recognized the status dynamic at work as blue-collar whites rejected the zero-sum society. "Working class voters," he later observed, "were persuaded that if you hitched your wagon to the poor, every time the poor moved up a rung on the ladder, they [would] take you down a rung," whereas those who attached themselves to the rich of the Republican Party would move up. In 1988 the Republican candidate, Vice President George H. W. Bush, made an indirect racial appeal in a campaign ad denouncing the Democrat, Governor Michael Dukakis of Massachusetts, for his release of a black criminal, Willie Horton, who had committed rape while on a weekend furlough program for state prisoners. One journalist surmised that the Willie Horton phenomenon reflected that crime had become a "shorthand *signal*" to white voters for the more general concern about social disorder, which included worries about status, morality, and race. The intense racialization of crime promoted by the media since the mid-1960s made it easy for the Willie Horton appeal to connect with white voters.[8]

If Reagan's rhetoric had polarized whites, the rising profile of the black activist Jesse Jackson in the Democratic Party in the 1980s advanced even further the tendency to give the parties racial identities. Jackson proved to be a divisive influence for many white Americans, especially Jews, whom Jackson alienated first when he publicly embraced the Palestinian leader Yassir Arafat and then aggravated during his 1984 campaign for president with his reference to New York as "Hymietown." A 1988 poll found that 59 percent of Jews believed that Jackson was anti-Semitic. Although most black leaders understood that Jackson's candidacy was mostly symbolic politics to register blacks' continuing racial interests, they deferred to Jackson's popularity among African Americans. In the end, black symbolic politics in the 1980s had the effect of making the Democratic Party look even more deferential to black interests, something that further alienated whites.[9]

Louis Farrakhan of the Nation of Islam exacerbated the continuing tension between blacks and Jews. Like Malcolm X a compelling orator, Farrakhan preached the virtues of education and family and deplored all drug and alcohol use. But in numerous speeches he also condemned white society, especially Jews, for the damage they had done to blacks. He called Judaism a "gutter religion." Throughout the late 1980s and 1990s, Farrakhan insisted that racial integration was a failure, that blacks ought to separate from the white-dominated American culture, and that the United States should pay reparations to blacks for wrongs done in the past. Although it was never clear that Farrakhan had a large following, neither were the condemnations of him and his message from other quarters of black America so emphatic that most whites knew for sure that his influence was marginal.[10]

In reaction to the electoral disasters of the 1980s, the Democratic Party in the 1990s attempted to move back to the center to reclaim white voters. A new, more centrist policy orientation emerged in the Democratic Leadership Council (DLC), which set as its first principles "We believe the promise of America is equal opportunity, not equal outcomes" and

"We believe the Democratic Party's fundamental mission is to expand opportunity, not government." The DLC backed Bill Clinton and Al Gore in the 1990s, and the Democrats' movement toward the center accounted for much of the party's electoral success.[11]

Continuing economic trouble left both whites and blacks insecure in the 1980s. In 1981 the U.S. economy had fallen into a deep recession that resulted in massive layoffs in industrial plants across the country, which continued the trend of deindustrialization advanced during the 1973–74 recession. Whereas in 1970 almost one-third of Americans worked in industry, by 1990 that fraction was down to just over one-fifth. Between 1979 and 1982, the number of jobs lost in the auto and steel industries reached almost 1.2 million. But just as whites were feeling most aggrieved, their status superiority to blacks began to widen again. The relative rise in blacks' incomes that had occurred during the 1960s and 1970s was reversed during the 1980s, and their earnings began to decline in relation to whites'. Whereas a college-educated African-American man earned about what a college-educated white male made in 1973, by 1989 the ratio of the black man's earnings to the white's had gone down by 13 percent. Those blacks with less education experienced similar declines. The relative decline of black incomes in the 1980s probably was due to both a surge of black college graduates that came during a time of recession and the relaxation of affirmative-action pressure during the Reagan administration, though economists were not certain.[12]

Still, the older dynamic of economic competition between blacks and whites did not return, not even in the hard times of the early 1980s. With industrial jobs disappearing in wholesale fashion, there were few opportunities for which to compete. Some economic competition arose in the service sector between blacks and Hispanics. In Miami and Los Angeles, some black joblessness probably owed to the presence of more Hispanics. But because that competition lay outside the status concerns of the vast majority of whites, it had relatively little impact on the larger national race consciousness. Black leaders such as Jesse Jackson proved reluctant to take positions that could be viewed as anti-immigrant.[13]

Groups continued to compete for residential space, and progress toward integrating urban neighborhoods and suburban towns remained only incremental. In 2000 the most segregated areas in the United States were some of the nation's largest metropolitan areas—New York, Chicago, Detroit, and several of the "Rust Belt" cities. In the 1990s both lenders and insurers were sued for redlining minority neighborhoods, and they paid millions of dollars in damages. The suits apparently had a salutary affect: one study revealed that between 1989 and 2000, the discrimination experienced by black and Hispanic homebuyers fell more than 25 percent. Over the course of the 1990s, residential integration advanced somewhat overall, the largest improvements taking place in the South and in areas of numerous military personnel. Between 1990 and 2000, America's still-growing suburbs went from 89 percent white down to 84 percent. One noteworthy counterforce, however, was the tendency among white-collar African Americans to move to black suburban enclaves rather than be isolated in an otherwise white neighborhood. In Atlanta a series of exclusive all-black suburban developments appeared, complete with golf and tennis clubs. "In my neighborhood, we have all the amenities we could have," a prominent black Atlantan noted in the 1990s, "and none of the hostility." He explained that "the whole integration movement was one where you were always worried. 'What do white people think of me, what impression am I making?' I think it's very healthy that that's no longer the case. These days, black folks are less interested in impressing white people than in satisfying ourselves."[14]

Persistent housing segregation meant continuing school segregation in the 1980s and 1990s, especially as the federal courts ceased to order busing and other desegregation remedies. In a series of decisions in the early 1990s, the Supreme Court allowed school boards to return to neighborhood schools and end efforts to compensate for segregation—particularly "magnet" programs to attract suburban students to inner-city schools. Along with continuing residential segregation and growing defections to private schools, these rulings accounted for some resegregation in American public schools in the 1980s and 1990s—thus reversing the two decades of spreading integration in the 1960s and 1970s. One study found that increasing segregation paralleled "a growing gap in quality between the schools being attended by white students and those serving a large proportion of minority students." Test scores and graduation rates among minority students also went down in the 1990s as the schools became more segregated.[15]

The Reagan administration worked to reduce the influence of the civil rights subgovernment that had emerged under Nixon. The budgets of both the Equal Employment Opportunity Commission (EEOC) and the Office of Federal Contract Compliance were cut significantly during Reagan's first years. Clarence Thomas, his appointee to head EEOC, focused the agency on individual cases of discrimination, rather than on imposing on corporations broad hiring goals and timetables as the agency had done in the 1970s. An African-American lawyer from Georgia, Thomas opposed quotas because he believed that affirmative action served only blacks who were already privileged. Thomas saw himself as fighting an entrenched civil rights establishment that had become elitist and removed from the needs of those who needed help. At the U.S. Commission on Civil Rights, Reagan put in as chair a black businessman who denounced "media-designated black leaders" who created a "new racism" in which "blacks and whites are not allowed to compete as equals." At the Justice Department, Reagan appointed as head of the Civil Rights Division William Bradford Reynolds, who withdrew support for busing and hiring quotas. Reynolds opposed the use of "disparate impact" evidence—use of facts that minorities were underrepresented in a group to prove that discrimination existed. Since the Nixon administration, statistics showing that minorities did not get their proportional share of jobs, admissions to higher education, or elected offices had been the main evidence used to justify quotas and set-asides. Reynolds failed to accomplish much of what he set out to do, in part because his aggressive assault on established policies spurred a broad coalition of opponents to focus their energies on him as much as his policies.[16]

Republican mastery of presidential politics in the 1980s meant that Ronald Reagan and George Bush had the opportunity largely to remake the federal judiciary. Reagan's four appointments to the high court effectively reversed the overall tendency of the federal courts to enforce strong remedies for racial discrimination. Bush's 1991 appointment of Clarence Thomas to fill the position vacated by Thurgood Marshall on the Supreme Court brought about an incident of intense racial politics. Liberals were incensed that the great legal advocate for equality was to be replaced by the black lawyer perhaps most opposed to Marshall's understandings of race policies. When a former EEOC employee charged him with sexual harassment in televised confirmation hearings, Thomas denounced his critics, saying that inquiry into his character was a "high-tech lynching for uppity-blacks who in any way deign to think for themselves." Thomas's confirmation only ensured that the court's future decisions would be highly scrutinized for their impact on the nation's racial politics.[17]

If the 1970s had left many Americans muddled and confused about race relations, Ronald Reagan had clarified the continuing ideological disagreements. In his simplistic but very persuasive way, he identified traditional, absolutist definitions for democratic values that most white Americans accepted. Liberty, equality, and democracy had to be colorblind, and the definitions of those values were to be the simple and obvious ones. For most whites, Reagan had provided needed relief from the frustration of the 1970s. His political opponents offered much evidence and many arguments for a more complex view with different policy outcomes, but most of the time he carried the day, and his influence on Americans' thinking about race lived well beyond his presidency.

I

The Reagan triumph advanced the critique of race policies that had emerged with the neoconservatives in the mid-1970s. Indeed, conservatism on all issues flourished, and it thrived not just because of the political triumph of the Great Communicator but also because of much stronger institutional bases for conservative philosophy and policy. By the early 1980s a growing conservative intelligentsia enjoyed significant financial support from philanthropists who had emerged in the 1970s to challenge the liberal influence of the Ford, Rockefeller, and Carnegie foundations. Businessmen and corporations funded the American Enterprise Institute, the Heritage Foundation, the Manhattan Institute, and other conservative think tanks. New magazines, new commentators, and in the 1990s a television news network emerged to advance conservative positions.[18]

Having charted a course for the conservative critique, some neoconservatives faded from the scene, and increasingly in the 1980s and 1990s blacks filled their places in the public debate. The Stanford economist Thomas Sowell emerged as a leading public intellectual to argue that quotas and other forms of special treatment demeaned those blacks who had honestly earned recognition and achievement. Sowell insisted that government intervention in hiring practices created a reluctance of white employers to take a chance on black workers. Walter Williams, another economist, presented evidence that the minimum wage worked against black economic development by making the cost of job creation so high for employers that the beginning positions for black teenagers never materialized.[19]

If Sowell and Williams raised controversial issues about blacks' economic lives, Shelby Steele, a black English professor, offered the sharpest critique of black attitudes in *The Content of Our Character*. Steele set forth opinions that rarely had been made openly by a black person. He questioned black nationalism for being "too infused with defensive grandiosity, too given to bombast and posturing" to serve a constructive purpose among African Americans. "Wherever one hears its themes today . . . it has that unmistakable ring of compensation, of an illusory black specialness that offers haven from inner doubt." He identified a habit among African Americans he called "race holding," which he defined as blacks' using race to keep from looking at themselves realistically. Race holding was a form of self-protection in integrated situations, wherein blacks in effect said to whites: *"I will reject you before you have a chance to reject me."* Steele insisted that such "integration shock" had erected imaginary boundaries of segregation where the old legal ones formerly stood and that it caused blacks to avoid opportunities, steer clear of arenas where they had not achieved, and segregate themselves in integrated situations. African Americans had come to rely, Steele contended, on the power that accrued to them as innocent victims of white supremacy. "It is a formula that binds the victim to his victimization by linking his power to his status as a victim."[20]

No argument of the black conservatives went unanswered. Liberals insisted that government hiring policies had brought blacks jobs they would not otherwise have gotten and that the minimum wage had significantly raised the standard of living for the working poor. Steele's critics accused him of dismissing the need to raise African-American ethnic consciousness to overcome the weight of centuries of oppression on black mentality. Along with vigorously stated liberal positions on economics and culture went some personal invective, aimed especially at Steele, for his alleged sycophancy to Republican power and white bigotry.

Conservative intellectuals focused most of their policy arguments on the failures of the welfare state. Having frequently said in his 1980 campaign that "in the 1960s we fought a war on poverty, and poverty won," Reagan cut welfare benefits and food stamps, thus reversing the rapid growth in those programs during the previous 15 years. By then many liberals had to admit that they had been wrong to believe that, as blacks attained more education, poverty among them would fall to the level of whites. In fact, black and white educational attainment converged in the late 1970s, but the portion of black families living below the poverty line stayed about the same—three times higher than whites. Daniel Patrick Moynihan had assumed in 1965 that when black men had a better chance at earning a decent living, the black family structure would more nearly mirror whites'. Even with fairer hiring and affirmative-action policies in the late 1960s and 1970s and the better overall economic performance of black men, African-American families were increasingly female headed. In part this reflected a century-old trend among whites as well as blacks away from dual-headed families and toward out-of-wedlock births, delayed marriages, female family headship, and children living with single mothers. But the rapidity with which the black families broke down in the 1960s and 1970s defied the slow historical trend. The portion of children born to unmarried women had been 20 percent among blacks in 1960, but it rose to 40 percent in 1970, and to about 60 percent in 1980. It would rise even more in the 1980s, by which time black family patterns overall were drastically different from those of all the other race and ethnic groups in the United States.[21]

The increase in single-family, female-headed households explained most of the continuing socioeconomic disparity between blacks and whites, because such families were by far the poorest in the country. Not only was there a much higher incidence of single women heading black families, but single black women usually stayed single, whereas white women typically married again after a few years. More inner-city black women were single, many people believed, because more black men were unemployed. A big racial disparity in unemployment had opened up with the recession of 1974–75, after which black male unemployment was twice as high as white male and growing wider.[22]

As the persistence of black poverty was acknowledged, discussion of its causes intensified. Whereas most liberal academics and civil rights activists pointed to the continuation of white racism, the sociologist William Julius Wilson countered in 1978 with an explanation of black poverty focused on the loss of industrial jobs from the inner cities. Education was becoming increasingly important in acquiring jobs, especially those that carried high and growing wage levels. Unskilled industrial jobs rapidly disappeared in the 1970s, and in alarming numbers the poorly educated fell into unemployment. Black men with steady jobs left the center cities during the 1960s and 1970s, and this altered the traditional composition of the black ghetto, which had, because of housing discrimination, previously forced middle-class black people to stay mostly in the inner city. Those who did not or could not leave ended up unemployed, on welfare, and often engaged in crime. Wilson's explanation failed to persuade some who doubted that ghetto dwellers were quite so stuck as he suggested and who contended that other forces were keeping blacks in poverty, particularly a ghetto "culture of poverty." "The welfare culture tells the man he is not a necessary part of the family," the conservative economist George Gilder wrote in 1981. "He feels dispensable, his wife knows he is dispensable, his children sense it." Comparisons with Asian, Hispanic, and West Indian immigrants pointed toward distinctive African-American shortcomings. The term "underclass" emerged to describe this cultural component of poverty, with the left inevitably condemning the term.[23]

The most influential argument about welfare policy came in 1984 from the political scientist Charles Murray, whose book *Losing Ground* provided much of the justification for the Reagan administration's welfare cuts. Murray insisted that welfare payments to poor women with children, food subsidies, and health and housing programs *increased* poverty by encouraging unemployment. Welfare policy encouraged idleness and discouraged work and saving. The aid to women with children penalized marriage and undermined the traditional family. All of this needed to stop, Murray insisted, and if we quit rewarding indolence and immorality, then people will change their behavior and it will end. Murray's critics responded that like Moynihan he was blaming the victim. Continuing racial discrimination and economic stagnation, not welfare, were the real reasons that welfare rolls increased in the 1970s, liberals argued. Murray's contention that welfare programs had made the poor even more poor was not really sustained by the evidence, but most people, including a growing number of liberal scholars, accepted his larger point that welfare programs had undermined traditional values about family and work.[24]

Over the course of the 1980s, the conformity of thought that had prevented a realistic critique of ghetto life broke down under the right's assault and the determination of William Julius Wilson to acknowledge ghetto realities. Wilson argued that intellectuals on the left, of which he was one, had to propose new ways for government to address the real problems, especially those that approached poverty from a structural economic perspective. With greater openness to realism, the real nature of ghetto life could be explored outside a particular policy agenda, and thus appeared such insightful works as the sociologist Elijah Anderson's *Streetwise*, an ethnography of ghetto life in a northern city in the 1980s. Anderson described how the intergenerational connection between young residents and "old heads," who in earlier times had handed down practical wisdom and taught functional values, had been lost in the ghetto life of the 1970s and 1980s. Now the dominant role model was the young black male who did not work or did so only grudgingly, and who supported himself mainly through drug trade. According to Anderson, he "shuns the traditional father's role," feeling "hardly any obligation to his string of women and the children he has fathered." Indeed, "to his hustling mentality, generosity is a weakness." For girls, the role model was a young woman who spent her few resources mostly for clothes, drugs, and alcohol. She might have a minimum-wage service job or be on welfare. "She may have one or two young children," Anderson observed, "whom she may dress up expensively" in order to compete with other young women for who has the cutest "prize."[25]

II

A new explosion of crime in the mid-1980s reinforced doubts about existing welfare policy. The national crime rate had declined in the early 1980s, but then it surged in 1986, especially among African Americans, with the crack cocaine epidemic. The murder rate for young black men in 1990 was 140 per 100,000; for young white men, 20. With the new crime wave came the broader recognition that African Americans were themselves the main victims of it. Historically, white police and courts tolerated black-on-black crime, and many African Americans had long insisted that the higher black rates were the result of white-supremacist policing. "In terms of misery inflicted by direct criminal violence," the legal scholar Randall Kennedy concluded, "blacks (and other people of color) suffer more from the criminal acts of their racial 'brothers' and 'sisters' than they do from the racist misconduct of white police officers." A political scientist observed that "racist white cops, however vicious" were only "minor irritants when compared to the viciousness of the black gangs and wanton violence." Because blacks at most income levels "are more likely to be raped, robbed, assaulted, and murdered" than

whites, Kennedy argued, "at the center of all discussions about racial justice and criminal law should be a recognition that black Americans are in
dire need of protection against criminality."[26]

But in fact much of the policy focus about black crime stayed on the
behavior of police. The disproportionate share of black men in U.S. pris-
ons was often taken as indisputable evidence that the police and the
courts meant to remove black men from the streets—not that black men
committed a disproportionate share of crimes. Black and white alienation reached such extremes in some places that justice seemed impossible. Kennedy offered as an illustration the sad reality of the 1987 situation
in New York in which a black teenager, Tawana Brawley, falsely alleged
that she had been abducted and raped by six white men. Black civil rights
activists in New York made "formulaic allegations of racial misconduct
without even bothering to grapple with evidence and arguments that
challenge their conclusions," and some continued to support Brawley
after her allegation had been exposed as false. To Kennedy, such attitudes
undermined "the credibility of all who protest against racial wrongs."[27]

A series of startling images emanating from Los Angeles in the early
1990s dramatized the continuing reality of racial conflict over police and
crime. In 1991, LA police captured a fleeing black motorist named Rodney King, and a bystander videotaped their severe beating of him. This
scene of violence was then run frequently on television. Charged with
violating King's civil rights, four policemen in 1992 defended their actions
to an all-white Los Angeles jury. Their acquittal sparked a riot as destructive as, and similar in character to, the 1965 Watts conflagration, though
this time there was even more focus on the victims of the riot. A television camera in a helicopter captured the beating death of a white truck
driver who happened to get caught at an intersection in the riot area.
Seven hundred Korean shopkeepers had their businesses destroyed, and
many were injured, in violence apparently aimed at punishing Asians in
particular.[28]

The 1995 murder trial of the black football player and actor O. J. Simpson, accused of killing his white former wife and her white male friend,
riveted the nation's attention on black attitudes toward crime. To most

white observers, the evidence pointing to Simpson's guilt was over-whelming. Most African Americans believed in his innocence, convinced that the Los Angeles police had planted evidence to convict him. Many blacks celebrated his acquittal. In the case of Simpson and other African Americans charged with crimes, Randall Kennedy observed, black jurors sometimes "nullified" the criminal prosecution of a black defendant, despite "belief beyond a reasonable doubt" that the defendant was guilty. Blacks continued to feel "a solidarity" against the police and the criminal justice system based on generations of white-supremacist treatment, and that was manifest in the way they rallied to Simpson. For most whites, one journalist wrote, the Simpson acquittal demonstrated that "race trumps spousal abuse, factual consistency [in court evidence] and just about anything else."[29]

The events of the early 1990s exhibited how racial images still pro-pelled human relations in the United States. The Los Angeles riot and the Simpson trial demonstrated that African Americans still suffered from the negative stereotype that disproportionate criminality unfairly assigned to all blacks, just as the Rodney King beating reinforced the belief among some minorities that whites were violent bigots. In the 1990s racial "profiling" became a controversial practice of police, one widely condemned and often officially abandoned. But in a racially alien-ated society in which personal security was so fundamental a concern, such practices were probably inevitable. In the late 1990s, Randall Kennedy subscribed to a "politics of respectability" for African Ameri-cans, similar to the concern for image that Booker Washington had pro-moted a century earlier. "In American political culture, the reputation of groups, be they religious denominations, labor unions, or racial groups, matters greatly." That would have dictated, Kennedy wrote, not celebrat-ing when O. J. Simpson was acquitted.[30]

By the 1990s there was tacit acceptance of the cultural dimensions of black poverty. President Bill Clinton supported a New Democrat welfare-reform plan that cut benefits and eligibility for millions of recipients. Louis Farrakhan and many of his followers—and some of his detractors—supported a "Million-Man March" to Washington in 1995 to

promote black-male family responsibility. The crime rate went down in
the 1990s as police departments and inner-city communities became
more effective at controlling the drug scourge. Cities governed previously by politicians who thrived on racial alienation chose leaders whose
first concerns were safety and business opportunity. As Americans
reached the end of the twentieth century, these were signs suggesting
that the racialization of crime and poverty had peaked and that the society was finding less polarized ways to think and act on its worst social
problems.[31]

III

Popular culture in the 1980s and 1990s offered less support for integrationist values than it had in the 1960s and 1970s. The commitment to tolerance and diversity of expression that had emerged in the 1970s
prevailed even more strongly, but the pursuit of common cultural
ground across races weakened. Some of this owed to a fatigue about
integrationism, a belief among some that the forces uniting groups were
weaker than the cultural differences dividing people. Part of it was also
the result of a growing sense among many that race did not matter and
that the culture simply needed to pay it less attention. Still another factor
was a more aggressively black-nationalist cultural perspective from some
African Americans. In 1988, Jesse Jackson announced that henceforth the
proper designation for black should be "African American," a term that in
his view carried more "cultural integrity" than "black" did. Within a
short time, most speakers and writers, black and white, had deferred to
Jackson, though those who were not adherents of black nationalism used
the two terms synonymously.[32]

A new musical form, rap, took American popular culture by storm in
the 1980s. Rap had emerged from the "hip-hop" culture of New York
streets in the mid-1970s, when the rhythmic, chanting music combined
with "break dancing" and graffiti to express the life experience of young,
mostly male black urbanites. Rap was immersed in the violence of

ghetto life, including the pressures of drugs and gangs, and in rejection of the dominant white society. Its slang-based lyrics were often misogynist, graphically sexual, and abundantly profane. The confirmation of the ghetto reality and the justification of the young men's existence did, of course, affirm the lives of one of the nation's most alienated groups.[33]

Although millions of white youths embraced rap and even some white rappers gained stardom in the 1990s, it hardly won the audience among Americans at large that rock and roll commanded in the 1950s and 1960s. Compared to other musical forms, rap lacked melody—to many an ear, it was entirely devoid of melody. At some level, listeners had to appreciate the message of rap—alienation from the dominant society, acceptance of drugs, free expression of masculine aggression. Those values were anathema to many Americans, and thus rap reinforced the image of black social pathology that was often projected in politics, media reporting of ghetto life, and policy discourse. To be sure, rock and roll had been condemned widely as undermining decent American life in the mid-1950s. But rock and roll became overwhelmingly popular among American youth, whereas rap appealed to a smaller segment of the white population. In a more permissive age, rap lyrics were blatantly sexual and violent in a way that rock-and-roll lyrics had never been.

Rap so dominated African American cultural expression, however, that the older traditions that had appealed strongly to white audiences— jazz, blues, gospel, and soul—were pushed to the background. New black artists either abandoned those genres or failed to make the airwaves as much as in the past. Themes of faith and salvation, of romance and love that had suffused African-American musical expression were rarely prominent themes in rap. To be sure, some defended rap as the legitimate descendant of bawdy blues, and African-American popular culture had often expressed despair. Still, the advent of rap in the 1980s meant that most blacks and whites lost the powerful point of connection in popular music that had nurtured interracial acceptance at earlier times.[34]

Many of the best films on race in the 1980s and 1990s reinforced the larger culture's preoccupation with ghetto pathologies and black violence, and they were made by young black directors. In 1989, Spike Lee captured black-white animosity in ghetto life in *Do the Right Thing*. In other films, Lee dealt honestly with color and class division among blacks. John Singleton in 1991 rendered the violence of ghetto life in a hard light in *Boyz N the Hood*. The notable exception to the emphasis on ghetto realism was *Glory*, Hollywood's 1989 recreation of the experience of black soldiers during the Civil War, which in fact celebrated blacks' heroism in defense of the nation and their freedom.

If television in the 1970s had promoted realism about race, its impact in the 1980s and 1990s reflected various crosscurrents in values. The most watched "race" show of the 1980s was Bill Cosby's situation comedy in which he played a doctor, Cliff Huxtable, married to a lawyer, thus creating a thoroughly upscale black home. Unlike Norman Lear's comedies in the 1970s, *The Cosby Show* rarely addressed race issues except to endorse African-American institutions, often through props. It reflected the desire of many affluent African Americans to remove themselves from the unsettled issues of racial integration in the United States. The show achieved popularity among whites because, one black critic argued, "the success of this handsome, affluent black family" taught "the fair-mindedness of whites who, out of their essential goodness, changed society so that black families like the Huxtables could succeed." In the 1990s television offered both greater variety of themes in all-black-cast programs and more shows with integrated casts. The growth of cable television made the medium's offerings more eclectic, which diminished the influence of the main networks' attitudes, brought specialized programming for blacks and Hispanics, and introduced to mass audiences much bawdy racial humor for the first time. Cable also advanced rap, which grew with the dissemination of music videos.[35]

Mass news communications in the 1980s and 1990s contributed little to closing the racial divide. The old racial stereotypes were all but gone from the visual representation of African Americans, but during the 1980s television and the media generally dwelt heavily on ghetto pathologies, especially gangs, crack, and crime. Preoccupied with reporting violence as always, the media covered intensely the outbreak of gang and drug violence that began in 1986 and continued into the early 1990s. This represented a kind of climax to the racialization of crime and poverty that had begun with the ghetto riots during the 1960s. Newsmagazines and television networks continued to exaggerate the number of black people among the poor, and they focused most heavily on the least sympathetic groups—unemployed adults—rather than on the more sympathetic elderly and young. By 1993 a backlash against the focus on black violence had occurred, and accusations about the media's malicious racial intent caused the newsmagazines and the television networks to change in the mid-1990s. They turned away from the ghetto focus but did relatively little reporting on race issues. The advent of round-the-clock news networks meant that viewers got many more hours of news coverage, but little of it focused on race matters, except for the major events— the Rodney King beating and trial, the Los Angeles riot, the O. J. Simpson trial, and the Million-Man March. Each of these in some way perpetuated the simplistic, negative view of race in America—black pathology and white racism.[36]

IV

Affirmative action remained the crucial issue in the 1980s and 1990s in the continuing national debate about who spoke for American values and who defined the meaning of equality. Opponents of affirmative action exposed the internal inconsistencies of the policy by asking hard questions. How do we distinguish between disadvantaged groups when no group is monolithically downtrodden? Do middle-class blacks deserve preference over poor whites? How much compensatory justice is enough? Opponents insisted that the government-mandated programs for affirmative action benefited relatively few blacks; that they had required a huge amount of time and emotional energy for a modest amount of good; and that affirmative action in education had become a panacea that helped people avoid the more fundamental problem of poor school performance among both blacks and Hispanics. At the level of morality or national values, conservatives were adamant that affirmative action was an affront to the most fundamental understandings of freedom and equality in the United States.

Supporters of the policy, on the other hand, still maintained that remedial action was necessary to overcome both the residual effects of past discrimination and the persistence of racial prejudice in the present. Powerful as it should have been logically, the justification based on race exploitation in history—and, indeed, very recent history at that—appeared not to convince many Americans of the need for remedial efforts. More compelling were the present-day examples of white bigotry—the refusal of restaurants to serve blacks and the harassment of the lone black family in a neighborhood—that appeared frequently. They provided vivid and immediate evidence that race still mattered in their nation. Proponents of affirmative action argued that to achieve equality of opportunity, never mind equality of results, American society needed special compensatory efforts to help historically disadvantaged groups.

Through the 1980s affirmative-action policies stayed largely in place, despite the denunciations by Reagan and his appointees and notwithstanding polls that showed that a large majority of whites opposed the policy as unfair. The use of quotas had not spread far beyond the originally protected groups—women and blacks, with Hispanics added along the way—but it had become entrenched and institutionalized. It had been accepted by big employers as a legitimate norm, and even by white employees, if often grudgingly. When the Reagan administration began to challenge the practice, it found that many businessmen did not want to give up quotas. "Businessmen like to hire by the numbers," one journalist reported in 1985. An economist reported in 1984 that as a result of affirmative action, recruiting efforts were broader, testing was made more directly relevant to jobs, new positions were advertised more widely, and evaluations were made far more open and objective. With women and blacks now well established in business bureaucracies, there were built-in constituencies for diversity.[37]

Whites also supported affirmative action, despite reservations about its fairness, because so few options were given. Often the choice presented was to support affirmative action or be labeled a bigot. American business had adopted an ethos of toleration and diversity—a market-driven acceptance of difference within the population. Within that framework, one could not afford to be seen as intolerant, a reputation that one chanced by opposing affirmative action.

By the 1980s another form of racial preference, the "set-aside" for minority contractors doing business with governments, had captured the attention of both the right and the left. Originated in 1969 by the Nixon administration to give a boost to "black capitalism," minority set-asides became a high priority for many local governments, especially those led by black politicians. In Atlanta, a city that rebuilt virtually its entire transportation infrastructure during the 1970s and 1980s, set-asides surpassed school desegregation and other remedial programs as the first priority of its black-dominated city administrations. Black businessmen received about 35 percent of the contracts let on Atlanta's big projects. Local governments around the country soon adopted the Atlanta policies as prerequisites for minority economic progress. African Americans viewed set-asides as the means by which they got a "piece of the economic pie." But close scrutiny of Atlanta's program revealed that in reality many of the minority contractors were fronts for white-owned construction companies and that much of the work awarded to genuine minority contractors was completed not by the black contractors but by whites added later. In the end only a handful of black builders and architects consistently worked on the many Atlanta projects, and while they thrived, little of the presumed benefit from the hundreds of millions of dollars actually trickled down to the average black person in Atlanta. For most white businessmen, set-asides were wasteful and unfair to white contractors already in business, but most came to accept them as simply part of the price of doing business in Atlanta. For other whites with a larger view, set-asides were the cost of peace in urban America.[38]

In 1989 the Supreme Court began to undermine support for various forms of affirmative action when it overturned a minority set-aside program in Richmond. "To accept Richmond's claim that past societal discrimination alone can serve as the basis for rigid racial preferences," Justice Sandra Day O'Connor wrote, "would be to open the door to competing claims for 'remedial relief' for every disadvantaged group." Lost in a welter of "shifting preferences based on inherently unmeasurable claims of past wrongs" would be "the dream of a Nation of equal citizens in a society where race is irrelevant to personal opportunity." In another decision the court objected to the use of disparate-impact evidence. The court's decisions provoked a strong reaction from civil rights advocates, who lobbied Congress to pass the Civil Rights Restoration Act of 1991, which specifically legalized the use of disparate-impact evidence. Conservatives denounced the law as a "quota" bill, but President Bush signed it—perhaps reflecting again the discomfort that many businessmen and some Republicans felt at being seen as hostile to minority opportunities.[39]

Still, the slim conservative majority on the Supreme Court forged ahead in its opposition to racial preferences. In 1993 the court ruled in the case of *Shaw v. Reno* that gerrymandering a congressional district in order to maximize the chances of electing a black candidate amounted to an unconstitutional race motive. The district at issue had been created by the North Carolina legislature in an effort to give the state, which had 12 congressional seats and a population almost one-fourth black, its first black congressman in the twentieth century. A many-sided geometric curiosity—as American electoral boundaries frequently have been—the district aroused the new conservative majority's opposition to race-proportional remedies. The court majority seemed to equate race-conscious districting with quotas and set-asides—mechanistic policies that continued racial thinking in a society attempting to become color-blind.[40]

In fact, the districting issue represented only one part of a complex history of manipulation of electoral and governmental forms. In the South after Reconstruction, whites altered both electoral districts and the forms of local government to diminish all remnants of black political power. They typically reduced the number of city council or county commission seats and elected representatives at-large rather than in districts; they made offices appointed rather than elected; and they often moved the appointing power for local offices to the state house. In the aftermath of the Voting Rights Act, whites in the Deep South attempted the same kinds of vote dilution, using at-large voting and majority-vote requirements for multimember bodies. At-large elections minimized the chances that a black enclave might have enough votes to choose a black or sympathetic white representative, because the overwhelming majority of whites in the South in the 1960s and 1970s simply would not vote for a black or a white openly sympathetic to blacks. Again, the democratic process secured white supremacy, even *with* the Voting Rights Act. But in the 1970s and 1980s, the federal judiciary's tough enforcement of one-man, one-vote principles largely stymied the effort to dilute black votes. Blacks got elected, and democracy lost much of its racial taint in the South.[41]

The hostility of conservatives in the 1990s to considering race in political districting quickly became opposition to all efforts against vote dilution. This damned what had been a crucial accomplishment of American democracy since 1965. Acquiring the right to vote and using it for significant results fulfilled for minorities the promise of the "consent of the governed," a right Americans had asserted in the Declaration of Independence. The many examples of black political power demonstrated objectively that American democracy now worked for blacks, something that served more the purposes of conservative interests than of black nationalists.

In the 1990s the courts began to waiver on affirmative action in higher education. In 1996 the Supreme Court allowed to stand a lower court's ruling that the University of Texas's admission policies used an unconstitutional quota mechanism. Some universities interpreted the decision as the signal to stop considering race in admissions decisions, while others continued the practice. In 1997 voters in California approved a measure outlawing all state-sponsored affirmative-action programs, including college and professional-school admissions, which resulted in a steep decline in black and Hispanic admissions to the state's prestigious professional schools. Then in 2003 the Supreme Court again upheld affirmative action in higher education in the case of *Grutter v. Bollinger*. Although the court reaffirmed that quotas were unconstitutional, Justice O'Connor found a compelling state interest in universities' admitting a diverse student body, and thus she and a slim majority approved of the use of race as a consideration in admissions. The left hailed the decision as a victory, and some institutions restarted their affirmative-action programs. Lawyers on the right vowed that the fight was hardly over.[42]

Through the 1990s many observers on the right insisted that affirmative action diverted Americans from attending to the more fundamental problems that shaped the lives of African Americans and other minorities. They argued that the real answer to the paucity of minorities in elite educational institutions was to improve educational preparation for all children, but especially inner-city students. By the 1990s it was widely recognized that many urban schools failed to give students an adequate background in basic skills, much less the higher academic achievement necessary for success at elite colleges. Many conservatives believed that parents in urban systems should be allowed to exercise "school choice" in order to opt out of bad public schools and choose private schools through the use of "vouchers"—education grants from public funds. In the mid-1990s a libertarian public-interest law firm represented a group of black parents in Milwaukee demanding such choice. By one account 90 percent of Milwaukee's black parents supported vouchers. The NAACP opposed the Milwaukee parents on the grounds that vouchers and school choice undermined public schools, which it believed were the only institutions that could practically be relied on to help poor students. For activists on the right, the opposition to choice and vouchers from the traditional civil rights establishment, regardless of local blacks' desires, demonstrated how narrow and self-serving the old attitudes were. At the end of the twentieth century, they remained as insistent on the need for vouchers as the NAACP and the teacher unions were united in opposing them.[43]

What people on the right did *not* say was that affirmative action had been a gift to their political interests. By standing so firmly for racial preferences, the political left had defined equality as *proportional racial representation*. This gave the right all other definitions of equality, including the one that most whites embraced—equality of opportunity without regard to racial consideration. Most white Americans interpreted equality of opportunity to mean no remedial action.

It was a sad reality that, as far as Americans had moved in overcoming the fundamental problems of race by the end of the twentieth century, they seemed to have reached the limits of their values. The disagreement over the meaning of equality appeared to have exposed a tragic flaw in the American character, the inability to settle finally on a path to a just and equitable society. The great nation faltered on how to realize its most ambitious goal.

There was also here a fundamental conflict between history and morality. As the record of human behavior, history teaches that people have thought and acted racially for centuries, and that such facts must be acknowledged to set policies for building a better society. History also amasses evidence of how past discrimination burdens those in the present in sometimes backbreaking ways. Hence a historical perspective supports affirmative action. But modern morality teaches that distinctions based on race are wrong and always have been. To perpetuate racial distinctions now is to extend the immorality of the past into the future. People had to choose between a moral and a historical logic; and whether or not they recognized it, most did choose.

THE BEGINNING OF THE BLEND

IN 1987 an eight-year-old asked her father why, when taking a standardized test at school, she should have to give her race. "Race isn't important," she stated emphatically. Well, the father explained with professorial confidence, the school needed to know if the little white girls like herself were doing as well as the black children in reading and math. "But what do you put down on the test if your father is white and your mother is black?" Caught in a logical trap unforeseen by virtue of a life lived entirely in a southern social order where race governed everything in some way, the father groped clumsily for an answer. Watching his discomfort was the eight-year-old's little sister, only four but full of confidence from just having starred in her preschool Thanksgiving pageant. She sensed that her father was in trouble, and she knew instinctively on which side of the generational divide her loyalties lay. The little sister moved in for the kill: "Yeah, Daddy, what do you put, what do you put down if your father is a Japan and your mother's a Pilgrim?"

As these children grew older, they became more aware of the real social differences that existed between blacks and whites, but despite many lectures on the history of discrimination, they remained resolute in their conviction that race was no more than skin deep. Whence came the commitment? They were taught at home and in school that racial distinctions were wrong, but that could not account entirely for their thinking. Once the schools and other institutions began consciously to avoid enforcing white supremacy, young people related naturally, often without regard to the older norms. They knew from school and other activities that black, white, Asian, and Hispanic children were essentially alike but just as varied in personality, which was the real way they judged their peers. What about the children who did not go to integrated schools? Popular culture had to have much of the responsibility for the attitudes of the Americans growing up after 1965: For all their questionable influences on children, television, movies, and music surely taught an ethic of equality, of color blindness, even while they recognized cultural difference. The emergence in the late 1990s of the brilliant young golfer Tiger Woods—of Asian, American Indian, and African-American racial mixture—provided a symbol for the irrelevance of, and resistance to, racial category. Woods simply refused to accept a designation, and his generation of Americans believed he was quite right in so doing.

At the end of the twentieth century, a great many Americans had decided that race would not matter in the future as it had in the past. W .E. B. Du Bois had rightly predicted in 1903 that the problem of the twentieth century would be the color line, but no equally authoritative voice a hundred years later was guessing that race would be *the* fundamental issue of the twenty-first century, not even those who insisted that race still does matter in America. If Americans' norm for race relations had been white supremacy at the beginning of the twentieth century, and if it changed to integration at the behest of civil rights activists in the 1950s and 1960s, by the end of the century it was racial and ethnic tolerance. However vague its meaning, the statement "Race doesn't matter" captured the broad commitment to tolerance that characterized the popular culture and civic life in the United States by the 1980s. It was as if a younger generation of Americans had gone back to the naïve faith of an old song that few of them had ever heard. "The faces that I see," Frank Sinatra had sung in 1945, "all races and religions, that's America to me."

By then powerful new demographic forces had encouraged Americans to think in new ways about the racial and ethnic makeup of their society. In 1960, 3.3 million foreign-born people lived in the United States, only 1.8 percent of the population and the lowest level of alien presence in the population in American history. Then in 1965 the Hart-Cellar Immigration Act was passed, and it effectively reopened the Golden Door to the masses from foreign shores by raising and equalizing the quota taken from each foreign nation and establishing liberal rules about accepting the family members of immigrants already here. More than 3 million new immigrants came in the 1960s, and almost 5 million in the 1970s—and that counted just the *legal* arrivals. Almost 8 million more came in the 1980s. A new immigration law in 1990 raised the quotas even more, and somewhere between 12 and 15 million immigrants, depending on the estimate of illegal aliens, arrived in the 1990s. There were significant numbers of political refugees from Asia and Central America, but the vast majority came seeking economic opportunity. The 2000 census reported 28 million foreign-born people in the country, but when the estimate of illegal immigrants and the children of those here legally were added, the best guesses went over 50 million. About half of the new immigrants were from Latin America, a third were from Asia, and perhaps an eighth from the Caribbean. By 2000 there were more Hispanic people in the United States than African Americans. The impact of immigration was concentrated in California, New York, Florida, Texas, and Illinois, though by the late 1990s much of the hinterland was experiencing a wave of the new immigration.[1]

Starting about 1976, some Americans had begun to get worried about the rising numbers of immigrants, but almost all of the concern focused on the illegal immigrants, mainly from Mexico and Central America. Indeed, most Americans were under the misapprehension that most immigrants were in the country illegally. After a full decade of debate, the Congress passed a law in 1986 making it illegal for employers to hire undocumented aliens, but it also extended amnesty to those who had been living in the country for four years. Concern about illegal immigrants ebbed and flowed for the rest of the century, but the only significant anti immigrant political effort came not surprisingly in California, which took in twice as many immigrants as any other state. In 1994, Californians passed, by a wide margin, a referendum that ordered the denial of health and education benefits to undocumented aliens. Court challenges in fact kept educational opportunities in place, but the effort showed the depth of concern among some Americans about the immigrant surge.[2]

Most Americans, however, accepted the new immigration as a certainty of the times. It was indeed a remarkable contrast to the nativism sparked by the immigrant surge a century earlier. Even those who experienced direct economic competition with new immigrants— African-American service workers, for example—offered only sporadic complaints about the impact of the new immigrants. Many Americans could see the economic contributions that immigrants made, from Hispanic housekeepers and construction workers to Korean shopkeepers to East Indian computer scientists. A lot of people had witnessed the diligence, intelligence, and kindly nature of most new immigrants. But most important, Americans' ideological journey in the twentieth century had brought them to a place where xenophobia and nativism were unacceptable. Most Americans understood that the rejection of white supremacy in the 1960s applied to discrimination against immigrants, many of whom were nonwhite. Now it was un-American to express nativist views. Moreover, the success of so many immigrants proved that the United States still assimilated the "wretched refuse" from other shores. It was still the land of freedom and opportunity, and many immigrant stories ratified faith in traditional democratic values.

The new immigrants vastly complicated Americans' historic impulse to bifurcate the social order into blacks and whites. Until the 1970s, Hispanics, American Indians, and Asian Americans were mostly included with whites. By the 1990s, to meet affirmative-action requirements in education, jobs, and politics, the U.S. government had separated Americans into four racial and ethnic categories—Indian, Asian, black, and white. Whites were asked further to designate themselves as either Hispanic or "Not of Hispanic Origin," which sent Hispanic activists to work trying to get recognized as a racial group. Hispanic and Asian Americans, the former now a larger group than blacks and the latter almost half as big, could point to their own histories of discrimination, but each group had manifested quite different responses from African Americans to prejudice—and from each other. Black immigrants from the Caribbean demonstrated group behaviors that diverged from African Americans'.

Soon a problem arose about people who did not fit into any one racial category, because they belonged to two or more groups. The longstanding "one-drop rule"—any person with one drop of African blood was categorized as black—finally was challenged. The creation of the official census category of "mixed race" caused even more skepticism about the efficacy of racial categorization.[3]

The demise of white supremacy had rapidly undermined the social stigma to interracial marriage. Polls had documented a precipitous fall since the 1960s in the number of Americans expressing disapproval of interracial unions. Exactly as Tom Heflin and Ben Tillman had predicted, the end of segregation had resulted in a tendency to what the white-nationalist leaders called "mongrelization." In the 1970s and 1980s, even in cities and small towns in the Deep South, one began to see a few black-and-white couples living in mostly white neighborhoods. More important, one knew them from parent-teacher associations and soccer teams, as their children participated in school and sports. Discrimination and harassment against them were not apparent, if they existed. During the 1990s, Americans hardly commented, and usually did not even know because the media stopped noting it, that among those joined in interracial marriage were a justice of the Supreme Court, the secretary of defense, and the president of the NAACP. By 1999 there were three million mixed marriages in the United States, about 5 percent of all marriages. Many more mixed couples cohabited. There were about five million mixed-race children in the country by 2003.[4]

The new immigration had contributed to the rapid increase in interracial marriages during the 1980s and 1990s. In 1997 one in seven babies born in California had parents of different races. The rates of marriage outside their race was as high as 50 percent among young Asians and Hispanics in the late 1990s, and the rates among young blacks was more than 10 percent. "This is the beginning point of a blending of the races," one demographer predicted in 1999. "You can expect that in these households racial or ethnic attitudes will soften, that identities will be less distinct, and that there will be an impact on attitudes in the communities surrounding these households. And this trend has real momentum behind it because it is so pronounced among young people."[5]

The new demographic realities thus pointed practically to values that regarded race and ethnicity as less important than other concerns. To be sure, Americans still pursued their fundamental needs for status and security. They continued to compete for economic opportunity, political power, and the use of space. But most Americans were far less oriented to the ideologies that encouraged ethnic or racial status competition—white supremacy or white nationalism—than they had been at the start of the twentieth century. Black nationalism persisted more among African Americans, but it clearly held much less sway in 2000 than it had in 1970. Status now was more clearly determined by wealth and occupation, though in a world of constant electronic communication, celebrity was the ultimate determinant of status in late-twentieth-century America.

But what values did prevail at the end of the twentieth century? Through all the political and economic turmoil after 1965, the United States economy recovered and even enhanced its strength, and out of that success came renewed faith in capitalist markets. Most Americans accepted the influence "the market" had on their lives, including its rewards for individual achievement and its privileging of economic liberty. Economic freedom still had a highly elastic meaning, encompassing the possibility of awful greed and exploitation, as Americans saw all too often in the 1990s and the early years of the new century. But it also meant that every person was responsible for his livelihood and accountable individually to market forces. Although by no means cleansed of discrimination, the American economy functioned for the most part to reward competence and enterprise and to penalize the timid and indolent. Most people in business insisted that race and ethnicity did not matter.

Democratic values of freedom, equality, and democracy still served to unite Americans. The United States protected civil liberties more vigorously than virtually any society in history, even extending them in practice to resident aliens. Attacked in 2001 by foreign-born terrorists who had been living in the United States, Americans demonstrated relatively little xenophobic reaction, and the government restricted the rights of only a small group of suspected terrorists. Most Americans at the turn of a new century still believed in equality before the law and equality of opportunity, even if the understandings of how to implement those meanings remained contested. Many Americans were disappointed in the shallowness of democratic discourse, the inordinate influence that monied interests exerted on the democratic process, and the behavior of many elected representatives. But their solutions to these problems typically have been more power to the people and not less.

During the last quarter of the twentieth century, Americans typically did not connect their instinctive assumption of democratic values to pride in nation. Indeed, most Americans, like many people in the West in the late twentieth century, held a healthy skepticism about nationalism because it had provided the ideological justification for violence and genocide in many places. American nationalism could threaten the need for security. When the country was attacked in 2001, American nationalism naturally surged again, demonstrating the great potential power of the latent sense of national honor when it was aligned with the more fundamental need for security. As "the American century" had shown so clearly, nationalism has great potential to shape the meaning of the people's values.

Thus over the course of the American century, the ideological underpinnings of society were altered fundamentally in some ways but conserved in others. The conflict between white supremacy and democratic values was exposed and addressed, even if many racial divisions persisted. Americans' sense of national honor expanded vastly and then contracted significantly. Nationalism seems to be expanding again in the new century, but no one can say today that it is a sure trend. Liberty and equality have been given much larger and more specific meanings, notwithstanding the great debate still going about how to define equality. It is not American chauvinism to say that liberty, equality, and democracy were given great power and substance in the United States in the twentieth century. It is true, and that truth has not been recognized as it should be in some quarters. But that represents an interpretation about the past, not a promise for the future. Indeed, Americans' achievements in expanding democratic values in the twentieth century create only responsibility to live up to them—and expand them further—in these times.

NOTES

Preface

1. The main theory supporting the assumption of the need for security and status is Abraham Maslow's "hierarchy of needs," which contains six levels of needs. The two most basic are physiological and safety needs, which are subsumed herein as "security." Maslow's other three needs—belonging, esteem, and self-actuality—are encompassed within my understanding of status. See *Motivation and Personality* (New York, 1954) and *Toward a Psychology of Being* (Princeton, 1962). My understanding of status is based mainly on the sociology of Max Weber. See *Max Weber: Essays in Sociology*, trans., ed., and with intro. by H. H. Gerth and C. Wright Mills (New York, 1946).

2. The economic historian Gavin Wright makes this point eloquently in "The Civil Rights Revolution as Economic History," *Journal of Economic History* 59 (June 1999), 286–87.

Chapter One

1. Phillip Shaw Paludan, *The Presidency of Abraham Lincoln* (Lawrence, Kans., 1994), 157; James M. McPherson, *Battle Cry of Freedom: The Civil War Era* (New York, 1988), 560; *New York Times*, November 7, 1862.

2. "Annual Message to Congress, 1862," *Abraham Lincoln: Speeches and Writings, 1859–1865* (New York, 1989), 412, 415.

3. For a recent discussion of American character, see Seymour Martin Lipset, *American Exceptionalism: A Double-Edged Sword* (New York, 1996).

4. Adrienne Koch and Willam Peden, ed., *The Life and Writings of Thomas Jefferson* (New York, 1944), 321–25, 344.

5. Alexis de Tocqueville, *Democracy in America*, ed. J. P. Mayer and Max Lerner (New York, 1945), 3, 473, 228, 235, 247.

6. Koch and Peden, *Writings of Jefferson*, 257, 256; Tocqueville, *Democracy*, 327, 315.

7. David R. Roediger, *The Wages of Whiteness: Race and the Making of the American Working Class* (London, 1991), 136; Eric Foner, *Free Soil, Free Labor, Free Men: The Ideology of the Republican Party before the Civil War* (New York, 1970), 60–62, 261–300; "Fourth Lincoln-Douglas Debate, Charleston, Illinois," *Abraham Lincoln: Speeches and Writings, 1832–1858* (New York, 1989), 636.

8. John Hope Franklin and Alfred A. Moss, Jr., *From Slavery to Freedom: A History of African Americans* (New York, 1994, 7th ed.), 165–66; Roger Lane, *Roots of Violence in Black Philadelphia, 1860–1900* (Cambridge, Mass., 1986), 7–18; Bruce Laurie, *Working People of Philadelphia, 1800–1850* (Philadelphia, 1980), 62–66, 124, 127, 155–58. On the significance of "whiteness" in nineteenth-century America, see Roediger, *Wages of Whiteness*; Alexander Saxton, *The Rise and Fall of the White Republic: Class Politics and Mass Culture in Nineteenth-Century America* (London, 1990); Jean H. Baker, *Affairs of Party: The Political Culture of Northern Democrats in the Mid-Nineteenth Century* (Ithaca, 1983); and Noel Ignatiev, *How the Irish Became White* (New York, 1995).

9. Susan-Mary Grant, *North over South: Northern Nationalism and American Identity in the Antebellum Era* (Lawrence, Kans., 2000), 5–15.

10. "Address at Sanitary Fair, Baltimore, Maryland," *Lincoln: Speeches and Writings 1859–1865*, 589.

11. David M. Potter, "The Quest for National Character," in *History and American Society: Essays of David M. Potter*, ed. Don E. Fehrenbacher (New York, 1973), 257.

12. David Herbert Donald, *Lincoln* (New York, 1995), 269; "'House Divided' Speech at Springfield, Illinois," *Lincoln: Speeches and Writings 1832–1858*, 426; Benjamin Quarles, *The Negro in the Civil War* (Boston, 1953), 184; Eric Foner, *Reconstruction: America's Unfinished Revolution* (New York), 49, 64.

13. "Address at Gettysburg, Pennsylvania," *Lincoln: Speeches and Writings 1859–1865*, 536.

14. Garry Wills, *Lincoln at Gettysburg: The Words That Remade America* (New York, 1992).

15. Edwin Stanton quoted in David Donald, *Lincoln Reconsidered: Essays on the Civil War Era* (New York, 1961, 2nd enlarged ed.), 8.

16. Vernon Lane Wharton, *The Negro in Mississippi, 1865–1890* (Chapel Hill, 1947), 80–97; Foner, *Reconstruction*, 262–63.

17. "The Meaning of July Fourth for the Negro," in *Frederick Douglass: Selected Speeches and Writings*, ed. Philip Foner (Chicago, 1999), 188–206; Ronald Takaki, *A Different Mirror: A History of Multicultural America* (Boston, 1993), 126–29.

18. Wharton, *Negro in Mississippi*, 82; Foner, *Reconstruction*, 70, 397.

19. 42d Congress, 2d Session, Senate Reports 41: *Testimony Taken by the Joint Select Committee to Enquire into the Condition of Affairs in the Late Insurrectionary States. Mississippi.* (Ku Klux Klan Hearings), Vol. 1, 570–75.

20. Ibid.; Foner, *Reconstruction*, 428.

21. Foner, *Reconstruction*, 229, 233, 238, 590, 574; Whitelaw Reid, *After the War: A Tour of the Southern States, 1865–1866* (New York, 1965 reprint), 564–65.

22. Foner, *Reconstruction*, 327–28, 375–76.

23. Ibid., 454–59.

24. Michael Perman, *The Road to Redemption: Southern Politics, 1869–1879* (Chapel Hill, 1984), 150–70.

25. Paul A. Gilje, *Rioting in America* (Bloomington, 1996), 98; Stephen Kantrowitz, *Ben Tillman and the Reconstruction of White Supremacy* (Chapel Hill, 2000), 67–79, 96–109.

26. Kenneth M. Stampp, *The Era of Reconstruction, 1865–1877* (New York, 1965), 194.

27. On ethnic nationalism, see Anthony D. Smith, *The Ethnic Origins of Nations* (New York, 1986); and Liah Greenfeld, *Nationalism: Five Roads to Modernity* (Cambridge, Mass., 1992).

28. On post-Reconstruction southern mythmaking, see Paul M. Gaston, *The New South Creed: A Study in Southern Mythmaking* (New York, 1970); and Gaines M. Foster, *Ghosts of the Confederacy: Defeat, the Lost Cause, and the Emergence of the New South, 1865 to 1913* (New York, 1987).

29. On sharecropping and tenancy, see Charles S. Johnson, Edwin R. Embree, and W. W. Alexander, *The Collapse of Cotton Tenancy. Summary of Field Studies & Statistical Surveys, 1933–35* (Chapel Hill, 1935).

30. William F. Holmes, *The White Chief: James Kimble Vardaman* (Baton Rouge, 1970), 55–56; 134–36; Holmes, "Whitecapping: Agrarian Violence in Mississippi, 1902–1906," *Journal of Southern History* 35 (May 1969), 165–85; Holmes, "Whitecapping in Mississippi: Agrarian Violence in the Populist Era," *Mid-America* 55 (April 1973), 134–48; C. Vann Woodward, *The Strange Career of Jim Crow* (New York, 1973, 3rd rev.), 87–88.

31. Joel Williamson, *The Crucible of Race: Black/White Relations in the American South Since Emancipation* (New York, 1984), 128; W. Fitzhugh Brundage, *Lynching in the New South: Georgia and Virginia, 1880–1930* (Urbana, 1993); Neil McMillen, *Dark Journey: Black Mississippians in the Age of Jim Crow* (Urbana, 1990), 236–37, 224; Wells quoted in Gilje, *Rioting in America*, 104.

32. W. E. Burghardt Du Bois, ed., *The Negro Artisan* (Atlanta, 1902); Sterling D. Spero and Abram D. Harris, *The Black Worker: The Negro and the Labor Movement* (New York, 1931); Robert Higgs, *Competition and Coercion: Blacks in the American Economy, 1865–1914* (Cambridge, Eng., 1977); Gavin Wright, *Old South, New South: Revolutions in the Southern Economy Since the Civil War* (New York, 1986).

33. Charles S. Johnson, *Patterns of Negro Segregation* (New York, 1943), 75–78; Howard N. Rabinowitz, *Race Relations in the Urban South* (New York, 1978), 226–54.

34. Rabinowitz, *Race Relations in the Urban South*, 125–225.

35. Edward L. Ayers, *The Promise of the New South: Life after Reconstruction* (New York, 1992), 141–46; *Plessy v. Ferguson* 163 U.S. 537 (1896); Charles A. Lofgren, *The Plessy Case: A Legal-Historical Interpretation* (New York, 1987).

36. George M. Fredrickson, *The Black Image in the White Mind: The Debate on Afro-American Character and Destiny, 1817–1914* (New York, 1971), 230; John Tyler Morgan, "The Future of the American Negro," *North American Review*, July 1884.

37. Fredrickson, *Black Image*, 228–55; Albion W. Tourgee, *An Appeal to Ceasar* (New York, 1884), 127; Frederick Ludwig Hoffman, *Race Traits and Tendencies of the American Negro* (New York, 1896). When the 1880 census was published and a

more accurate count of blacks was compared with the erroneously low figure from 1870, most observers drew the conclusion that the black population was booming. One commentator sympathetic to black interests estimated that in a hundred years there would be four times as many blacks as whites in the South.

38.   Thomas Nelson Page, "A Southerner on the Negro Question," *North American Review*, April 1892; Philip Alexander Bruce, *The Plantation Negro as a Freeman: Observations on His Character, Condition, and Prospects in Virginia* (New York, 1889); J. L. M. Curry, "The Negro Question," *Popular Science Monthly*, June 1899.

39.   James Bryce, "Thoughts on the Negro Problem," *North American Review*, December 1891; Frederick Douglass, "The Future of the Negro," *North American Review*, July 1884.

40.   David A. Jasen and Gene Jones, *Spreadin' Rhythm Around: Black Popular Songwriters, 1880–1930* (New York, 1998), 1–10; Robert C. Toll, *Blacking Up: The Minstrel Show in Nineteenth-Century America* (New York, 1974); Saxton, *Rise and Fall of the White Republic*, 177.

41.   Eugene Levy, *James Weldon Johnson: Black Leader, Black Voice* (Chicago, 1973), 79–81; Jasen and Jones, *Spreadin' Rhythm Around*, 1–132.

42.   This assessment of popular-culture and mass-communications usage of coon imagery is based on examinations of several southern newspapers in the 1890s and early 1900s, including the *Atlanta Constitution, Atlanta Journal, Nashville Banner, Nashville American, Memphis Scimitar,* and *Birmingham Age-Herald.*

43.   Thomas D. Clark, *The Southern Country Editor* (Indianapolis, 1948), 189–209, 58, 311–17.

44.   David B. Parker, *Alias Bill Arp: Charles Henry Smith and the South's "Goodly Heritage"* (Athens, 1991); *Atlanta Constitution*, March 2, February 2, April 28, March 16, 1890; October 14, 1891.

45.   Rabinowitz, *Race Relations in the Urban South*, 334–35.

46.   C. Vann Woodward, *Origins of the New South* (Baton Rouge, 1951), 254–55.

47.   Woodward, *Strange Career of Jim Crow*, 74–96; see also Michael Perman, *Struggle for Mastery: Disfranchisement in the South, 1888–1908* (Chapel Hill, 2001).

48.   Johnson, *Patterns of Negro Segregation*, 77; Edward L. Ayers, *Vengeance and Justice: Crime and Punishment in the 19th-Century American South* (New York, 1984), 173–74, 185–222; Howard N. Rabinowitz, "The Conflict Between Blacks and the Police in the Urban South, 1865–1900," *The Historian* 39 (November 1976), 62–76; Alex Lichtenstein, *Twice the Work of Free Labor: The Political Economy of Convict Labor in the New South* (London, 1996); Mary Ellen Curtin, *Black Prisoners and Their World, Alabama, 1865–1900* (Charlottesville, 2000).

49.   Louis R. Harlan, *Separate and Unequal* (Chapel Hill, 1958).

50.   Nell Irvin Painter, *The Exodusters: Black Migration to Kansas after Reconstruction* (New York, 1976).

51.   Ray Stannard Baker, *Following the Color Line: An Account of Negro Citizenship in the American Democracy* (New York, 1908), 112–18, 133.

52.   Ibid., 125–29; Lane, *Roots of Violence*, 23.

53.   Seth Scheiner, *Negro Mecca: A History of the Negro in New York, 1865–1920* (New York, 1965), 46–54; Leslie H. Fishel, Jr., "The North and the Negro, 1865–1900, A

Study in Race Discrimination" (unpublished Ph.D. dissertation, Harvard University, 1953), 127–63, 438–64.

54. John Bodnar, Roger Simon, and Michael P. Weber, *Lives of Their Own: Blacks, Italians, and Poles in Pittsburgh, 1900–1960* (Urbana, 1982), 232–66.

55. Fishel, "North and the Negro," 163, 463, 158; Baker, *Following the Color Line*, 158.

56. Lane, *Roots of Violence*, 1–5, 82–176.

Chapter Two

1. Newspaper account from the *Montgomery Advertiser*, reprinted in the *Nashville American*, October 19, 1904.

2. Heflin quoted in Malcolm C. McMillan, *Constitutional Development in Alabama, 1798–1901: A Study in Politics, the Negro, and Sectionalism* (Chapel Hill, 1955), 305; Heflin Scrapbook 6, Box 848, Heflin Papers, Amelia Gayle Gorgas Library, University of Alabama, Tuscaloosa, hereinafter identified as Heflin Papers, used with permission of Senator Howell Heflin.

3. August Meier, *Negro Thought in America* (Ann Arbor, 1963), 40–50; Louis R. Harlan, *Booker T. Washington: The Making of a Black Leader, 1856–1901* (New York, 1972), 224–28.

4. Washington, *Up from Slavery*, in *Three Negro Classics*, ed. John Hope Franklin (New York, 1965), 146–50.

5. Louis R. Harlan, "The Secret Life of Booker T. Washington," *Journal of Southern History* 37 (August 1971), 393–416.

6. Booker T. Washington [hereinafter referred to as BTW], "An Address at the National Peace Jubilee," October 16, 1898, in the *Booker T. Washington Papers*, ed. Louis R. Harlan et al. (Urbana, 1972–1984), IV, 490–93, hereinafter cited as *BTWP*; BTW, "A Statement on Lynching," in the *Birmingham Age-Herald*, *BTWP*, V, 91; and BTW to Emmett Jay Scott, ca. June 5, 1899, *BTWP*, V, 125. The article, "Lynching in the South," was included in BTW's book *The Story of My Life and Work*, reprinted in *BTWP*, I, 149–54.

7. For examples of BTW's speeches that emphasized black progress, see "An Address before the National Educational Association," July 10, 1896, *BTWP*, IV, 188–99; "A Speech at the Institute of Arts and Sciences," September 30, 1896, *BTWP*, IV, 211–23; "An Address before the Christian Endeavor Society," July 7, 1898, *BTWP*, IV, 438–41; BTW to Randall O. Simpson, October 22, 1903, *BTWP*, VII, 302–4.

8. BTW, *Up from Slavery*, 88–91, 147.

9. "An Abraham Lincoln Memorial Address in Philadelphia," February 12, 1899, *BTWP*, V, 32; "An Address on Abraham Lincoln to the Republican Club of New York City," February 12, 1909, *BTWP*, X, 32–36.

10. BTW to Louis G. Gregory, January 19, 1904, *BTWP*, VII, 401–2.

11. BTW to Timothy Thomas Fortune, November 7, 1899, *BTWP*, V, 256–57.

12. BTW, *Up from Slavery*, in *BTWP*, I, 347.

13. McMillan, *Constitutional Development in Alabama*, 305.

14. Dixon, *The Leopard's Spots: A Romance of the White Man's Burden, 1865–1900* (New York, 1902), 244.

15. Stephen Kantrowitz, *Ben Tillman and the Reconstruction of White Supremacy* (Chapel Hill, 2000), 217–21; Thomas Dixon, Jr., "Booker T. Washington and the Negro: Some Dangerous Aspects of the Work of Tuskegee," *Saturday Evening Post,* August 19, 1905.

16. Dewey W. Grantham, Jr., "Dinner at the White House: Theodore Roosevelt, Booker T. Washington, and the South," *Tennessee Historical Quarterly* 18 (June 1958), 116–18, 125; William F. Holmes, *The White Chief: James Kimble Vardaman* (Baton Rouge, 1970), 99; Felton quote from newspaper clipping, reel 718 in the Papers of Booker T. Washington, Library of Congress, Washington, D.C.

17. BTW to Theodore Roosevelt, October 2, 1901, *BTWP*, VI, 221. For a sample of evidence of BTW's commitment to combating lily-whiteism, see BTW to Theodore Roosevelt, September 27, 1902, *BTWP*, VI, 527; BTW draft letter to *Montgomery Advertiser,* ca. September 1901, *BTWP*, VI, 536–39; BTW to Francis Jackson Garrison, October 14, 1902, *BTWP*, VI, 547; and BTW to Thomas Ruffin Roulhac, October 29, 1902, *BTWP*, VI, 561–62.

18. *Leslie's Weekly*, February 4, 1904.

19. *Tom Watson's Magazine,* June 1905; C. Vann Woodward, *Tom Watson: Agrarian Rebel* (New York, 1938), 380.

20. Dixon, "Dangerous Aspects of the Work of Tuskegee."

21. An Editorial in the *Montgomery Advertiser*, August 16, 1905; BTW letter to the editor, *Montgomery Advertiser*, August 20, 1905, *BTWP*, VIII, 341–44.

22. BTW to Charles William Anderson, September 13, 1905, *BTWP*, VIII, 356–57; Three Reports of Pinkerton Detectives, October 22, 1905, *BTWP*, VIII, 418–21; BTW to Francis Jackson Garrison, October 5, 1905, *BTWP*, VIII, 394–96; Garrison to BTW, October 12, 1905, *BTWP*, VIII, 402–3.

23. Louis R. Harlan, *Booker T. Washington: The Wizard of Tuskegee, 1901–1915* (New York: 1983), 307–18; Thomas G. Dyer, *Theodore Roosevelt and the Idea of Race* (Baton Rouge, 1980), 114–16; *BTWP*, IX, 131.

24. Walter White, *A Man Called White* (New York, 1948), 3–12; Roberta Senechal, *The Sociogenesis of a Race Riot: Springfield, Illinois, in 1908* (Urbana, 1990), 195.

25. Harlan, *Wizard of Tuskegee*, 318–20.

26. David Levering Lewis, *W. E. B. Du Bois: Biography of a Race, 1868–1919* (New York, 1993), 299–301; Harlan, *Wizard of Tuskegee,* 45; S. P. Fullinwider, *The Mind and Mood of Black America: Twentieth Century Thought* (Homewood, Ill., 1969), 47–71.

27. Du Bois, *The Souls of Black Folk* in *Three Negro Classics,* 215.

28. Lewis, *Du Bois,* 226, 243–45.

29. Ibid., 233–37; 286–87.

30. Du Bois, *The Souls of Black Folk* in *Three Negro Classics,* 240–52.

31. Lewis, *Du Bois,* 321–23.

32. *Crisis,* August 1912.

33. BTW, "Is the Negro Having a Fair Chance?" *Century,* November 1912; BTW, "My View of the Segregation Laws," *New Republic,* December 4, 1915.

34. Harlan, *Wizard of Tuskegee,* 60, 85–86, 320–21. Du Bois condemned Washington's ownership of the *Age* and alleged secret ownership of other newspapers, as an attempt to control the black press. It is important to recognize that such race leaders as Vardaman and Watson owned newspapers and that Tillman, Dixon,

Felton, and the other white-nationalist leaders had ready access to the pages of one or more papers. Du Bois and Trotter certainly used the *Boston Guardian* and other newspapers to vie with Washington for leadership of African Americans.

35. August Meier and Elliot Rudwick, "The Boycott Movement against Jim Crow Streetcars in the South, 1900–1906," in *Along the Color Line: Explorations in the Black Experience* (Urbana, 1976), 267–89; Ray Stannard Baker, *Following the Color Line: An Account of Negro Citizenship in the American Democracy* (New York, 1908), 148.

36. John Michael Matthews, "The Georgia 'Race' Strike of 1909," *Journal of Southern History* 40 (November 1974), 613–30.

37. *Crisis*, March 1911; August 1912; July 1912; Kenneth L. Kusmer, *A Ghetto Takes Shape: Black Cleveland, 1870–1930* (Urbana, 1976), 75–80.

38. Allan H. Spear, *Black Chicago: The Making of a Negro Ghetto, 1890–1920* (Chicago, 1967), 36–41.

39. Senechal, *Sociogenesis of a Race Riot*, 2.

40. Ibid., 108–48.

41. Thomas Woofter, Jr., ed., *Negro Problems in Cities: A Study* (New York, 1928), 26–33; *Crisis*, December 1910; February 1912.

42. Morton Sosna, "The South in the Saddle: Racial Politics during the Wilson Years," *Wisconsin Magazine of History* 54 (Autumn 1970), 31; Nancy J. Weiss, "The Negro and the New Freedom: Fighting Wilsonian Segregation," *Political Science Quarterly* 84 (March 1969), 61–79; Kathleen Long Wolgemuth, "Woodrow Wilson's Appointment Policy and the Negro," *Journal of Southern History* 24 (November 1958), 462–63.

43. Thomas Cripps, *Slow Fade to Black: The Negro in American Film, 1900–1942* (New York, 1977), 41–69; Donald Bogle, *Toms, Coons, Mulattoes, Mammies & Bucks: An Interpretive History of Blacks in American Films* (New York, 1999, 3rd ed.), 3–10.

44. Ed Guerrero, *Framing Blackness: The African American Image in Film* (Philadelphia, 1993), 12–15.

45. Al-Tony Gilmore, *Bad Nigger! The National Impact of Jack Johnson* (Port Washington, N.Y., 1975), 9–30.

46. Ibid., 32–38.

47. Ibid., 40–71.

48. Ibid., 77–120.

Chapter Three

1. James R. Grossman, *Land of Hope: Chicago, Black Southerners, and the Great Migration* (Chicago, 1989), 70; Chicago Commission on Race Relations, *The Negro in Chicago: A Study of Race Relations and a Race Riot in 1919* (Chicago, 1922), 86.

2. Carole Marks, *Farewell—We're Good and Gone: The Great Migration* (Bloomington, 1989), 35–36; *Crisis*, June 1917, 63–66; "Additional Letters of Negro Migrants," *Journal of Negro History* 4 (October 1919), 440; "Letters of Negro Migrants," *Journal of Negro History* 4 (July 1919), 332; Grossman, *Land of Hope*, 18.

3. James R. Grossman, "*Blowing the Trumpet: The Chicago Defender and Black Migration During World War I*," Illinois Historical Journal 78 (Summer 1985), 82–96.

4. Michael Homel, *Down from Equality: Black Chicagoans and the Public Schools, 1920–1941* (Urbana, 1984), 88.

5. John Dittmer, *Black Georgia in the Progressive Era* (Urbana, 1980), 186–91; Malaika Adero, ed., *Up South: Stories, Studies, and Letters of This Century's African American Migrations* (New York, 1993), 54; *Montgomery Advertiser*, September 21, 1916, quoted in Chicago Commission, *Negro in Chicago*, 85.

6. Grossman, *Land of Hope*, 66; Woodson, "The Exodus during the War," in Adero, *Up South*, 11; "Additional Letters of Negro Migrants," 461.

7. Joseph A. Hill, "The Recent Northward Migration of the Negro," *Opportunity*, April 1924; "Additional Letters of Negro Migrants," 464.

8. James Weldon Johnson, *Along This Way: The Autobiography of James Weldon Johnson* (New York, 1931, 1990), 319–20.

9. Bernard C. Nalty, *Strength for the Fight: A History of Black Americans in the Military* (New York, 1986), 101–6.

10. Ibid., 109–24; Charles S. Johnson, *"Public Opinion and the Negro,"* Opportunity, July 1923, reprinted in *The Opportunity Reader: Stories, Poetry, and Essays from the Urban League's* Opportunity Magazine, ed. Sondra Kathryn Wilson (New York, 1999), 441.

11. Nalty, *Strength for the Fight*, 109; Neil McMillen, *Dark Journey: Black Mississippians in the Age of Jim Crow* (Urbana, 1990), 302–3. Du Bois's leading biographer has suggested that his support came partly from the promise, not fulfilled, that he would get an officer's commission in military intelligence to examine "Negro subversion," David Levering Lewis, *W. E. B. Du Bois: Biography of a Race, 1868–1919* (New York, 1993), 556.

12. McMillen, *Dark Journey*, 302–3.

13. Johnson, *Along This Way*, 308–38; Eugene Levy, *James Weldon Johnson: Black Leader, Black Voice* (Chicago, 1973), 75–98.

14. Johnson, *Along This Way*, 308.

15. Ibid., 315.

16. *Buchanan v. Warley* 245 U.S. 60 (1917); Robert L. Zangrando, *The NAAACP Crusade against Lynching, 1909–1950* (Philadelphia, 1980), 51–71.

17. Johnson, *Along This Way*, 305.

18. Sterling Spero and Abram L. Harris, *The Black Worker: The Negro and the Labor Movement* (New York, 1931), 299–302; George B. Tindall, *The Emergence of the New South, 1913–1945* (Baton Rouge, 1967), 164; Eric Arnesen, *Brotherhoods of Color: Black Railroad Workers and the Struggle for Equality* (Cambridge, Mass., 2001), 65–70.

19. Herbert Aptheker, ed., *A Documentary History of the Negro People in the United States, 1910–1932: From the Emergence of the N.A.A.C.P. to the Beginning of the New Deal* (Secaucus, N.J., 1977), 279–82.

20. Allan H. Spear, *Black Chicago: The Making of a Negro Ghetto, 1890–1920* (Chicago, 1967), 201–22.

21. Homel, *Down from Equality*, 80; Olivier Zunz, *The Changing Face of Inequality: Urbanization, Industrial Development, and Immigrants in Detroit, 1880–1920* (Chicago, 1982), 375–77; Spear, *Black Chicago*, 210–22.

22. Homel, *Down from Equality*, 11, 20, 48; Stephen Grant Meyer, *As Long as They*

Don't Move Next Door: Segregation and Racial Conflict in American Neighborhoods (Lanham, *state tk,* 2000), 45–46. The NAACP challenged the constitutionality of the covenants, but in 1926 the U.S. Supreme Court ruled that they amounted to private agreements, not state action that might be governed by the Fourteenth Amendment's equal protection clause. See *Corrigan v. Buckly* 271 U.S. 477 (1926).

23. Meyer, *As Long as They Don't Move Next Door,* 38–46.

24. August Meier and Elliott Rudwick, *From Plantation to Ghetto* (New York, 1976, 3rd ed.), 240–42.

25. Homel, *Down from Equality,* 27–34, 189–90; Kenneth L. Kusmer, *A Ghetto Takes Shape: Black Cleveland, 1870–1930* (Urbana, 1976), 182–84.

26. August Meier and Elliott Rudwick, *Black Detroit and the Rise of the UAW* (New York, 1979), 3–33; Claude A. Barnett, "We Win a Place in Industry," *Opportunity* (March 1929), in *African Americans in the Industrial Age: A Documentary History, 1915–1945,* ed. Joe W. Trotter and Earl Lewis (Boston, 1996); Spero and Harris, *The Black Worker,* 153–56, 178, 180.

27. Peter Gottlieb, *Making Their Own Way: Southern Blacks' Migration to Pittsburgh, 1916–1930* (Urbana, 1987), 98–99, 102; Harvard Sitkoff, *A New Deal for Blacks: The Emergence of Civil Rights as a National Issue: The Depression Decade* (New York, 1978), 37–38; Kusmer, *A Ghetto Takes Shape,* 198.

28. Lizabeth Cohen, *Making a New Deal: Industrial Workers in Chicago, 1919–1939* (Cambridge, Mass., 1990), 165–66; John Bodnar, Roger Simon, and Michael P. Weber, *Lives of Their Own: Blacks, Italians, and Poles in Pittsburgh, 1900–1960* (Urbana, 1982), 232–37, 255–59.

29. Spear, *Black Chicago,* 187–88, 208.

30. Nancy McLean, *Behind the Mask of Chivalry: The Making of the Second Ku Klux Klan* (New York, 1994), 130; Leonard Moore, *Citizen Klansmen: The Ku Klux Klan in Indiana, 1921–1928* (Chapel Hill, 1991), 20; Philip Jenkins, *Hoods and Shirts: The Extreme Right in Pennsylvania, 1925–1950* (Chapel Hill, 1997), 65–70.

31. Moore, *Citizen Klansmen,* 21; John Higham, *Strangers in the Land: Patterns of American Nativism, 1860–1925* (New Brunswick, N.J., 1955), 156.

32. Moore, *Citizen Klansmen,* 184–88; J. Mills Thornton, III, "Alabama Politics, J. Thomas Heflin, and the Expulsion Movement of 1929," *Alabama Review* 21 (April 1968), 82–112.

33. Mary Gambrell Rolinson, "The Garvey Movement in the Rural South, 1920–1927" (unpublished Ph.D. dissertation, Georgia State University, 2002), 48; Meier and Rudwick, *From Plantation to Ghetto,* 246–47; John Hope Franklin and Alfred A. Moss, Jr., *From Slavery to Freedom: A History of African Americans* (New York, 1994, 7th ed.), 358.

34. Franklin and Moss, *From Slavery to Freedom,* 357–59.

35. *Crisis,* January 1921; David Levering Lewis, *W. E. B. Du Bois: The Fight for Equality and the American Century, 1919–1963* (New York, 2000), 80.

36. Lewis, *Du Bois: The Fight for Equality,* 37–84.

37. James Weldon Johnson, *Black Manhattan* (New York, 1931), 263; on the hidden honor of pariah people, see Weber, *Essays in Sociology,* trans., ed., and with intro. by H. H. Gerth and C. Wright Mills (New York, 1946), 189–90.

38. Nathan Irvin Huggins, *Harlem Renaissance* (New York, 1971); David Levering Lewis, *When Harlem Was in Vogue* (1979).

39. Ann Douglas, *Terrible Honesty: Mongrel Manhattan in the 1920s* (New York, 1995), 353–57, 420.

40. Ibid.

41. James Weldon Johnson and J. Rosamond Johnson, *American Negro Spirituals* (New York, 1969) 12, 17.

42. James Weldon Johnson, *God's Trombones: Seven Negro Sermons in Verse* (New York, 1927) 2–3.

43. Melvin Patrick Ely, *The Adventures of Amos 'n' Andy: A Social History of an American Phenomenon* (New York, 1991), 11–114; for examples of the racist short fiction, see the works of Irvin S. Cobb and Octavus Roy Cohen. Cohen's stories were collected in such books as *Dark Days and Black Knights* (New York, 1923) and *Assorted Chocolates* (New York, 1922).

44. Donald Bogle, *Toms, Coons, Mulattoes, Mammies & Bucks: An Interpretive History of Blacks in American Films* (New York, 1999, 3rd ed.), 26–52.

45. Robert J. Norrell, "Caste in Steel: Jim Crow Careers in Birmingham, Alabama," *Journal of American History* 73 (December 1986), 675–76; Sitkoff, *A New Deal for Blacks*, 36.

46. Sitkoff, *A New Deal for Blacks*, 37.

47. Homel, *Down from Equality*, 98; Kusmer, *A Ghetto Takes Shape*, 184, 197.

48. August Meier and Elliot Rudwick, "The Origins of Nonviolent Direct Action in Afro-American Protest: A Note on Historical Discontinuities," in *Along the Color Line: Explorations in the Black Experience* (Urbana, 1976), 312–32.

49. Dan T. Carter, *Scottsboro: A Tragedy of the American South* (Baton Rouge, 1969); James Goodman, *Stories of Scottsboro* (New York, 1994).

50. Theodore Draper, *American Communism and Soviet Russia* (New York, 1960); Mark Naison, *Communists in Harlem during the Depression* (New York, 1983); Robin D. G. Kelley, *Hammer and Hoe: Alabama Communists during the Great Depression* (Chapel Hill, 1990).

51. Sitkoff, *A New Deal for Blacks*, 47–53, 70–79.

52. Eric Foner, *The Story of American Freedom* (New York, 1998), 204.

53. *Time*, August 17, 1936; David Potter, *The South and the Concurrent Majority* (Baton Rouge, 1972) 68, 76–77.

Chapter Four

1. Roi Ottley, *'New World A-Coming': Inside Black America* (Boston, 1943), 186–202.

2. Ibid.

3. *U.S. v. Carolene Products Co.* 304 U.S. 144 (1938); Robert M. Cover, "The Origins of Judicial Activism in the Protection of Minorities," *Yale Law Journal* 91 (June 1982), 1287–1316.

4. *New Negro Alliance v. Sanitary Grocery Co.* 303 U.S. 552 (1938); August Meier and Elliot Rudwick, "The Origins of Nonviolent Direct Action in Afro-American Protest: A Note on Historical Discontinuities," in *Along the Color Line: Explorations*

in the Black Experience (Urbana, 1976), 326; *Missouri ex rel. Gaines v. Canada* 305 U.S. 337 (1938).

5. John B. Kirby, *Black Americans in the Roosevelt Era: Liberalism and Race* (Knoxville, 1979), 114.

6. Scott A. Sandage, "A Marble House Divided: The Lincoln Memorial, the Civil Rights Movement, and the Politics of Memory, 1939–1963," *Journal of American History* 80 (June 1993), 136–43.

7. Nell Irvin Painter, *The Narrative of Hosea Hudson: His Life as a Negro Communist in the South* (Cambridge, Mass., 1979), 255–67.

8. Ralph Bunche, *The Political Status of the Negro in the Age of FDR*, ed. Dewey W. Grantham (Chicago, 1973), 69–101, 253–476; Adam Fairclough, *Race and Democracy: The Civil Rights Struggle in Louisiana, 1915–1972* (Athens, 1995), 50.

9. Linda Reed, *Simple Decency and Common Sense: The Southern Conference Movement, 1938–1963* (Bloomington, 1991); Patricia Sullivan, *Days of Hope: Race and Democracy in the New Deal Era* (Chapel Hill, 1996).

10. *Ladies' Home Journal*, September 1941.

11. *Life*, February 17, 1941.

12. Andrew Buni, *Robert L. Vann of the* Pittsburgh Courier: *Politics and Black Journalism* (Pittsburgh, 1974), 299–320; *Crisis*, December 1940.

13. Horace R. Cayton, "Fighting for White Folks?" *The Nation*, September 26, 1942; *Pittsburgh Courier*, December 21, 1940.

14. Bernard C. Nalty, *Strength for the Fight: A History of Black Americans in the Military* (New York, 1986), 162–203; Harvard Sitkoff, "Racial Militancy and Interracial Violence in the Second World War," *Journal of American History* 48 (December 1971), 667.

15. Sitkoff, "Racial Militancy," 668; Ottley, *New World*, 311; Daniel Kryder, *Divided Arsenal: Race and the American State during World War II* (Cambridge, Eng., 2000), 168–207.

16. Nalty, *Strength for the Fight*, 143–203; George B. Tindall, *The Emergence of the New South, 1913–1975* (Baton Rouge, 1967), 712; Richard Polenberg, *America at War: The Home Front, 1941–1945* (Englewood Cliffs, N.J., 1968), 125; Fisk University, Social Science Institute, *A Monthly Summary of Events and Trends in Race Relations* [hereinafter identified as "Fisk *Monthly Summary*"], March 1945.

17. Fisk *Monthly Summary*, January 1945.

18. Paula F. Pfeffer, *A. Philip Randolph, Pioneer of the Civil Rights Movement* (Baton Rouge, 1990), 240–80.

19. Richard M. Dalfiume, "The Forgotten Years of the Negro Revolution," *Journal of American History* 55 (June 1968), 91; Merl E. Reed, *Seedtime for the Modern Civil Rights Movement: The President's Committee on Fair Employment Practice, 1941–1946* (Baton Rouge, 1991), 35; Charles S. Johnson, *To Stem This Tide: A Survey of Racial Tension Areas in the United States* (New York, 1943), 3, 7–21.

20. Polenberg, *America at War*, 116; Kryder, *Divided Arsenal*, 102–17.

21. Fisk *Monthly Summary*, June 1944; Robert J. Norrell, "Caste in Steel: Jim Crow Careers in Birmingham, Alabama," *Journal of American History* 73 (December 1986), 679–80; Nelson Lichtenstein, *Labor's War at Home: The CIO in World War II* (Cambridge, Eng., 1982), 79–80.

22. Fisk *Monthly Summary*, August 1943; January 1945; Bruce Nelson, "Organized Labor and the Struggle for Black Equality in Mobile during World War II," *Journal of American History* 80 (December 1993), 952–88.

23. Fisk *Monthly Summary*, January 1945; *The Gallup Poll*, 1945, Vol. 1, 528.

24. Reynolds Farley and Walter R. Allen, *The Color Line and the Quality of Life in America* (New York, 1989), 298.

25. Robin D. G. Kelley, "We Are Not What We Seem": Rethinking Black Working-Class Opposition in the Jim Crow South," *Journal of American History* 80 (June 1993), 104.

26. Dalfiume, "Forgotten Years," 99–100.

27. Meier and Rudwick, "The Origins of Nonviolent Direct Action," 328; *Steele v. L&N Railroad* 323 U. S. 192 (1944); Fisk *Monthly Summary*, January 1945.

28. Pete Daniel, "Going Among Strangers: Southern Reactions to World War II," *Journal of American History* 77 (December 1990), 893; Cayton, "Fighting for White Folks?" *The Nation*, September 26, 1942; Fisk *Monthly Summary*, January 1945.

29. Tindall, *Emergence of the New South*, 714–15; Daniel, "Going Among Strangers," 891; Robert J. Norrell, *Dixie's War: The South and World War II* (Tuscaloosa, 1992), 41.

30. Howard Odum, *Race and Rumors of Race: Challenge to American Crisis* (Chapel Hill, 1943), 57, 67–89, 97.

31. Hazel Erskine, "The Polls: Race Relations," *Public Opinion Quarterly* 26 (1962), 137–49.

32. Ronald Takaki, *A Different Mirror: A History of Multicultural America* (Boston, 1993), 378–82.

33. Arnold R. Hirsch, *Making the Second Ghetto: Race and Housing in Chicago, 1940–1960* (Cambridge, Eng., 1983), 2–20; Fisk *Monthly Summary*, September, November 1943; June 1945.

34. Carey McWilliams, "The Zoot-Suit Riots," *New Republic*, June 21, 1942.

35. Dominic J. Capeci, Jr., and Martha Wilkerson, *Layered Violence: The Detroit Rioters of 1943* (Jackson, 1991).

36. *New York Post*, August 2, 1943; Dominic J. Capeci, Jr., *The Harlem Riot of 1943* (Philadelphia, 1943).

37. Thomas Sancton, "The Race Riots," *New Republic*, July 5, 1943.

38. Johnson, *To Stem This Tide*, 104; Elazar Barkan, *Retreat of Scientific Racism: Changing Concepts of Race in Britain and the United States between the World Wars* (Cambridge, Eng., 1992), 203, 279–340.

39. Philip Gleason, "Americans All: World War II and the Shaping of American Identity," *Review of Politics* 43 (October 1981), 483–518; Archibald MacLeish, *The American Cause* (New York, 1941); Reinhold Niebuhr, *The Children of Light and the Children of Darkness* (New York, 1944), xi; Gunnar Myrdal, *An American Dilemma: The Negro Problem in Modern Democracy* (New York, 1944), lxvii–lxix.

40. Johnson, *To Stem This Tide*, 103; *Look*, May 1, 1945.

41. Barbara Dianne Savage, *Broadcasting Freedom: Radio, War, and the Politics of Race, 1938–1948* (Chapel Hill, 1999).

42. Fisk *Monthly Summary*, April 1944; Clayton R. Koppes and Gregory D. Black, "Blacks, Loyalty, and Motion-Picture Propaganda in World War II," *Journal of American History* 73 (September 1986), 383–406.

43. Hazel Erskine, "The Polls," 137–49.

44. John Dittmer, *Local People: The Struggle for Civil Rights in Mississippi* (Urbana, 1994), 25; Charles M. Payne, *I've Got the Light of Freedom: The Organizing Tradition and the Mississippi Freedom Struggle* (Berkeley, 1995), 25–29; Stephen G. N. Tuck, *Beyond Atlanta: The Struggle for Racial Equality in Georgia, 1940–1980* (Athens, 2001), 40–73; Meier and Rudwick, "The Origins of Nonviolent Direct Action," 358; Sullivan, *Days of Hope,* 195–212.

45. *Shelley v. Kraemer* 334 U.S. 1 (1948); *Morgan v. Virginia* 328 U.S. 373 (1946); *Henderson v. United States* 339 U.S. 816 (1950); Mark V. Tushnet, *The NAACP's Legal Campaign against Segregated Education, 1925–1950* (Chapel Hill, 1987), 105–37.

46. Jules Tygiel, *Baseball's Great Experiment: Jackie Robinson and His Legacy* (New York, 1983).

47. Doug McAdam, *Political Process and the Development of Black Insurgency, 1930–1970* (Chicago, 1982), 77–103; Aldon D. Morris, *The Origins of the Civil Rights Movement: Black Communities Organizing for Change* (New York, 1984), 4–6; Gavin Wright, *Old South, New South: Revolutions in the Southern Economy since the Civil War* (New York, 1986), 236–69.

48. Fisk *Monthly Summary,* May 1946; Hirsch, *Making the Second Ghetto,* 53–54; Stephen Grant Meyer, *As Long as They Don't Move Next Door: Segregation and Racial Conflict in American Neighborhoods* (Lanham, 2000), 104; Fisk *Monthly Summary,* January 1945.

49. Jon Wiener, "His Way," *The Nation,* June 8, 1998; Kitty Kelley, *His Way: The Unauthorized Biography of Frank Sinatra* (Toronto, 1986), 107; Fisk *Monthly Summary,* January 1945.

50. Kari Frederickson, *The Dixiecrat Revolt and the End of the Solid South, 1932–1968* (Chapel Hill, 2001), 48; John Egerton, *Speak Now Against the Day: The Generation before the Civil Rights Movement in the South* (New York, 1994), 369–70.

51. Harvard Sitkoff, "Harry Truman and the Election of 1948: The Coming of Age of Civil Rights in American Politics," *Journal of Southern History* 37 (February 1971), 597–616.

52. Frederickson, *The Dixiecrat Revolt,* 137.

53. Egerton, *Speak Now Against the Day,* 444–46.

54. Ibid., 453–54.

55. Kelley, *His Way,* 109–10; Wiener, "His Way."

56. Kelley, *His Way,* 109–10; Wiener, "His Way."

Chapter Five

1. *Memphis Commercial Appeal,* June 9, 1950; Robert Gordon, *It Came From Memphis* (New York, 1995), 11–26.

2. Brian Ward, *Just My Soul Responding: Rhythm and Blues, Black Consciousness and Race Relations* (London, 1998), 30.

3. Ibid., 33–36.

4. Pete Daniel, *Lost Revolutions: The South in the 1950s* (Chapel Hill, 2000), 131; David L. Chappell, "Hip Like Me: Racial Cross-Dressing in Pop Music before Elvis," in *Media, Culture, and the Modern African-American Freedom Struggle,* ed. Brian Ward

(Gainesville, 2001), 108.

5. Peter Guralnick, *Last Train to Memphis: The Rise of Elvis Presley* (Boston, 1994), 100–1.

6. Ward, *Just My Soul,* 52–60, 134, 165.

7. Gordon, *It Came From Memphis,* 19–23; Ward, *Just My Soul,* 161–69.

8. Ward, *Just My Soul,* 104–7.

9. Donald Bogle, *Toms, Coons, Mulattoes, Mammies & Bucks: An Interpretive History of Blacks in American Films* (New York, 1999, 3rd ed.), 143–47.

10. Donald Bogle, *Prime Time Blues: African Americans on Network Television* (New York, 2001), 13–55.

11. Henry Louis Gates, Jr., *Colored People: A Memoir* (New York, 1994), 19–23.

12. Ibid., 19–27.

13. John H. Johnson with Lerone Bennett, Jr., *Succeeding against the Odds* (New York, 1989), 155–59, 207.

14. Hazel Erskine, "The Polls: Race Relations," *Public Opinion Quarterly* 26 (1962), 137–49.

15. Brenda Gayle Plummer, *Rising Wind: Black Americans and U.S. Foreign Affairs, 1935–1960* (Chapel Hill, 1996), 195–200; Mary L. Dudziak, *Cold War Civil Rights: Race and the Image of American Democracy* (Princeton, 2000), 62.

16. Kenneth R. Janken, "From Colonial Liberation to Cold War Liberalism: Walter White, the NAACP, and Foreign Affairs, 1941–1955," *Ethnic and Racial Studies* 21 (1998), 1074–95.

17. Julia Anne McDonough, "Men and Women of Good Will: A History of the Commission on Interracial Cooperation and the Southern Regional Council, 1919–1954," (unpublished Ph.D. dissertation, University of Virginia, 1992), 556–70.

18. Editor's comments attached to letter, Frank K. Kelly to E. J. B. Rose, May 8, 1956, in the Papers of the Southern Regional Council, Atlanta University, Folder 852. Works that emphasize the importance of the Cold War in enabling or precipitating the civil rights movement, see Dudziak, *Cold War Civil Rights,* and Plummer, *Rising Wind;* Penny M. Von Eschen, *Race against Empire: Black Americans and Anticolonialism, 1937–1957* (Ithaca, 1997); Philip A. Klinkner with Rogers M. Smith, *The Unsteady March: The Rise and Decline of Racial Equality in America* (Chicago, 1999); Thomas Borstelmann, *The Cold War and the Color Line: American Race Relations in the Global Arena* (Cambridge, Mass., 2001).

19. William H. Chafe, *Civilities and Civil Rights: Greensboro, North Carolina, and the Black Struggle for Freedom* (New York, 1980), 13–41; Robert J. Norrell, *Reaping the Whirlwind: The Civil Rights Movement in Tuskegee* (New York, 1985), 59–110; John Dittmer, *Local People: The Struggle for Civil Rights in Mississippi* (Urbana, 1994), 32–41.

20. C. Vann Woodward, *The Strange Career of Jim Crow* (New York, 1973, 3rd rev.), 143; Adam Fairclough, *Race and Democracy: The Civil Rights Struggle in Louisiana, 1915–1972* (Athens, 1995), 106–9.

21. Mark V. Tushnet, *Making Civil Rights Law: Thurgood Marshall and the Supreme Court, 1936–1961* (New York, 1994), 137–67.

22. Robert Fredrick Burk, *The Eisenhower Administration and Black Civil Rights* (Knoxville, 1984), 102–6.

23. Robert Mann, *The Walls of Jericho: Lyndon Johnson, Hubert Humphrey, Richard Russell, and the Struggle for Civil Rights* (San Diego, 1996), 87–88.

24. *Shelley v. Kraemer* 334 U.S. 1 (1948).

25. Kenneth T. Jackson, *Crabgrass Frontier: The Suburbanization of the United States* (New York, 1985), 196–213.

26. Ibid., 241; Burk, *Eisenhower Administration*, 112–13.

27. Arnold R. Hirsch, *Making the Second Ghetto: Race and Housing in Chicago, 1940–1960* (Cambridge, Eng., 1983), 241.

28. Jackson, *Crabgrass Frontier*, 223–29; Thomas J. Sugrue, *The Origins of the Urban Crisis: Race and Inequality in Postwar Detroit* (Princeton, 1996), 76.

29. Hirsch, *Making the Second Ghetto*, 59, 186 Stephen Grant Meyer, *As Long as They Don't Move Next Door: Segregation and Racial Conflict in American Neighborhoods* (Lanham, state tk, 2000), 112–13, 126–29.

30. Hirsch, *Making the Second Ghetto*, 22–100.

31. Ibid., 86, 186–87.

32. Ibid., 185–86.

33. Ibid., 199.

34. Ibid., 61–62; Sugrue, *Origins of the Urban Crisis*, 235; Carolyn Martindale and Lillian Rae Dunlap, "The African Americans," in *U.S. News Coverage of Racial Minorities: A Sourcebook, 1934–1996*, ed. Beverly Ann Deepe Keever, Carolyn Martindale, and Mary Ann Weston (Westport, 1997), 85.

35. Hirsch, *Making the Second Ghetto*, 196; Michael Homel, *Down from Equality: Black Chicagoans and the Public Schools, 1920–1941* (Urbana, 1984), 187–88.

36. Sugrue, *Origins of the Urban Crisis*, 83–84; William Julius Wilson, *The Declining Significance of Race: Blacks and Changing American Institutions* (Chicago, 1978), 79–82.

37. Sugrue, *Origins of the Urban Crisis*, 126–28; Burk, *Eisenhower Administration*, 103.

38. Herbert Hill, "Racial Inequality in Employment: The Patterns of Discrimination," *Annals of the American Academy of Political and Social Science* (January 1965); Sugrue, *Origins of the Urban Crisis*, 95–105.

39. Sugrue, *Origins of the Urban Crisis*, 113–17; Hill, "Racial Inequality," 33–38, 42; Burk, *Eisenhower Administration*, 103.

40. Reynolds Farley and Walter R. Allen, *The Color Line and the Quality of Life in America* (New York, 1989), 214; Wilson, *Declining Significance of Race*, 89–91.

41. Michael Reich, *Racial Inequality: A Political-Economic Analysis* (Princeton, 1981), 51–52; Farley and Allen, *The Color Line*, 298; Karl E. Taeuber and Alma F. Taeuber, *Negroes in Cities: Residential Segregation and Neighborhood Change* (Chicago, 1965), 39–41.

42. Michael J. Klarman, "How *Brown* Changed Race Relations: The Backlash Thesis," *Journal of American History* 81 (June 1994), 81–118; for an opposing view to Klarman, see Gerald N. Rosenberg, *The Hollow Hope: Can Courts Bring About Social Change?* (Chicago, 1991).

43. Woodward, *Strange Career*, 154; Dittmer, *Local People*, 50–51; J. Mills Thornton, III, *Dividing Lines: Municipal Politics and the Struggle for Civil Rights in Montgomery, Birmingham, and Selma* (Tuscaloosa, 2002), 393–94.

44. Aldon D. Morris, *The Origins of the Civil Rights Movement: Black Communities Organizing for Change* (New York, 1984), 31.

45. Robert J. Norrell, "Labor Trouble: George Wallace and Union Politics in Alabama," in *Organized Labor in the Twentieth-Century South*, ed. Robert H. Zieger (Knoxville, 1991), 253, 257.

46. Ibid., 253–54; Dittmer, *Local People*, 46–55; Stephen J. Whitfield, *A Death in the Delta: The Story of Emmett Till* (New York, 1988), 15–31.

47. Whitfield, *Death in the Delta*, 107, 145.

48. Thornton, *Dividing Lines*, 20–40.

49. Ibid., 53–67.

50. David J. Garrow, *Bearing the Cross: Martin Luther King, Jr., and the Southern Christian Leadership Conference* (New York, 1986), 19–20; Thornton, *Dividing Lines*, 65, 74.

51. Rosenberg, *Hollow Hope*, 113–15; Garrow, *Bearing the Cross*, 66.

52. August Meier and Elliot Rudwick, "The Origins of Nonviolent Direct Action in Afro-American Protest: A Note on Historical Discontinuities," in *Along the Color Line: Explorations in the Black Experience* (Urbana, 1976), 389.

53. J. Mills Thornton, "Challenge and Response in the Montgomery Bus Boycott," *Alabama Review* 30 (July 1980), 163–235.

54. Claybourne Carson, ed., *The Papers of Martin Luther King, Jr.* (Berkeley, 1992), III, 71–73.

55. Ibid., 71–73, 135–36.

56. Keith D. Miller, *Voice of Deliverance: The Language of Martin Luther King, Jr., and Its Sources* (New York, 1992), 87–100; Garrow, *Bearing the Cross*, 60–61.

57. Miller, *Voice of Deliverance*, 63.

58. Ibid., 17–24.

59. Ibid., 48–52, 67–70.

60. Ibid., 72–79.

61. Ibid., 126, 134–36, 191–92.

62. Garrow, *Bearing the Cross*, 66–73, 83–86, 97–103.

63. Erskine, "The Polls," 140–41; Thornton, *Dividing Lines*, 96–97.

64. Norrell, *Reaping the Whirlwind*, 104–7.

65. Mann, *Walls of Jericho*, 156–65.

66. Ibid., 195–224; Steven F. Lawson, *Black Ballots: Voting Rights in the South, 1944–1969* (New York, 1976), 140–202; Norrell, *Reaping the Whirlwind*, 121.

67. David Halberstam, *The Fifties* (New York, 1994), 675.

68. Robert J. Donovan and Ray Scherer, *Unsilent Revolution: Television News and American Public Life* (Cambridge, Mass., 1992), 6; Gates, *Colored People*, 25.

Chapter Six

1. George B. Leonard, "Midnight Plane to Alabama," *The Nation*, May 10, 1965.

2. *New York Times*, February 28, 15, 1960.

3. Aldon D. Morris, *The Origins of the Civil Rights Movement: Black Communities Organizing for Change* (New York, 1984), 188–94.

4. *New York Times*, April 8, 1960; *New York Times v. Sullivan* 376 U.S. 254 (1964).

5. C. Vann Woodward, *The Strange Career of Jim Crow* (New York, 1973, 3rd rev.), 170–71; *New York Times*, March 6, February 28, 1960; David J. Garrow, *Bearing the Cross: Martin Luther King, Jr., and the Southern Christian Leadership Conference* (New York, 1986), 151.

6. Garrow, *Bearing the Cross*, 171, 168; Gerald N. Rosenberg, *The Hollow Hope: Can Courts Bring About Social Change?* (Chicago, 1991), 151–54; Claybourne Carson, *In Struggle: SNCC and the Black Awakening of the 1960s* (Cambridge, Mass., 1981).

7. Garrow, *Bearing the Cross*, 265; Steven F. Lawson, *Running for Freedom: Civil Rights and Black Politics in America since 1941* (New York, 1997), 78–79.

8. Hugh Davis Graham, *The Civil Rights Era: Origins and Development of National Policy, 1960–1972* (New York, 1990), 27–28.

9. Garrow, *Bearing the Cross*, 156.

10. *New York Times*, May 15, 21, 1961; David Halberstam, *The Children* (New York, 1998), 310–13.

11. Garrow, *Bearing the Cross*, 157.

12. J. Mills Thornton, III, *Dividing Lines: Municipal Politics and the Struggle for Civil Rights in Montgomery, Birmingham, and Selma* (Tuscaloosa, 2002), 140.

13. *New York Times*, April 12, 1960.

14. Thornton, *Dividing Lines*, 257.

15. Ibid., 124–25, 251–52.

16. Garrow, *Bearing the Cross*, 161–67.

17. Ibid., 170.

18. Pat Watters, *Down to Now: Reflections on the Southern Civil Rights Movement* (New York, 1971), 141–218.

19. Adam Fairclough, *Better Day Coming: Blacks and Equality, 1890–2000* (New York, 2001), 268–69; Garrow, *Bearing the Cross*, 227.

20. Garrow, *Bearing the Cross*, 187–88.

21. Allen J. Matusow, *The Unraveling of America: A History of Liberalism in the 1960s* (New York, 1984), 83–85.

22. Dan T. Carter, *The Politics of Rage: George Wallace, the Origins of the New Conservatism, and the Transformation of American Politics* (New York, 1995), 105–6.

23. Marshall Frady, *Wallace* (New York, 1968), 141–42.

24. Thornton, *Dividing Lines*, 299; Garrow, *Bearing the Cross*, 227.

25. Garrow, *Bearing the Cross*, 227, 264, 274.

26. Andrew Young, *An Easy Burden: The Civil Rights Movement and the Transformation of America* (New York, 1996), 226, 208; Garrow, *Bearing the Cross*, 264.

27. Garrow, *Bearing the Cross*, 247.

28. Ibid., 247–60.

29. *New York Times*, May 8, 1963.

30. Robert J. Donovan and Ray Scherer, *Unsilent Revolution: Television News and American Public Life* (Cambridge, Mass., 1992), 6; Fairclough, *Better Day Coming*, 278; Halberstam, *The Children*, 388.

31. Thornton, *Dividing Lines*, 323, 313–14; *New York Times*, May 4, 1963.

32. Daniel M. Berman, *A Bill Becomes a Law: Congress Enacts Civil Rights Legislation* (New York, 1966), 139; Garrow, *Bearing the Cross*, 260–62; Robert Mann, *The Walls of Jericho: Lyndon Johnson, Hubert Humphrey, Richard Russell, and the Struggle for Civil Rights* (San Diego, 1996), 304; *New York Times*, June 9, 1963.

33. Garrow, *Bearing the Cross*, 275–76.

34. E. Culpepper Clark, *The Schoolhouse Door: Segregation's Last Stand at the University of Alabama* (New York, 1993), 213–37; Carter, *Politics of Rage*, 150.

35. Matusow, *Unraveling of America*, 90.

36. *New York Times*, June 15, 17; July 8, 13, 15, 21, 30; August 7, 8, 1963; Paul Burstein, "Public Opinion, Demonstrations, and the Passage of Antidiscrimination Legislation," *Public Opinion Quarterly* 43 (Summer 1979), 157–72; Rosenberg, *Hollow Hope*, 130; Martin Luther King, Jr., *Why We Can't Wait* (New York, 1964), 111; Garrow, *Bearing the Cross*, 273.

37. *New York Times*, August 29, 1963.

38. "I Have a Dream," in *A Call to Conscience: The Landmark Speeches of Dr. Martin Luther King, Jr.,* ed. Claybourne Carson and Kris Shepard (New York, 2001), 81–87.

39. Donovan and Scherer, *Unsilent Revolution*, 18; Dan Nimmo and James E. Combs, *Nightly Horrors: Crisis Coverage in Television Network News* (Knoxville, 1985), 16.

40. Carter, *Politics of Rage*, 156–79.

41. Mann, *Walls of Jericho*, 326–27, 354; *New York Times*, October 31, 1963.

42. Mann, *Walls of Jericho*, 317, 390–91, 400.

43. Ibid., 383, 361.

44. Charles and Barbara Whalen, *The Longest Debate: A Legislative History of the 1964 Civil Rights Act* (Cabin John, Md., 1985).

45. *New York Times*, August 7, 8, 1963; Thomas J. Sugrue, *The Origins of the Urban Crisis: Race and Inequality in Postwar Detroit* (Princeton, 1996), 210.

46. Carter, *Politics of Rage*, 207–15.

47. *New York Times*, July 19–29, 1964.

48. John Dittmer, *Local People: The Struggle for Civil Rights in Mississippi* (Urbana, 1994), 137–38.

49. Ibid., 242–71.

50. Ibid., 272–302.

51. Thornton, *Dividing Lines*, 442–82.

52. David Garrow, *Protest at Selma: Martin Luther King, Jr., and the Voting Rights Act of 1965* (New Haven, 1978), 43–45, 63; *New York Times*, January 26, 1965.

53. Donovan and Scherer, *Unsilent Revolution*, 19.

54. Garrow, *Protest at Selma*, 88; Special Message to the Congress: "The American Promise," March 15, 1965, *Public Papers of the Presidents of the United States: Lyndon B. Johnson, 1965* (Washington, D.C., 1965), I, 281–87.

55. Garrow, *Protest at Selma*, 91.

56. "Address at the Conclusion of the Selma to Montgomery March," in *A Call to Conscience: The Landmark Speeches of Dr. Martin Luther King, Jr.,* ed. Claybourne Carson and Kris Shepard (New York, 2001), 119–32.

57. Donovan and Scherer, *Unsilent Revolution*, 20.

Chapter Seven

1. *Los Angeles Times*, August 14–16, 1965.

2. Robert J. Donovan and Ray Scherer, *Unsilent Revolution: Television News and American Public Life* (Cambridge, Mass., 1992), 71–74.

3. Geoffrey Hodgson, *America in Our Time* (Garden City, N.J., 1976), 266.

4. Nathan S. Caplan and Jeffery M. Paige, "A Study of Ghetto Rioters," *Scientific American* 219 (August 1968), 15–21.

5. Allen J. Matusow, *The Unraveling of America: A History of Liberalism in the 1960s* (New York, 1984), 194.

6. *Time*, August 6, 1965.

7. *Time*, July 16, 1965; David J. Garrow, *Bearing the Cross: Martin Luther King, Jr., and the Southern Christian Leadership Conference* (New York, 1986), 437–45, 455, 469–72.

8. Office of Policy Planning and Research, United States Department of Labor, *The Negro Family: The Case for National Action* (March 1965), 3.

9. Ibid., 4–47.

10. Lee Rainwater and William L. Yancey, ed., *The Moynihan Report and the Politics of Controversy* (Cambridge, Mass., 1967), 410; Nicholas Lemann, *Promised Land: The Great Black Migration and How It Changed America* (New York, 1991), 175–76, 181; *New York Times*, November 15, 1965.

11. Kenneth Clark, *Dark Ghetto: Dilemmas of Social Power* (New York, 1965); Oscar Lewis, *Five Families: Mexican Case Studies in the Culture of Poverty* (New York, 1959); Roger D. Abrahams, *Deep Down in the Jungle* (Hatboro, Pa., 1964); Elliot Liebow, *Tally's Corner: A Study of Negro Streetcorner Men* (Boston, 1967), 50–55; William Julius Wilson, *The Declining Significance of Race: Blacks and Changing American Institutions* (Chicago, 1978), 109.

12. *New York Times Magazine*, September 11, 1966.

13. *Commentary*, January 1963.

14. Russell Kirk, *The Conservative Mind: From Burke to Santayana* (Chicago, 1953), 8, 45–52, 142.

15. *National Review*, January 25, 1956; July 4, 1957; *U.S. News and World Report*, June 24, 1963.

16. Claybourne Carson, *In Struggle: SNCC and the Black Awakening of the 1960s* (Cambridge, Mass., 1981), 215–306; *New York Times*, June 17, 1966; *Time*, June 1, 1966.

17. Stokely Carmichael and Charles V. Hamilton, *Black Power: The Politics of Liberation in America* (New York, 1967), 44.

18. Matusow, *Unraveling of America*, 355–57.

19. *Time*, September 16, 1966.

20. Michael Novak, *The Rise of the Unmeltable Ethnics: Politics and Culture in the Seventies* (New York, 1971), 15–19, 35, 71–72.

21. *New York Times*, August 6, 1966; Garrow, *Bearing the Cross*, 489–502; Matusow, *Unraveling of America*, 204–5.

22. Hazel Erskine, "The Polls: Demonstrations and Race Riots," *Public Opinion Quarterly* 31 (1967), 655–77; Erskine, "The Polls: Speed of Racial Integration," *Public Opinion Quarterly* 32 (1968), 513–24.

23. Richard Lentz, *Symbols, the News Magazines, and Martin Luther King* (Baton Rouge, 1990).

24. Herbert Hill, "The AFL-CIO And the Black Workers: Twenty-five Years After the Merger," *Journal of Intergroup Relations* 9 (1982), 37–38.

25. *New York Times*, September 21, 1966.

26. *New York Times*, November 9, 10; December 29, 1966.

27. *New York Times*, April 5, 1967; Garrow, *Bearing the Cross*, 562.

28. Garrow, *Bearing the Cross*, 562–64.

29. August Meier, "On the Role of Martin Luther King," *New Politics* 4 (Winter 1965), 1–8.

30. *Newsweek*, May 15, 1967.

31. *The Kerner Report: The 1968 Report of the National Advisory Commission on Civil Disorders* (Washington, 1968 [1988 reprint]), 35–107, 362–88; Lemann, *Promised Land*, 191; *U.S. News and World Report*, March 11, 1968.

32. *Newsweek*, February 27, 1967; January 8, 1968; Baldwin quoted in Randall Kennedy, *Race, Crime, and the Law* (New York, 1997), 26.

33. Martin Gilens, *Why Americans Hate Welfare: Race, Media, and the Politics of Antipoverty Policy* (Chicago, 1999), 104–32.

34. *New York Times*, August 18, 1967.

35. *Newsweek*, May 15, 1967; Matusow, *Unraveling of America*, 365; *Time*, August 4, 18, 1967.

36. Robert Weisbrot, *Freedom Bound: A History of America's Civil Rights Movement* (New York, 1990), 319; Robert G. Weisbord and Arthur Stein, *Bittersweet Encounter: The Afro-American and the American Jew* (Westport, 1970), 139–42; C. Eric Lincoln, *The Black Muslims in America* (Boston, 1961), 166.

37. Weisbrot, *Freedom Bound*, 237–41; Tamar Jacoby, *Someone Else's House: America's Unfinished Struggle for Integration* (New York, 1998), 158–226.

38. *Time*, July 28, 1967.

39. *U.S. News and World Report*, October 26, 1970; John G. Condren, "Changes in White Attitudes toward Blacks: 1963–1977," *Public Opinion Quarterly* 43 (month tk 1979), 463–76; Andrew M. Greeley and Paul B. Sheatsley, "Attitudes toward Racial Integration," *Scientific American* 225 (December 1971), 13–19.

40. Earl Black and Merle Black, *Politics and Society in the South* (Cambridge, Mass., 1987), 175–258.

41. On post–civil rights movement disappointments in the South, see Robert J. Norrell, *Reaping the Whirlwind: The Civil Rights Movement in Tuskegee* (New York, 1985); J. Mills Thornton, III, *Dividing Lines: Municipal Politics and the Struggle for Civil Rights in Montgomery, Birmingham, and Selma* (Tuscaloosa, 2002); John Dittmer, *Local People: The Struggle for Civil Rights in Mississippi* (Urbana, 1994); and Charles M. Payne, *I've Got the Light of Freedom: The Organizing Tradition and the Mississippi Freedom Struggle* (Berkeley, 1995).

42. Reynolds Farley and Walter R. Allen, *The Color Line and the Quality of Life in America* (New York, 1989), 298; Reynolds Farley, *Blacks and Whites: Narrowing the Gap?* (Cambridge, Mass., 1984), 131.

43. Jacoby, *Someone Else's House*, 253–54; Timothy Minchin, *Hiring the Black Worker: The Racial Integration of the Southern Textile Industry, 1960–1980* (Chapel Hill, 1999), 43–66; Farley and Allen, *The Color Line*, 289, 264.

44. Clifford Mason, "Why Does White America Love Sidney Poitier So?" *New York Times*, September 10, 1967.

45. *Newsweek*, May 1, 1967.

46. Matusow, *Unraveling of America*, 367–73.

47. Ibid., 396–97.

48. Arthur M. Schlesinger, Jr., *Robert Kennedy and His Times* (New York, 1968), 940; Matusow, *Unraveling of America*, 396.

49. Matusow, *Unraveling of America*, 206–8, 396–98.

50. Ibid., 424–26; Dan T. Carter, *The Politics of Rage: George Wallace, the Origins of the New Conservatism, and the Transformation of American Politics* (New York, 1995), 324–70.

51. Matthew David Lassiter, "The Rise of the Suburban South: The 'Silent Majority' and the Politics of Education, 1945–1975" (unpublished Ph.D. dissertation, University of Virginia, 1999), 531–32.

52. Carter, *Politics of Rage*, 351–70; Matusow, *Unraveling of America*, 411–39.

Chapter Eight

1. *Newsweek*, May 5, 1969; *New York Times*, April 20, 21, 1969; *U.S. News and World Report*, May 5, 1969.

2. *Newsweek*, May 6, 1968; *U.S. News and World Report*, February 24, 1969; William Van Deburg, *New Day in Babylon: The Black Power Movement and American Culture, 1965–1975* (Chicago, 1992), 78; *Newsweek*, February 10, 1969.

3. *U.S. News and World Report*, September 21, 1970.

4. Ibid., March 1, July 19, 1971.

5. Tamar Jacoby, *Someone Else's House: America's Unfinished Struggle for Integration* (New York, 1998), 308–35, 352.

6. William Van Deburg, *New Day in Babylon: The Black Power Movement and American Culture, 1965–1975* (Chicago, 1992), 17–18; Jacoby, *Someone Else's House*, 256; Thomas Byrne Edsall with Mary D. Edsall, *Chain Reaction: The Impact of Race, Rights, and Taxes on American Politics* (New York, 1991), 157.

7. Van Deburg, *New Day in Babylon*, 131.

8. Donald Bogle, *Toms, Coons, Mulattoes, Mammies & Bucks: An Interpretive History of Blacks in American Films* (New York, 1999, 3rd ed.), 231–66; Ed Guerriro, *Framing Blackness: The African American Image in Film* (Philadelphia, 1993), 69–112.

9. J. Fred MacDonald, *Black and White TV: African Americans in Television since 1948* (Chicago, 1992), 117–223.

10. Van Deburg, *New Day in Babylon*, 131.

11. John Erlichman, *Witness to Power: The Nixon Years* (New York, 1982), 221–24; Hugh Davis Graham, *The Civil Rights Era: Origins and Development of National Policy, 1960–1972* (New York, 1990), 302, 309, 313, 322; Nicholas Lemann, *Promised Land: The Great Black Migration and How It Changed America* (New York, 1991), 3–4, 20, 108, 203; *U.S. News and World Report*, February 3, 1969; Kevin P. Phillips, *The Emerging Republican Majority* (New Rochelle, 1969).

12. Lemann, *Promised Land*, 209.

13. William Julius Wilson, *The Truly Disadvantaged: The Inner City, the Underclass, and Public Policy* (Chicago, 1987), 14–15.

14. Graham, *The Civil Rights Era*, 312; Daniel Patrick Moynihan, *Maximum Feasible Misunderstanding: Community Action in the War on Poverty* (New York, 1969); Lemann, *Promised Land*, 213; Edsall, *Chain Reaction* 106–7.

15. Graham, *The Civil Rights Era*, 279–96, 327; Glazer, *Affirmative Discrimination: Ethnic Inequality and Public Policy* (New York, 1975), x.

16. Graham, *The Civil Rights Era*, 325, 334–35; *New York Times*, August 7, 1969; *Wall Street Journal*, September 26, 1969; *U.S. News and World Report*, April 7, 1969.

17. Graham, *The Civil Rights Era*, 341–42, 442–43, 448; Glazer, *Affirmative Discrimination*, 36–37.

18. Graham, *The Civil Rights Era*, 389; Glazer, *Affirmative Discrimination*, 53.

19. John Higham, *Strangers in the Land: Patterns of American Nativism, 1860–1925* (New

Brunswick, N.J., 1955), 278; Shad Polier to Friend, September 26, 1963, in Southern Regional Council Papers, Series I, folder 46; American Jewish Committee, Executive Board Meeting, November 1–3, 1963, Statement on Quotas and Race Relations, in Southern Regional Council Papers, ibid.; Nathan Glazer, "A Breakdown in Civil Rights Enforcement?" *The Public Interest* 6 (Winter 1971), 107.

20. Graham, *The Civil Rights Era*, 446; *New York Times,* September 26, October 5, 9, 1972; *Newsweek*, September 18, 1972.

21. Graham, *The Civil Rights Era*, 343, 363.

22. Ibid., 362.

23. Shelby Steele, *The Content of Our Character: A New Vision of Race in America* (New York, 1991), 18; Glazer, *Affirmative Discrimination*, 38, 49.

24. *U.S. v. Jefferson Co. Board of Education* 372 F.2d 836 (1966); *Green v. County Board of New Kent Co.* 391 U.S. 430 (1968); *Alexander v. Holmes County* 396 U.S. 19 (1969); Graham, *The Civil Rights Era*, 319, 382.

25. Graham, *The Civil Rights Era*, 320; J. Harvie Wilkinson, III, *From Brown to Bakke: The Supreme Court and School Integration, 1954–1978* (New York, 1979), 135.

26. Wilkinson, *From Brown to Bakke*, 202, 142; Reynolds Farley and Walter R. Allen, *The Color Line and the Quality of Life in America* (New York, 1989), 143–45; Karl E. Taeuber and Alma F. Taeuber, *Negroes in Cities: Residential Segregation and Neighborhood Change* (Chicago, 1965), 2, 94; Reynolds Farley, *Blacks and Whites: Narrowing the Gap?* (Cambridge, Mass., 1984), 201; Jacoby, *Someone Else's House*, 263–64.

27. Wilkinson, *From Brown to Bakke*, 150; *U.S. News and World Report*, August 30, September 13, November 8, February 28, 1972.

28. Jacoby, *Someone Else's House*, 259–67.

29. *U.S. News and World Report*, April 10, 1972; Jacoby, *Someone Else's House*, 259–69, 281, 302.

30. *U.S. News and World Report*, August 16, 1971; February 28, January 24, May 29, 1972; Dan T. Carter, *The Politics of Rage: George Wallace, the Origins of the New Conservatism, and the Transformation of American Politics* (New York, 1995), 432.

31. Wilkinson, *From Brown to Bakke*, 156–57, 151–52.

32. Wilkinson, *From Brown to Bakke*, 203–6; Jacoby, *Someone Else's House*, 293; Ronald Formisano, *Boston against Busing: Race, Class, and Ethnicity in the 1960s and 1970s* (Chapel Hill, 1971); J. Anthony Lukas, *Common Ground: A Turbulent Decade in the Lives of Three American Families* (New York, 1985).

33. *U.S. News and World Report*, June 19, 1972; Wilkinson, *From Brown to Bakke*, 148, 222–27.

34. Gary Orfield and Susan E. Eaton, *Dismantling Desegregation: The Quiet Reversal of Brown v. Board of Education* (New York, 1996), 301; Jacoby, *Someone Else's House*, 510.

35. Wilkinson, *From Brown to Bakke*, 172–73.

36. Steven F. Lawson, *Running for Freedom: Civil Rights and Black Politics in America since 1941* (New York, 1991), 201.

37. Edsall, *Chain Reaction*, 101–6.

38. Farley and Allen, *The Color Line*, 298.

39. Lester C. Thurow, *The Zero-Sum Society: Distribution and the Possibilities of Economic Change* (New York, 1980), 178–88.

40. Richard G. Niemi, John Mueller, and Tom W. Smith, *Trends in Public Opinion: A Compendium of Survey Data* (New York, 1989), 73–92.

41. Lemann, *Promised Land,* 201.

42. Earl Black and Merle Black, *Politics and Society in the South* (Cambridge, Mass., 1987), 71; Paul M. Sniderman and Thomas Piazza, *The Scar of Race* (Cambridge, Mass., 1993), 176.

43. Peter Steinfels, *The Neoconservatives: The Men Who Are Changing America's Politics* (New York, 1979), 5.

44. Glazer, *Affirmative Discrimination,* xiii.

45. Wilkinson, *From* Brown *to* Bakke, 253–306.

46. Morton J. Horwitz, "The Jurisprudence of *Brown* and the Dilemmas of Liberalism," in *Have We Overcome? Race Relations since* Brown, ed. Michael V. Namorato (Jackson, 1979), 179.

47. William Raspberry in the *Washington Post,* June 30, 2003.

48. Lawson, *Running for Freedom,* 160.

49. Christopher Jencks, *Rethinking Social Policy: Race, Poverty, and the Underclass* (Cambridge, Mass., 1992), 112.

Chapter Nine

1.   *Columbia World of Quotations,* 1996, No. 32942. Reagan apparently first said this in 1965.

2.   Dan T. Carter, *The Politics of Rage: George Wallace, the Origins of the New Conservatism, and the Transformation of American Politics* (New York, 1995), 432; *New York Times,* February 15, 1976; Lou Cannon, *President Reagan: The Role of a Lifetime* (New York, 1991), 518–23.

3.   Shelby Steele, *The Content of Our Character: A New Vision of Race in America* (New York, 1991), 9.

4.   Thomas Byrne Edsall with Mary D. Edsall, *Chain Reaction: The Impact of Race, Rights, and Taxes on American Politics* (New York, 1991), 179.

5.   Ibid., 164, 182.

6.   Eduard Bonilla-Silva, *White Supremacy and Racism in the Post–Civil Rights Era* (Boulder, 2001); Michael K. Brown, *Whitewashing Race: The Myth of a Color-Blind Society* (Berkeley, 2003).

7.   Bond quoted in *National Review,* May 20, 1993; Paul M. Gaston, "After Jim Crow: Civil Rights as Civil Wrongs," in *The Southern State of Mind,* ed. Jan Nordby Gretlund (Columbia, 1999), 39.

8.   Ibid., 175, 224.

9.   Murray Friedman, *What Went Wrong? The Creation and Collapse of the Black-Jewish Alliance* (New York, 1995), 342.

10. Ibid., 331–39; William L. Van Deburg, ed., *Modern Black Nationalism: From Marcus Garvey to Louis Farrakhan* (New York, 1997).

11. "The New Orleans Declaration," Statement Endorsed at the Fourth Annual DLC Conference, March 1, 1990, www.ndol.org.

12. Edsall, *Chain Reaction,* 200; Claudia Goldin, "Labor Markets in the Twentieth Century," in *The Cambridge Economic History of the United States,* III, ed. Stanley L.

Engerman and Robert E. Gallman (Cambridge, Eng., 2000), 559, 606.

13. David M. Reimers, *Unwelcome Strangers: American Identity and the Turn against Immigration* (New York, 1998), 32–37.

14. *New York Times*, April 4, 2001; *American Prospect*, January–February 1999; *Discrimination in Metropolitan Housing Markets 1989–2000 Report* (HUD No. 02-138), November 7, 2002; *New York Times*, December 9, 2001; Tamar Jacoby, *Someone Else's House: America's Unfinished Struggle for Integration* (New York, 1998), 505.

15. Gary Orfield and Susan E. Eaton, *Dismantling Desegregation: The Quiet Reversal of Brown v. Board of Education* (New York, 1996), 301; *New York Times*, July 20, 2001.

16. Edsall, *Chain Reaction*, 187–88; Nina J. Easton, *Gang of Five: Leaders at the Center of the Conservative Crusade* (New York, 2000), 193–96; *Newsweek*, January 30, 1984; *Engineering News-Record*, March 14, 1985; *U.S. News and World Report*, March 18, 1985; Raymond Wolters, *Right Turn: William Bradford Reynolds, the Reagan Administration, and Black Civil Rights* (New Brunswick, N.J., 1996).

17. *New York Times*, October 12, 1991.

18. Easton, *Gang of Five*, 83.

19. Thomas Sowell, *Race and Economics* (New York, 1975); Sowell, *Markets and Minorities* (New York, 1980); Sowell, *Ethnic America: A History* (New York, 1981); Walter E. Williams, *Youth and Minority Unemployment* (Stanford, 1977).

20. Steele, *Content of Our Character*, 14, 24–25, 49, 52, 66.

21. Nicholas Lemann, *Promised Land: The Great Black Migration and How It Changed America* (New York, 1991), 200; Reynolds Farley, *Blacks and Whites: Narrowing the Gap?* (Cambridge, Mass., 1984), 200, 170, 138; Christopher Jencks, *Rethinking Social Policy: Race, Poverty, and the Underclass* (Cambridge, Mass., 1992), 18.

22. Farley, *Blacks and Whites*, 39–42, 169; William Julius Wilson, *The Declining Significance of Race: Blacks and Changing American Institutions* (Chicago, 1978), 89–92.

23. Wilson, *Declining Significance of Race*, 88–121; George Gilder, *Wealth and Poverty* (New York, 1981), 122; Jencks, *Rethinking Social Policy*, 15–16.

24. Charles Murray, *Losing Ground: American Social Policy, 1950–1980* (New York, 1984); Jencks, *Rethinking Social Policy*, 13.

25. William Julius Wilson, *The Truly Disadvantaged: The Inner City, the Underclass, and Public Policy* (Chicago, 1987); Elijah Anderson, *Streetwise: Race, Class, and Change in an Urban Community* (Chicago, 1990), 103.

26. Jencks, *Rethinking Social Policy*, 181–89; Randall Kennedy, *Race, Crime, and the Law* (New York, 1997), 20, 11–12.

27. Kennedy, *Race, Crime, and the Law*, 7.

28. Lou Cannon, *Official Negligence: How Rodney King and the Riots Changed Los Angeles and the LAPD* (New York, 1997).

29. Kennedy, *Race, Crime, and the Law*, 295; *Newsweek*, October 16, 1995.

30. *Newsweek*, October 16, 1995; Kennedy, *Race, Crime, and the Law*, 21.

31. Jacoby, *Someone Else's House*, 533–38.

32. Tom W. Smith, "Changing Racial Labels: From 'Colored' to 'Negro' to 'African American,'" *Public Opinion Quarterly* 56 (1991), 496–514.

33. Martha Bayles, *Hole in Our Soul: The Loss of Beauty and Meaning in American Popular Music* (New York, 1994), 341–62.

34. Although not precisely the same argument as herein, Bayles's *Hole in Our Soul*

makes a powerful case for the decline of African-American music within a broader cultural context. Ibid., 287–392.

35. Steele, *Content of Our Character*, 11; J. Fred MacDonald, *Black and White TV: African Americans in Television since 1948* (Chicago, 1992), 224–310.

36. Martin Gilens, *Why Americans Hate Welfare: Race, Media, and the Politics of Antipoverty Policy* (Chicago, 1999), 133–53; Carolyn Martindale and Lillian Rae Dunlap, "The African Americans," in Keever et al., *U.S. News Coverage of Racial Minorities*, 128–29.

37. Jencks, *Rethinking Social Policy*, 13; Nathan Glazer, *Affirmative Discrimination: Ethnic Inequality and Public Policy* (New York, 1975), vii, xiv–xv.

38. Jacoby, *Someone Else's House*, 377–499.

39. *City of Richmond v. J. A. Croson Company* 109 S. Ct. 706 (1989); *Wards Cove Packing Co. v. Atonio* 490 U.S. 642 (1989).

40. *Shaw v. Reno* 509 U.S. 630 (1993).

41. Kousser, *Shaping of Southern Politics: Suffrage Restriction and the Establishment of the One-Party South 1880–1910* (New Haven, 1974) 45–62; Frank R. Parker, *Black Votes Count: Political Empowerment in Mississippi after 1965* (Chapel Hill, 1990); Chandler Davidson, ed., *Minority Vote Dilution* (Washington, D.C., 1984); J. Morgan Kousser, *Colorblind Injustice: Minority Voting Rights and the Undoing of the Second Reconstruction* (Chapel Hill, 1999). For an alternate view, see Abigail Thernstrom, *Whose Votes Count?: Affirmative Action and Minority Voting Rights* (Cambridge, Mass., 1987); and Stephan Thernstrom and Abigail Thernstrom, *America in Black and White: One Nation Indivisible* (New York, 1997).

42. *Hopwood v. State of Texas* 84 F.3d 720 (5th Cir., 1996); *Grutter v. Bollinger* 288 F.3d 732 (2003).

43. Easton, *Gang of Five*, 323.

Epilogue

1. David M. Reimers, *Unwelcome Strangers: American Identity and the Turn against Immigration* (New York, 1998), 65–86; Steven A. Camarota, "Immigrants in the United States—2000: A Snapshot of American's Foreign-Born Population," *Backgrounder* [Center for Immigration Studies], January 2001.

2. Reimers, *Unwelcome Strangers*, 65–153.

3. *New Yorker*, July 24, 1964.

4. *USIA Electronic Journal*, August 1997.

5. *American Demographic*, November 1999.

A Note on Theory and Bibliography

1. George M. Fredrickson, *The Comparative Imagination on the History of Racism, Nationalism, and Social Movements* (Berkeley, 1997), 89–90; *Max Weber: Essays in Sociology*, trans., ed., and with intro. by H. H. Gerth and C. Wright Mills (New York, 1946).

2. *Weber: Essays in Sociology*, 180, 188.

3. Ibid., 190.

A NOTE ON THEORY AND BIBLIOGRAPHY

THE SOCIOLOGY of Max Weber informs this work theoretically, because it provides a coherent language and logic for understanding the relationship of race, class, and political power in the social order. In an essay entitled "Class, Status, Party," Weber identified the three main sources of power in modern societies. Each of the three is a distinct analytical category within the social order, but authority among the three components overlaps and interacts in shaping social reality. Weber's observations were prescient for the study of race relations in twentieth-century America, and in a direct, if not always explicit, way they guide the arguments that follow. Weber rejected Marx's presumption that a class was "infallible" in perceiving its interests. He understood property ownership to be the main determinant of economic power, but he believed that class interests depended on the kind of property owned. Similarly, occupation shapes economic power according to the kind of work done. For classes to be influential in the social order, Weber believed, they have to be "communalized," or imbued with a sense that they belong together. In the history of the United States, the evidence for a consistent class-based communal sense strikes me as inconsistent and episodic, unless one focuses exclusively on a very small group of the wealthiest people, and even there class consciousness is often mystified by ethnic concerns.[1]

Weber wrote that the pursuit of status, defined as the social estimation of honor, is the largest influence in the social order. Class is usually an important factor in determining status, but status groups are also formed on noneconomic bases. "Propertied and propertyless people can belong to the same status group, and frequently they do with very tangible consequences," Weber wrote. Within a status group "above all else a specific *style of life* can be expected from all those who wish to belong" to the group, and restrictions are put on "social intercourse"—marriage, for example—among those who stay in it. In the United States, "races" have effectively functioned as status groups.[2]

The competition among status groups, I have argued, was the main engine for action in the history of American race relations since the Civil War. Americans have sought economic opportunity, political power, and space in which to live. In these three arenas, status groups—almost always understood in racial and ethnic terms—have vied for success and dominance over competing groups. Americans have often defined our success by how fully our status group is dominating others. The competition for status extended past the time that white supremacy shaped American race relations, just as the ideological struggle over the meaning of Americans' values has continued since the 1960s. The dynamic of status competition in the post–civil rights movement years explains much of why race remains a foremost issue in American life in the early years of the twenty-first century. Well after the civil rights movement had undermined white-supremacist ideology, most whites retained a sense of belonging to a racial status group and acted accordingly, notwithstanding the frequent avowals of "color-blindness."

African Americans have been the most clearly defined status group in the United States, though their status has been deemed so negative by the white group as to make them pariahs. "But even pariah people who are most despised," Weber wrote, "are usually apt to continue cultivating in some manner that which is usually peculiar to ethnic and to status communities: the belief in their own specific 'honor'." Whereas privi-

leged status groups focus on their superiority in the present and their glorious past, pariah status groups look to the future, and perhaps to the
next life. Their "sense of dignity . . . must be nurtured by the belief in a
providential 'mission' and by a belief in a specific honor before God," he
suggested. "The 'chosen people's' dignity is nurtured by a belief either
that in the beyond 'the last will be the first,' or that in this life a Messiah
will appear to bring forth into the light of the world which has cast them
out the hidden honor of the pariah people."[3]

The conscious and unconscious growth of communalization of
blacks shaped the narrative of the first half of the book. By 1938 that
process had developed sufficiently that most urban black communities
had begun a movement to acquire civil rights—to vote, to get an equal
education, to have a fair chance at a job. By the mid-1950s a convergence
of influences—changes in popular representations of African Americans,
the emergence of powerful new forms of communication, and the brilliant presentation of ideological conflict within American thinking—
resulted in the mass communalization of African Americans, and the
national civil rights movement thus ensued. After 1965 the negative status
that whites had imposed on African Americans sharply abated as white-
supremacist ideology was made largely illegitimate, but a black ethnic
nationalism emerged to replace it as a communalizing influence.

Weber used "party" to mean more than the modern form of a group
organized to influence electoral politics. He included all the conscious
efforts of groups—classes, status groups, or even interest groups or occupations—to acquire social power through planned action to dominate a
community. He explained that parties must have well-developed legal
and governmental institutions to achieve their goals. There have been
many such Weberian "parties" in American life, and the competition
among them has shaped much of the history explored herein. The emergence of African-American status "parties" in the twentieth century, primarily organizations to advance black civil rights, is crucial for
understanding when and how activism succeeded.

Weber's thoughts about nationalism have guided many who have
tried to ascertain its significance in the nineteenth and twentieth cen-

turies. "Nations" are political communities that usually refer to ideas "of common descent and of an essential, though frequently indefinite, homogeneity," which makes them like ethnic groups. Nations often embrace faith in their "providential mission," their existence as a "chosen people," and they insist on achieving "autonomous polity." The characterization of nationalism applies to the United States from the Civil War forward, but it also describes much of what happened in the American South after the war in the creation of a competing southern white ethnic nationalism.

For facts and much historical interpretation, this book relies on the work of a great many scholars, journalists, and activists who have written about American race relations since the Civil War. Historians, social scientists, and journalists have been working for more than a generation to answer questions about the emergence of the civil rights movement and its relative successes and failures. The first important explanation, and probably still the most influential single interpretation, was C. Vann Woodward's in his 1955 work *The Strange Career of Jim Crow*, revised in 1966 and 1973. Woodward offered a distinctly political interpretation for both the creation of the system of segregation and its undoing. The failures of Populism in the 1890s cleared the way for white unity in a codified imposition of white supremacy, and then in the 1960s the national legislature, prodded by a series of demonstrations in the South, declared illegal the segregation and disfranchisement that had been imposed seventy or so years before. To be sure, Professor Woodward accounted for many nonpolitical realities in his interpretation, but the essence of his answer to the big questions about causation remained political. Other historians, most notably Steven Lawson and Woodward's students J. Mills Thornton, III, and J. Morgan Kousser, have also emphasized political forces as the most salient cause for, and limit on, racial changes. Their books are cited in the notes, as are the works of other authors mentioned in this section.

A wide assortment of scholars and journalists writing mainly in the 1980s and 1990s explained the civil rights movement's rise and fall by looking at the actions and strategies of the protestors themselves. The works of August Meier and Elliott Rudwick, David Garrow, Taylor

Branch, Adam Fairclough, Charles Payne, John Dittmer, Willam Chafe, David Colburn, J. Mills Thornton, III, Diane McWhorter, and Claybourne Carson dissected the lives of protestors and their organizations during the 1950s and 1960s. Most were focused on Martin Luther King, Jr., and the national civil rights organizations, but some looked at activists working within local movements. All explored protest strategies and often emphasized the "moral" appeals made by activists, and thus they suggested both political and ideological motives but usually without explicit acknowledgment of possible categories of explanation. Many of these works, and certainly the ones that have been most consistently read, have noted a variety of "other" influences—usually economic and social changes. Often, however, these are simply listed, rather than being arranged in some direct relationship to one another.

During the 1970s and 1980s, sociologists used "mobilization" theory to address the ways that broad structures influenced the process of changes in race relations. They suggested that successful protest efforts in the 1960s resulted from the increasing urbanization among African Americans, their rising incomes and educational levels, and the strengthening of black institutions during the 1940s and 1950s. The mobilization interpretation emphasized broad social and economic development that provided the strengthened community support for a broad-based movement of social protest. It was put forward initially by Anthony Oberschall and then advanced by Doug McAdam and Aldon Morris. Again, however, the connections between the improving black economic and social profile and the actual onset of sustained protest strike me as weak, and the argument itself as somewhat circular.

During the past decade, other scholars have emphasized the importance of American foreign policy to shaping racial changes by arguing that American interests abroad provided crucial impetus for acceptance of the changes pushed by black activists. In these interpretations, the momentum for change coincided with the U.S. involvement in major wars. These writers emphasize especially the importance of the Cold War in advancing the civil rights movement of the 1950s and 1960s. The political scientists Philip Klinkner, Rogers Smith, and Mary Dudziak and the historians Thomas Borstelmann, Brenda Gayle Plummer, and Penny M. Von Eschen are the most notable exponents of this interpretation. Although there was abundant commentary about how U.S. race problems hurt American influence in world affairs after World War II, almost all of the evidence came from the pro–civil rights and diplomatic communities. One is hard-pressed to find Cold Warriors from the South who spoke out for expanding civil rights, and none of the ones who did had significant political influence. The domestic impact of the Cold War clearly undermined activism in the 1950s, and to a lesser extent in the 1960s, and the United States's most extensive Cold War commitment, the war in Vietnam, clearly undermined the civil rights movement.

In part one, discussions of American ideology owe much to the work of Eric Foner, Garry Wills, and David M. Potter. Understandings about Reconstruction are based in part on Foner's study of that period, and the interpretation of the post-Reconstruction South relies mainly on Professor Woodward's analysis and that of Paul M. Gaston. Professor W. Fitzhugh Brundage's work on lynching guided my thinking about racial violence. Howard Rabinowitz's explanation of the origins of segregation shaped much of my view on that subject. George Fredrickson's study of white racial thinking was indispensable to developing my viewpoint of late-nineteenth-century race ideologies. August Meier did much the same for black thought. Although my views on Booker T. Washington are decidedly different from Louis Harlan's, his research on the Tuskegeean was indispensable in formulating my understanding. Similarly, I relied on David Levering Lewis's work on W. E. B. Du Bois, even as I developed a different interpretation of the black intellectual and protest leader. On the Great Migration, James Grossman's study of migrants to Chicago shaped much of my understanding. The writing of James Weldon Johnson was by far my largest influence on the 1920s. Harvard Sitkoff shaped my knowledge of race relations in the Great Depression, and Eric Foner's writing about ideology in the 1930s was crucial to my views on that issue. August Meier and Elliott Rudwick supplied essential research on the history of black activism throughout the first half of the twentieth century.

In part two, the works of John Dittmer and Charles Payne on Mississippi, Adam Fairclough on Louisiana, and William Chafe on North Carolina informed much of what I wrote. Professor Sitkoff's work taught me much about the 1940s, though we come to different conclusions about the significance of activism in that time. Diane McWhorter's compelling story about Birmingham provoked me to think again about the significance of that city to racial change. The historian J. Mills Thornton's study of three Alabama communities was, however, the single largest influence for understanding the dynamics of activism in the South. David Garrow's works on the career of Martin Luther King, Jr., were absolutely crucial to my understanding of the full range of the SCLC leader's actions. Keith Miller's study of King's ideas and rhetoric shaped much of how I have interpreted his ideological impact. Robert Mann's engrossing narrative of congressional politics brought the Washington story about civil rights to life for me. Henry Louis Gates's memoir gave a fresh perspective for how the movement was perceived by African Americans not on the front line. Brian Ward's study of the origins and influence of rock and roll is one of our most important studies of culture in the United States. The works of Arnold Hirsch, Thomas Sugrue, and Kenneth Jackson taught me a great deal about racial matters in the North in the 1940s and 1950s. Herbert Hill's research on employment discrimination and the racial divisions within the labor movement filled an important need in my understanding. On politics and race in the 1960s, Allen Matusow and Dan T. Carter provided invaluable studies.

In part three, the works of sociologists, political scientists, and journalists were most important for shaping my views, though the historians Hugh Davis Graham and J. Harvie Wilkinson provided incisive interpretations of politics, law, and government in the late 1960s and 1970s. Among the journalists, the works of Thomas Edsall, Tamar Jacoby, Nicholas Lemann, and Nina Easton were immensely informative. The sociologists William Julius Wilson, Reynolds Farley, and Christopher Jencks made sense of the post-1965 developments with true commitment to clarity and complexity. I also benefited particularly from the work of the political scientist Martin Gilens on media treatment of poverty in the United States.

INDEX